Homeless Mysteries, Homeless Intimacies

Other Books by Mark Jay Mann

Collection of Wordstreams
Astrology for the Absolute Beginner
Afterlife Lovestreams

Homeless Mysteries, Homeless Intimacies

By
Mark Jay Mann

Published by:

Breakthrough Enterprises
P.O. Box 5511
Eugene, OR 97405

Copyright © June 2011 by Mark Jay Mann and
Breakthrough Enterprises

All rights reserved. No part of this book, including artwork and photographs, may be used or reproduced without written permission from the author or publisher.

ISBN: 978-0-9648470-5-7

Dedicated to the homeless women, children and men throughout the world. May these individuals, as well as all of us, find the emotional security and physical sustenance that will allow us to reach our potentials and make the world a more caring place to live.

ACKNOWLEDGEMENTS

I want to acknowledge Doug Hoss, of Doug Hoss Media Productions, who has provided invaluable editing, design and formatting services. He has been objective, encouraging and consistently creative as he assisted me in making my revisions and finalizing the eBook and print book formats.

I want to express a special thanks to Susan Astle Paradis, for her proofreading and editing services. Her feedback and encouragement have been instrumental in assisting me to create the new edition of this book.

I want to thank my granddaughter, Iris Keuter, who created the cover design for these new editions of this book.

TABLE OF CONTENTS

February 17 ~~ FADING AWAY 3
    ~~ MORNING VISIONS OF LOVE AND DEMONS 5
    ~~ YOUNG LOVERS 7
    ~~ CHALLENGES AND FEARS 8
    ~~ HOMELESS MURDERS. WHO ARE THE MURDERERS? 11
    ~~ ACCOMPLICES TO MURDER 12
February 18 ~~ LISTENING TO MUSIC FRAGMENTS 16
February 19 ~~ A NEAR DEATH EXPERIENCE 17
    ~~ PEACEFUL REVERIE 20
February 21 ~~ THE DANGEROUS LURE OF THE TREASURE MARKET 21
    ~~ THE TREASURE THEATER 23
    ~~ FIRST MEETING WITH JUSTINE 23
    ~~ FIRST DAY WORKING AT THE TREASURE MARKET 27
February 22 ~~ BEDTIME RITUALS 29
    ~~ BEDTIME DANGERS 29
    ~~ LAUNDROMAT COMFORTS 31
February 25 ~~ WALTER AND THE ALIENS FROM ANOTHER PLANET 33
February 27 ~~ FIRST ENCOUNTER WITH ESOLA 34
February 28 ~~ EXQUISITE PERIL 36
March 2 ~~ CHOOSING TO LET PARTS OF MYSELF DIE 40
March 3 ~~ WHERE I LIVE 43
    ~~ TAKING A CRAZY RISK 45
    ~~ ANOTHER HORRIBLE ENCOUNTER WITH THE BUTCHER 45
    ~~ MUST STOP THIS MANIAC 47
March 4 ~~ NIGHTMARES 49
    ~~ FALLACIOUS 51
    ~~ UNCARED FOR PEOPLE AND PLACES 51
    ~~ JEREMIAH'S SEARCH FOR THE CHRIST CHILD 52
    ~~ THE ATTACK OF THE BAG LADY 53
March 7 ~~ THE MYSTERIOUS EXOTIC DANCER 55
    ~~ THE TRUE WEALTH OF OUR CIVILIZATION 57
    ~~ THE THAILAND FLAG 57
March 8 ~~ RANTS AND REVERIES 59
March 9 ~~ THE HOLY SKYSCRAPER AND QUEEN AVARICE 61
    ~~ MY PAST AND PSYCHOLOGICAL BREAKDOWN 62
March 10 ~~ THE CAMPFIRE AT THE FREEWAY FIELDS 66
    ~~ RANSACK AND THE BUTCHER 69
    ~~ MEANINGFUL COINCIDENCES 72

March 11 ~~ JUSTINE IN A DREAM 73
 ~~ WALTER'S FEAR OF THE SPACE ALIENS 74
 ~~ JEROME THREATENS ME 75
March 13 ~~ A BREAKFAST SURPRISE 76
 ~~ ATTRACTIVE WOMEN 78
 ~~ JUSTINE DESERVES BETTER 81
 ~~ INTERVIEW WITH THE TEENAGE GIRL 82
 ~~ THE CURSE OF THE BAG LADY 86
 ~~ MYSTERY SOUNDS IN THE WAREHOUSE 87
 ~~ NEIGHBORLY STREET SHARING 87
March 14 ~~ QUEEN AVARICE ENTERS MY DREAM-WORLD 90
 ~~ RANSACK CONFRONTS THE BUTCHER 91
March 16 ~~ WRITING IN MY JOURNAL 94
 ~~ TESTING THE BUTCHER 97
 ~~ THE UNEXPECTED JOYS OF A HOT SHOWER AT THE TREASURE
   MARKET 98
March 17 ~~ THE COSTUME PARTY 101
 ~~ JEROME SCARES ME 106
March 18 ~~ QUEEN AVARICE BEYOND THE FIELD OF GOLD 108
 ~~ FOLLOWING QUEEN AVARICE 108
 ~~ CAUGHT LIKE A FLY 110
March 19 ~~ RETURNING THE DREAM DOLL 110
March 20 ~~ WAILING SIRENS 111
 ~~ RANSACK'S DISPLAY OF VIOLENCE 112
March 21 ~~ SOMETHING STRANGE IS HAPPENING AT THE BUTCHER'S
   STORE 113
March 22 ~~ WALTER TAKES ME TO SEE THE SPACE ALIENS 115
March 27 ~~ QUEEN AVARICE AND THE GOLDEN UMBRELLA 118
March 29 ~~ DEAD ZONES 119
March 31 ~~ UNREAL DREAMS OF ROMANCE 121
 ~~ THE BURNSIDE SHELTER 122
 ~~ RAUL 123
 ~~ FADING AWAY ON THE GRAND DRAGON BOAT 124
April 2 ~~ CARISSA ASKS ME VERY PERSONAL QUESTIONS 124
April 4 ~~ A PERFORMANCE I DID NOT WANT TO SEE 127
April 5 ~~ RANSACK DEMANDS REPAYMENT 129
April 6 ~~ TAROT READING FROM ESOLA 134
April 7 ~~ SOAKING WET 136
 ~~ LIVID AND BILLY BUZZ 138

April 9 ~~ CHARLES AND LOUISE	139
April 10 ~~ SHAPE-SHIFTING WOMEN IN MY DREAMS	141
~~ QUEEN AVARICE LOSES HER BLUE SCARF	142
~~ THROWING IMAGINARY ROCKS AT GLASS WINDOWS	144
April 11 ~~ JEREMIAH AND THE CHRIST CHILD	144
~~ ANOTHER HOMELESS MURDER	146
~~ CARISSA ASKS ME HOW I WOULD SOLVE THE HOMELESS PROBLEM	146
April 16 ~~ RELUCTANT NIGHT AT THE SHELTER	149
April 20 ~~ CHALLENGES FROM ESOLA AND JUSTINE	150
April 22 ~~ LOST CLOTHES AND DISTURBING DREAMS	153
~~ SEARCHING FOR MORE CLOTHES AND SLEEPING GEAR	155
~~ LIVID'S OFFER	159
April 24 ~~ CARISSA VISITS THE WRONG SHELTER	160
~~ HOMELESS MAN DYING ON THE STREET	161
~~ WHY ISN'T JUSTINE MARRIED?	162
April 25 ~~ CHARLIE WANTS TO LIVE AND DIE IN NEW ORLEANS	164
April 26 ~~ TAKING ANOTHER CHANCE TO SEE THAI WOMAN DANCE	166
~~ JEROME MIGHT BE FOLLOWING ME	167
April 28 ~~ THE GRAND DRAGON BOAT AT THE TREASURE MARKET	168
April 29 ~~ THE HOMELESS CONTINUE TO BE MURDERED	169
April 30 ~~ TWILIGHT BY THE RIVER	170
May 2 ~~ THE BAG LADY ATTEMPTS TO MURDER ME AGAIN	172
~~ JUSTINE TALKS ABOUT HER LOVE RELATIONSHIP	172
~~ QUESTIONED BY THE POLICE	176
~~ LOOKING INSIDE THE PAGODA CABIN OF THE GRAND DRAGON BOAT	176
May 4 ~~ WALTER GIVES ME SOMETHING TO HIDE	177
May 5 ~~ AN UNEXPECTED JOURNEY TO ANOTHER WORLD	180
May 6 ~~ FINDING NAOMI'S RED PURSE AND UNEXPECTED AWARDS	182
May 7 ~~ GETTING RID OF A SOURCE OF CORRUPTION & GREED	190
~~ ESOLA AND JUSTINE NOTICED A CHANGE IN ME	190
~~ DOES ESOLA HAVE PSYCHIC ABILITIES?	191
May 10 ~~ RANSACK'S SCARY SAGA	193
~~ TRYING TO CONFRONT JEROME	199
May 11 ~~ HOWARD AND SUSAN	200
May 12 ~~ IMAGES OF JUSTINE AND THE TREASURE MARKET	201
~~ RAUL, THE EVIL STREET URCHIN	202
May 14 ~~ CARISSA'S PROBING QUESTIONS	203

May 15 ~~ USING WORK TO REPRESS DESIRE	205
May 16 ~~ HOMELESS KILLINGS CONTINUE	205
May 17 ~~ THINKING ABOUT TRYING TO MEET THE THAI DANCER	206
~~ VISITING THE HOUSE WHERE THE THAI DANCER LIVES	207
May 19 ~~ A CURE FOR JUSTINE'S TENSIONS	208
May 21 ~~ RANSACK CONTINUES HIS DEMAND FOR A LITERARY REPAYMENT	210
~~ THE BAG LADY'S STRANGE DISAPPEARANCE	212
May 22 ~~ POSSIBLE HELP FOR BILLY BUZZ	213
May 23 ~~ THE BLOWOUT BETWEEN JUSTINE AND CHRIS	214
~~ MY RETURN TO THE THEATER	218
May 24 ~~ DRAMATIC INVOLVEMENT	219
May 25 ~~ CARISSA SEARCHES FOR A FRIEND'S FATHER	220
~~ JUSTINE'S CONCERNS	220
May 30 ~~ THE NIGHT OF THE PLAY	221
~~ I BECAME THE PLAY	222
~~ RESISTING THE LURE OF THE RING	223
May 31 ~~ CAPTURED, TIED AND GAGGED	223
June 6 ~~ SECOND WEEKEND OF THE PLAY	229
June 7 ~~ RANSACK'S MYSTERIOUS ACTIVITIES	230
~~ LIVID'S DESPERATE GOAL TO HELP BILLY BUZZ	231
~~ MY MYSTERIOUS PROTECTOR	232
June 8 ~~ QUEEN AVARICE SLUMMING AT A DELI	233
June 9 ~~ QUEEN AVARICE BUYS ME A STEAK DINNER	235
June 11 ~~ CARISSA SHADOWS ME	236
June 13 ~~ THE ENDING OF THE PLAY	238
June 14 ~~ TRYING TO RESIST INVOLVEMENTS	239
~~ ESOLA'S SAD MOOD	240
June 18 ~~ SUCH A WASTE	242
~~ CARISSA SHARES INFORMATION ABOUT THE HOMELESS KILLERS	245
~~ WHAT SHOULD I DO WITH THIS INFORMATION?	247
~~ TELLING RANSACK ABOUT MY SUSPICIONS	247
~~ FEAR OF BEING FOLLOWED	248
June 20 ~~ COULD I HAVE BEEN A WARRIOR IN MY PAST LIFE?	248
~~ SPACE TRAVEL	250
June 21 ~~ GIVING ESOLA THE RING & RECEIVING HER GUIDANCE	251
~~ INSIDE THE PAGODA CABIN OF THE GRAND DRAGON BOAT	253
June 22 ~~ VISITING THE HIDEOUT OF THE BEINGS FROM ANOTHER WORLD	255

June 23 ~~ BILLY BUZZ OVERDOSES	257
June 25 ~~ WHO WILL SEE JUSTINE'S CANDLELIGHT IN THE WINDOW?	257
June 26 ~~ TRYING TO MAKE BETTER SENSE OF MY RANTING AND RAVING	258
June 27 ~~ PROTECTING THE TREASURE MARKET IN MY DREAMS	259
~~ BILLY BUZZ AND LIVID	260
~~ I'M BEING TARGETED	260
June 29 ~~ DREAM OF THE HOMELESS KILLER	261
~~ CARISSA'S FEARS	262
July 2 ~~ ESOLA AND THE MYSTERIOUS RING	262
July 5 ~~ A COMMUNITY GATHERING ON HOMELESSNESS	266
July 10 ~~ JEREMIAH AND THE NEW CHRIST CHILD	268
July 16 ~~ JUSTINE'S CONCERNS	269
~~ CONFRONTING AND CONTROLLING FALLACIOUS	271
July 18 ~~ THE CONFERENCE ON HOMELESSNESS	271
July 20 ~~ ASTROLOGY READING	274
~~ IS THIS THE TIME FOR ME TO ACT?	279
July 21 ~~ A CHANGED MAN	279
July 24 ~~ JUSTINE SHARES HER SECRET ROOM WITH ME	283
July 25 ~~ ANOTHER HOMELESS MAN MURDERED	290
~~ THE FINAL STRAW	290
July 26 ~~ REACHING OUT FOR HELP	292
~~ MEETING WITH KEN	292
~~ CARISSA'S UNREASONABLE DEMAND	294
July 27 ~~ SURVIVING THE MYSTERY OF THE MURDERS	295
July 28 ~~ WAKING UP FROM A NIGHTMARE	305
~~ CARISSA'S MOTHER	307
~~ NOT A FUTILE EFFORT	310
~~ QUEEN AVARICE'S POWER	312
July 29 ~~ VISITING CARISSA IN THE HOSPITAL	313
~~ ENTERING THE HOLY SKYSCRAPER	315
~~ LIBERATION FROM THE AMERICAN MONEY DREAM	320
~~ REACHING OUT TO JUSTINE	321
August 6 ~~ FEELING AT HOME	323

PREFACE

I first wrote this novel during the years from 1989 to 1991. In part I wanted to express my dissatisfaction and dismay at the political, economic and social policies of the 1980s that led to so many people becoming homeless and the increase in poverty in the United States. I also wanted to write a novel that focused on aspects of life I value (love, spiritual development, community activism), and of course, I wanted to write an entertaining novel.

In 2011, I decided that I would return to the novel, revise it and publish it as an eBook.

Now in 2020, I am publishing a new edition in eBook and paperback formats with a different cover design and minor revisions. Sadly, the problems of homelessness, poverty, systematic racial injustices, income inequality and climate change have worsened in the United States, and I feel this novel seems even more relevant 30 years after it was first written.

In writing about the mysteries and intimate relations the main character experiences while being homeless in Portland, Oregon, I have tried to convey optimism that profound transformative and evolutionary systematic changes are occurring. I believe these changes will lead to a more inclusive, caring and just society. I hope readers not only find this fictional book thought-provoking, entertaining and encouraging, but will also inspire more involvement by all of us to bring about the positive, transformative, personal and societal changes.

Mark Jay Mann
November 2020

Nobody wants to be alone Nobody wants to die

> Jeremy "JT" Lindsay
> JT AND THE CLOUDS
> From the album, *Caledonia*

One must have chaos inside oneself to give birth to a dancing star.

> Friedrich Nietzsche
> From *Occult Preparations for a New Age*

Our normal waking consciousness, rational consciousness as we call it, is but one special type of consciousness, whilst all about it, parted from it by the filmiest of screens, there lie potential forms of consciousness entirely different...no account of the universe in its totality can be final which leaves these other forms of consciousness quite disregarded.

> William James
> From *The Varieties of Religious Experience*

February 17 ~~ FADING AWAY

On some clear nights I can remember fading out of my familiar street surroundings on an ancient Chinese Grand Dragon boat floating up into the sky toward faraway stars. I imagine myself standing on the deck of this magnificent flying boat outside the pagoda-shaped, multi-storied cabins. The boat has intricate carvings on its hull and majestic amber sails spread wide on three tall masts. I stay with this vision as I stare up into the night sky until the boat disappears slowly into the darkness beyond my consciousness.

I often fade away from my here and now awareness of the freezing stings of cold rain—of intersections at street corners that require agonizing decisions of which way to go, decisions that I'm not always prepared to make—of store windows displaying things I can't buy—of jagged cracks in grey sidewalks that have depths I can't fathom—of streets that never seem to have a destination.

When I first became homeless, I would fade out, only later to have my everyday street reality come rushing back into focus, often jarring me with its harsh colors and strident sounds, forcing me back to my street life. I would often experience a profound sense of fear or anxiety—a catch in my breath. I was not sure if I was afraid of something I had just experienced outside my consciousness in another reality, or if I was experiencing a fear of having to return to this reality.

Now it seems more often I fade back to my everyday reality in a gentler manner, and I'm able to look around me slowly, taking in my surroundings with feelings of peacefulness and renewal. I'm not sure why this change has occurred, but I have come to believe that my whole being is somehow benefiting from these journeys my mind takes, even though I can never remember anything about what I have experienced. Maybe one day I will.

I often fade out in a transfixed pose of reverie sitting or standing on the sidewalk. It usually doesn't present a problem for me in my current condition. Since I'm homeless, even if I'm noticed in my temporary catatonic states, staring off into the unknown, people probably think I'm crazy, or drunk or drugged out. So I appear normal—normal as a stereotypical homeless man in his late thirties might seem to others. I don't even take street drugs or prescription drugs for that matter. And I only have a drink occasionally. I do look a little scruffy—but my dark brown hair is generally well-groomed—not long, but not cut short either—no beard—no mucus flowing from my nose—but, yes, I am often staring blankly out into somewhere, looking like I might be crazy.

I fade out even if I know I may never come back, may get lost in mazes of insanity. Or that I may face dangers, monsters, evildoers hidden in the shadows of other dimensions. I am willing to take these chances, to take journeys that may end in the death of my consciousness or being. Sometimes I believe I fade out of this reality to keep myself sane.

At times I wonder if I fade out in search of the roots of my being beyond our oppressive society. Sometimes I must prove to myself that I wasn't created in a big vat in a blackened factory that manufactures outcasts in order to provide the bored upper-class citizens of this nation an ample supply of easy prey and convenient scapegoats to deflect blame from them, those who are really to blame for our society's ills, because of their greed.

Maybe I fade out to get away from the results of their greed.

I fade out of this reality, and when I do, I hope I am caring for my new self who's not fully developed yet—my creative soul who's developing inside me—that I've hidden away in some private place within my psyche, where I can nurture it and protect it until it's strong enough to express itself through me and transform me into the person I want to be.

Being homeless now for almost six months feels like an eternity. However, I do recognize that I now seem to be able to sustain my awareness of this street reality for longer periods of time. I am also willing to remember more and more of my past. I feel as if I have almost returned to the land of the rational. I'm a college graduate. I worked in a regular, fairly good-paying job for most of my twenties and early thirties. I was a married man, a homeowner, about to start a family—and then everything fell apart.

I started writing in my journal about six months ago, right after my mental breakdown. Well, that's what the psychiatrist called it. I now think of it as a mental liberation. Anyway, when I started writing my journal, I knew it was necessary to help me stay connected to this reality and maybe one day to become more aware of the other places I go when I fade out. I know that I have to keep myself together, to stay connected to this reality despite my mental wanderings—for the sake of my new developing soul.

Even in my most discouraged and fearful moments, I know my life may be different one day. I don't know how because in this reality I don't believe we live in a healthy, peaceful, loving or creative environment. But for some reason, I feel a tiny, very tiny bit of hope. That doesn't make sense to me—it's like being lost in a cave, and every once in a while, seeing a light flicker across the cold stones. Does the flickering light come through some opening that lets in the sun from the blue sky outside the cave, meaning there is a way out of this blackness? Or is the light just a hallucination in my crazy mind? Doesn't matter, I suppose. The little flickering of light, when it comes, is comforting, and I need all the comforting I can get wherever it comes from.

I believe I have a special purpose to fulfill in this life, and that I have to develop my new soul to fulfill this purpose. If I didn't have a special purpose here in this reality, why would I come back? I could believe in my special purpose with the fullness of my heart, if I didn't feel so lonely in this reality—and lately, so often afraid of the violence I see on the streets, terrified of being killed. I have become deeply afraid that I am going to be killed in the streets of this city, and I don't know if I can do anything to change my destiny. Since being out here on the street these past six months, I don't think my concerns about how many people want to get rid of us reflect paranoia. According to the news, homeless people are being murdered by some crazy serial killer or vigilante group, for god's sake!

~~ MORNING VISIONS OF LOVE AND DEMONS

I am writing about my mind's secret journeys and my fears even before I get out of my sleeping bag this morning—it's past dawn. One moment it is dark inside me and in the sky, and another moment I open my eyes and the sky is light, boosting my urge to live. When dawn arrives each day, new opportunities are being born. I have to believe that.

I'm lying in an alley next to a red brick apartment building, one of my favorite old buildings. Perhaps if I were financially able to, or more importantly, wanted to live again within four walls, this type of building would be where I might rent an apartment.

I woke up to the sound of a woman's voice saying, "Come back to bed, hon. Come back under the covers next to me. It's so warm and cozy. I miss your body…"

In my sleep I reached out to someone who was not there. I reluctantly opened my eyes and then looked up to see if I had overheard someone talking in a nearby apartment—to see if the woman's voice had come from an open window in an apartment above me, but it seemed like all the windows of the apartment building near me were closed. I noticed a small, multi-faceted glass crystal in the shape of a drop of water, hanging in the window above me, and for a moment I became mesmerized by reflections of light emanating from this ornament. Since becoming homeless one of the few luxuries I have is time to linger and enjoy beautiful sights and sounds often hidden in the otherwise ugly and discordant structures of this modern utilitarian city.

I thought of the woman's sultry voice again—"Come on back to bed, hon"—and for a few seconds I entertained the idea that perhaps I can now hear through walls. Or perhaps I was with the woman of my dreams in another reality, and that's why I fade out so often. Anyway, it was a nice way to wake up with an intimacy that seemed real for a few seconds.

I realize now that I was probably remembering a special moment in my relationship with my wife before my breakdown, and before she left me. I still cherish the cuddling and caring moments we shared, even if we were not meant to stay together. I'm surprised at how easy it is for me now to write about our breakup with such acceptance—it wasn't easy for me to accept then, but time has allowed me to recognize she needed to leave me, and I needed to lose everything, including her.

Once I fully woke up, I sat up and propped my back against the side of the building, still trying to keep warm in my sleeping bag and blankets. I am starting a new journal today. Past, present, future and beyond time, all blend together in my journals. I may be crazy, I may be destitute, but I do want to record whatever I am feeling as fully as I can—my passion and fury, my serenity and contentment, my loneliness and fear, my joy and laughter. As I write these feeling words, the different emotions they describe flow through me quickly like changing water currents. Images of me as different characters in a play expressing these different emotions flashed through my mind. It seems I have no control over when I might feel one emotion or another. Perhaps thinking I can live life fully in the condition I am is delusional, but I know I need to try. I like thinking of life as a theatrical or movie production—unscripted and improvisational—so it doesn't matter if I actually have any control over when I might feel one emotion or another. I just have to perform whatever part the circumstances of this drama of life calls for and as fully as possible. Imagining playing different roles in ever changing scenes of a play is comforting to me, and seems to help me get through painful moments of loneliness and scary moments where I fear for my safety.

I've finished a few journals since my emotional breakdown. In the last journal after I finished an entry, I started going back to the beginning of these entries and quickly writing a title. I don't know why I started doing this, but I'm enjoying it. I write these titles trying not to think about or judge if the title really reflects what I am writing about. Maybe it's my way of desperately trying to stay focused within the vast irrational universe in which I seem to be floating. But it does seem to help me to squeeze out, condense and define the essences of my experiences. It brings closure in my streams of thought—it seems paradoxical to me to bring closure to entries by writing titles that are at the beginning of the entries, but I believe that beginnings and endings do not just follow a straight line, but sometimes fold back upon themselves. I imagine time flowing in graceful curves and cycles. I don't know where I come up with these ideas…I'm just a street person, trying to survive and make sense of things.

Right now I need to get up and get inside somewhere for a few moments where it's warm. It's cold out here. A cup of coffee and a muffin would be nice. Maybe it is ok that I'm working a few hours a week. I now have a little money to spend. This pittance allows me to afford to do my laundry more and not always have to scrounge around for food people throw away. But I can't get pulled back into the type of lifestyle that did so much damage to me. I have to be careful how many hours I work at the Treasure Market each week. I like being there too much and that worries me.

I just saw a cat, or a rat, or perhaps a demon scurry across the alley into the shadows down a ways from me. I believe in all possibilities and I'm afraid of all possibilities! Another reason to get up and to get out of this alley so I can find somewhere warm and a little bit safer.

~~ YOUNG LOVERS

I'm finally sitting in a warm coffeehouse with a hot cup of coffee and a bran muffin, my backpack and plastic bag sitting beside me. It took longer than I figured to walk to this coffeehouse, and it's so damn cold outside. It's taking a little while for the heat of the coffee cup to warm my hands, but now I can relax a little.

I don't have enough money to buy a newspaper, but I expect I will soon find one that someone has left behind. I believe reading leftover newspapers is an example of one of the many ways homeless people like myself provide a useful recycling service to society, even if it is not appreciated. I should charge for this service, if I knew who to charge, if I knew who would pay me.

While I'm waiting for someone to leave a newspaper, I just noticed a young couple sitting on a couch across the room. They are cuddling together, and being so openly loving to each other.

I stopped writing in my journal for a few moments to watch them. I put my pen down on the table. Sat back in my chair. They are animated in their interactions, giggling, smiling, and often stopping in motion to look into each other's eyes, seeming to share such deep feelings.

It was difficult for me to pry myself away from their happy, intimate displays of love.

But I turned away from looking at them, took a sip of coffee and began writing in my journal again.

I try not to invade other people's spaces or privacies—at least in a way they will notice. Often all I can do is just observe other people's lives, but I still try to do it in as noninvasive way as possible.

~~ CHALLENGES AND FEARS

The worst thing about my homelessness is being without someone to love. Someone to lay next to at night, cuddling, sharing warmth, and passionate intimacies. I miss sharing the everyday moments, being romantic with someone who thinks I'm as special as I think she is. I'm not just referring to sex, though I definitely miss that, too. But I know I'm not ready to be responsive to someone else now. I have a different purpose. To nurture a new side of myself to see if I can become someone I hope would be a loving companion, and someone who could contribute to the good of society using my creativity.

I suppose the next worst thing about being homeless is a fear that someone might attack and kill me—I hate to keep dwelling on this, but every day out here on the streets I have to face this fear that someone will kill me, and no one would know about it or worse, even care. As I walk and sleep on the streets of this beautiful city, dodging gangs and other people who seem weirder than I feel, I can't help but imagine myself being beaten, stabbed or shot, lying in a spreading pool of my blood in some dirty alley in terrible pain, near death.

I've seen a lot of violence on the streets during these last five months. Destructive, vicious street gangs roam around looking for property to destroy and people to victimize. I experience at times outbursts from angry, bitter street people who seem to hurt a lot worse than I hurt. Knives are popular street weapons, but there are also plenty of guns around, more than I would have expected. Fortunately, I haven't been shot at yet, nor has someone tried to shoot or knife me. I've also seen a lot violence by police toward who seems like innocent homeless people, many who are black and brown skinned. I try to keep myself invisible as much as I can, not only to the mainstream society, but also to the outcast society that I've fallen into.

Another thing that gets to me often about being homeless is the differences between what some people have and what other people don't have. Being hit in the face day in and day out with the outrageous discrepancy between what some people have and others don't have can get me pissed off, but I can deal with my anger better than I can deal with my loneliness and fear. My anger keeps me warm, while my loneliness and fear make the winter cold even more uncomfortable. No matter how uncomfortable I feel at times living on the street, I've realized that I cannot go back into mainstream society until my creative soul has developed and become stronger and mature enough to remain free in an enslaved society. I'm not that concerned about being hungry, cold or dirty. I've gotten numb to these things even though the pains in my stomach, the chill in my shoulders, or the itch in my crotch can make me feel depressed at times.

I have decided to use the word "slave" to describe mainstream citizens. It may be inappropriate in this day and age in the U.S to use this word to describe citizens of our society. I acknowledge that I am a privileged white man and if I weren't crazy and determined to protect my new soul, I could go back and get a job that would probably be considered middle-income. I acknowledge that despite my craziness, even as a homeless man, I don't have to worry about police profiling me or stopping me for some minor infractions. I don't have to worry about being brutalized or even killed by some bad police officer if I don't act compliantly—I don't have to worry about this because of my white skin. I know I am privileged, but I don't want to feel privileged at the expense of others just because of the color of my skin and the color of theirs. Besides, my soul doesn't feel that privileged anyway.

I'm not trying to co-opt that word related to African-Americans who have endured worse racial injustices than I have. I just feel strongly that our unequal economic and power system in the U.S. is trying to enslave all of us, of all races. I feel that we are all slaves to an unjust profit-driven system—not a positive collective human-driven system. For me, the word slave in modern times relates to an economic system that is harming non-white races more directly, but is also harming white people, more and more who are being limited to low-wage, dead-end jobs, and cannot afford suitable housing, necessary health care, and also have to endure the brunt of devastating climate disasters. And, who has the time to embrace a higher quality of life that allows an individual to develop their spiritual and creative side when they cannot make ends meet, or are working so hard to be paid a little higher income—or trying to avoid being a victim of our systemic racial injustices?

But in my current state of being, I just want to drop out of it all—all of these injustices. I'm not able to help improve this unjust society that attempts to enslave all of us in an autocratic, top-down system of income inequality as well as racial injustices. I can't deal with it. I'm sleeping on the street in my own state of poverty, because I can't do anything else now. I don't feel capable of trying to diminish the pain of the homeless, of black people, of all races who are non-white. I can't get beyond my own inner pain. I know I selfishly exist in my own pain. I don't want anyone to be a slave to some elitist, mostly white masters in our current top-down society. Yet I am consumed with battling my own demons so I can free myself fully from my past connections to the lure of unequal privileged comforts that comes at the expense of the well-being of others. I am consumed by protecting my new creative soul so that it can survive and one day grow into a more compassionate soul—and then maybe I will be able to be more helpful to others. Maybe one day I'll be able to contribute to transforming this unjust system for the better. I just can't do it now. I hope that in the future I'll be healed, strong, involved and helpful, but I can't imagine when that time will come.

One day at the city library I explored the various meanings of the word "slave." I wrote these definitions down in one of my earlier journals, and I want to rewrite them now at the beginning of this journal to remind me of what I have left and can't go back to. One definition was "a person entirely under the domination of some influence or person."

The dominating influences of our society are money and the people who are the masters, mostly white, rich corporate CEOs and investors. We have the royalty of the rich, the slave workers, and then there are the outcasts. We who are homeless are the outcasts. From what I've seen on my time living on the streets these past few months, there seem to be more African-American, Latinos and Native American individuals and families who are a part of the homeless outcasts. I think the cause of this might not just be because of poverty, but because of the discrimination non-white races have to endure related to housing, the criminal justice system, health care, education and so on.

That day at the library I identified another definition of a slave in our modern society: "One who has lost the power of resistance; one who surrenders himself to any power whatsoever; a drudge (one who labors like a slave)."

Actually, the word "drudge" seems like a good label for most middle-class people in our society, especially white people who have succumbed to their privileges and surrendered to the dream of becoming as rich and famous as their masters. But I think the word "slave" has a broader meaning. It seems that so many people in the mainstream have lost the power of resisting the illusion of attaining material wealth.

Since I am writing this journal for my own private emotional release, and hopefully one day for creative purposes, I'm not going to worry too much about what others might think about me using the word "slave" in the broader way that I am. Even in my confused state of mind, I know I am not using it to diminish the terrible things others are still experiencing because of racial discrimination. I know I am trying to keep focused on the underlying beliefs that not only led to enslaving black people centuries ago in the first place, but now in modern times have expanded to enslave all races in so often meaningless jobs that only benefit the rich and powerful. I also have to admit that I want to use this controversial word to keep me riled up and to scare myself so I won't be tempted to return to that slave existence.

I stopped writing for a few minutes. I got myself so upset writing about these things. I have to get myself out of this worrying mood—OK, I do tend to worry about many things at times—but now I want to get myself into a more peaceful state of mind. When I wrote earlier about going to the public library, I felt a glimmer of lightness come into my feelings. I love the city library and also Powell's Bookstore. I have spent hours in each since I became homeless, reading about philosophy, spirituality and politics. I have been reading plays, novels and poetry, and also writing in my journals surrounded by the wonderful array of books. It is not only warm and comfortable in the library—I'm doing something I know I was meant to do before I got channeled into sales work while still a teenager. My readings are helping me form my own philosophy of life, my own political views, and my own creative urges. All of these viewpoints are developing within me, and having the precious time to read what I want to is one of the few good things about living on the street. I'll have to go back to the library soon. Hanging out at the library might help me regain a peaceful state of mind...at least for the brief periods of time I am allowed to stay there.

I see someone has left a newspaper on a table nearby. I'll go get it so I can get my mind off my homeless struggles. I want to see what's happening in the world I've left behind. I don't know why I care, but I do.

~~ HOMELESS MURDERS. WHO ARE THE MURDERERS?

No—No—No—The horrible headline of today's newspaper reported that another one of us was found murdered yesterday—again, brutally killed—hacked to death, just like the others. Four homeless people murdered in the past month—three men and one woman. The homeless man killed last night left a family behind. A wife and two children, who were sleeping in a car near where he was killed. Not too far from where I generally hang out, on the side of the river across from downtown.

The killer has attached the same note to all of his victims—"You are unable to take care of yourself. You are a burden to society and not worth keeping alive. The survival of the fittest keeps our nation strong. Your death makes sure the deserving continue to thrive."

The reporter wrote a brief summary of how the survival of the fittest statements of this serial killer relate to Social Darwinism. Wealth was said to be a sign of natural superiority, and not achieving wealth was a sign of unfitness. It seems that a further extension of this theory is that only the strongest and most successful are fit to survive in our society.

So the poor and the outcasts of society should be allowed to die—or be killed—so they won't be a burden to the others who are more worthy of living. Just another excuse for the powerful to oppress the common folk. And kill the homeless.

Apparently the police don't really know if it's one person or a group of people killing us, even though all the killings are done in the same horrible, systematic way.

But I know who the murderers are. I'm sure most of the people in this coffeehouse, and those who walk by outside on the street, know too. Despite those who are actually using their knives to kill helpless homeless men and women, the real murderers are those people in our vicious society who have more than enough to not care about the poor and homeless, and those others who are striving so hard to have more than enough, that they are also too busy to care.

So many citizens of all classes in our society are accomplices to these murders—accomplices to the many ways other than murder that we are dying on the streets of the U.S. and around the world.

~~ ACCOMPLICES TO MURDER

I stopped writing in my journal a while ago, and went out into the street to look into the eyes of these accomplices to murder. Maybe I was being inappropriate, but I couldn't help doing this. I don't really blame everyone. It's just that so few people really do anything to help others. I speak from experience, living on the other side when I had a job. Running from home to work to recreation to home to work to wherever else I thought I was supposed to be going—on and on, and every once in a while, I would feel concern about the travesties of the world. Then I quickly forgot about all of these travesties as I tried to make ends meet and find some enjoyment in life. I failed at both of those efforts, and also did nothing to try to change the travesties occurring in the world.

But I stood on the street a few moments ago and looked into the eyes of people walking, not with a passive, blank stare, but with an in-your-face glare. I felt the difference. I hoped that the people walking by could see the difference in my eyes, in my expression. I know I was being irrational, but I was trying to make these people feel some shame. I was trying to find some remorse in their eyes for being accomplices to the murders of homeless people and many others living in poverty in our nation and in our world.

As usual, today most people completely ignored or looked away quickly as they caught my eye. These reactions gave people walking by me an appearance of programmed automatons. These people had no expressions on their faces, and they were so unwilling to acknowledge me. I was looking for any kind of reaction—even anger. But I wasn't trying to provoke violence, just a reaction, or acknowledgement. The murder of another homeless man made me more determined to reach into the souls of these people rushing by me.

I began to concentrate and thought I could begin to see flickers of recognition behind the blank stares of certain people. I tried to focus more clearly and open myself to what feelings lay hidden behind their expressions, and I began to see some concern, some compassion, even some guilt. While I was recognizing or imagining these emotions in various individuals, I also began to recognize anger and frustration in some of them. But these people walking by were not acknowledging these emotions, nor were they openly acknowledging me.

Then I felt shocked to see glimpses of life activities when I looked at some people. As I looked at one man I saw him playing catch with his son in their backyard. When I looked at another man, I saw him in the kitchen cooking dinner with his wife. They were laughing together. I looked into the eyes of a woman, and saw her gardening, talking to a rose bush she was planting. These images shook me out of my purposeful anger, and I began to wonder what I was really visualizing.

Suddenly out of the corner of my eye I saw someone stop and walk back toward me. I felt momentarily disoriented as I tried to regain my focus on the present moment. I looked at him, a middle-age man in a stylish dark grey suit. He had short black hair with streaks of grey and seemed like he would be a business salesperson or professional of some type. I braced myself for his anger.

Instead, when he spoke, he expressed concern. "Are you ok? Are you feeling ok? You seem like you are experiencing some pain or hurt. Can I help? Can I call an ambulance?"

I wasn't expecting to hear someone's concern so I didn't know what to say right away. He stood there waiting for me to respond. Getting back in touch with my feelings of anger, I finally said, "I'm not in pain in the way you think I am. I just read that another homeless man was killed last night. And I felt angry about how people like you can go on with your lives, knowing how many of us are being killed, and how many more of us are dying in the streets from hunger or lack of medical care, while you live your privileged lives."

He kept looking at me with the same concern in his eyes. He finally said, "I didn't realize another homeless person was murdered last night. I am so sorry to hear that. But do you really feel all of us are responsible for one deviant person's actions?"

"Yes, I do. How can you enjoy your fancy clothes? Your fancy haircut? Your fancy earring? Your expensive shoes? How can you enjoy all your luxuries when there are people like us out here who have nothing and others who are dying and being killed?"

He looked down for a moment. Then he looked back into my eyes and said,

"Of course, you are right. How can I enjoy these things? How can we enjoy these things? All I can say is that I think a lot of people do care and try to do what they can. I know I do. It may not be enough ..."

He saw my scowl, and I started to turn away to pick up my backpack and bag. I was thinking, what's the use talking to these people? It just makes me more frustrated. When I stare and glare, at least I'm venting my feelings—throwing emotional darts, silently screaming, and somehow it helps me to release my anger. But to talk with someone from the slave world who is a true believer in the status quo makes me feel worse, makes me not just angry, but sad as well.

"Wait, wait," I heard this guy say, and something in his voice that seemed sincerely concerned caused me to turn back with curiosity. He continued, "I want to tell you something. Can I take just a little more of your time?"

I nodded. My mind and emotions really go in all directions. Just in the last little while I've felt loneliness, then fear, then anger, then also a little sadness. But now I was feeling like laughing, actually not at him, but at his question to me. Do I have time to listen to him? It's not a matter of time. Time doesn't exist for me out here on the street. It is a matter of giving up hope, of protecting what little I have, or can have. Did I really want to make a connection to everyone passing me by? Probably not. I just wanted to make others feel as badly as I do. Maybe that would be a start of some change. I don't know. But yes I have all the time in this world.

Somehow I managed to focus on what he was saying, "Listen, I work for an advertising agency, and a few of us have been feeling the need to do something about homelessness. Honestly. I know you are thinking that I'm just saying this to make you feel better about me. But you don't know me and I don't know you, so it wouldn't really matter what you feel or think about me. One reason I stopped is because I thought you might need some emergency care—you did seem in so much pain. Now that I've listened to you, it has made me think of a project some of us want to work on to try to bring people's attention to the need there is to help homeless people like yourself. Talking with you has given me a great idea. Would you mind if I video you staring at people? And then we could put a voiceover where you could say the kinds of things to the public that you just said to me. We would be willing to use it as a public service announcement to get people engaged in helping the homeless. What do you think?"

I instinctively answered that I could not be involved in this project right now. He looked at me and started to say something. I think he was going to challenge me about being hypocritical, but then his cell phone rang. He said to whoever had called him that he'd be right there. Then he looked back at me. "I'm late for a meeting, gotta go. Please think about it. Please. You can do something to help us help the homeless." He gave me his card and as he ran away, he yelled back to give him a call.

After he left I looked at his business card and I did feel amazed. I stared at the card for a while, and thought about throwing it away. This is a dilemma for me—here's an opportunity for me to do something positive about homelessness, but I can't get involved with mainstream society in the condition I'm in. And there is a part of me that feels it would not do any good anyway. The rich people are too powerful.

I put the card in my backpack with my old clothes and notebooks, and sat down to write about what just happened and to see if I could sort some of this out. I don't know what I will do about this connection. I'm frightened about getting involved with the slave society again.

I had made one verbal connection, but I felt more excited about my ability to see the emotions and images behind the eyes of people as they walked by. This person did seem to care. But so many others just looked away and hid very sad and sometimes scary emotions. I realize that what I think I'm seeing could just be my imagination. I don't really know if I'm psychic or delusional—or a bit of both.

In terms of my attitudes toward society, I can admit to myself in the privacy of my journal that my attitudes may be a bit extreme. Just a bit. But I need to keep this extremist attitude so I don't allow myself to slip back into old patterns, my old lifestyle where I put financial security above my own creative development. I just can't allow myself to do it. I feel my labels and analogies have truths in them. I know there are a few people out there who are not slaves, even if they live the slave life. I feel that within everyone there is the potential for a new creative and compassionate soul to be born and nurtured and developed. But it's difficult for slaves to get in touch with their caring and compassionate sides when they're trying to fulfill the obligations and duties of regular society. The slave society is really geared toward the production of income for the wealthy, not for the development of caring souls.

What the fuck am I writing about here? I was trying to stare down the accomplices to the murders of homeless people, not trying to find the good potentials in the souls of people. Not to justify their lack of action, their lack of taking responsibility for the ills of our society. It is so hard for me to stay angry at other people. And now I have to worry about my own inaction.

Ahhh, I need to stop thinking about these murders and murderers, slaves and accomplices. I need to get my thoughts and emotions in a more positive place. I really do have to get away from these depressed and angry feelings… when I feel this way all I can do is keep moving and hope that something comes along that will lift my spirits. I need to find some soothing music to listen to.

February 18 ~~ LISTENING TO MUSIC FRAGMENTS

One of the most difficult parts of being on the street for me is not being able to listen to the music that my soul needs when it needs it. It took me until the early afternoon to find a place where I could listen to music that helped to lift my spirits. The search for music did help me get my mind off of the murders.

I can actually hear a variety of sounds on the streets. I hear people's car radios blaring out, usually some rap or pop music vibrating with a heavy bass. I get surprised that the street pavement beneath such cars doesn't crack. Street musicians can be delightful, but many can't even carry a note. I can go by the dormitories at one of the colleges and hear a lot of music, but it's like listening to five different types of music at one time. Kind of strange.

I hear country music outside of a street-level apartment on southeast Belmont almost every time I walk by. Once I went to sleep nearby and the next morning, I could hear country music until about 7:00 am, probably until the person went to work. Country music brings back memories of growing up in the South, and brings images of a lovesick cowboy or cowgirl pining away by a cactus under a prairie moon. Actually, I grew up on the bayous near New Orleans, but I can still relate to the sadness of Southern country music.

I have found a few taverns where rock and blues are played on the weekends, and where I can stand outside on the sidewalk or in the alley and listen. I have to be careful, though, because certain kinds of blues can really bring me down, touch me deeply, give force to my loneliness, cause me to cry. I cry often in the darkness of the night. It both exorcises and exercises my soul. It's like running an emotional mile, while at the same time getting rid of my emotional toxins. I sleep better after I have a good cry.

I've been trying to find a place where I can hear classical music, but I haven't yet found a place I can depend on. Or maybe down here in the gutter I'm not allowed to hear such exquisite music.

Most of the time I hear streams of sound fragments. I hear a yell connected to a horn connected to a screech connected to a gas exhaust explosion connected to a bell connected to an angry outburst, connected to violins of an orchestra connected to a cloth ripping connected to a bang and crunch of an auto accident. When I close my eyes, I imagine that my internal film director, whom I call Fallacious, has hired a composer to create a symphony of city sounds. Every once in a while, I can make it work and I am actually entertained. But I really miss the choice, the choice of listening to what I want.

There are good things about America, like heating vents, laundromats, libraries, used bookstores—and music. I just feel that our society has been captured by greedy groups of people who have no real concern for others. It's for this reason I'm forsaking many wonderful things like the choice to listen to what music I want when I want to. I won't buy into the luxuries of this society anymore. I'll just have to settle for the fragments of music that come to me haphazardly as I walk the streets.

Yesterday after the terrible mood I was in, I walked around most of the day, and I did hear some enjoyable music from time to time. Then in the evening, I stood outside a church and listened to someone playing the organ. It definitely helped me feel better. I stayed there for a while before I found a place to sleep, and I slept well, which surprised me. I thought I would have a horrible nightmare.

February 19 ~~ A NEAR DEATH EXPERIENCE

My nerves are burning around my shoulders and neck, and my hands are still shaking as I try to write in my journal. I can't believe that I was almost chopped to death in broad daylight by some maniac butcher with a meat cleaver. I've never been so scared in my life.

I had this premonition a few days ago when I wrote in my journal that I thought I might be killed by someone. Maybe this is the person who is killing homeless people? Even if he isn't the serial killer, he probably will kill a homeless person one day.

A few minutes ago, this meat cutter came running out of his store, yelling at me, wildly swinging a meat cleaver. I had been standing in front of his store staring into space for—I guess I lost track of time. When I walk by this store I often think of my father. He was a wholesale produce and meat salesman, and I blame him for most of the wrong paths I've taken in life. I know that's unfair, and maybe I'll fully accept responsibility for my choices one day.

But I can't really remember where my mind had gone to. All of a sudden my mind refocused, and I was back standing on the sidewalk, only to find this butcher charging me like a pit bull, screaming that he was tired of chasing bums away from his store. He was a giant man with a goddamn huge pot belly. His vicious face flushed with anger as he screamed at me. The streaks and stains of blood on his white apron scared me as much as his screaming, but the dark metal meat cleaver scared me even more.

In seconds he was in front of me, swinging the meat cleaver towards my neck. My head jerked to the right away from his swing, and I collapsed onto the sidewalk dodging the cleaver. I felt the wind of the metal blade as it swept inches above my head. I had no idea I could act so fast. I guess I really do want to live.

The next thing I remember was lying on the sidewalk, looking up at his big hulk of a body standing over me. I saw him bring the meat cleaver high up over his head, preparing to bring the sharp slicing edge down on me. I couldn't move. When I think of it now it's like all feelings, thoughts, and the ability to act had drained out of my body. I had become frozen with this stop-frame fear, my usually wandering mind focused totally on the meat cleaver's sharp edge.

The butcher started to bring the meat cleaver down. I think I came close to leaving my body just to avoid the pain. Then someone grabbed the giant's arm from behind, and pulled it back. I watched as another butcher, a shorter, thinner man, held his arm. Then I saw a woman rush up behind the butcher and also grab onto his arm to try to restrain him.

The other butcher was yelling, "It's not worth it to hurt this bum. You'd go to jail. Is it worth it to go to jail for this bum? Think about it." The woman was repeatedly screaming, "Get a hold of yourself, Al."

The killer butcher was struggling, staring at me with hatred. What did I do to him? He doesn't even know me. The only thing I've ever done is walk past his store, and sometimes stand in front of it for a while. Maybe more than just a little while—but I don't do any harm to anyone.

After a few mesmerizing moments of watching this killer butcher being restrained, I came to my senses, jumped up, grabbed my backpack and bags, and ran down the street. I looked over my shoulder and saw that he had broken away and was running after me. I ran through the intersection at the end of the block, dodging cars. Halfway down the next block I looked over my shoulder again and realized with relief that he'd given up. He was yelling something I couldn't understand. To be on the safe side I kept running for another block. Eventually I slowed down and walked until I got down here to the industrial section by the river.

I'm still trying to catch my breath, and get control of myself. It's damn scary realizing how suddenly, quickly and easily I could be killed with no warning. One minute alive, the next minute dead.

This near-death experience confirms my belief that I won't die from starvation or from eating garbage food or what passes for food in this city's shelters. My death will not be caused from cancer, AIDS, a heart attack, a terrorist's nuclear bomb, or from being run over in my sleep by a goddamn street cleaner—and I'm sure I won't have the opportunity to die from old age. Unless I can change my destiny, I'm going to be killed or murdered by someone who simply wants me dead. Having just looked into the eyes of such a person, having just escaped his attempt to kill me, I...I'm just trying to gain control of myself. I'm still in shock. I'm sitting here in an alley between two buildings hopefully hidden from view. All I can do is sit here in what I hope is a safe place, safe from everyone, and write.

My hands are still shaking. It's hard to believe this is all happening. I can still see his eyes. He would have killed me with that meat cleaver if he hadn't been restrained. Right there in broad daylight I would have been attacked and killed. An image just shot through my mind, the meat cleaver hitting the side of my neck, slicing through...my head falling onto the sidewalk.

Why am I imagining this? Why dwell on it? Because it almost just happened, goddamnit! Maybe I have to think and write about it to get it out of my system. I definitely don't want to carry this around with me for the rest of the day or for the rest of my life. I have enough troubles, enough demons to deal with.

I know my presence on the streets triggers lots of people's anger and hostility. Something about my condition brings out the worst in people. Living on the streets I've gotten used to people yelling or screaming at me. When it happens I leave quickly. I almost didn't leave quickly enough today. I almost didn't get away from that maniac.

I really do believe that most Americans would prefer people like me dead. Almost daily I experience expressions of disgust on the faces of mainstream people as I try to survive on the street. But it's quite another thing to experience a huge monster of a man swinging a meat cleaver at me.

It's amazing that I can write clear sentences because I feel completely unnerved. Hell, I just escaped a killer! Yet, as usual, I'm using my journal to calm myself, to try to make sense of this crazy, mean world I'm living in. I don't want to die at the hands of some mean bastard like him. That would be an awful way to die. I don't want to die by any means, which is strange given the situation I'm in. Like, what do I have to live for? Sometimes I'm not so sure...and even if I seem aimless to others most of the time, I'm aware of my purpose and that keeps me going, that makes me want to stay alive. I need to protect my infant creative soul and I like to think of my aimlessness as a disguise. It makes me feel more in control of my chaotic life.

However, from now on I'll try to direct my aimlessness away from that asshole's shop and his meat cleaver at least for a day or two. I must have walked along every street in this neighborhood, hundreds, maybe thousands of times, going back and forth between the river and the residential areas. I don't think I've stood in front of his store any more than any other store in the area. As a matter of fact I usually hang out near Casey's Cafe, the next street over.

Even as I write this I know I have to go back to the butcher's shop. I can't let him run me off. "The Butcher's Block", I'll call his street. A side of me wants to stand up to the bastard. This neighborhood is one of my favorite places to be, goddamnit. This is where I hang out. What right does he have to run me off?" "The right of his meat cleaver," my other side answers. I have a terrible feeling he'll come looking for me. That's ridiculous. I have to stop thinking about the goddamn Butcher.

~~ PEACEFUL REVERIE

I would like to know where worn out, broken people go to heal or get recycled. Down here in the industrial section I imagine that I look to others like a discarded piece of junk. Not that I mind being seen that way. It's just that I am still alive and feel like I have some worth. I'm not dead yet, and I don't want to be thrown into some fenced-in junkyard beside some old warehouse. Since being on the street I've often wondered when the U.S. will create containment centers to imprison us without homes so that we won't offend the royalty and the lower slave classes.

Right now I'm sitting on a loading dock of an empty warehouse, feeling quite safe from the Butcher, and safe from the nasty stares of people less prone to using violence as a way to relieve their frustrations.

After writing that last sentence, I put my pen down and stared at the unrestrained branches of a maple tree growing in an area between the sidewalk and the street close by. My mind must have gotten lost in the twisted branches for a while. I became aware again of my surroundings, took a deep breath and felt happy to be alive. I've learned to not question these feelings of contentment when I experience them—I imagine them as brief breaks in a dark, clouded sky that allows blue skies and a bright sun to be seen.

It is now late in the afternoon, still an hour or so before dark. From here I can't see the downtown skyline, or the streets full of spastic traffic. I can see the river, and large ships that have sailed in from the Pacific Ocean to load or unload their cargo. It has been a peaceful afternoon for me, which I needed after what occurred with the Butcher. I don't know where my mind journeyed, but I'm sure it was a peaceful place. Maybe I'll be able to sleep well tonight after all.

February 21 ~~ THE DANGEROUS LURE OF THE TREASURE MARKET

I slept well most of the night, but woke up feeling anxious. I felt like going to the Treasure Market to talk with Justine and Esola, but I decided not to do it.

I am reluctant to rely on or become emotionally involved with other people right now. As painful as that may be to me at times, I'm not relationship material in the condition I'm in. If I reached out to Justine and Esola, and they responded and we became closer, there's a chance I would be lured back into the slave society. I fear I would be taking the first step back toward the repression and perhaps death of my new soul. It's not strong enough to withstand the forces of a society where only money, comfort and luxury have any worth. I don't think Justine and Esola are ruled by these things, but to relate to them—to reach out to them I would have to return to the prison I've just escaped from.

I just remembered watching Justine the last time I was working at the Treasure Market. She was sitting at her desk looking through various papers while I cleaned furniture in the workroom. From time to time she would take her right hand and run her fingers through her hair. It was a sensual motion. I enjoyed seeing the movement of the dark curls as they fell back on her neck.

So I'm using this memory as an anecdote for my knotted emotions. But Justine is only my employer for a few hours each week. She's nothing more. She can be nothing more. Fortunately—and I write that word now with difficulty—she is in a relationship and there is no possibility of romance between us.

I do enjoy working at Treasure Market. It might look like an antique or second-hand furniture and jewelry store but to describe it as a second-hand store doesn't capture the magical aspects of its atmosphere and merchandise. To describe it just as an antique store is even too limiting. I think the word "treasure" captures the essence of the place. It contains treasures that seem to have been brought back from history of different parts of the world, from exotic, faraway places, some ancient, some from the future, even from a different dimension. Everything in the store has a beauty or a power and seems to be encased in the time period and land where it was made.

Sometimes when I'm in the store I seem to be transported to a Byzantine place where men in colorful robes with daggers hanging by their sides and women with faces covered by scarves are bartering. Or sometimes I feel like I'm in an old English village mansion standing around dark, hand-carved wood furniture.

Justine seems about my age, in her mid-thirties. She is Esola's daughter, and manages the store. I remember when I first allowed Justine to lure me into working a few hours for her. A few hours at a time is all I will allow myself to work in their store. I had walked by the Treasure Market often, and was truly impressed by the dense fantasy land of lamps, mirrors, clocks, cabinets, chests, tables, jewelry, old paintings, chandeliers, rugs, fabrics and other objects I could see as I stood outside looking in through the large store window. I would often see Justine talking with customers, cleaning or fixing something. When the days were dry, she would put furniture and things out on the sidewalk in front of her store. I would sit a short distance away, leaning against a tree or against a nearby building, writing in my journal, trying to keep my mind focused on the array of objects I could see being displayed. I would notice Justine as she came outside to organize her display, or to interact with customers. Sometimes she would turn and look at me for a few moments. I worry often that store managers will be upset about my presence so near their stores. I realize the effect I have on owners of small stores. I have to admit that sometimes I use this effect - their fear that I will scare away their customers - to needle some of them who I feel are particularly paranoid or who are just plain mean.

But I certainly didn't feel that way about Justine. I never had the feeling that Justine was actually worried about my presence. She just had some kind of curiosity, and later I realized she just wanted to acknowledge that I was there. After I got to know Justine, I realized one of her special qualities is her willingness to take the time to truly become aware of others around her. Her focus doesn't seem to be superficial or judgmental, but seems to always be on recognizing the uniqueness of each person. I have learned that she insists on honest interaction. A part of her seems to reach out for an emotional connection while another part seems to remain at a distance, like a director trying to determine how best to use the cast to create an effect the scene called for. Justine is involved in the city's theater as an actress and director. She loves drama. And when I think of drama I think of her mother, Esola.

I had frequently witnessed the spontaneous performances of Justine's mother while sitting outside on the sidewalk near the Treasure Market. Esola's a tall, large woman, big-breasted, with graying hair. She sometimes has an air of dignified royalty about her. Other times she seems like a street vendor, full of emotion, bursting out with laughter or anger. Justine would sometimes get pulled into Esola's mini-dramas, and I would be pleasantly entertained as I watched them. Later I found out Esola's true character is that of a gypsy. She fascinates and enchants me, but unsettles me at times with her accurate predictions, psychic assessments and pronouncements.

~~ THE TREASURE THEATER

I was initially drawn to this area, not by Esola's Treasure Market, but the building next to it—The Treasure Theater. Both buildings have old, dark wood exteriors, and seemed to have been designed by the same architects. Tall buildings with large glass windows on the first floor facing the street and with dark shingled pitched roofs—the Treasure Market is taller, probably five stories tall. The Treasure Theater is a two-story building.

I later found out that the theater and the store are both owned by Esola and Justine as two separate businesses. Justine manages both. The Treasure Theater puts on established plays as well as new plays written by local writers.

I will soon need to face and perhaps write about my emotions related to my experiences with theater and plays. I have not been ready to deal with this part of my past life. But I feel amazed that I found a place like the Treasure Theater, and even more amazed that I not only met, but am working part-time for the owner of the theater.

~~ FIRST MEETING WITH JUSTINE

The day I met Justine, I had been sitting on the sidewalk under the huge maple tree near the street between the theater and the market. The afternoon was unusually warm for February. I had my journal open and was ready to write, but I couldn't get my mind to work. As had been happening all too often to me, my mind seemed to be in a disintegrated state, pieces of thought and fantasy floating off in every direction. But then Justine just walked out of her store, walked straight up to me and asked if I wanted to make a few bucks helping her move some furniture. I would normally have said no without thinking, even though I was starving. But as I looked into her eyes, I couldn't say no. I couldn't say yes, either, and I must have looked pretty stupid with my mouth open, just staring up at her.

"Can you speak?" she finally asked.

I nodded.

She stood for a moment with her hands on her hips, looking at me. "Are you on drugs?" she finally asked.

I shook my head, "No". She looked at her watch. I remembered being mesmerized by her presence. As she stood there, her expression seemed a mixture of a soft unconditional acceptance of who I was and yet of a strong expectation for me to meet my responsibility at the moment—at least the responsibility of responding to her. I had forgotten what meeting the expectations of others meant.

Somehow, though, I was able say, "I'm sorry. I was deep in thought. I ..." And I didn't know what else to say.

"Look, that's okay. You know, I've seen you around. I've seen you writing in your notebook. I thought you might be homeless, but I wasn't sure. I'm cautious about giving handouts to street people. It's just that I could really use some help moving furniture in the store right now and I'd be willing to pay you for your work. I'm up against a deadline."

Without thinking further, I said, "Yes, I'll help. If it doesn't take too long." What a lame response. Of course, it wasn't that I had any time demands. I was just protecting myself.

She did look surprised at my response, but then just said, "No, no, moving this furniture won't take that long. By the way, my name is Justine. What's yours?"

I told her my name was Gibson Calhoun, and she said "I used to know someone named Gib. Do you prefer Gib or Gibson?"

"I've always asked that people call me Gibson, but it doesn't really matter." I still can't believe I said that to her. Of course it matters to me.

I remember she said to me, "No, I'll call you Gibson. It kinda goes better with the image of a writer."

"I'm not a writer." I said, probably more vehemently than I should have. I am not a writer in the way she thinks I am a writer. I write for my soul, not for others.

Then she said to me, "Oh I've seen you writing in your journal so often. I just thought...but I don't mean to pry. Anyway, Gibson, we need to get going if we're going to get the furniture ready before the customers come."

She turned and walked back toward her store. I got up and followed her. It meant a lot to me that she hadn't pried further about my writing.

As I entered the store, I felt a deep sense of awe. I had entered a place where so many beautiful objects were, objects that people all over the world, from all different time periods had made, used, and enjoyed. I followed her up two flights of stairs.

"I have some furniture to bring downstairs that someone will be here to get in about twenty minutes. I'm shorthanded today," she said as she looked over her shoulder. "We have an elevator we can use, in case you're wondering or were worried about having to carry furniture down two flights of stairs."

"I hadn't thought that far ahead," I responded. "I've just been admiring all of these beautiful things."

"Well, there are five floors, and a basement—many rooms full of these things. I usually have two crews of furniture movers but recently I've lost some of them and need to hire more. I also need someone for part-time help but it's difficult to find a person who only wants to work a few hours a week."

"I'm sure a lot of homeless people would be willing to work whenever you'd need them."

"Not you?" She looked inquiringly at me with her dark eyes.

"I don't know how to answer that right now. I don't know if I'd be able to commit myself to…to anything so structured."

She laughed. "So structured?" she asked. "A few hours every once in a while? That's too structured?"

I surprised myself that I was able to smile. "I know it sounds weird, maybe even irresponsible, but it's more that I'm …" I could only think of words like "crazy" and "emotionally unstable," but I couldn't say them, and I stopped smiling in my confusion.

She must have noticed that my mood had changed. She shrugged and said, "Whatever it is, you don't have to explain. I suppose you are doing what you need to do."

I felt my anxiety dissolve when she said that. It was simple. So non-judgmental. I felt relieved that I didn't have to explain myself further. After a few moments, I asked her how she finds all those wonderful things in the store.

"My mother and father moved here from Greece about forty years ago and started this store. They already had many contacts in Europe, but they continued to develop more contacts in other parts of the world and the U.S. They tried to fill the store not only with expensive antiques, but also inexpensive furniture, fabric, jewelry and other specialty house crafts and decorations that anybody could buy regardless of how much money they have. We buy from garage sales and from auctions. We buy locally when we can, but we feel it is important to bring culturally-diverse, artistic and well-made housewares from other parts of the world."

She pointed to a dark wooden table with six chairs that we had to get out from behind a couch and a cabinet. We started moving the furniture aside.

As we moved it, she continued to talk about the store. "My father died about eight years ago and I started helping my mother run the store. Then a couple of years ago she asked me if I wanted to start running it for her. So I manage the store now, but she still continues traveling to buy merchandise. She has a special eye for unique and beautiful jewelry and decorative fixtures."

"I have noticed your mother."

Justine laughed and said, "I bet you have."

"I see you and Esola often go to the Treasure Theater, actually mostly you. Are you involved the theater?"

"Yes, we own and I manage both buildings. Theater is my real passion in life. My mother has been very supportive of me developing a theater company in that building. I think she decided that I would stick around and help her with the store if I was operating a theater company. She was wise to offer that to me. It's a good mix…we have all the sets that we want from our used furniture, and for right now it's working well for both of us."

After we brought the table downstairs, I helped her unload some furniture from a truck out back. Then she gave me $30 for about a half hour of work. "This is more than I would normally pay for such a short time, but you really helped me out of a bind today."

I thanked her and started to leave, but she said, "Listen. Gibson, if you do decide you need some work, I can always use some help around here. Maybe we could agree on something like setting a limit on the hours I could pay you on a weekly basis, and whenever you want to work you could just stop by and we could tell you what we need to have done. It could be cleaning, moving furniture, maybe painting or repairing something. I will need to hire some more regular movers, but I could always use some extra help for a few hours a week. What do you think?"

Right on the spot I agreed to it. I knew that I wanted to spend more time in the store and perhaps in the theater—and more time around Justine. It wasn't the money I was interested in, even though I didn't mind the idea of having a little money to spend. At the same time, I feared being drawn into the slave life again. I feared putting my vulnerable creative soul at risk. I am trying not to work at the Treasure Market too often.

It's been okay, though. A few days ago I worked a couple hours right before noon unloading furniture. Justine wasn't at the store when I was working and I missed seeing her. Esola said she was with her boyfriend preparing for a new stage play. I guess he is an actor.

I can allow myself to enjoy being around Justine even though I know our relationship cannot become romantic.

~~ FIRST DAY WORKING AT THE TREASURE MARKET

As I'm sitting here writing in my journal about Justine, I'm also remembering with special feelings how pleased she had seemed when I walked through the front door of the Treasure Market a few days after that first meeting. She had jumped up from her desk, walked hurriedly around the counter, and said, "Gibson, I'm so glad to see you. I was hoping that you meant it when you said you'd work for me." I replay often in my mind her spontaneous expression of warmth at that moment, and I suppose I like to fantasize she had a different kind of feeling toward me than she really does have.

"Yes, I'd like to take you up on your offer if it's still there," I said.

"Sure it is. You can start any time you want."

"Is it still all right for me to just come when I want and work for a couple of hours or so?"

"Sure it's all right," she smiled. "Do you want to work today? There are things that need to be done around here."

Justine showed me the back room where the store merchandise is stored before it is put out on one of the sales floors. The work room is a large room next to the main floor sales room. A number of doors lead to and from the work room. One door leads to a loading dock, and another door leads to the front sales floor where Justine has her desk behind a counter. Another door leads to the repair shop. On that first day she introduced me to Harold, a handyman who also works occasionally for her repairing furniture and other store merchandise. Harold's a sixty-five-year-old man who's apparently been with the store for many, many years. He greeted me gruffly, but said that he looked forward to seeing me around the store. Then he turned and went back to work. Justine explained to me that Harold mostly keeps to himself.

Then I remember Justine stopping and looking at me for a moment. "Are you a loner, too, Gibson?"

I remember feeling panicky at that moment, thinking I made a mistake agreeing to work for her. I did not feel, and still don't feel that I am capable of explaining myself. How can I explain my new infant soul? Or Fallacious? I need to be a loner at this time, but, god, I want so much to be with a woman I love. All I remember saying to Justine at that moment was that I was a loner.

"I'll try to respect that. Gibson." She smiled, and I felt such mixed feelings. I felt like I want to tell her that I wasn't really a loner, but I also felt a sense of relief that she wasn't going to pry further into my confused emotions.

She just continued showing me around the store. She told me I would be working mostly by myself in the work room loading and unloading furniture, taking and getting merchandise to and from different rooms of the store, cleaning and putting together merchandise, sanding and doing some minor repairs. She said I could ask her or Harold if I had questions about anything, but that I'd be working under her supervision, which I definitely was pleased to hear. As I looked around the workroom with all the furniture, lamps, rugs, mirrors and boxes of small items, I could see that there would always be something for me to do.

Esola was not in the store during that first day. The day I met her is another story, which I'll have to write about soon.

After Justine showed me around she brought me back to the front counter where she has her desk. She asked me what I wanted for a wage and I told her I didn't know. The concept of consistently having money again seemed unreal to me. She said that she would start me at $10.00/hour, and then would be willing to increase it if I came regularly and things worked out between us.

I remember now the expression on her face as we shook hands on the deal. I realize that this may just be the illusions of a lonely street man, but I felt like she was welcoming me into her heart. I don't think of Justine in sexual terms. Well, in a way I may think of her sexually, as I enjoy seeing her feminine body in her tight jeans, and her lovely facial features, her dark skin, and her curly, wild, long black hair. But I've tried to resist sexual fantasies about her. After all, what's the use? I'm just a hollow vehicle, a dead person carrying around an infant soul inside who is too undeveloped to be sexual. And besides, she's just being a nice person, a warm person. I can enjoy how lovely she is and still relate to her as a nice boss, a nice person. I can feel fortunate for her opening her store to me, and being open to tolerate my eccentricities. I can't ask for more, and where I am in my life, I shouldn't.

What's strange for me to remember is how right it felt to be in the store walking around with Justine that day. I didn't feel the need to be defensive at all about my need to make my own schedule. Even now I think I couldn't be more fortunate to have this work opportunity. Working for her gives me a little money for food, so that I don't have to rely totally on what other people throw away or leave behind at tables in public places.

February 22 ~~ BEDTIME RITUALS

As night begins to take over the city, I begin my ritual of preparing my bed. This ritual for me is a little more complicated than just pulling back the sheets and covers.

The act of making my bed involves finding the right pieces of cloth or cardboard to keep the wind or the rain or heavy morning dew off me as I sleep. It involves finding the right nooks or crannies that I can fit into without changing my basic body shape or personality structure.

Sleeping places do affect my personality, given the fact that my psyche is in a continual state of dissolving and reforming—as it reforms it picks up essences of the environment in which I live and sleep. It sounds esoteric, but I suppose it's more psychotic.

If I sleep in a huge water or sanitation pipe, my sleep is sporadic because I fear being flooded with the city's shit during the night, even if I know that the pipe is not being used. Needless to say, I have a fitful sleep when I make my bed in a pipe. If I sleep in an abandoned building, how relaxed I am depends on how hidden my bed is. All sorts of violence goes on in abandoned buildings.

Tonight I am in one of these abandoned warehouses, and I'm on the third floor of the building hidden away behind some large boxes near the fire escape. I am writing a little before I go to sleep. I haven't slept in this building before, but it is on the east side, not too far from Casey's Café. I had a premonition before I came into this building that I shouldn't. But I haven't proven to myself that I am really psychic, and I felt tired, and the door was unlocked, so I decided to test fate. Now that I made my bed, I think I made the right—wait, I hear noises downstairs, yelling and laughing. I hear metal scraping along the concrete floors and masculine hooting and howling. I have to find a way out of here.

~~ BEDTIME DANGERS

The howling and hooting of this gang actually saved my life, or at least some intense pain. I'm in a 24-hour Laundromat right now, where I'm trying to calm my nerves.

When I heard the gang climbing the stairs, I jumped up, grabbed my backpack and blanket, ran to the fire escape door, and slipped outside. I instantly felt my stomach sink as I realized that there was no fire escape stairway. I was standing on a platform high in the air with no way down except back through the warehouse. I turned back to the door and looked through its wire mesh window just in time to see a gang of cocky, rough-looking white young men come into the room, joking and jostling with each other. A couple of them carried chains and what looked like metal clubs. One of them carried a bag. He must have been their leader because he motioned and the others formed a circle around him. I heard him say that now was the time to count how much charity the rich had decided to give to them. The others howled and yelled obscenities and beat their metal clubs on the floor. The leader reached in the bag and pulled out a wallet. He opened it up and took out money and some credit cards, laying them in piles. The other gang members made crude noises again.

The leader again reached into the bag and pulled out what looked from where I was like a small piece of cloth. But the leader let me know what it was by holding it up and turning it, whistling and then saying thanks to the woman the panties belonged to for leaving on them the scent of her body for all of them to use. The others yelled and howled and stomped. I turned away from the window and sat with my back to the door feeling sick again. My insides were being torn from both fear and disgust.

I turned back to the window and forced myself to watch the gang complete their ritual of counting what they had obviously stolen from others. I had to be prepared to at least try to defend myself if they decided to come out onto the fire escape. When they were through dividing their money, I heard one of them say that he wanted to play pool at a bar and someone else said, "Let's go. I want to beat your ass."

I started to feel relief until I heard one of them say that they should come with him down the fire escape. The others agreed and started in my direction. I stepped back from the door and desperately looked around. The only way off this platform was to jump. I quickly looked down, it seemed a long way down to the concrete alley. If I jumped, I'd break every bone in my body, but then again, maybe that would be preferable. A quick death.

I looked over to my right and saw a drain pipe extending from the roof to the ground. I knew they were almost at the door. I threw my backpack over the edge of the platform. Then I climbed on the railing of the platform and jumped toward the drain pipe. I managed to hold on and started sliding down the pipe. I heard the door open, and then heard someone above me yell, "Look, some asshole's been out here listening to us."

I was still 15 or 20 feet from the ground, when suddenly I felt a part of the thin metal drain pipe break, and I fell to the pavement. I landed partly on my backpack, which along with all of the layers of clothes I wear, seemed to cushion my fall. As I jumped up, I heard someone above yell. "Go get him."

I realized quickly that I didn't break anything. I picked up my backpack and started to run down the alley to the street. My left side felt sore and bruised, but I just kept running, zig zagging down alleys and streets.

I finally came here to this Laundromat to feel some security and warmth around me. I decided I might as well wash my clothes while I was here. I don't think I will get much sleep tonight after what just happened.

Maybe this gang is killing homeless people. I thought for a while about this possibility, but it didn't seem right. I wasn't getting a psychic recognition, and I have to be careful about giving too much credence to my psychic abilities, especially after what just happened at the warehouse, which I felt would be a safe place to sleep.

~~ LAUNDROMAT COMFORTS

I'm waiting for my load of laundry to finish in the washing machine (I could only afford one load and the small container of soap tonight) before I put it in the dryer, but already I feel much better.

I wonder how I look to the mainstream slaves who dress so expensively. From my viewpoint I don't always look like a bum. I don't have dirt caked or streaked on my face. I'm not glassy-eyed with baggy pants and a hunched-over posture. Yet I do have stubble growth and wrinkled clothes most of the time.

I'm a little over six feet, and weigh about 165 pounds. I weighed about 195 before I became homeless, but I wouldn't recommend this lifestyle change as a weight control method for everyone.

Some days I wear blues or blacks because it doesn't show the street filth. On other days I like to wear outrageous and incompatible colors to offend other people's complacency. But most days I just wear my brown shirt and blue jeans.

Except for my reveries, I try my best to not look too grogged out, drugged out, dirty, and crusty. Even out here on the street I sometimes imagine that I want to be ready if I do meet the woman of my dreams. Just because I have isolated myself and have nothing, doesn't mean I have to look like a slob. And it doesn't mean that a chance for a meaningful relationship is totally out of the question. So I keep myself looking as clean and neat as I can. Such a romantic encounter really is out of the question but I keep battling with myself. It's not even a matter that it could never happen; it's a matter that I should never let it happen.

You don't have to have a home to stay clean. Sometimes I think that the main advantage of a home is that you can hide more of what you have that is dirty. True, it's more difficult to stay clean on the street. Public restrooms are not so friendly to the homeless anymore, if they ever were. I used to be able to sleep in stalls just a few months ago, but now they have taken doors off of many of the public toilets.

I try to wash myself in public restrooms when they're not too busy. I can wash my face easily, but that's about it before Mr. Joe Public Slave comes in, and

I have to leave so I don't create a scene. I make it a point to wash my hair every few days even if it's just with the soap in the restroom. I'm not saying my hair is in a healthy condition but at least it doesn't look grimy or too wild.

The shelters have showers, but I don't like the shelters. Shelters make me feel like just one of the stray rejected cattle that are herded over to a barn in the back pasture out of sight of everyone while the masters wait for the truck that'll take us to the slaughterhouse. I know that's a little extreme but it's what I think.

If I were in a small, rural town I probably couldn't be easily distinguished from the regular working slaves of the farms, logging camps, or the mills. But here in the city even though I may be clean most of the time I contrast with the slick, expensive clothes, hair styles and jewelry that the city slaves wear. People spend a hell of a lot of money on looking nice. I have nothing against that in itself. I enjoy the beauty and the variety of the different fashions. Women look sexy, independent, creative, in control. Personal statements. Fine. It bothers me that they're looking that way so expensively while people are starving all over the world. I don't see that much creativity in men's clothes but still these guys in their designer pants and T-shirts coming out of the local health spa look pretty damn handsome and I know that they spend a hell of a lot of money on themselves, too. Everyone seems to look like fashion models. So how can a homeless person like myself even hope to look decent enough to fit in? We don't fit in, which is why we are on the street wearing used clothes uniforms that set us apart. But still I make sure I'm clean most of the time, even if I don't look the shiny-gel-blow-dry-French-powdered-clean that the mainstream slaves look.

I just put my load of clothes in the dryer. During these winter months I'm spending as much time as I can in Laundromats. I hang out in Laundromats for a number of reasons. One, it's warm. Two, there are a lot of magazines lying around, and sometimes there's a TV. Three…well, I don't have another reason, except the obvious—it's a comfortable place to spend some time.

I know washing my clothes so often is expensive in a relative sense. If I hired a financial planner, I'm sure that I'd be told that I'm spending too high a percentage of my meager income on washing my clothes. But maybe he wouldn't be taking into account that the same money being used for my laundry is also being used to cover partial rent, heat and entertainment expenses. And what's more I can often pick up clothes in the discarded clothes box. I realize that even though I wash my clothes often I still really do look homeless. I can get the dirt out of my clothes but I can't wash out my scroungy outcast appearance. I don't mind that really. I need to keep the line clear between the regular slaves and myself. Anyway, it's the warm air of the Laundromats and the feel of clean clothes against my skin that are important to me. Thank god for Laundromats. There are some things in America that I still like and that's one of them.

February 25 ~~ WALTER AND THE ALIENS FROM ANOTHER PLANET

After doing my laundry, I found a place to sleep nearby that seemed safe. I can't become afraid of sleeping at night. I have to get my sleep or I probably will go crazy. Or more crazy. I decided to find a place to sleep near downtown. I thought that would be safer than where I usually sleep on the east side of the river. I don't know why I thought the downtown area would be safer. It seems I have to not only protect myself from gangs, but also a serial killer and a butcher. Maybe I don't have to worry about the Butcher unless I go by his store again.

I found an alley that I've slept in before and that seemed out of the way of heavy traffic. And I quickly fell asleep.

Sometime during the night, probably early morning, this old drunk, Walter, twenty or thirty years older than me, stumbled into my alley way and woke me up. He had a bottle of cheap wine with him and offered me some. I sat up and took one drink of the wine, and had to listen to him ramble on about his life, or someone else's life.

He asked me at one point in a whispery voice, "Have you seen them?"

He looked around nervously. I looked around too, and all I could see were the shadows and a car or two rolling by in the street beyond the alley. "No, Walter," I said, "I don't think I've seen them."

He looked at me for a long time without speaking. Then he said, "I don't know if I can trust you." He tried to get up but was having difficulty.

I reached out to him. "Wait, Walter...you can trust me. You've seen me on the street these past months. We've talked. I'm just like you, trying to survive out here."

He took another drink of wine, and finally decided he could trust me. He said he had uncovered a secret, an alien race of beings, who looked like humans and might be trying to take over the earth. He said that he is not sure about that, but he is scared. He said he was sleeping in an alley one night, hidden underneath his cardboards and rags. These beings walked into the alley and started making strange unearthly sounds. Walter said he looked out between his cardboard, and described how one of the alien beings took off his head and started turning the ears like a radio dial. He said this alien being started talking into his head's nose like a microphone, and spoke in a language he didn't understand. Walter said he was afraid he would be noticed, but the alien eventually put his head back on, and they left the alley. Walter said he followed them to their apartment building, and has spent the last four months following them to their meetings. Lately, though, he has been afraid he has been noticed, which is why he is going to different alleys to sleep. And he said he decided just tonight to tell someone else so that if they killed him, at least someone else would survive to warn the world.

I thanked him for the honor and moved my cardboard down the alley to try to get some sleep. He yelled at me not to tell anyone, and that he would soon have proof that these aliens are coming for me and the rest of the world. I nodded to him, and before I fell asleep, I realized that it was comforting to have Walter next to me in the alley tonight, even if he was crazier than I was, and I smiled to myself as I realized he even provided me a fanciful bedtime story.

February 27 ~~ FIRST ENCOUNTER WITH ESOLA

Just a few minutes ago I was walking by a Greek restaurant and I heard some wonderful Greek music. Hearing this lively, passionate music reminded me of the first time I met Esola, Justine's dramatic mother. I had just come into the store to work, when one of the salespeople said that Justine had run out on an errand but Esola was somewhere in the store. I went looking for her. When I saw her, she was swaying to a slow romantic gypsy song playing on a stereo in one of the back rooms.

I stood in the doorway watching this delightful older woman holding her arms out from her sides even with her shoulders, moving gracefully to the music. She noticed me out of the corner of her eye but kept dancing. She motioned with one of her hands for me to come into the room. "Come join me, young man," she said. I stayed where I was.

She stopped dancing and came up to me. "What? You want me to give you a performance? Do you have money to put into my bosom?"

"No, I ..."

"No, of course not. Men want everything for free." Then she laughed. "You must be...wait, don't tell me." She put her hand to her head. "You must be Gibson Calhoun, the homeless man that my daughter hired to work around here."

"Yes, and you must be Esola."

"I'm happy to meet you Gibson. Do you know that I am the one who suggested to Justine that she hire you?" The music had stopped. She walked to the stereo, turned the record over and started the other side.

"No, I didn't." I don't think I sounded disappointed.

Esola looked back at me and said, "She told me that she had also been thinking about talking with you. Does that make you feel better?"

"I...I'm not sure what you mean. I was just trying to find Justine to ask her what she wants me to do. I didn't mean to interrupt your..."

"Gibson, please don't say, 'I didn't mean to …'" she interrupted, "Don't apologize. Just do exactly what you do and do it passionately. I didn't mind if you saw me dancing. I enjoyed it, even if I gave you a bad time for just staring at me." She looked at me and laughed. "I'm just this way. At my age I can be any way I want. And to dance before a man is still a pleasure. You want a glass of wine, Gibson?"

"I don't know. I came to work a couple of hours."

"There will be plenty of time for that. Come share a glass of wine with me. Today is a very special day, which is why I'm being so sentimental and dancing to old Greek gypsy songs. Exactly forty years ago today I met my dear husband. We had been married thirty-seven years when he died. Don't you think this is a day worth celebrating?" She grabbed my arm and pulled me toward a table with a bottle of wine sitting on it. "Come celebrate with me. This is not part of your job so you can say no, but I'd like you to celebrate with me, Gibson. It will also be a good introduction for us, don't you think?"

She refilled her glass and poured another one for me. As she handed the wine to me, she said, "I like you Gibson. I can tell you are a good man. I don't know why you are living the life of a bum, but I know you are a good man." She laughed with a full spirit.

I laughed, too. "Thank you, I guess," I said. "How about this, though. I'll celebrate with you if we don't discuss my life…as a bum."

Esola laughed again and raised her glass. "I'll agree to that for today, for this celebration. But tomorrow all agreements are off. I can be as nosey as I want. A deal?"

I reluctantly raised my glass and clinked it against hers. "You can try to be as nosey as you want."

"I like a challenge, Gibson. But, you know, I am psychic. I won't have to ask you too many questions anyway." She laughed and took a sip of her wine. I felt uneasy.

I drank a few glasses of wine with Esola, and listened to her talk about her deceased husband. She cried and she laughed and I have to admit that I laughed with her and found that I did have tears in my eyes at times. I completely forgot about working or anything else…until Justine came.

When she came into the room, I was a little drunk, I think, and I just stared at her, feeling an excitement in my chest. She stood there at first with a questioning look on her face, like she couldn't believe what she was seeing. Before she could say anything, Esola said, "Gibson is so wonderful. He's been celebrating with me, Justine. Celebrating forty years since I met your father."

"I know, Mama. I know you met Papa forty years ago."

I thought about saying, "I came to work," but instead I said, "Your mother is wonderful. But I'm sorry. I'm not in any shape to work now."

She seemed so serious. I thought I had lost this job after only being hired for a short time.

She came into the room, maintaining her serious expression. She said, "All I can say is that you two better have saved a glass of wine for me." As she poured herself a glass, her expression softened and she said, "Gibson, there'll always be work around here. There'll be plenty to do whenever you come again. Especially if you are willing to put up with my mother."

I looked at Esola, and she just raised her eyebrows and her glass of wine. "Let's toast to that," she said, and laughed.

By this time, it was almost closing. Esola and Justine asked if they could buy me dinner. I said no. And I left the Treasure Market. I remember later sitting alone on a transit bench. It was drizzling. I was cold and hungry and drunk. I kept asking myself why I couldn't have just gone with them and let them buy me dinner? Why couldn't I have? I kept asking myself what was wrong with me. But I knew that I had made the right decision, no matter how I was feeling at the time. I knew I couldn't get too close. I just couldn't get that close. I ended up going to a grocery store and buying a small container of yogurt and a banana.

My first memory of Esola was of her celebrating. She's delightful to be around even if she enjoys giving me a bad time.

I don't have any money so the sooner I get back over to Esola's Treasure Market and do some work today, the sooner I'll be able to eat. I guess I could always scrounge around at the Yamhill Market to find leftovers at the tables in the mall area, but that's just not appealing to me right now.

February 28 ~~ EXQUISITE PERIL

I'm sitting in Casey's Cafe eating a bowl of chili. It's early evening. I had quite an eventful few hours at the Treasure Market this morning. I had been working about half an hour when Justine rushed into the store and dropped the stack of files she was carrying onto her desk. Then she hurried into the workroom and said, "Gibson, could you do something for me? I know that I keep asking you to bail me out of emergencies. Maybe I'm stretched too thin, but I have to get some props over to the theater for a dress rehearsal they're having tonight. Can you help me? It's only a table, a few chairs, a lamp. Let's see, what else? Well, just a few more things. I need help loading them onto moving carts and rolling them over."

I helped her load up the items that the theater was going to use. She told me about the play as we worked. It sounded like an interesting one. An avant-garde play about two germs in a hospital room talking about the diseases they can inflict on modern people. About how technology is helping them, the germs, grow stronger as much it's helping people combat the germs. I told Justine that it sounded kind of weird. I told her that somehow when I saw the old furniture that she was loading up into the van, it seemed like the play would be more traditional, about an English family's loves and conflicts. She laughed and said that of course part of the satire and humor in the play involves the human-like way the germs are presented.

"Maybe the germs should be a male and female and they fall in love, which changes their desire to inflict diseases on people," I said. That idea just popped into my mind.

Justine looked at me for a moment without saying anything. "Interesting idea, Gibson. This is a strange avant-guard, black humor play, but…having these germs fall in love could provide an unexpected dramatic twist. I'll talk to the director about your idea."

When we entered the theater, I realized that this was the first time I had been in one since high school, and as I walked into the backstage area, I felt this rush of excitement. It was strange. I mean, since I had rarely been around theater in my life, I didn't know where my excitement was coming from. But I felt it.

I helped Justine unload the furniture, then as she talked with the director, I walked around the stage, looking at the dark wood, the tall curtains, the ropes, the pulleys, the lights. It was like an empty, hollow cavern, but I knew it was waiting for the magic of the drama, of the play to begin. I was enjoying how connected I felt to this atmosphere, this place.

I remembered enjoying a high school play when I was about 16 years old before the death of the creative part of myself. I think it was a Tennessee Williams play. Someone was exquisitely in love with someone else but some tragic thing happened. I can't remember what. And I'm sure I didn't understand anything that was actually going on. What I remembered as I walked around the stage earlier today was the thrilling atmosphere of the performance, the play, the audience. The depth of expression. The deepest sharing I can imagine.

Those memories seem so dreamlike. They have been so far away but they seem closer now. Yet, I don't know what to do with them. Lost opportunities. Such wrenching pain I feel when I bring these images to my mind. I've lost so much.

On the way back to the store, Justine told me that she had told the director of my idea, and he really liked it. She said he wished the idea had been presented to him earlier, but he felt it was too late now to change the play. I told her I was truly surprised that she had liked the idea.

"Justine, I enjoyed being in that theater so much. I haven't been in the theater for such a long time."

"Gibson, I know what you mean," She responded. "As much as I've been involved in theater, I have not lost the sense of magic I feel when walking onto the stage, even an empty stage. She used the word, "magic," the same as I had thought and felt earlier when I had walked on the stage.

She continued, "Theater is my life. Managing the store is temporary. At least it seems temporary now. I am doing this to help my mother. I'm good at it, but I don't love it like I do working in the performing arts. I am planning on one day finding someone else to manage the store."

"Doesn't it bother you that you are sacrificing the work that you love in order to manage this store?" I asked.

We had entered her office area in the Treasure Market, and she sat at her desk. I sat in one of the chairs nearby. "I'm not really sacrificing anything. I'm doing both," she answered.

"It seems that it would be difficult to really do both well."

"It is difficult but I do it. Of course I don't have too much time for anything else. Like developing my relationship with Chris, or starting a family. The man I am seeing now is an actor, but we have a rather rocky relationship. He goes into these melodramatic fits all the time. He plays hurt, betrayed, ignored. He is a good actor. He has much more control of his emotions on stage than off, which is not all that uncommon for actors. I should know better getting involved with another actor, but he has a lot of attractive sides…settling down and making a commitment is just not one of them. He's not ready to make a commitment at all. So I'm able to devote most of my attention to my work, on and off the stage." She stopped talking and shook her head. "I can't believe I'm telling you all this. Just don't tell my mother anything I've just told you. Understand?"

I nodded.

"How did you become interested in theater?" I asked her.

"When I was a child my parents took my sister and me to plays. I think my mama and papa wanted to be actors, but never did. But it's also in me. I love taking on a role, stepping into the feelings of someone different than me. I enjoy creating entertainment—expressions of pleasure, passion. There's something that excites me about a group of people performing before another group of people—and being able to rise together to peaks of feelings and understandings. I enjoy the intimacy of drama. It's so much more interactive than film." She expressed such a glow of excitement as she talked.

"One of my first memories as a child is of Papa taking me to an opera. I remember being in awe of everything. The extravagant beauty of the opera house with its chandeliers, mirrors, red carpeting. How well-dressed everyone in the audience was. Just how many people were in the lobby, tall and fancy-dressed people milling around. Then everyone was seated, and I looked up into the galleries and imagined that one day they would be looking at me on stage. Can you imagine? I did not want to be in the galleries, where all the fancy-dressed people were. I wanted to be on the stage. Then the huge curtain pulled open and I became mesmerized with the elaborate and fancy sets and the costumes of the opera singers. Then they begin to sing. I felt like I had entered some wondrous fantasy land, and I never wanted to leave."

Justine laughed and said, "What I didn't realize was that my papa had not planned on taking me that night, but Mama was not feeling well. He thought that I was too young to sit through an opera, and he didn't want to have to leave before it was finished. Years later, when I was older, he told me how surprised he was that I did sit through the opera thoroughly entranced. After that night, he began taking me to all sorts of performances. Plays. Dances. Concerts.

"As I got older I began going to more experimental and political theater on my own. I enjoy it all, traditional, experimental. There needs to be a balance, I think. When I went to college, I got my degree in theater.

"But while I was growing up my sister and I, and our friends, used the entire store as our stage. All through school I went out for acting, dancing, any performing arts that I could. My parents really encouraged me."

"You were very fortunate. I didn't have that encouragement, or my life might have been a little different than it is now."

"Tell me about it."

"You know, I have to get upstairs and clean the mirrors that you wanted ready today. I won't be able to finish that job if I don't get going." I got up and started walking away.

Before I left the room, she called after me, "You know I'm the boss here. I don't mind if the mirrors aren't finished today."

I stopped and looked back at her. "Actually I don't have anything really to tell you. So I'd just as soon go finish the mirrors."

She frowned and said, "OK, Gibson, but one day I want to know all about your secret past. Not talking about it makes me even more curious. What are you hiding?" Then she smiled and shrugged. "I'm just kidding, of course. You don't have to tell me anything, but I want you to know how curious you are making me."

Oh god, if I didn't like Justine and Esola so much, and if I didn't like being in the Treasure Market so much, I'd quit. I wish I had the strength to quit. It may be too risky for me. It may be my downfall.

March 2 ~~ CHOOSING TO LET PARTS OF MYSELF DIE

Luckily, Casey's Cafe is not too busy tonight because I just feel like staying here and writing more. Drinking coffee and writing until closing time. The luxurious life. What more could I want? I have my pen and paper, time and few tidbits to eat, hot coffee. I'm a rich man. But I have more even. I am developing my new soul.

Since I paid for my coffee, the manager of Casey's can't force me to leave, but actually I haven't seen him tonight anyway. He's not a bad person, just a little bit cantankerous. I know he is worried about making money so I don't blame him specifically for being an asshole sometimes. I blame the society we all have to live in for not meeting up to higher, more caring standards.

After wrestling with myself for these months since my breakdown I think I have finally identified two events that threw the switch on what I consider my natural development. One occurred when I was a teenager, the other when I was in my late twenties. My visit to a stage theater has made me realize how right I am about this. But I didn't want to talk with Justine about it.

I remember the day I had to choose to not join a theater project at the high school because of my father. A drama teacher was recruiting students to write short plays, and then she would choose three of the plays to be performed before the entire student body during the following semester. I wanted to join the drama project more than anything else in the world. I had written some brief skits and had shown them to the drama teacher. He said that I had a flair for dialogue, and he encouraged me to join the group. I couldn't get my work hours changed and my father had been trying to convince me that I should not cut back my work hours because I would stand a better chance of getting a promotion than if I were working part-time or had fewer hours.

I was going to choose the theater over my work, but I didn't. I don't feel like writing right now about the sudden tragedy that happened to our family, which forced me to make the choice I did. Once I made the choice, I didn't go see any of the plays of the theater project. As a matter of fact I haven't seen a play all through the years of my mainstream life. I just shut that part of myself off.

Becoming a success was so important to me because I was impressed by the things that money and prestige could bring. When I was a teenager my family could barely make ends meet. I had a friend whose father was a successful executive for a large corporation. Whenever I stayed at this friend's house I was completely overwhelmed by the amount of money he had available to him. I was amazed by the amount of material things he had and the privileges that his father's money bought him. I was very impressionable. Here was someone who had all the records and clothes he wanted, was being provided guitar lessons, had a pool table in his basement, a huge freezer that always held four different flavors of ice cream, and a TV in his own room.

Needless to say, we didn't have those things at home. Our black and white TV very seldom had a clear picture on it. We were lucky if we had ice cream once a month. I wanted to be a success so that I could have the material things that my friend had. I wanted to work hard so I could become an executive and bring home a high salary. I wanted to drive a fancy car, and wear the most fashionable clothes, and attract the most beautiful women. I wanted to not only be successful. I wanted to have access to the good life, the privileged life. I hated my lower-class existence. I felt that I had nothing.

But later, too late, I realized that these materialistic dreams were wrong, and that I had turned my back on my creative self.

The second major turning point occurred when I married a woman who I didn't really love. It was more than that, though, because by making that decision I also turned away from another woman who had aroused feelings of love and passion in me.

When I had finished college, I started going with Kristen, the woman who was to become my wife. I didn't feel deeply in love with her, but I enjoyed being with her. Her family was well-connected and wealthy. Oh my god, what an asshole I was. Then I met this other woman, Sally Waters, who often came into the store where I worked. She was trying to build something, a greenhouse, I think. She had this wonderful smile, and she asked me to have coffee with her and help her draw a proper diagram of the greenhouse she wanted to build. I accepted, which surprised the hell out of me. She was so vivacious. We had a very strong attraction to each other and I remember that I felt extremely alive around her, and I even wrote some poetry about her, which I never ended up showing her. Then one day she invited me out to her place and I had never before experienced the fullness of love as I did when I was with her that one time. But the next day I proposed to Kristen. My fatal flaw is that I am often spontaneous in the wrong direction—and out of fear.

I've tried not to think about why I turned away from Sally. She was a bit offbeat. She was into the counterculture and wore unusual clothes. Since I was only thinking of my image at the time, I chose the woman who would be a more traditional wife. And that's when another part of me died.

I did love my wife in some ways. It's just that I didn't feel a deep love, a passion for her. I didn't feel the rush of excitement, I don't know, that special romance. We really didn't share a lot in common. We both worked. We both wanted to achieve material comfort.

I think she is a good person. We began to have problems once my breakdown started to occur. She couldn't understand what was going on, and at first I didn't either. I didn't want to go to counseling. So we had nowhere to go but to split. She finally met someone special, divorced me, and moved back to Louisiana where we had both grown up.

I know now that even counseling would not have helped. It was not a matter of me being able to make psychological or social adjustments. Maybe I would have been able to recognize my needs more quickly, but I feel that my needs don't really fit into the mainstream society. So I'm just another one of those outcasts that can't or don't want to make it in the regular world.

Before my breakdown, Kristen and I had been talking about finally starting a family. I regret that this possibility has ended for me—well, I'm still young enough. It may still happen. In some reality.

So I've been able to write about my past a little more. As difficult and unpleasant as it is for me I have to remember more. More about my father, my mother, Sally and other people and events. I have to bring all this painful muck to my consciousness so I won't have any hidden revengeful stray sides of myself to sabotage my new soul.

I think I'll let it rest right now. I want to walk for a while. I will try to come back to these thoughts about my past later. It's cold outside and the hot coffee has been wonderful. I'm lucky the owner of Casey's still hasn't come back. He's knows I'm homeless and doesn't like me hanging out in his café. But I like this place. Small little café. The next block over from the Butcher's store. Why did I have to think of him?

I just looked out the window of the café. The block directly across from the café is a paved parking lot and across the parking lot I could see the backs of stores, one of which is the Butcher's store. I couldn't tell which one but it didn't matter. I'm just obsessed with my would-be killer.

March 3 ~~ WHERE I LIVE

I have a river running through my home. A huge river with at least twelve bridges that span the waters. I mostly sleep on the northeast side of the Willamette River in the vacant lots that run under the maze of freeways near the Burnside Bridge. Or in or close to warehouses nearby. I sometimes sleep on the west side of the river, just for a change of scenery, or because I am too tired to walk back over one of the bridges.

The northeast side of the river—further north and east than where I usually hang out—is the part of Portland that seems to have been set aside for the poor, minorities and outcasts. Portland allows us homeless to make our sleeping quarters bordering this section of town. They'd rather us be in it, but we've spread out all over the city like mold on an unkempt bathtub. They keep trying to find ways to scrub us away, but there are too many of us.

Some of the street people tell me they used to make their homes in the northwest section of town on the hillside. But this part of town became too uppity and too yuppie and the hillside was developed for expensive condos. Pearl District has become so upscale it is difficult for a homeless person like me to walk through it without feeling we're intruders in the king's estate.

I really don't mind staying mostly on the northeast side of the river. I like the northeast side. It's easy to cross the Burnside Bridge or a little further down, the Morrison Bridge, to go downtown, which I do as many mornings as I can to visit the Holy Skyscraper.

But most of the day I stay in the northeast because it's, well, it's my living room, kitchen, bedroom and den. I can do most everything I want to do on this side of the river. Further south on this side of the river, not far from my bedroom in the fields under the freeways, is one of the industrial sections of Portland with lots of warehouses, some of them vacant. There's a certain type of garbage that can be found here. Wholesale garbage. Different types of discarded materials that can be used to make tents or makeshift sleeping bags. One has to be careful, though, because some of the wastes in this section can be rather toxic. Everything has a risk.

A little ways east of the industrial section, up from the river, is a commercial section with a number of restaurants, stores, repair shops and office buildings. Restaurants or cafés can have some good leftovers if you're there at the right time. Sometimes you can make a friend with a dishwasher or waiter who will save you some food.

Still further east, away from the river, the residential areas start and intermingle with more shops, cafés, and office buildings. This residential section consists of mostly middle-class people who are up-and-coming, struggling, duped working fools who have bought totally into the American dream without asking who's being exploited, or what percentage of them will ever achieve their dreams and remain healthy and sane. These people throw away a lot of good, useful things. There's also a lot of trees in this section, and so it's like walking in my northeast side garden.

The Butcher's Block is on the northeast side in the commercial section. Esola's Treasure Market is also on this side but fortunately not close to the Butcher's Block. On the other side of the river, near downtown, is Powell's Bookstore (a new and used bookstore that takes up an entire city block and is one of the closest things to heaven on earth that I know of, and the Holy Skyscraper, one of the shrines I often travel to pay homage to. Why, I don't know. I think the Holy Skyscraper contains people who think they are making their way to heaven by accumulating and climbing on stacks of money. I'm uneasy about my attraction to this building, but I'm not ready to confront or at least try to understand this contradictory part of myself.

The main city library is also downtown.

For beauty and culture, I prefer the northwest side of the river where the young yuppies intermingle with the artists, minorities, the gays and lesbians. I like the old Victorian houses in this section, and the whole area sparkles with creativity. I come here especially when I need to nurture my infant creative spirit. In this section there is also a hospital that has some good sleeping places around it. And there's a few good parks to hang out in.

I'm not talking about a great distance to any of these sections. I don't want to be one of those people who have a home bigger than they need. And, besides, I share this home with a lot of other people who live in the streets of this city.

Sometimes I need to write about my surroundings to prove to myself that I really know where I am. And writing about my surroundings like this helps me keep my bearings. My journal is my compass and my anchor to the real world. I am admitting, for the time being, that the world of the American, noncaring, soul-selling masses is the reality that I have to keep anchored to, though not necessarily a part of.

~~ TAKING A CRAZY RISK

I'm leaning against the building right outside Casey's Café. Next to Casey's is Nature's Joy, a natural food store. I would buy more food in Nature's Joy, except I don't cook and it wouldn't make much sense to buy bulk food. And besides, I don't usually have money to buy food anyway. But the people at Nature's Joy have been very nice to me, and sometimes give me food. And since I know it is organic, eating Nature's Joy food gives me a feeling that I can be healed. I try not to analyze this too deeply, but their raw vegetables and fruits not only taste better, they also make me feel better.

When I have money to spend, I usually spend it next door at Casey's Café, which is just a regular American greasy spoon type of eating place, but the coffee and food is cheaper. I like sleeping in the alleyway behind Casey's because they have a kitchen vent that somehow warms the area in the alley next to a large waste container that hides me from the street. The owner of Casey's isn't willing to give free or leftover food to homeless people like myself, but I try not to let this type of behavior get to me—I just don't want to be pissed off and angry all the time.

I can see the back of the Al's Meat Store across the street. His meat store extends for the entire block, and there's a large parking area where trucks come and load and unload meat and other food items. I feel a mixture of caution and anger as I look over at the back of Al's store.

For some crazy reason I feel the urge to walk around to the front of the Butcher's store. I want to see where I was almost killed or at least almost horribly disfigured yesterday. That may sound a little melodramatic to someone who hasn't experienced a meat cleaver swinging by his head. I'm realizing this event isn't something that will be easy to forget.

~~ ANOTHER HORRIBLE ENCOUNTER WITH THE BUTCHER

This did not turn out the way I expected. That was my problem. I didn't focus on what might or might not happen when I went to get a better view of the front of Al's Meat Store. My pulse is racing and I know it was stupid of me to go so near the front of the store again. It seems my mind and emotions get hooked on certain people and places and I can't get unhooked no matter how dangerous or unpleasant being around them might be.

I was standing cautiously on the street corner across from the Butcher's Block. I could see the butcher's store, Al's Custom Meats, and could see strings of sausage hanging in the store front window. The lettering of Al's Custom

Meats was done in the color of blood. On one side of the store's name is painted a roast chicken. On the other side is painted a ham. Below the name was painted a heifer grazing on a spot of green grass. Probably right before it was slaughtered. How cute, I was thinking. How benign looking. I almost felt like going over there and staring through the window again, but I got control of myself.

I kept walking back and forth from Casey's Café to the street corner where I could see Al's Meat Store. I think part of me wanted to prove that I could be in the area and another part of me want to see if the asshole was going to attack someone else. I know that the Butcher will seriously hurt somebody one day and I don't know what to do about it.

About an hour and a half after I'd been hanging around the Butcher's Block, another homeless man walked past me and crossed the intersection going towards the direction of the Butcher's store. This man seemed to be over 50 years old, grey beard, very thin, with his grey hair having the usual homeless matted, dirty look. He carried one bag swung over his shoulders.

I started to yell to the man to warn him, but I didn't. Maybe another part of me really couldn't believe that the Butcher would actually attack someone else. I wanted to believe that maybe he had just had a bad day when he tried to attack me.

But as this other homeless man walked by the meat store, goddamnit if the Butcher didn't come running out again. At least this time he wasn't carrying his meat cleaver. I heard him yell at the guy, who turned his head to look back but kept walking. The Butcher ran after him and pushed him from behind so hard that he stumbled and fell on the sidewalk. I couldn't believe it. I stood there for a moment, shocked.

I came to my senses when the Butcher started kicking him while he was trying to get up. I started to cross the intersection. I guess I had some foolish notion of helping the poor guy. I also was looking to see if anyone else would be coming to his aid. By the time I had crossed the intersection he had rolled away from the Butcher, had managed to get to his feet and run. I saw his pack lying on the sidewalk. The Butcher picked it up and threw it into a trash can near the front entrance of his store.

I had stopped, and was about to head back across the intersection when the Butcher turned and saw me. "You!" I heard him shout. "I told you never to come back here. You're dead, man. You're dead if I catch up with you." He started running toward me.

At first I couldn't move. Everything seemed so ludicrous. Here right in broad daylight this Butcher was yelling that he was going to kill me again, and other people were just walking by with scarcely a glance. I remained in this inert state of consciousness for only a few seconds before I turned and ran. I looked back after I had run almost a block, and the Butcher had stopped at his intersection. He stood just staring at me. I stopped and turned to stare at him. He started across the intersection, and I took off running again. I glanced back over my shoulder, and saw that the Butcher had stopped again. So much for a grand display of courage on my part. I'm going to have to learn how to defend myself, even though my best defense seems to be in knowing how to duck into the shadows, dodging the attacks. But what if that's not enough?

How often does this insane man go on his rampages? We must have really made his day, two homeless men he was able to scare all within a few minutes. It's kind of frightening, but I have this feeling he's going to hurt someone, maybe already has. I have a vague feeling of an obligation.

Maybe he really is the one who is killing homeless people around the city. It would be too coincidental, but even if he isn't the one killing homeless people, he is too out of control, and I think he will hurt someone one of these days.

~~ MUST STOP THIS MANIAC

I've been walking around thinking about what I could do to stop this man who seems so out of control and dangerous. I didn't think it would be any good to call the police. But then I thought about Ransack. He's often at the Campfire in the freeway fields and he's always telling bullshit stories about his past life working for the CIA. It's difficult to tell how old he is, but he seems like he is in his 50s. He has long blond graying hair, a handle bar mustache, a long-pointed beard on his chin, and wears a cowboy hat and a brown jacket with frills. He looks like pictures I've seen of some western showman, like Wild Bill Hickok. Ransack is over six-foot tall and has a well-built frame that adds to his commanding, charismatic personality. I have never seen him be violent but I sense in him a coldness, even through his dramatic storytelling.

Ransack says that he used to be a hit man working for some small branch of the CIA. His duties included searching for things that the CIA wanted found, and then killing whoever had the things after they were found. He said he got his nickname from how thorough he was at his job. He describes often, and with obvious pride, how he would completely ransack and destroy each place searched. When he tells this story he bows his head, slowly shakes it back and forth, and says it was never a pretty sight when he was finished. Ransack has told us that a few years ago, after he had to assassinate an innocent woman when she was at the wrong place at the wrong time, he began to hate himself and his job. So he said he quit and went into hiding. He vowed to devote his life to helping the disadvantaged, but he decided to keep the name Ransack to remind him of his past that he's trying to overcome.

I don't know whether or not to believe anything Ransack says but he looks mean. He has many stories of how the CIA has sent other agents to track him down and kill him to prevent him from talking about classified secrets. He describes how he has survived these attempts. He either reads a lot of spy novels, or has had a hell of a frightening life.

He once told me that he had lived in Texas for a while as Willie Nelson's bodyguard. He said that period of time was one of the highlights of his life, but he had to leave the job because it was too public. Ransack always talks about times when he was younger; how he was a mean son of a bitch but as he's gotten older and let his hair grow longer, he said he has become a lot nicer. He says that he sleeps on the street to protect himself. The thing about Ransack is that he never sleeps around the Campfire. I've never seen him sleep anywhere else on the streets and I've never seen him anywhere around a shelter. I wonder if he's really homeless.

Maybe I should hire Ransack to put a stop to this crazy Butcher bullying homeless people. Hire him, hell. I don't have any money. I should just ask him to stop this goddamn maniac. Ransack says he's trying to do good these days. Putting the Butcher in his place would be doing us homeless people immense good. I know it's just a matter of time before the Butcher will stick that meat cleaver into somebody if he hasn't already. I'm a little hesitant to get more involved with Ransack but something has to be done about the Butcher. If I can get Ransack to stop the Butcher, all I'm doing is turning violence back upon itself. There can be no harm in that.

First I'll have to find Ransack, and then I will have to convince him to use his special-ops, violent persuasive skills to change the Butcher's mode of behavior into something that would allow us homeless to walk past his store without fearing for our lives.

I went immediately over to the freeway fields looking for Ransack. It's still early afternoon but I thought by chance he might be there. When I got there, I was told that he had been at the Campfire a couple of days ago but that he said he wouldn't be around for a couple of days. Ransack said something about going out to ride some horses. Now who the hell does Ransack know who has horses? I don't know what to believe about him. But I'll keep checking back.

I left the freeway fields and came back downtown crossing the Morrison Bridge. After buying some fruit at the Yamhill Market I sat on a bench across the street in a park by the river. I don't know why I came back downtown unless it was to get as far away as I could from the Butcher's neighborhood. I don't want to let him keep me away from one of the areas where I hang out and sleep, but right now I don't want to deal with it.

I'm in a strange mood. I know I will sleep on this side of the river tonight which I don't do too often. It's something about the way they make buildings these days. I think they're making buildings with strong toxic materials that keep the slaves in a drugged state of compliance. I swear that when I'm downtown for too long I begin to feel a little stranger than usual, almost like I might be willing to return to the slave life. I'm caught between the Butcher on the other side of the river and dangerous toxic buildings on this side of the river. I must try to do something about the harmful rampages of the Butcher, at least.

March 4 ~~ NIGHTMARES

Last night I had to endure one of my reoccurring nightmares ~

Forever, or so it seems in these nightmares, horrendous flying machines, mechanical night dragons, rain fiery breaths of destruction down onto the houses and buildings of this city, forcing people to run from their burning homes, screaming and shivering, filling the streets in every direction. These mechanical flying monsters cast huge spotlights over the crowd in the streets, and incessantly blast abusive and threatening tirades over loud speakers to the homeless and to the people they have just forced into the city streets below. Tirades about how useless these people have become—how they do not deserve their homes—how they are costing businesses money by their low productivity and demands for higher wages and health care and education for their children. I saw frightened faces of children cowering in the arms of their parents, who are trying to protect them. I woke up hearing children crying.

I often dream of ghostly abandoned skyscrapers transformed into faces with glassy, hollow eyes and grotesque mouths full of jagged, rotting teeth. I dream of wrecked cars screeching in pain around us. In my dreams I often experience the destruction of the homes of this city; I experience the fiery breath and the brutal questions of the mechanical night dragons; I experience these nightmare images that seem to go on forever, until I awake yelling and twisting, trying to protect myself.

I seldom remembered my dreams before I became homeless. Now it seems as if some strange, deranged foreign filmmaker has moved his production company into the back of my mind. Now it doesn't matter if I am asleep or awake, Fallacious (the name I've given this evil film maker that exists inside my psyche) will turn on his projector and I will see crazy, sometimes horrible images of the world becoming chaotic, inhuman, unfeeling -and often I am caught in the middle of frantic mobs grasping after the homes and security they are suddenly losing.

In these dreams, some people who have just been forced out of their homes become angry and decide to take their wrath out on the street people, the people who have already been homeless. In some of these nightmares I'm with a small group of homeless people at the end of a dark alley with nowhere to escape, and suddenly a mob of angry people having just seen their homes destroyed, pour into the entrance of the alley. These people are holding clubs and knives. They have expressions of intense hatred on their faces.

We shout back that it's not our fault they've lost their homes. We have no control, no power over the flying mechanical monsters. But the mob won't listen. They come closer and closer, until suddenly they're on us, and I awake from my nightmare just as a huge spiked club is being swung toward my head by a man wearing a designer blue suit, a red tie and white shirt. These nightmares reinforce my feelings that often the fashionable, expensively dressed slaves of our society are trying to hide their darker selves.

If I had my way I would dream different dreams—dreams of floating through shopping mall crowds and patio barbeque parties, trying to make the material-minded masses become awake, trying to evoke compassion out of their complacent credit card hearts, before our humanity becomes bankrupt, before mechanical night dragons decide to destroy everything out of disgust. I would ask the people in these places questions.

Questions that I have a difficult time answering even when I am awake—questions about compassion, justice, greed, and about masses of people locked out of opportunities to make a better life for themselves and their children. Questions about why the moon bothers to shine its magical light of love down onto these cities of people living uncaring, upscale lifestyles, while so many humans are living and dying on the streets.

But I don't dream these things. Fallacious won't co-operate with my wishes. It seems my sadistic internal filmmaker likes horror films more than he likes romantic, idealistic films that shows the higher potentials of humans. I am caught somewhere in between the horror and the ideal. Maybe one day I will be able to have more control over my dreams and the images I often see in my waking life. Maybe one day I'll write and direct my own films—that possibility seems so unattainable to me now.

~~ FALLACIOUS

Fallacious not only creates frightful and unsettling dreams that I have to endure, he sometimes makes me see strange images and visions when I look into the sky. I see events unfolding. I see human epic movies played out—battles between the rich and the poor. I see class wars in the United States. The rich are wearing armor black jackets covering their fancy suits and black helmets, and using brief cases as shields. The poor have a few guns and knives, but mostly have broken pieces of plastic as weapons and garbage can lids as shields.

Sometimes the battle wages through the day and into the night. The rich win for a while and then become complacent, allowing the poor to win for a while. But the poor never really win. They fight a guerilla warfare, hidden in old buildings, setting traps for the rich soldiers, and sniping and throwing rocks from within dark hideouts. The rich then become angry and send huge missiles, destroying whole buildings. The only thing that the poor have going for them is that there are more of them, more to die.

I get so tired of these battles. I've never liked epic movies anyway, and I can't stand watching something where I know how it's going to end. Fallacious is so transparent. He's knows the rich are too powerful. One day I hope I'll be able to gain control of Fallacious. Just to punish him for what he's done to me. I'll make him edit old Ronald Reagan movies, old Bush Jr. news conferences, and cable talk shows that masquerade as news.

~~ UNCARED FOR PEOPLE AND PLACES

So much of the city is tarnished, defiled, stained. Benches, walls of buildings and houses, metal street signs and posts, sidewalks, fountains, sculptures. The gritty and grimy textures of the places I have to sit and lie and touch often give me a gutter feeling about my life. And seeing faded brown and washed out gray walls reminds me of the psychiatric ward.

I go through times on the street where everything seems so disgusting and dirty, and I wonder how I can live in the filth much longer. Colors of discarded wastes and lack of care. Soul-draining colors exist on uncared-for structures that form so much of the landscape of even this beautiful city. At least I do have the options of changing my environment sometimes to get away from these faded colors, the grime and the filth. I try to walk to the brighter places when I am feeling oppressed by my surroundings—to places with more vibrant and fresh colors. But sometimes these upscale surroundings make me feel worse because they seem to mock me and the homeless life I am a part of. The more beautiful places in the city are out of reach of so many people who struggle each day just to find a little bit to eat.

If more people could share in the wealth of this world, all would certainly enjoy better things in life, simple items of convenience, places of beauty. Until everyone can share in it though, I'll stay on the street—in the uncared for places that we, the poor, are contained in—but it doesn't always make me feel good.

~~ JEREMIAH'S SEARCH FOR THE CHRIST CHILD

Jeremiah, Portland's self-ordained, white, homeless street priest with wild grey hair just came up to where I was sitting and blessed me. He said that I looked like I needed a friend, and that Christ could be that friend if I wanted. I nodded. I'd heard it all before from Jeremiah. I have to give him credit though. He's persistent as hell. He sat by me and talked for a while about how Christ is alive and has been reborn, he thinks, somewhere in Portland. I just nodded. I knew the story better than I wanted to about how he moved to Portland from Savannah, Georgia, after he had a vision that Christ had just been reborn here.

Jeremiah's always talking as if he's in front of some congregation preaching about the second coming. He's entertaining unless he's preaching directly at me, and then it depends on what mood I'm in. I didn't mind listening to him preach today. As a matter of fact, I welcomed it as a needed distraction from my low mood. I even got into it a little bit. I asked Jeremiah how he was going to locate the new Christ child. He said he goes around from church to church each Sunday, and one day he will recognize the Christ child. Jeremiah explained that he looks for Him outside of churches, too, on the street, in school yards. Everywhere. He said he wants to be prepared to serve Him when he when he finds Him.

At one point Jeremiah looked at me with the vice-like expression he sometimes gets on his face, and he said, "You don't believe me, do you brother?"

"Jeremiah, I believe you," I half-lied. Who am I to say anyone else is crazy? I told him I really hoped he found the Christ child. It would solve one area of disagreement that's been plaguing people for over 2000 years.

Jeremiah smiled at me and put his hand on my head and mumbled something. Then his mood abruptly changed and he became less preachy, more discouraged. He told me about a nine-year-old homeless child he had found unconscious a couple of mornings ago behind one of the shelters on the east side of the river. He took the child to the shelter managers, and eventually the child was taken to Emmanuel Hospital. Jeremiah said the child was almost dead from malnutrition and also had traces of heroin in his system. The shelter managers couldn't identify who the child belonged to, so Jeremiah said that he'd probably be sent to a foster home.

I felt depressed. So many women and children are on the streets. I didn't realize how bad it was until I became homeless myself. I just thought street people were mostly single men who were failures, who couldn't make it in the real world. Now I know different, but it's so sad to see the mothers and children. It makes me angry that so few people with jobs and incomes and homes care enough to do something about it. I thought at least this young child will have a chance to stay alive even if he is destined to become just another slave.

Jeremiah got up to leave, saying he was going to visit the child in the hospital. I was left again with my discomfort.

~~ THE ATTACK OF THE BAG LADY

After Jeremiah left, I was sitting on the bench, minding my own business, writing in my journal, when this crazy bag lady came and sat down on the same bench not too far away from me. I'd seen her around, and I always tried to stay clear of her. The word on the street is that she carries knives around in her bags, and waves the knives around when she gets angry. She is supposed to have hurt some people quite seriously, and has spent time in jail and the psychiatric wards. I wonder how she keeps getting knives. I wonder how she keeps getting released. I know why—our society's inhumane priorities.

So here she was sitting on the same side of the bench at the picnic table. I glanced nervously up from my journal, and saw that she was staring at me. Her mouth was set in a sneer, and I thought that I heard her growling. She had a purple scar that stretched across her chin. Her graying, dirty brown hair spilled out of a red bandanna tied around the top of her head.

I quickly looked back down to my journal. I was scared shitless. My peaceful, albeit chilly, afternoon on an out-of-the way city bench had suddenly turned into a potential horror story. I was about to get up and leave.

"What are ya writing?" she asked in a raspy voice.

I jumped as she stuck her hand in one of her bags, but relaxed when she pulled out an old rag and blew her nose.

"I asked ya what are ya writing? Are ya deaf?"

"I...I'm just writing my private thoughts," I said quickly.

"Ya writing 'bout me, ain't ya?" she said, glaring at me, sticking her chin out. Her scar seemed more menacing to me than before.

"No, no I'm not writing about you. Really, I'm not. I'm just writing about personal things."

"Let me see then." She reached her hand out. How many people had she mutilated with that hand? I realized that I was walking on very thin ice here. I had been writing about her. I had just written in my journal, "Just my luck. This crazy psychotic old woman has just sat down beside me to ruin my afternoon in the park."

"I don't let anybody read my journal," I finally said, hoping foolishly that she would accept that and leave me alone.

She stared at me for a long time, during which I don't think I breathed. Suddenly she stuck her hand into her purse again, and this time did pull out a long bread knife that looked mean and dangerous in her hand.

I jumped up from the bench and started backing away. She jumped up and lunged at me. Backing up, I just missed being stuck by the knife. She yelled, "I'm going to read your goddamn journal. I know you've written vulgar and nasty things about me."

"What are you trying to do?" I yelled. "You can't just go around stabbing people."

"Ya wanna bet?" she yelled as she came toward me.

I turned and started running. As I ran down the street, I glanced over my shoulder and saw that she was not following me. I could still hear her yelling, "You can't run forever. I'm going to find ya, and I'll get that damn journal. You can't write nasty and vulgar things about me and think ya can get away with it."

I thought about reporting her to the police, but I decided that the police would probably arrest me and charge me with vagrancy.

This is all I need. A crazy bag lady stalking me, ready to cut my throat and read my journal. As if I didn't have enough people with knives ready to kill me each day. What is going on here? I'm just trying to be a peaceful poor person. I'm not trying to bother, hurt, or make anybody angry or mad. Why can't all these crazy people just leave me alone? Why are they attracted to me?

I just don't like the idea of having to look over my shoulder all the time. There's the Butcher. There's the bag lady. And then there's the fanatic who's killing homeless men. Maybe I'm making too much of this. I'm still alive, aren't I? I have to get into living each moment at a time and quit worrying about whether or not some crazy person is going to kill me. I've convinced most of myself, except, it seems, my intestines. I've got to go find a toilet very quickly.

March 7 ~~ THE MYSTERIOUS EXOTIC DANCER

Yesterday afternoon, after I left the freeway fields and talked with Jeremiah, I stayed downtown. Then right before dark, as I was walking along this street in the northwest section, I saw an unusually beautiful and tall house that seemed to stretch into the clouds, as if it were a thousand stories high rather than the three stories it was. It was a narrow building built on a rise. Vines climbed the corners and spread along the windows. I thought of fairy tales just looking at it.

Two huge maples stood in the front yard. I walked across the street to get a better look at the house. It was then I noticed the huge flag hanging in one portion of the front window, draped in front of curtains. I didn't recognize the country the flag belonged to.

While I was standing there, I began to hear music, the exotic sounds of flutes and stringed instruments. The music was very faint, even so I was immediately mesmerized by its slow, lilting, hypnotic cadence. Since the house sat on the corner of the street, I was able to walk around it to see if I could hear any better. A tall hedge completely blocked the view of the house from this side. I walked further and noticed an alley behind the house.

I walked down the alley. Even though I could barely see the house through the dense shrubbery and trees, I was able to hear the music more clearly. Maybe there were windows open somewhere? Wild and thick bushes, trees and smaller shrubbery bordered the back of the property. As I walked closer, I could hear the music even louder.

I walked back and forth behind the house, and finally found what looked like a pathway. I started to make my way through the shrubbery. The bushes, vines and thin limbs of trees parted easily. I tried to be as quiet as I could. Finally I was able to see the house clearly. It stood beyond the large backyard which was completely hidden from the outside world by this natural fence of nature.

My eyes were instantly drawn to a woman dressed in an exotic costume. Her blouse was black, her skirt gold and black. She wore a headband of golden material around her long black hair, which extended down past her shoulders. She wore many bracelets on her arms, with colors of gold, red, and blue.

I stood hidden in the shrubbery, and watched this woman dance to the music. The cadence was still very slow. She stood still and moved her arms and hands and shoulders in rhythm to the music. Then the music began to increase in cadence, and her movements increased. I became mesmerized by the strange but beautiful movements of her arms and legs and feet as they curved and flowed faster and faster, moving in so many different directions, yet they seemed to move together in sublime coordination.

When the music ended, I caught my breath, and realized that I must have been in some kind of a trance. I looked at the woman who was now standing still. She seemed to be looking directly at me. I crouched quickly behind a bush. I waited for her to start screaming, but she just remained still. I also remained in my crouched position, tensed, waiting for her to do something.

Finally she turned and walked over to a table by the back door on which some equipment sat. Soon another song started, and she walked back to the same spot and began dancing again.

I breathed a sigh of relief and decided to just sit and enjoy this performance. I thought about how rare it was these days for me to feel a part of something special.

The light was fading as the evening approached. I figured that she would soon be finishing and when she did, I would go look for something to eat and a place to sleep. But she kept dancing into the evening, and when it became dark, she lit some candles and a lantern. Her movements created shadows with the light and her performance seemed even more mysterious.

At one point I stopped watching her long enough to look at the rest of the house and thought I saw someone standing behind one of the second-story windows near the right corner of the house, but whoever it was moved away after a few moments.

As this woman danced and danced, I became more and more relaxed. At first I tensed after each dance because the woman remained still, and seemed to be looking in my direction, but eventually she would turn and put on another piece of music.

Without intending to, I eventually fell asleep. I slept the rest of the night. I woke up startled, then slowly got my bearings. It seemed to be just after dawn, and from where I lay it felt as if I were in the country. I could hear no city sounds.

I slowly stood up, and began to stretch the soreness out of my body, but then I noticed that a small red glass bracelet was hanging on one of the thin branches of the bush I was hiding behind. I looked at the house but nobody was there, and I couldn't see any movement in the windows. I took the bracelet and noticed that symbols of some kind were painted on it. She must have known I was there the whole time, but why would she just let me, a stranger, watch her? And why would she give me a bracelet?

I carefully put the bracelet in my backpack, and decided to go somewhere and buy a cup of coffee, and try to ponder the meaning of this strange event. I had discovered a wonderful secret, a special place and was able to see a mesmerizing dance performance. I hoped that if I came back, I'd be able to see the woman dance again.

Walking back through the thick shrubbery I wondered which country these people were from. I walked back around to the front of the house, and took another look at the flag. I drew a sketch of it in my journal, marking the colors, and decided to go to the library to see if I can identify it.

~~ THE TRUE WEALTH OF OUR CIVILIZATION

When I walk into the downtown city library I feel instantly at ease. I feel I'm in the presence of the true wealth of our civilization. I feel soothed by the large, immaculately clean rooms with their huge windows, light pine-wood ceilings, walls, and tables.

I try not to go into most public buildings. Somehow I feel like my new essence will be captured and only my slave self will be allowed to leave. I feel most vulnerable when I am in buildings. I have so much to lose. But I don't feel that way when I come into the library. I feel like I belong here and I feel invigorated, especially after I become involved in the written word. My anxieties ease, and I begin to feel quite comfortable. I imagine myself as an apprentice to a vast but hidden spiritual wisdom, buried in the written words found in libraries. I know that the secrets of the universe can be found in the language of books, magazines, and newspapers. I wonder how many people who use and work in the library know the treasures they handle each day.

~~ THE THAILAND FLAG

I've just found out that the flag in the window of the house is from Thailand. The beautiful, exotic dancer is from Thailand.

My first thoughts were of Bangkok, and I had visions of a wild city of huge pagodas, of temples with layers of golden, curving roofs. I also imagine stretches of white sand beaches sparkling in the daylight and with young tourists partying through the night.

I've also read about drug and prostitution enterprises in counties like Thailand. I envision knifed-murdered victims being thrown into murky rivers. I envision crowded, hot, and humid streets with strange, sinister half-human, half-demon figures lurking in shadows.

I have to admit that I don't really know a damn thing about Thailand, but it has to have something special going for it if the woman who can dance such a magical dance is from that country. Given my ignorance about Thailand I have spent the last couple of hours reading more about it. The facts about the country don't really matter to me at this moment. Only the dancer does.

When I sat down at my table a few hours ago, I placed the glass bracelet she gave me by my journal. Occasionally I glanced at it while reading, and I wondered what the squiggles and symbols mean. I wonder what it means that she gave me the bracelet, and that she was willing to let me know that she knew I was watching her. I have this strong desire to go back to the house and try to meet her, talk with her. Isn't her giving me the bracelet an invitation?

Fallacious just flashed the image of my Controller across the big screen in my mind, and the Controller demanded to know the purpose of my wanting to talk with this dancer. What do I want? I just want to enjoy the company of a woman I find attractive. I can envision sitting somewhere, perhaps in her backyard after she'd danced, listening to her explain the meaning of her performance. Or just listening to her tell me about her homeland and how she came to the United States—listening to her tell me about her experiences since she came here, and what her life is like now.

But I have so little to share with her. My past contains nothing of interest. I lived so long as a slave not really being alive. And my present life is sort of a blur, a dream that eludes my consciousness from moment to moment. What would I share? I would be taking and I wouldn't be able to give. I'd better just stay at a distance and enjoy what she is willing to let me enjoy. She'll be just another one of my safe fantasies.

I'll have to be careful about how often I go over to the Thai dancer's house. I don't want to be caught, or to ruin a good thing. I don't even know if I'll be able to catch her dancing again, but I will go back. I don't think I'll be able to stop myself. She seems to create a powerful emotional effect with her dancing. I better be careful how much I let myself watch her. I don't know what I am afraid of unless it's the fear of being totally under her control. Becoming a slave to her. I have a thing about not ever wanting to be a slave again. Maybe I was a slave in a few of my past lives. I didn't use to believe in reincarnation, but now I do. Must be Esola's influence.

Ok. Ok. I have to get my mind off of this dancer and figure out what's next in my busy schedule of things to be done. God, I hate that concept, "Things to be done." Unfortunately I do have something that has to be done. I have to find Ransack to see what he's done about the Butcher. I'm going to walk over to the freeway fields to see if I can find him.

Just a thought before I leave. I can't stand the nerdy man who's at the library counter. I think his name's Gerald. He's the only one at the library who's questioned my coming here. One time after I'd been in the library for four hours he came up to me and asked if he could help me. At first I couldn't understand why he thought that I needed help, but then I realized that it was his way of probing to see if I was just hanging out, and whether or not I intended to stay in the library until closing time. He's so uptight. I can't let people like that get to me. I have to find antidotes to their poisonous dispositions.

March 8 ~~ RANTS AND REVERIES

I just walked by a fancy downtown hotel where I was able to see through the front doors into the lobby. The discrepancy between the luxury and opulence I saw in that lobby and the poverty and pain on the streets sometimes makes me feel sad, often angry. Today I struggled not to feel angry. Just to let it go, I kept telling myself. I see it around me all the time. Perhaps my run-ins with the Butcher have made me more on edge. And my talk recently with Jeremiah about the terrible conditions of children has disturbed me. As I looked through the glass doors of the hotel I could see marbled floors and counters, huge vases containing large plants, lavish chandeliers, large chairs and couches, giant paintings on a wall. I could see well-dressed men and women standing around talking with each other. They seemed to be from an advanced time and place compared to the world of the street people, where time has stood still, not allowing us to advance and partake of the basic needs of a wealthy modern society.

I walked away from the hotel feeling disgust at the extravagance while so many other people were starving, becoming sick and dying.

I won't apologize for being homeless. I won't lower my head and turn away my eyes. You've put me on the street, Mr. and Ms. USA. You have chosen to ignore my existence. You have chosen to ignore the social problems at a time when I know they could be solved if you cared. You have sold out to material security. You won't ask the right questions because you don't want to know the answers. You don't want to change your greedy lifestyles, give up your designer clothes, your new hair styles, your many costly playthings, your dinners out, your frequent vacations. I am not inferior to you just because I don't have or do these things anymore!

These dark currents that flood my mind and emotions, I won't apologize for them. I travel on frightening streams of despair and through a dense undergrowth of anger. Yet somehow I find myself returning again and again to civilization, to civility. I don't want to hate anyone, but I blame everyone. Right now I just want to be left alone. I don't want hand-outs or harassments. I've given up on the idea that we could all join together to solve the deep problems we face. I've given up on thinking that we could join together to find our way to more decent homes for everyone. I just want to be left alone.

Dazed by everything that is around me and the nothing that I have, I sometimes sit rocking back and forth on a transit-stop bench. I have no energy, my mind is slack, without focus, numb. I don't think I can take it. But what can I do? I won't even consider suicide. I don't know if it's because I have some insane urge to live despite my despicable circumstances, or if it's because I'm a coward.

Probably a little of both. I would be afraid of missing something if I committed suicide—perhaps that big opportunity in the sky. Why I believe that, I don't know. Perhaps the lottery propaganda of America still has control over me. I've known of many homeless people who've bought lottery tickets with their last dollars. Of course, they probably had just drunk a gallon of wine, and didn't really know what they were doing. We, the underlings and slaves of America, are reduced to begging and gambling against unfair odds for a chance to partake of, not the good life, but just life.

My mind comes up for air. I write to forget. My pen is like a needle and syringe, pulling thoughts out of my brain, and injecting in their place a sedated state of consciousness. I write to enter a trance. I write so I can be doing something. I write because I am alive, and I have to talk to somebody, even if it's to my journal. It's better than talking out loud to myself. People look at me like I'm crazy. I am a little crazy, but I don't like those looks that people give me when they think I'm not only a bum but also crazy. They ignore me mostly when they think I'm just a bum. But if they think I'm crazy, they get this wide-eyed, defensive look.

I rock back and forth. I hear the transit coming down the track. I don't look up. I just sit and listen to the rumbling get louder. My body feels the rumbling, and then the transit stops. I wait. Nobody tells me to leave. The transit starts rumbling away, and I realize I have been holding my breath.

I'm not supposed to use this transit bench without using the transit, but when you're on the street you get used to using what's provided free to regular citizens. I take what I can get, even some dazed moments on a transit bench.

Where will I go next? That question comes up often, and I guess it's like a wide-open road or a dead end, depending on if I actually get up and go somewhere or not. Right now it seems like I am at a dead end.

I look up into the sunset and see the streaked red horizon. I can almost remember feelings of security and romance I've experienced when I've seen such beautiful sunsets in my past. I try to recapture these feelings now. I wish I was enjoying this sunset with someone special. An image of Justine flashed in my mind—but she lives in a different world than I do. And she already has someone else with whom she can enjoy sunsets.

Perhaps I should not be feeling so down. After all I have a sunset, a transit bench, and a number of shelters and soup kitchens I could go to, if they were not already filled. So I'm a little down and out. What's the big deal. Life's like that. If I wait until the next rainbow perhaps I'll find a pot of gold—but I know that's only the mainstream trying to fool me again with their goddamn lottery propaganda. I'm not going back into their spiritless prisons even if I somehow found that pot of gold.

March 9 ~~ THE HOLY SKYSCRAPER AND QUEEN AVARICE

The building across the street is one of those silver and mirrored skyscrapers, a sleek metal-and-glass holy corporate shrine housing thousands of frenzied and, in their own minds, purposeful human beings, dressed in the latest fashion uniforms, performing their sanctimonious materialistic duties to their executive gods. The building is named after one of the largest banks in the country and probably has offices for all sorts of financial service businesses. I call it the Holy Skyscraper, and despite how I fight against it, I feel compelled to come here many workday mornings to look at it, to be near it. Consciously, I don't just disdain what the Holy Skyscraper represents, I totally reject and abhor it. But there must still be some pathetic robber baron floating around inside of me, hiding from me waiting to betray my best interests, the best interests of the common good. I have to remain vigilant to resist these decadent urges.

I'm sitting across the street now on this cold, crisp Friday morning. When I come here in the morning before the workday starts, I sit across the street on the steps of a five-story, older sandstone building. It looks like a courthouse or a library but it's neither. The steps are wide, spreading across almost the entire front of the building. Nobody seems to care if I sit here and write in my journal and watch people across the street going in and out of the Holy Skyscraper.

I have identified certain people who enter in the morning on a regular basis. I hesitate to write that they are going to work. It is difficult for me to imagine that anyone really works in the Holy Skyscraper. I imagine they perform their materialistic rituals of accumulation and reverence around piles of cash and in front of wall size computer monitor that shows where vast sums of money are being held in offshore accounts around the world. I even imagine they enslave magicians to change dirt to precious metals and gold using ancient alchemy. I also imagine that when they enter this building and reach their greedy offices, they change into black and gold hooded robes.

A limousine just drove up to the entrance of the Holy Skyscraper, and yes, Queen Avarice emerged from the backdoor of the limousine and walked quickly into the Holy Skyscraper. I've given her this name because she appears to be one of the royalty, ruling over others. Her clothes are always opulent, whether she wears a suit or dress, and the way she carries herself is what some might call majestic, but I tend to describe her demeanor as arrogant. At any rate, I do recognize that she is a beautiful woman, and always seems to exude the highest levels of confidence that money can buy. I sometimes see her walking out of the building surrounded by her entourage of peons or apprentices, probably to a restaurant nearby, or to an important other skyscraper nearby.

Her shoulder-length blonde hair appears more golden today, glowing. Maybe she has been more successful than usual recently in reaping her riches at the expense of others.

I have entertained the idea of going into the Holy Skyscraper one day. Sometimes I feel I want to confront the people who use this building for their greedy practices—but then I worry that if I actually did enter the Holy Skyscraper, I would ask for their forgiveness and blessing. Luxury can sometimes seem so damn pleasant and comfortable. Why wouldn't I want to live in places that rise up to the heavens above the squalor and dirt near the earth? Who wouldn't? Most of the time I know that I wouldn't. Every once in a while I doubt my resolve.

~~ MY PAST AND PSYCHOLOGICAL BREAKDOWN

Now that I've seen Queen Avarice come to work I think I'll do something I'm not comfortable with. Still, it has been something I've been thinking about all morning. I think I'll try writing about myself. Since experiencing what the psychiatrist called my psychological breakdown, I haven't been able to remember too much about my past. Maybe it's just that I haven't wanted to remember. But for my new soul's sake I have to remember. So if my mind, my pen and Fallacious, my internal filmmaker, will co-operate, I'll begin.

Where to start? My birth—I was born in the deep south, in New Orleans, and grew up between New Orleans and Lafayette. My roots were Cajun gumbo, Sunday school, 4th of July picnics with family and neighbors, listening and dancing to music, exploring the bayous, dodging snakes and alligators, and discriminating against non-white, non-Christian people. Thank god, somehow I never bought into discriminating against others, so having to wrestle with racial and religious prejudice wasn't something that plagued me as an adult, and certainly didn't cause my psychological breakdown.

I was told by my father before he died that maybe I'd be able to work myself up to be a sales manager, and eventually I might become a stock broker, and if I saved and invested wisely, I could one day be worth a million or more dollars. In my teen years I was duped into adopting the dream of working in a building like the one across the street, but in the battle to reach my dream, I experienced a meltdown.

I haven't been able to sort out all of the reasons I experienced a breakdown. I've only been homeless for about six months, and during this time it seems like Fallacious has had complete control of my mind. Just lately I seem to be more successful and wrestling control of my thinking back from Fallacious. After my mental breakdown, my thinking was dulled further by prescription drugs and I slept for long periods of time. I ran out of these drugs after a few weeks and decided not to get any more. These anti-depressants eased the physical discomfort I felt but I knew I needed to remain more in control, or at least more awake, if I were going to survive on the street.

I allowed a part of myself to die when I was about 16 years old. During my high school years I was a team player, who endured football, drank with the boys, had a few girlfriends. But secretly I liked drama, dance, music and literature. I found out I could speak well in front of groups. I could act and I liked to write poetry. But my father, who was a wholesale food salesman, kept badgering me to follow in his footsteps. Not exactly in his footsteps, but he wanted me to take a job as a stock clerk in a local department store. He had arranged this job offer from a close friend of his.

After some inner turmoil, I was about ready to say no to this job. I had planned on becoming involved in theater at my high school, and if I took the job, I would not be able to spend the time needed for rehearsals and performances. Our family was barely able to make ends meet, and I had some good friends who were from very well-off families. I spent a lot of time over at their houses, and I wanted the luxuries that they had. I was torn between wanting to follow this creative urge I felt, even if it meant being a starving artist, and wanting to satisfy my Mom and Dad, and yes, another part of myself to start on a path that might lead to financial riches.

One day, I walked onto the stage at my high school. It was empty, but as I stood on the dark floors and looked out at the empty seats, I felt an excitement deep in myself, and I knew I wanted to be a part of the upcoming theater production. I planned on saying no to my father, and decided not to take the job.

But about the same time I was on that stage, my father was driving home from work, and he had a massive heart attack that killed him instantly. After I recovered from the shock of his death, I knew I would have to go to work to help support our family. My younger sister was just turning 12 and couldn't work. My mother had been a stay-at-home mom, and she was basically unskilled and would only be able to find low-paying service jobs as a waitress or assembly worker or house cleaner. She did work at these types of jobs and provided as best she could for us.

I took the sales job, and then decided, what the hell, since I wasn't going to be able to do what I really wanted to do, I would put all my energy to pursuing the dream to become rich. Wasn't this the essence of America? To allow a common poor person to use his (mostly men were thought to do this) individual drive to rise above his pathetic conditions to become rich, powerful and worthy of the blessings of the royal elite.

But I found it wasn't going to be so easy to achieve my American Dream. I worked and eventually went to community college, completing a transfer degree. Then I finished a Bachelor of Science Degree in Business Management and finally my MBA. I finished with a huge student loan, but by this time I had worked my way up to being a store manager, and felt I was on my way to the fortune I would be able to make one day.

While taking college courses, I did sneak in some writing and literature courses, but it was too emotionally painful for me to try to become involved in theater activities. I decided it was better that I let that part of myself remain dead.

The management positions kept me busy, and in my late twenties, I married Kristen. We moved to Portland, Oregon so that I could accept a promotion to assistant regional sales manager. My wife and I bought a house, and planned on starting a family, but we were both working, and she wanted to put it off for a few years, which turned into seven years.

Then one day last year, I noticed my mind often drifted into trances and daydreams. I began to read poetry at work and often forgot to write out the work schedule for my sales people. Somehow, I was still able to maintain my composure at work, but then the recession hit, and I lost my job. When I told my wife, she used this moment to tell me she had been having an affair with someone she loved, and they were going to move back to Louisiana together. She filed for a divorce.

I didn't start fully fading away from everyday realities and responsibilities until my wife actually left me. Then I found that I couldn't balance my checkbook, and didn't really care. I was able to keep my house for a while, but then lost the house when I couldn't make the mortgage payments.

I thought about contacting my younger sister to borrow money, but she was in the Peace Corp and I knew she would not have any money. We hadn't kept in touch. My mother had died of cancer before I had been transferred to Portland. My sister, who had become a licensed nurse, mainly took care of my mother during the last period of her illness, but I also helped when I could. My mother's death affected both of us deeply, but my sister decided she wanted to devote herself to community service.

I had not maintained relationships with family and friends in Louisiana so there weren't others I could turn to for help, and I'm not sure if I would have anyway. Even though I was not all that clear headed, I knew I was being forced into a new direction in my life, and I wanted to be cut off from my past.

I spent about a few days in an emergency hospital psychiatric clinic in Portland. They said that I had experienced a temporary psychological breakdown. Which may be true, but I know it was more than that. It was a death and a birth. It was like going to a hospital to give birth to a new part of myself, my creative soul. Only they didn't think of it that way. They kept me drugged for a few days. Then they eased up on the drugs, and when they found that I was coherent, they released me with instructions to continue taking the meds. Since their mental health services were cut severely, I guess I wasn't crazy enough for them to feel they had to continue taking care of me. Probably to my benefit.

By this time though, I had begun to understand what had happened. I had experienced a vision of the rebirth. And was happy to be on my journey with my new creative infant soul developing within me.

When I got out I had nowhere to go. I didn't really care. My car had been repossessed before I had lost my job. So the streets of this city became my home. Why all of this actually happened, I am only now beginning to allow myself to think about.

Even though I am still drawn to the dream encased in the Holy Skyscraper across the street, I know I will fight myself to never return to the slave life. I hate that there's some remnants of my old soul still hanging around inside of me. Which confuses me and means that I can't entirely trust myself. Would I sell my new creative soul if someone walked out of the Holy Skyscraper and offered me a job? The fact that I would even ask myself that question pisses me off…and scares the hell out of me.

All right, I've had enough of this autobiographical bullshit for today. What's going on over at the Holy Skyscraper?

Here comes Lord Lucre walking from the parking garage. He's a little late. Who's that with him? Ah, that's why he's late, maybe. They stop and kiss, then he turns and hustles into the building. She stands and watches him until he goes into the building. She then looks into her purse, and pulls out something—a pocket mirror? She's touching up her lipstick, maybe changing color, while people rush by her. The image, the image…they can't lose the image. Hey, what's this? Another man comes up to her and pinches her butt. That's Prince Privilege. I've seen Lord Lucre and Prince Privilege together before. Prince Privilege is young, in his late twenties or early thirties. He's tall and thin, wears wire rimmed glasses and seems bookish, unlike Lord Lucre, who is handsome and well-built, and appears to be an up-and-coming manager type who can dazzle the women just with his sexy stare. But Prince Privilege? He seems so quiet and shy. This woman, I'll call her…Princess Supercilious. She puts away her lipstick and pocket mirror, puts her arm in his and they walk off together away from the Holy Skyscraper. Hmmm. Very interesting. Prince Privilege has definitely surprised me. I'll have to keep track of this new tryst unfolding out in front of the Holy Skyscraper.

Now that I've witnessed all this royal drama, I guess I'll go try to find something to eat. I've been here a couple of hours. Writing about myself has taken a lot out of me. My past is still so confusing, and painful. It was such a waste. But I know I need to start remembering and dealing with who I was so that my new soul won't be attacked by any hidden saboteurs, sides of myself that still want to strive for power and money at the expense of caring and creativity. As I write this I also feel I want to have something good to remember about my past. I have to get in touch with those good memories. I know that I need these memories for my new soul to build on. But enough of this self-reflection for now.

March 10 ~~ THE CAMPFIRE AT THE FREEWAY FIELDS

Last night I spent the early part of the evening at the Campfire. It's been a cold night, colder than usual, and I needed a good fire and some company. I also wanted to see if Ransack would be there, which he was.

Homeless people have settled into the fields underneath the freeways just north of the Burnside Bridge, east of the river. I usually go to the freeway fields after dark because I don't like to see what it looks like in the light of the day. But at night, when various fires glow in different parts of the fields, I can almost believe that this place is a campground in the natural wilderness.

The Campfire is in the section of the fields nearest the river and directly under one of the freeways, so it is protected from the rain. The same group of homeless people hang out in this area at night, and sometimes I join them. I call it the Campfire because when I was thirteen years old my mother sent me to church camp. We sat around a big fire at the church camp each evening, the girls on one side of the fire and the boys on the other side telling stories late into the night. What the church camp leaders didn't realize was that after the campfire sessions, when everyone was supposed to be going back to their cabins, some of the boys would meet some of the girls and go off into the woods to make their own fires. What did they expect from thirteen and fourteen-year-olds—especially at a youth church camp?

Granted, this situation I'm in now certainly isn't a church camp, even though our street evangelist, Jeremiah, tries to turn it into one whenever he's around.

But Jeremiah wasn't there last night, thank god.

When I got to the Campfire, Ransack was in the middle of a story so I decided to wait until he was alone before I asked him about the Butcher. He was telling a story of how earlier that day he'd come upon a group of five white-power skinheads who were beating up a black man. He described how he jumped into the middle of them and knocked the first one out with a blow to the side of the head. Ransack often talks about how he's able to incapacitate and even kill people with simple chops or blows with his hands. Once the leader was knocked out, the other skinheads momentarily became confused, which allowed Ransack to get the black man on his feet. He wasn't hurt too badly, and immediately joined Ransack in attacking the other skinheads.

While he described this action one of the other regulars, Billy Buzz (his street name), sat by the Campfire, leaning against his girlfriend, Livid. Billy Buzz is always drugged out. He lives to get high. He's nineteen years old, and someone said that he ran away from his home about 5 years ago to get away from his abusive father. Apparently Billy Buzz escaped into drugs and eventually to the streets.

As Ransack talked, whatever consciousness Billy had left slowly faded, and his head dropped into Livid's lap. Livid is from Amsterdam and can't be more than fifteen or sixteen, but she insists she is twenty-one. Her hair has streaks of auburn and blonde through long brown hair. She sometimes wears jeans, but mostly she wears a short skirt with tights and high heels. She says last year she was brought to Portland by a businessman who had become her lover in Amsterdam, and promised to take care of her. Shortly after arriving in Portland, the businessman became embroiled in some kind of legal hassle he had to deal with, and he quickly dropped her. She decided to stay in Oregon, and has become a prostitute to survive. She says her real name is Liv, but people on the street have started calling her Livid because of her volatile temper. Livid says she doesn't think Liv is a Dutch name, but that her mother happened to be in love with Liv Ullman at the time she was born. I've heard Livid say, "I can't stand Liv Ullman's movies. They are so fuckin' serious and depressing and are so slow. Liv Ullman is pretty I guess. She's just so serious. I don't think I'm like her in any way."

Ronald and Hawley were also there last night. Ronald and Hawley always seem to be around each other even though they get into terrible arguments and shout and sometimes get into fist fights. Ronald is a staunch conservative. He's twenty-six, and spent his early twenties in the army. He was going to make a career of it until he broke his right knee and was medically discharged. He wears his hair in Army crew cut fashion, and somehow always seems to be neat and clean even though I know he's homeless. I thought I looked unusually clean for my condition, but Ronald's appearance makes me look like the street bum I am.

Ronald is constantly talking about how great America is, how we all should feel lucky to be in America. He hates foreign terrorists and communists, doesn't believe the cold war has ended, but does believe that the Al Qaeda terrorists have to be tracked down, tortured and executed without trials wherever they are hiding. He can't stand people who take government hand-outs, and says he works for what little money he gets. He says that one day he'll get a job that will allow him to get back on his feet, or he'll go to school. He also says there are plenty of opportunities for him and all of us to rise up from our condition. He says when he eventually achieves success, it'll mean more because he has been so down and out. He says that this is what makes America great—that people who are down-and-out can crawl over others to reach the top. He actually says that.

Ronald thinks that Hawley is one of the Communists everyone in America has to fear. Hawley insists he is not a Communist, just an anti-corporate American. Hawley believes all Americans have to take to the streets to bring down the elitist totalitarian system, the plutocracy that is controlling and ruining the United States and the world. He believes it's about time the disadvantaged rise up and fight for what's right. He says he's mainly nonviolent, even though Ronald seems to push to the edge of violence sometimes. Hawley's a little older than Ronald. He spends a lot of time working for progressive organizations and attending demonstrations. He says he's dedicating his life to bringing about social change.

There were others in the vicinity of the Campfire. But a few had smaller fires going. Like the two old winos, Willie and Danny, who sat by themselves around their own fire. They're drunk most of the time, and hang out across the Burnside Bridge near downtown. Sometimes a few mentally ill older women wander through the Campfire area. Then sometimes I see Louise and Charlie, an older couple who are always together. Louise is black and Charlie is white, and they also come from the New Orleans area, like me. Louise talks to herself, but can communicate with others pretty well when she wants to. Other than Louise, Charlie and Walter, I don't know much about any of these older folks.

Then there is Jerome, the shadow man. He's a black Gulf war veteran who doesn't talk much and remains in the background most of the time. He seems to be the kind of Post-Traumatic vet that is waiting to explode. It's like the pin has been pulled many years ago, and the grenade inside of him is just taking a little longer before it causes havoc and destruction. We have no choice but to remain around him at these campfires because when he comes to them nobody has the courage to get up and move to another location. One day I am going to try to talk to Jerome. I don't know why, but even though I was never in military, I feel a strange bond to him.

Walter used to be at the Campfire a lot until he started chasing aliens. Now we don't see him around all that much.

~~ RANSACK AND THE BUTCHER

After Ransack finished his story about beating up on the skinheads, Hawley held up his fist and yelled "Right on! The skinheads are the army of America's right-wing fascists, who are trying to dominate the world."

I could tell that Ronald started to respond, but Ransack said, "You're right. The skinheads are probably supported by a large number of so-called respectable citizens of the U.S. But they will never dominate the world. There are too many decent people who will fight against them."

Someone passed around a bottle of wine, and after a while Ransack stood up and started walking away. I jumped up and caught up with him. I told him about the Butcher and asked him if he could do anything. He asked me what I wanted him to do.

I told him I didn't know. "I thought you'd know more about handling someone dangerous like him than I would."

Ransack smiled, "Yes, I do know a number of ways to handle someone like him. I just wondered if you wanted me to kill the bastard or just mess him up a little. Perhaps break his meat chopping arm, or his knee cap, or both."

"Kill him? Mess him up? I don't want you to do anything so drastic," I responded. "I just want you to scare him, stop him somehow from harassing us. Maybe you could walk by his store and if he comes out you could stand up to him. Maybe he'll back down and will think twice about harassing a homeless person again."

"That's fine but what happens if he doesn't back down?"

It became very clear to me that if it came to a fight, which it probably would, Ransack might severely hurt or even kill the Butcher. I must have blocked the idea of violence out of my mind when I thought about Ransack helping. But I feel something has to be done about the Butcher's dangerous behavior. I told Ransack to do whatever he thought needed to be done, but try to avoid violence and don't even think about killing him. Definitely do not kill him. I can't believe I am even in a situation where I would be making a decision about whether someone would be killed or not. I'm just trying to protect myself and other homeless people.

He laughed at me. "You're not being realistic, Gibson. You can't solve problems like this by being reasonable. But don't worry. If I do anything about the Butcher, I'll do it quietly, or at least in a way nobody can track me." Ransack stopped walking and stood thinking for a few moments. He looked at me, then said, "Actually, I just decided. I am going to do this for you but I am going to ask something in return."

"What?" I felt an immediate attack of panic. Am I selling my soul? A soul that isn't even fully developed?

"You don't have to worry. It's not going to involve doing anything illegal or dangerous. Ever since I've seen you around the fields, I've thought about asking you to do something for me. Now I'll just make it a part of the payment for helping you take care of this little problem you and other homeless people seem to be having with the Butcher. You'll understand when I tell you but I don't want to tell you until I see if I can do anything about the Butcher. I'd like you to show me where his shop is."

I felt sort of assured. What could he want me to do if it isn't illegal or dangerous? Surely it wouldn't be anything that's too much of a hassle if it didn't involve breaking the law or danger. It would be worth doing him a favor to stop the Butcher from going on his rampages.

I took him to the Butcher's Block, and from across the street pointed to the shop. It was closed, as were the other shops on the street. I stood a block away while he crossed the street and looked around. After a little while he came back to me and said that he'd do something about it, but he didn't know what. He told me that he'd let me know in a few days when the job was done.

We then pooled our money together and bought a couple of quarts of beer and walked back down to the industrial section. We sat under the overhang of a building and as we drank our beer, Ransack talked about where he'd been these last couple of days. He said that he'd seen this woman in a bar whom he'd known many years ago, and he became worried that she could identify him and tip off the CIA where he was hiding. He said that he followed her for a few days, broke into her house, and rummaged through her things (neatly, he said, so that she wouldn't know he'd been there) to see if he could find whether or not she was still linked to the CIA. He said that he couldn't find anything, but he said that he had decided to make plans to leave the U.S. for a while. Perhaps go to Asia or Africa.

I asked Ransack why he talks about these things to people, like me, who are almost strangers to him. I asked him if he didn't worry that someone like me would turn him in. He said that he decided long ago that he had to trust some people. He looked at me with a very cold look and said, "Besides, Gibson, I know more about you and the others around here than you think. I still have some of my connections that let me get information I need on people. Most people don't realize how extensive the big-brother spy network really is. Secret organizations of this government are constantly keeping track and prying into the day-to-day activities of everyone."

"Even a homeless man like myself?" I said incredulously.

"Yes like you because you descended to the streets from such a conventional life. You are easy to track and to know about. My life has been undercover so long my true identity has been totally erased. Most homeless people are more like you than me.

"But anyway, Americans are generally a naive, stupid group of people. Their greatness came when they could depend on their bold and arrogant actions to dazzle or bully their way to success, but now the world has become vastly more sophisticated than Americans are capable of dealing with. Americans don't seem to want to know that they have sold their souls to the true devils in the Pentagon and in secret business organizations whose sole purpose is to keep a select few in power. You see, Gibson, I was trained by these people. I know how they think. I can smell them out. I know when a place is safe or not. I can tell who it's safe to tell my story to. And if I'm wrong, I have confidence that I can survive a surprise attack just like I have survived all my encounters these last twenty years. And if I don't survive…well, that prospect is what keeps me young and alert."

Ransack took a drink of his beer and shook his head laughing. "You know what I have become in my old age, Gibson? A storyteller. I sit around the fires at night and lecture or tell stories to a group of down and out street people, most of them too drunk or too drugged out to even know what I am talking about."

"Do you miss the action?" I asked.

"No, because I've stayed in the action. Only now I'm more in control of what actions I take and I am able to have more choice in the outcomes."

He didn't say more, and when I asked him to explain, he looked at me with his cold look, a look that I hadn't seen on him except for tonight, and he told me not to ask him about what he does, just let him tell me what he wants to tell. I felt truly frightened of Ransack at that moment. It was like he had changed into a different person. But then he smiled and changed back into the person with whom I was more familiar. He started telling me about some other story in his past and eventually I felt more relaxed.

Later after we had gone our separate ways, I began to worry that perhaps it had been a mistake to ask Ransack to do something about the Butcher. Maybe I should have just stayed away from the Butcher's Block and tried to forget about what he was doing to the street people. What will he want me to do in repayment for his help?

~~ MEANINGFUL COINCIDENCES

I've been walking along the major streets of Grand Avenue and Martin Luther King Avenue this hour or so. Back and forth. North and South. I've wanted the busy night traffic to keep me company. The blur of the headlights and the sound of the cars can pull me into a trance sometimes where I can leave my worries and fears for a while.

I feel a little better now about asking Ransack to help out. I brought the image of the Butcher back into my mind. Fallacious cooperated in flashing the Butcher's nasty face before me, and in replaying the scary incident of him almost slicing my head off with his meat cleaver. I was almost killed I reminded myself. Twice. Ransack is right. Some people can't be reasoned with. You have to beat the shit out of them to make them more decent to live around. But I know that I could not beat the shit out of the Butcher. I am not a trained fighter or big and strong enough to have an effect on his monstrous hulk. And perhaps Ransack really won't have to hurt the Butcher too badly.

I thought about my father being a wholesale meat representative but I couldn't imagine him ever being like the Butcher. My father was misguided but not mean, vicious, violent. Yet I have to admit because the Butcher looms so large in my mind, I seem to become angry because he cuts and sells meat just like my father did at times in his work. It almost makes me believe in a master plan. I leave the lifestyle represented by my father, and then the universe turns loose a maniac like the Butcher on me. Well, even if it's true, even if the universe is that mean, I won't accept it. The Butcher is going to be dealt with. If Ransack doesn't do it, I'll find another way. But I think Ransack will be able to do it.

Shortly after becoming homeless, I picked up a book from the free book bin at the library about the magic of time. I only read part of this book, and then I lost it in an alley where I was sleeping one night. But I remember reading in this book that there are no random events in life. I read that life unfolds in meaningful patterns, and what we think of as coincidences have meaning for us if we could understand these patterns. I think the author was trying to say each individual has things to learn and develop and express in life, and that we will keep drawing to us experiences, people and events that will challenge us to develop qualities of being that we are meant to develop.

There are no random events, no senseless coincidences. All recurring patterns have meaning. But what meaning does meat cutting and sales have for me? Whatever it means I'm not ready to become a vegetarian, even though my current life style does not provide me the opportunity to eat meat that often anyway...as I wrote that I managed to make myself smile. I can't be so serious all the time

I'm sitting on this bus bench thinking about how tired and sleepy I am, but having brought those frightening images of the Butcher back into my mind, I am a little uneasy about going into the darkness to find a place to sleep. Maybe I need to keep walking around for a few more hours until I get so tired I won't care what happens to me. I'm sure nothing is going to happen to me tonight. At least not in this reality. I don't know about in my dreams, though, but there's nothing I can do about that.

March 11 ~~ JUSTINE IN A DREAM

Last night I dreamed of Justine standing at the counter, daydreaming, staring at something through one of the front windows of her store. I am watching her from the workroom behind her. And then I walk toward her, as I come in front of the counter she looks at me and smiles at me. She smiles at me because I'm me, not just to be sociable, and despite that I am homeless.

I stood looking at her expression, intense, spontaneous, a clear expression of energy, a look that sees inside of me. Receptive, but in her own terms. I remember thinking, "Why do you look that way at me? What do you see in me?"

I've watched Justine since I've started working for her and I've noticed that she doesn't look that way at everyone. She is more formal, though very personable, when she interacts with most people. I wish that I had the courage to ask her. But it's probably nothing. It's probably Fallacious playing his usual tricks on me again. I can't allow myself to be vulnerable to her yet.

I woke up feeling good, except now I'm feeling the pressure of the dawn pressing down on me as I struggle to awake. I'm warm now, but when I move I will be cold and I have to move because I have to take a piss. Life is unrelenting in its incessant demands.

I don't have money to wash my clothes today but I feel chilled throughout my body, and need a shot of hot air. I walked over to the Laundromat near SE Salmon that has air vents from their dryers pointed out toward the sidewalk. I stood for at least an hour under the invisible shower of wonderful hot air, protected from the cold.

While I was being warmed by this air vent I decided that I would still come here to the Holy Skyscraper after I finished warming myself. For some reason I cannot take the cold today. I didn't even want to walk here to the Holy Skyscraper. Eleven or twelve blocks to the bridge, then at least another fifteen or so blocks to the Holy Skyscraper. Normally I don't care how far I walk. Walking is a state of being for me. So is feeling cold. But today I'm having a hard time handling goddamn cold states of being.

I had to make a decision. I had a little less than two dollars. I had to decide whether to buy myself a cup of coffee or ride the bus to downtown. As much as I wanted a cup of coffee, I decided to ride the bus. Now I'm here at the Holy Skyscraper, and I feel like I made the right decision. I hope I'm not getting sick. The cold has never bothered me so much before.

I knew that I had to make a little money today. I needed to eat some food, get some nutrients in my body, and I didn't want to spend the time outside scouting around the back of restaurants. And tonight I've got to find a warm place to sleep. It's times like these that I think I should be living in San Diego or Miami. Or in Hawaii. I wonder if there are many homeless people in Hawaii.

~~ WALTER'S FEAR OF THE SPACE ALIENS

I saw Walter this afternoon walking along SW 11th Avenue around Burnside. I tried to get his attention, but he was walking as if he were deep in thought; his head was down. I haven't seen Walter around too much lately, but I think he's changed in some ways. For one thing he almost always had a bottle in his hand before. If he wasn't drinking he had just finished drinking and he tended to talk to himself or to anybody who would listen. He would go back and forth from telling stories to being belligerent.

I never knew Walter to be a paranoid kind of person. He'd been on the streets for a long time, and had become a wino, but wasn't incoherent all the time. I've had a few pretty decent conversations with him at different times. But lately, ever since I ran into him in that alley and he started telling me about seeing aliens from another planet, I guess he has kind of become…well, crazy. Even if he had seen aliens, who would believe him? At any rate, I've decided it wouldn't do any good to try to tell him he's wrong about the aliens, but if he keeps this paranoid shit up he'll probably end up in the psychiatric ward.

I crossed Grand Avenue, and caught up to Walter. When I came up beside him he was startled for a moment until he recognized me.

"Walter, you are really scared these days. What's going on?"

"What do you mean asking a question like that?" he answered gruffly. "As if everything is normal. You of all people should know that the world as we know it is on the verge of being destroyed by these horrible, conniving aliens, and being one of the few people who know it, I have to fear for my life. I have to keep moving. You're one of the few people who also know. You better keep moving, too, buster."

"Come on, Walter. How are you so sure you've seen aliens?" I thought maybe if I could pin him down he might have to acknowledge that he's deluded himself.

"If I could show you what I've seen, you would not ask such a stupid question. I've seen things that would boggle your mind. Ah, maybe it's better that you don't believe me…for now. You might be safer. When the time's right I'll prove to you that I've really seen aliens. Until then leave me alone. Just get away from me. We'll both be safer."

Walter turned and ran off down a side street. Well, so much for my amateur psychological efforts. That guy has really gone off the deep end. Too bad. I liked him.

~~ JEROME THREATENS ME

I've been hanging around the freeway fields all afternoon looking for Ransack. I don't like being in these fields during the day. I like to come here after the darkness of night cloaks some of its ugliness and despair.

The grey overcast sky makes walking through these fields a more gloomy and grim experience than usual. The fields seem so barren, even though strewn with syringes, used toilet paper, empty wine bottles. The harsh realities of our existence.

Where's the idyllic country field. This is a city's undeveloped vacant lot, a little bigger than most lots, and probably only undeveloped because nobody's figured out yet how to use it to exploit somebody else.

When I first arrived in the fields I saw Jerome sitting under a tree sharpening one of his huge hunting knives. I decided to try to talk with him. I took a deep breath, walked over to him and sat done in front of him. "Mind if I sit down here?" I asked.

He didn't answer. Kept sharpening his knife in long steady stokes across a dark stone. His short hair made his long, square face seem large and powerful. I saw a long scar on his right cheek that extended underneath his chin. I almost thought about getting up and walking away right away, but instead I said to him, "Jerome this may sound strange to you. It certainly sounds strange to me but since I've seen you around here I've been interested in talking with you." I felt like I was talking to myself. "Do you feel like talking?"

For the longest time he didn't say anything. He kept sharpening his knife and didn't even acknowledge that I was there. Then suddenly he reached out with startling speed, grabbed my right hand and pulled it toward him so my right arm was stretched out in front of me. He then laid the flat edge of the blade of his huge hunting knife on my arm and slid it toward him, slicing off some fine thin hair off.

Still holding my arm Jerome stared at me with a look that gave me the creeps. He looked intense but there was something else. As strange as it seems, there was a longing look. I can't describe it any other way, but he said, "I won't talk to you. I can't talk to you. Don't ever ask me again." Then he let go of my arm and started sharpening his knife again. I got up and quickly walked away. He was very clear. No doubt about it. No matter how drawn I feel to him, we are absolutely not going to get to know each other better. I wonder why he said that he can't talk with me. Forget it. I'm sure it's safer not to know.

I've been sitting here now at the edge of the freeway fields for hours it seems. Being around this ugly-looking place so long in daylight and that incident with Jerome has made my overcast mood even darker. I need a change of scenery. I think I'll walk to some other section of the city and come back later tonight to see if Ransack's at the Campfire. I'll walk over to the Northwest area. The beauty and culture there will be a good antidote for the poisons that have invaded my emotions today.

March 13 ~~ A BREAKFAST SURPRISE

This morning I woke up with someone standing over me. I was lying on my cardboard in the back alley behind Casey's when I opened my eyes and found myself looking at two thin, bare legs. As my eyes travelled a little higher I saw the hem of a skirt, so I more or less assumed it was a teenage girl probably around 16 or 17. Thinking back on it I suppose that seeing it was a teenage girl kept me from being scared out of what little of my mind that was awake.

I lifted my head and looked up into her face — definitely not our kind, from the street. She was well-groomed, wearing wire-rimmed glasses, her brown hair neatly pulled back into a long braid, and clean, very clean.

We stared at each other for a moment, and I began to wonder what she was doing, standing and staring at me. I wondered, "What could she want? Is she going to give me money, ask me for help…?"

Finally, she said, "I've got some food here, if you want it." And she held out something wrapped in a paper napkin. I didn't reach for it because, quite frankly, I was stunned and still groggy from sleep, so she made a move to lay the bundle of food beside me.

"Here, take this," she said. "I have to get back to work before they see me. You know, the manager may call the cops if he sees you now that it's light out. Why don't you get out of the way, behind that trash bin? I'll bring you a cup of coffee in a few minutes if I can." She was gone so quickly, I would have thought I'd been dreaming except that I could see the bundle of food beside me.

I sat up and lifted a corner of the napkin wrapped around the food. I saw a coffee cake and a couple of hard-boiled eggs. Amazing. I stared at this feast for a while. I picked up one of the eggs. It felt warm. I must have been in a trance. Then suddenly I remembered her warning. I looked quickly at the door that led into the back of the café to see if I was being observed, but the door was closed. I grabbed my food and my sleeping bag & pack, and settled behind the trash bin making sure I was out of sight.

I lay the bundle of food on my lap, then for the first time sat back and took notice of the morning. It was overcast and chilly. Lucky for me it wasn't raining. I took a bite of the coffee cake, and tasted the nuts and the cinnamon. I closed my eyes enjoying these rare tastes to the fullest. Then I took a bite of one of the eggs, and steam filtered up before my eyes. I was in heaven.

I heard the door open and footsteps coming toward the trash bin, so I sat very still as if I could become invisible by not moving. Someone walked to the edge of the trash bin and stopped. I held my breath, clutched my food, and stared at the edge of the bin. A movement caught my eye at the bottom edge of the bin, and I saw a small hand set a paper cup of coffee on the ground in front of me.

"Here's a cup of coffee," I heard the girl say.

I waited for a moment before saying thanks. I bent forward and picked up the paper cup by its handles. I smelled the aroma and instantly felt warmer. Then I realized that she was still standing by the bin.

"Can I ask you something?" she asked.

"Yeah, of course."

She hesitated. I wondered what she could want from me. For the first time, I realized that I had been accepting this generosity assuming that this was an expression of charity. Over the months on the streets, I had begun to realize that among the majority of stingy, uncaring people there are a few who are giving and caring.

"I…would like to talk with you. I want to ask you some questions about your life. I'm doing a project for school on the homeless, and I want to interview someone who is homeless for the project."

I looked at my wonderful breakfast in front of me, and thought, "Why not?" I said to her, "OK, ask away. You mind if I eat while we talk?"

"I can't interview you now," she said. "I'm still working. I'm a dishwasher at Casey's. Could you meet me this afternoon about two at the park down the street?"

My first reaction was "hell no, I don't want to stick around here all day." But then, I thought, "I could go to the Holy Skyscraper and still be back by two, even though I really didn't know what time it was."

"I'll try to meet you at two, but I'm not too good at keeping track of time these days."

"Here," she said as she placed her small watch on the ground at the corner of the trash bin. I still couldn't see her.

"No, hey, I don't want to take your watch. What are you doing? You don't even know me. Keep it."

"It's a cheap watch, besides I feel like I can trust you. You can give it back later when we meet," she said, and she walked off. This girl had a way of not taking no for an answer, and yet at first she seemed sort of shy. I realized suddenly that I wasn't sure if I would remember what she looked like. I had seen her so briefly, and I had been half asleep. Oh hell, I thought, she probably knows what I look like. I picked up the watch and put it in my pocket. Then, I sat back to enjoy the warm breakfast and hot coffee. This day had started off like a charm. As I sipped my coffee, I hoped the day wouldn't become more complex than I was used to dealing with in my stripped-down, emotional, street-life state of being.

~~ ATTRACTIVE WOMEN

After finishing my unexpected delicious breakfast, I walked downtown to the Pioneer Square. It's a sunny day, and I'm feeling pretty good now, except for having to see a multitude of attractive women who have decided to come to the Pioneer Square this morning.

Seeing attractive women from the condition I am in—homeless and broken—is both a wonderful and a painful experience. It's the one thing that tears at my resolve to remain separate from the mainstream slave life. I need someone to share my self and my feelings with. I need to share deeply with someone. I have realized that when I was in my early twenties I was able to express my feelings more than I am now. I was able to reach out to a woman, and to be responsive. When I first met my ex-wife, even though I had been a slave for a few years, I was still able to be responsive and express myself with love, even if we really didn't belong together. I think there is a part of me that believes we are meant to share love in different ways with different people. There are soul mates, and then there are other special people with whom we can share love.

At any rate, as the years went on, I lost the capacity to love—I just lost the feeling and the desire. The slave life kept eroding my sense of self-expression and my capacity for intimacy, kept eroding it like waves of acid washing onto my soul, until all that was left was a barren desert, devoid of passion and responsiveness. I was only able to live out my slave role—nothing else. I maintained my role for many years until I broke down. I just broke down.

I've let myself open now to the bittersweet memories of being with Sally Waters, my first real love, the woman I turned away from to marry my ex-wife. I've only realized since my breakdown how much I blocked out about her during my marriage and how special she was to me. After my breakdown, when I would think about Sally, I felt a long overdue sense of loss. Then I felt angry. Then depressed. Now I think these feelings are more the result of the lack of romance in my life at this time as they are about losing the first woman I loved.

Years back, Sally and her brother Stephen, both in their early twenties at the time, had inherited a substantial amount of money and about fifty acres of land when their parents were killed in a car crash. Sally and Stephen lived a hippie life-style out on their land, and most people in town disapproved of them. I had just finished my graduate degree, but was working all the time at the department store. Most of the time, all I allowed myself to think about was work and my goal of becoming a manager one day. I was going out with Kristen, the woman who was going to become my wife.

During all those years before my breakdown, I kept buried deep in my mind the memory of the afternoon I got off work and Sally was waiting for me. And then during my breakdown those memories erupted like a warm erotic dream. Sally was blonde, and on that one special day she was wearing a yellow sun dress and I could tell that was about all, except for her sandals. She asked if I wanted to come out to her place with her. She said that she wanted my advice on what she needed to make her greenhouse larger. She also said that she wanted to spend some time with me to get to know me better. She said that she appreciated how nice I had been to her, especially when most of the people in town were so uptight and disapproving.

I did go with Sally to her place in the country. When we arrived nobody else was there, and I was amazed to see how nice her ranch style house was. She said that it had been her parents and even though she really didn't like the style, it was what they had to live with. I remember thinking that she said it as if it were a shack or like the small apartment I lived in at the time. I would have given anything to live in a stylish house like hers. Of course, she had decorated it inside with strange colorful hanging cloth, and there were plants all around, and the smell of incense. All over the living room she had plush pillows. No other furniture.

At first she took me out back to the greenhouse, and I helped her figure out what she needed. The day was hot, and at one point she took my hand and let me through a wooded area behind her house to a creek. She took off her clothes and dove into the creek. She yelled to me to take off my clothes and join, which though I was a little self-conscious, I did. When we got out we kept our clothes off and walked back to the house. She put music on her stereo and we made love in her living room in the midst of many pillows.

Sally drove me back to town, and when I arrived home late, everyone was upset. I was supposed to be having dinner with Kristen and my mother. When I hadn't shown up, Kristen had called the store and someone had told her that they had seen me drive away with Sally. Kristen was, of course, really upset and left my apartment to go home. I was upset too, and I went out in the backyard to try to figure things out.

I didn't want to hurt Kristen, but I had never before experienced the fullness in relating that I had experienced that day with Sally. We had worked a little together on the green house. We had talked about all sorts of things. Sally was a photographer and she had shown me some of her work. She liked taking photographs of all types of people, and had a wonderful ability to capture a wide range of expressions and emotions. She had a lot of pictures of townspeople, and I was surprised when she showed me pictures of me at work, talking with customers. I told her that I used to write, but now I didn't have that much time. She said that she felt sad about that and hoped that I would start writing again. And then when we made love she was so open and responsive, and quite frankly at first I felt a little intimidated, but she helped me get over my insecurities. I had the most physical pleasures that I have ever experienced.

So I stood out on the deck of my apartment that evening, thinking to myself that I should go after Kristen, but I really wanted to just go back to Sally's house. She had asked me to stay the evening with her. My mother came out onto the deck to talk with me, and she said she knew about me going with Sally. She didn't ask me anything about how I felt. She just said that I needed to think of my future, and that I was on the right track in my work, and she felt that I would be getting the promotion I wanted soon. She said that Kristen would be such a good wife. She said that I should think hard about ruining my reputation by chasing after someone who probably would never settle down.

She said that she and my father always wanted me to be able to have the things that they could not provide me. She said before my father died, he said he felt I had the potential to be a great success in business and management and she said he was so proud of me. She hugged me and said she was also proud of how hard I worked, and she wanted so much for me to be successful and happy.

I let her pull me back into my father's and her dream for my future, and I went over later that night to ask Kristen to marry me. The next day Sally showed up at the store, and I told her I had asked Kristen to marry me. She didn't say anything. She smiled and shook her head and walked away. Again, by making that choice I know now that I killed so much of my real self.

Now I'm homeless and broken, unfit for a relationship, outside the realms of life where relationships exist. I need to be with someone, to love someone, to share with someone but I can't let myself right now…so again I've let my feelings of self-pity and loneliness spill out onto these pages. Now I have to straighten up, reaffirm my purpose despite my loneliness, and get on with my street life of self-imposed isolation. To hell with love. To hell with relationships. To hell with memories of first loves. To hell with attractive women. They're just illusions, lures to trap my new creative soul, to pull it back into the slave life. I have to remain alone, but damn, it sure hurts sometimes.

~~ JUSTINE DESERVES BETTER

I decided to leave Pioneer Square and work for a few hours before I needed to meet the young girl who gave me breakfast this morning.

While I was working, I heard Justine talking with her boyfriend, Chris, in the next room. When he sees me he seems to sneer and never says hello. Maybe I'm imagining the sneer, but I don't think so. I have to admit he is good looking, very good looking. He has the square-jaw type of handsome face, blonde hair, blue eyes, muscular build, fashionable slacks and shirt and coat—he looks like a model or a movie star. I have to remind myself that he is emotionally unstable, like me…but in a different, apparently a more obnoxious way. I keep my emotional instability more to myself, or at least I try to.

I just don't understand why Justine is with Chris. Well, I guess if she is considering his handsome face, wavy blond hair, his tall, muscular body and the fact that he is an actor, I can understand why—reluctantly. But he has such an arrogant disposition, and that does not seem to fit with Justine. I just don't understand why she is with him.

It's none of my business, really. But I do like Justine and I don't want her to be hurt. What am I thinking? She's a grown woman. She can handle this type of life challenge. I can't. I have to remain focused on my own life challenges, not hers.

Justine came into the room where I was working and said, "Goodbye Gibson. It was nice to see you here today. I'm going over to the theater to work on some rehearsals with Chris …"

Just then Chris called impatiently from the front door, "Come on, Justine. We have to get going."

She frowned and shook her head, but then waved goodbye to me with a smile as she turned to leave.

~~ INTERVIEW WITH THE TEENAGE GIRL

Somehow, a little before 2:00 p.m. I found myself sitting on one of the benches in the park where I was supposed to meet the girl who gave me breakfast earlier in the day. I realized I was still hungry. I began counting the change in my pocket to see if there was enough to buy some yogurt, when I saw her walking across the street and into the park. She noticed me, and started walking in my direction. She was a thin girl and she had taken her sandy hair out of the pony tail and it was shoulder length. She wore a white blouse and a dark blue skirt, and was carrying school books against her chest and a brown purse with a shoulder-length strap. She looked like the type of school girl who always made the best grades, had no social life, and didn't know anything about real life. The kind of girl who couldn't find time for boys.

She came over to the bench and sat down. "Thanks for meeting me," she said. She looked down at her books, and started arranging them to take notes.

"Thanks for breakfast."

She nodded shyly, "I didn't just give you breakfast because I wanted to interview you."

"Well, I wouldn't mind if that had been your only reason. I thoroughly enjoyed the food."

"I feel sorry that there are so many homeless and poor people. I feel someone should help them…and you."

"I wish more people felt like you do. Maybe there wouldn't be so many homeless people. Or at least maybe we wouldn't be so hungry all the time," I smiled.

She went on in her serious manner, "A social worker came to our class to talk about homelessness, and she said that we should not give beggars or homeless people money because they mainly use it to buy alcohol or drugs. She said that we should give them food if we wanted to give them something. Do you think she is right?"

"Is this the first question of the interview?" I asked, smiling.

"I suppose so," she answered, and finally she also smiled. "I just sort of dove in, didn't I? I have so many questions." She became serious again. "As I told you, I have this project I'm doing on the homeless. It's for my high school social studies class. I plan on interviewing various homeless people."

"Why did you choose me?"

"I've seen you around."

"Lying around or standing around." I joked. She seemed so nervous or bothered or something. I needed to try to lighten her up.

She thought for a moment. "Both. A few Saturdays, when I've come to work early, I've seen you sleeping in the alley. I've seen you a few times during the week in the afternoon, standing at the corner. You've also come into the café a few times and ordered coffee."

"I don't remember seeing you."

"I didn't serve you. I just wash dishes. You're lucky, by the way, that the boss was busy in the back. He doesn't like what he calls bums or street people coming into the café. He doesn't want the waitresses to serve them. But they do it anyway when he's not looking. Everyone thinks he is an asshole."

She saw me raise my eyebrows, and she smiled, and said, "I'm just being honest. I'm sure you've heard worse."

I nodded, and said, "Well, I don't usually stay in the café. When I have money, I just buy it to go."

"Lucky you do."

I told her that I realized she had risked her job giving me breakfast that morning and that I appreciated it. She smiled and said that when she wants to do something and believes its right, she will take risks. She said it with such firmness that it was like the sun coming out from behind clouds. Perhaps this girl wasn't as timid as she seemed.

"Speaking of risks, here's your watch back."

As she took it, she nodded and looked as though she was thinking, "See, I knew I could trust you."

I told her I was as ready as I would ever be to answer her questions, but that she would have to risk me not making sense sometimes because I have little control over my mind these days. She asked if I had psychological problems. I told her that her vocabulary was very sophisticated, that most people would just ask if I was crazy. She seemed startled by my blunt statement, and expressed concern that I would be hurt by being called crazy. I told her that it didn't bother me, because I did think I was a little crazy, a harmless crazy though. A harmless, homeless crazy man. She asked if she could learn more about my problem, and I said that maybe we could get to that but first I wanted her to ask easy questions.

"Okay," she said, and looked down at her notebook, "How long have you been homeless?"

"A little over six months."

"Do you have any children?"

That question surprised me. "No, I don't have children."

"Were you married?"

"Yes."

"And you didn't want children?"

"Now, I didn't say I didn't want children. I said I didn't have children. My wife and I were planning to have children before we divorced."

I looked at the girl. This line of questioning was making me feel a little uncomfortable. "What does this have to with me being homeless?"

"Part of my project will be on the effects of homelessness on children."

"Well, I don't know if I am the right person for your project because I don't have any children."

For some reason I felt irritated, and I knew I sounded like it.

"I'm sorry if I made you upset. I just ...actually, I can change my main theme..."

My irritation quickly dissipated as I saw her looking down at her notebook. I thought I could see tears in her eyes.

I said, "Wait a second. You seem to be more upset than I am. I'm not angry at you. I guess I'm just a little uncomfortable talking about children. I really wanted to have a family. It's sometimes difficult for me to think about not being with someone I love and to not have a family... but I don't understand why you are so upset."

Suddenly she blurted out this whole terrible story about how her father had just died of a sudden, unexpected heart attack, and how her mother has never worked in her whole adult life, and that her mother hasn't been able to find work, and if she doesn't find work she, her mother, and her nine-year old brother and herself will become homeless.

"I found a part-time job, but my mother hasn't found one. I'm so afraid. But I'm trying to prepare myself. I'm trying to find out what it is like being homeless, having to live on the street."

"What is your name?" I asked. I didn't know what I was going to do or how I was going to get out of this. I wasn't used to dealing with other people's crises or emotions since mine had been blown apart in my breakdown.

"Carissa. My father gave me that name."

"Look, Carissa, there are a lot of places that will help your mother since she has you and your brother to take care of. How old are you?"

"Sixteen."

"And your brother is nine?"

She nodded.

"I bet your mother right now is finding a job, or is at one of these agencies getting assistance."

"No she isn't. She's drinking. My mother started drinking after my father died, and she doesn't do anything else."

This situation was definitely getting more complicated than I wanted or was capable of dealing with.

"Are you really doing a school project on the homeless?"

"Yes, yes, I am. I need to do this project. I want to get a good grade so I can pass my class at school. But I...I also need to do it to be prepared in case we become homeless. Both reasons are important to me. My father taught me that to survive you can't be afraid of the future, you just have to make sure you've learned as much as you can about what you may have to deal with so you can be prepared for what you have to face."

"I feel badly about your father, and your mother, and if you feel it's going to help, I'll answer your questions."

Then she hit me with her next big surprise. She told me that she wanted to do in-depth studies of one or two homeless people's lives. A single man. A single woman. And a family. She wanted to know if I would be willing to let her follow me around a few times, and for me to show her where I sleep, and what I do with my day and night.

I felt really uncomfortable with this. I still do. But I agreed to at some point let her follow me around for a day.

I think I agreed when she looked at me, and I saw her eyes were still red with her tears, and she looked so forlorn and afraid. Maybe it's that I have had so few such opportunities to be a hero to somebody in need. Or maybe it's just that I can't stand other people feeling emotionally distraught. I have to find a way to get over being so sensitive about others' problems. It doesn't fit well with surviving on the streets. I need to become more hardened.

"I'll go along with this," I told her, "But with a few conditions. One is that you only ask easy questions. Second, that you don't often cry around me. Or if you have to, at least you have to smile and laugh a lot, too. Three, I don't have to be anywhere at a certain time."

"Wait, how will we know when to meet? I work. I go to school. I have to help around the house. We have to arrange some times."

"I'm just not good with time these days. I'm just not ..."

"I know. I know," she said. "The best times for me are Thursday and Sunday afternoons after three. I work all the rest of the days after school. I will come by this park between three and four, and if you are here, you're here. If you're not, you're not. I'll just know you can't make it. If I don't see you after a few tries, I do know where to find you ..."

"Yes, you do know where to find me on some mornings. I guess I can agree to trying to meet you on your days off," I said, and deep down I knew that I would try to make it there on those days. I knew that I was getting myself into trouble. What is it in me that feels I should respond to Carissa? Is it ego? I didn't realize that I even had an ego left. Is it that I feel the need to help those in need? I have never had that affliction before. Anyway, I will try to be there on those days at least a few times, and see what I can do to help her understand and prepare herself. Of course, even if her family became homeless she wouldn't live the kind of life I live. She'd be in a shelter and possibility would have better care. At least the chances are that she would be. The more I think about it, the more I'm getting intrigued—I'm going to be a survival teacher. A street survival teacher. It could be interesting.

Before she left, she smiled and said, "I can't say I will always ask easy questions, but I will try to smile as much as I cry."

I like her. I decided that it would be nice to spend more time around her.

~~ THE CURSE OF THE BAG LADY

I was getting ready to leave the park when I saw someone running toward me out of bushes. It was the goddamn bag lady, and again she had one of her knives in her hand.

"What are you doing?" I yelled as I started to run away. "You can't keep trying to kill me with your knife." That was useless to say because indeed she was continuing to try to kill me with her knife.

"Give me that journal, goddamn you," she was yelling at me. "I am putting a curse on you. You are going to die a painful death for writing terrible things about me."

"I'm not writing terrible things about you," I yelled as I kept running away. "Please believe me."

"You have to show me. You have to prove to me. I need to see it."

But I just kept running, and eventually got away from her. I think I heard her say at one point, "If I don't get you, the curse will."

Oh shit, that's all I need. A curse. And an undefined curse at that. My demise could be the result of anything. I'm sure I don't believe in curses. I'm sure of that.

~~ MYSTERY SOUNDS IN THE WAREHOUSE

It's almost evening—I've walked back to the east side of the river and have been sitting on the steps of another abandoned warehouse—kind of in a daze. I'm not sure how long I've been sitting here. I believe time has abandoned me.

The bag lady ruined what was a pretty good day. I am just beginning to feel a little more relaxed. I faded away there for a while, and somehow I'm feeling better. I wish I knew where my mind went, but I do feel better now.

Someone's banging on something inside the warehouse, and I already feel guarded, tense. Could it be a gang? After what's been happening to me lately with the gang, the butcher, the bag lady, the curse, and even Jerome, I've got to be more on guard, but I don't like feeling this way. There goes my sense of peacefulness, such a fleeting moment of feeling at ease.

The door on the right side of this loading dock just banged open. I stopped writing and braced myself, ready to run. But out came a young child, maybe two years old. Right after him came a young woman, who scooped the child up and disappeared back into the warehouse so fast she seemed like an apparition. The after-image imprinted on my memory was of a woman in her twenties wearing a maroon long jumper over a light-colored blouse, her long strands of black hair were flying around her like a magical cape.

I can still hear the banging and I'm becoming curious enough to find out what it's about. Seeing the child and the woman has made a difference in how safe I feel, enough that I've decided to go into the warehouse to see what's going on.

~~ NEIGHBORLY STREET SHARING

I slid open the heavy metal door, and peered into the deserted warehouse. I tried blinking my eyes, hoping to speed my adjustment to the dark. The few rays of dusty light from the high windows spotlighted the concrete floor. As I stood in the doorway, listening to the banging, the eeriness I felt kept me from moving any further. Shortly after the banging stopped and from somewhere came the unexpected sounds of children running and yelling. Until then I hadn't heard my own heartbeat banging on my ears.

I walked through one large room and passed huge concrete, graffiti-covered pillars. At the far end of the room I passed through a doorway and saw a Hispanic man standing in the middle of the room near a bicycle cart. He held a large wrench in his hand. He looked up and stared at me. I recognized him. I've often seen him and his family around the freeway fields and other places in the city. They have a boy about two years old and a girl two or three years older. I glanced around the room, looking for the others. They must be playing in another room, I thought.

I looked back at the man. He asked if I could give him a hand. He said that he could use help steadying the wheel he was trying to straighten. He was shorter than me, about medium height, a thin man with a black moustache, full, curly black hair and an intense look in his dark eyes. He wore corduroys, and a woolen sweater underneath his green army jacket. A yellow bandanna around his forehead helped to contain his hair. He seemed to be in his early thirties. I felt strangely at ease with the matter-of-fact way he was asking me for help. He seemed far from threatening.

I walked over and took hold of the wheel as we introduced ourselves. He said his name was Carlos. He told me earlier that day the cops had run him and his family away from their camping place near the Banfield Freeway, and in the process the cart rolled down an incline and crashed into a concrete wall, bending the basket and one of the wheels. He didn't seem angry as he spoke, and I asked him about that. He said he didn't feel angry. He said what mattered was that his family was all right and that he was with them. He said he was thinking about taking his family away from the city again. I asked why he didn't take them to a shelter. He looked up from his work with a disgusted expression on his face. He said if he had to for the children's sake he would take them to a shelter for a night or two, but he didn't like how they made him feel, like he was a refugee in a foreign country. He said in shelters he also felt so constricted, and he'd rather be free to make camp wherever they wanted.

His two children ran into the room, stopping when they saw me, obviously startled. Carlos assured them it was ok and introduced us. The girl's name was Dolores. She had hair like her mothers, though not as long. The boy's name was Juan. Both children were thin and had the wrinkled, ragged look of the streets, but they also were lively, and once they saw their father had accepted me, they continued their play.

Carlos finished straightening the wheel and was putting it back on the cart when his wife, Laura, came into the room. With hardly a pause she said that she had some food prepared and there was enough for me if I wanted to eat with them. Carlos put his wrench down and I found myself following him into the next room.

It was then I realized I was operating as if I were in a dream, a dream in which I had been visiting a neighbor's house, helping him fix a bike, and now I was being asked to stay for dinner. The strange mixture of shadows and diffuse lighting helped to create and maintain this unreal atmosphere. Though the warehouse rooms were cold and musty I felt warmer than I had all afternoon.

And it was such a pleasant dinner. Chicken and vegetable soup cooked on a kerosene stove. A blue and white checkered table cloth had been laid on the floor with a vase of flowers in the middle. Carlos said he would open the bottle of wine since they were having a guest. As he was opening it, he told how they always carried one bottle of wine with them. It was one of the few ways they kept beauty and pleasure in their lives despite their financial situation. Smiling, he announced it was time for some pleasure. I told Laura what a wonderful dinner and atmosphere she created. She was pleased with the compliment. She explained how they usually ate vegetables with rice or beans, sometimes a little cheese, but every once in a while they could afford chicken or some other meat. Laura looked at Carlos with an expression of admiration and trust, and said he always provided for them.

With a serious look Carlos shook his head, saying all he was able to do lately was get enough work to feed them. His voice thickened as he continued saying he wanted more for them, like a clean, decent apartment, enough clothes so they could be comfortable winter through summer, the medical care they needed. He said that he was plagued with fear that one of them could become seriously sick.

While we ate Dolores couldn't stop asking me questions. Laura was busy feeding Juan as well as herself. Carlos and I spoke some but were content to let Delores have the stage. At the end of dinner Dolores looked at me as she told her dad she wanted to dance. Carlos leaned back and grabbed a guitar that had been leaning against their boxes and bags. He began to play some music, and Laura sang. We watched Dolores dance both gracefully and spontaneously, to her parents' music and singing. After a while she ran off with her brother to play.

I sat with them into the evening, all of us sharing our experiences on the streets. With sleepy voices Laura and the children got up saying their goodnights. She put the children to sleep on mats laid in the corner of the room, then laid down with them. Carlos told me they took turns watching the children throughout the night. It was the only way to feel safe from intruders, gangs or psychopaths, like whoever is killing homeless people.

That brought me back to reality. Carlos said he hoped he would find another job soon so he could rent an apartment. He said that he had become more afraid the last few months because he noticed an unsettling change in people, homeless as well as people who seem to have money for the basic needs. He said he felt there is a desperation brewing, and he didn't know if he wanted to be on the street when it erupted.

I offered to stay and take a turn guarding the family, but he said that he'd rather be alone with them. I thanked him again for dinner. He thanked me for helping with his bicycle cart. I left them, walking away from the wonderful atmosphere of sharing, away from the warehouse and the dream-like quality it had.

I decided to sleep underneath the loading dock just outside the warehouse. I enjoyed the time with them. I feel full with the good meal, and I feel glad to be alive. Such a rare feeling for me these days. It almost makes up for running into the Bag Lady earlier in the afternoon.

Even though they were a family, and wanted to be more a part of the slave life, they didn't seem like slaves. Maybe it's because they're still outcasts. They were so decent and caring. Is that because they at least have each other to sooth the hurt and humiliation that comes with living on the street?

March 14 ~~ QUEEN AVARICE ENTERS MY DREAM-WORLD

I had a fitful sleep last night. I woke up a few times thinking I heard a child crying. Each time I'd listen for a while, but could hear nothing unusual. Unfortunately, each time I would also remember the incidents with the Butcher and the Bag Lady. Then I couldn't fall back to sleep until I had tossed and turned for what seemed like hours. I also had one of my terrible nightmares last night.

To my shock, Queen Avarice was in this nightmare. I feel awed and a bit disturbed that Fallacious has brought her into one of my dreams. Queen Avarice's mansion had just been destroyed by three of the mechanical monsters, hovering over it, shooting streams of fire down onto its roof and sides. I saw her run out into the street in a silk robe, barefoot. I saw someone knock her down, and as she fell she scraped her head on the curb of the street. I watched Queen Avarice stagger to her feet, blood streaming down the sides of her face, mingling with tears and strands of her blonde hair. I could see her so well. I could see the anguish on her face, and she seemed more human and vulnerable than I think of her being. I wanted to reach her, to help her. But as I started running, she turned running away as if she were frightened of me. I tried to yell that I just want to help her, and that I knew what it was like to be homeless, that I could show her how to survive, maybe even take care of her. But suddenly I was in a dark alley with no escape, and I remember cursing Fallacious for not letting me reach Queen Avarice. He splices his horrible endings into dreams whenever he tires of torturing me. I waited for the mob, knowing that I'd have to endure the swinging of the spiked club by the man in the pinstriped suit before I could awaken.

When I awoke from this nightmare it was after dawn. I lay quietly, listening as more and more cars and trucks also roared to life. I felt strange about Queen Avarice being in one of my dreams. Having sold her soul to greed—which I imagine she has, based on her regal and extravagant appearance—how vulnerable can she be?

I finally got up and went inside the warehouse to see how Carlos and his family made it through the night. When I reached the room where they had been sleeping, I saw they had gone. I felt surprised and also disappointed as I stood in the doorway of the cold, damp, deserted room where I had such a warm and pleasurable time just the night before.

Something was lying on the floor of the room across from where the children had been sleeping. I went to see what it was. Stooping over, I picked up the limp and well-loved rag doll the children must have forgotten. I wondered how upset Delores would be when she found it was missing. I held the soft doll in my hand and decided to keep it until I ran into the family again.

Before going to sleep tonight I want to put this doll with her forever smile sewn onto her loving face at the corner of my sleeping place close to my head, close to Fallacious, the director of my torturous dreams. Perhaps with it near me I'll be protected from the night dragons with their ranting and raving questions, from the angry mobs, from the cowering spirits that roam this city night and day. Dolls like this which have been loved so much could have special protective powers. It's worth a try.

~~ RANSACK CONFRONTS THE BUTCHER

After dark I found Ransack at the Campfire. He told me he had dealt with the Butcher. He said it so matter-of-factly that I was taken aback. For a moment I thought he wasn't going to say anything more about what had happened. He did continue though and told me that a few days ago he had waited for the Butcher to leave the store after it was closed. He said he went up to the Butcher and warned him that the next time he hears of a street person being harassed by him that he would come and hang him up on one of his meat hooks and lock him in his freezer.

"What did he say?" I asked.

"He got pissed off and came at me. The next thing that he knew was that his big bulk of a body was flat on the ground. I almost broke his right hand and shoulder. I didn't, but I think he got the idea that I wasn't someone he should mess around with. He promised not to harass anyone again, and I left. So the job's done."

"It's difficult to believe that he would back down so easily," I said.

"That's because you haven't lived in the world of brutal, forceful persuasion, my friend. The Butcher is not a killer, he's a bully. Most bullies don't really know how to hurt or kill anyone. Most bullies don't have the patience to learn the deadly arts of combat, and they usually end up hiring someone else, like me, to do their dirty work. The first thing that professional killers like us are taught is that it's detrimental to go around bullying other people. It's a waste of our energy, and it's like a champion boxer fighting a kid on the street. You lose your self-respect and prestige going into those kinds of uneven battles.

"The Butcher agreed to my conditions because he was scared shitless. He has a sore hand and shoulder, which as he uses the next few days will remind him of how powerless he really is. I don't think you'll have to worry about him anymore."

As I listened to Ransack I saw a spark in his eye. I could tell he had become invigorated, enlivened by this experience. He was in his element. I told him that he looked like he had enjoyed standing up to the Butcher. And he said he did, very much so. I couldn't help wondering why he left the CIA, why he had left a position that was so powerful. I asked him why he couldn't have become another type of secret agent—I was trying to think of how to describe another type of agent.

He interrupted me by laughing again and slapping me on the back. "Listen, Gibson, there are no other types of secret agents in the government who are more altruistic than others. CIA agents and other kinds of secret agents are all-high-class mercenaries. Like I've said before, the reason I got out is because the killing started to bother me, and I knew that it would just be a matter of time before I would be killed either by the enemy or by our side. I proved that I was a good agent and I felt like I had to move on. It was a mixture of survival and a need to help people rather than hurt or kill people. I know what you're thinking. Yes, to help people I sometimes have to hurt or kill people, but not always. And, you know Gibson, sometimes you ask too many questions. I keep telling you that it's not safe to ask an ex-CIA agent too many questions. I'll tell you what I want to tell you."

"Yeah, I guess you're right," I said. "You've told me that before, and I keep forgetting. Well, look, Ransack, I really appreciate you doing this for me, actually for everyone on the street."

"Believe me, it was my pleasure. I tell you what you do. Sometime during the next few days you go stand outside of the Butcher's store and if he harasses you let me know."

"If he doesn't kill me first. I don't know if I have the courage to test it out. It was pretty scary almost being killed by his meat cleaver."

"I'll tell you, Gibson, nothing will happen. You can trust me about this."

I told him that I might do it. I told him that I'd feel better if he would come with me, but he said that he didn't have time, and that he had to leave town for a few days. I thanked him again and left the freeway fields.

I don't feel right about how easily Ransack said that he was able to scare the Butcher. In some ways it makes sense that being thrown to the ground and hurt could be quite convincing. On the other hand, the Butcher seems like the kind of raving maniac who would keep attacking someone even if it meant someone would take revenge on him.

I don't know. I suppose I will have to go back and stand outside the Butcher's store to see if Ransack's encounter with him really made a difference. It might be a good way to get over some of my fears. Of course, it might also be a quick way of getting myself killed. If he does attack me, I guess I'll know for sure that I have some kind of psychic abilities, though I may not have much chance after that of using it. The street life is really a lot more dangerous than I realized. I should have known that the law of the jungle would exist in this level where people have so little, and have so little reason to abide by civil rules of behavior. My only protection is to remain as invisible as possible, but this doesn't always seem to work. When it doesn't, I just have to try to be fast on my feet.

Before I left Ransack told me that he'd talk with me later about what I owed him. I had forgotten about that. "I don't have any money, Ransack," I said in exasperation. What the hell do I owe him? Oh god, I hope it's not doing something like delivering secret documents…what can he want me to do? "Don't worry, Gibson. I know you don't have any money." he said. "What I want you to do won't cost you anything, and it won't be all that painful…" He smiled and walked away.

Not all that painful? Not all that painful? This is not good.

March 16 ~~ WRITING IN MY JOURNAL

Sometimes when I write about my life and what I do and think about each day, I feel I'm legitimizing my existence—this lonely homeless existence. I'm not meaning to legitimize it. It's just that this is what my life is about right now. I would rather be writing a story about two lovers overcoming all obstacles to be together, or about a hero overcoming evil or an epic drama in which the victim courageously fights against tremendous odds to rise triumphantly from misfortune, or a comedy in which everyone laughs and feels good, or a slice of life drama in which a person gains spiritual insights through a series of meaningful experiences.

But I can't seem to make up stories right now. My writing is not about art. My writing is for my survival. My mental and emotional survival. I write to enter into a space defined by words. This space has become my home. It's the only home I know I can come back to time and time again, knowing it'll still be here. Even if I lose my notebook. I know I can get another one. I know I can build a new home out of my words. I don't care whether or not anybody reads them. As a matter of fact, I've become a recluse, choosing to remain hidden within my home of words.

Wait, I'm not really a recluse. I talk to people. I'm friendly. Actually, I like to be around people. It's just that it's not easy to sustain relationships right now, to know where I belong. I do know I don't belong in the mainstream society, which is where most people exist. I maintain my daily life on the edges, but many others who inhabit these surroundings with me have been damaged in ways that normal relating is outside their abused capacities.

I know I've also been damaged, yet I feel fortunate that I feel something new and creative is growing inside of me. The damaged part of myself can't maintain a relationship, the new side of myself isn't ready. So I write. I write not to legitimize my old self, but my new self, to cope with the changes and doubts within myself and the dangers of street life. I write to remain alive.

Sometimes I wonder how I could have let myself become the way I am—I realize, though, that like a rubber band I had been stretched and twisted and turned and twisted until I finally had to let go and then I found myself unraveling out of control. When I stopped unraveling, and I'm not sure I have stopped yet, I found myself out on the street, unable to rebound, with nothing to hold on to.

I used to be able to control situations so well. I used to be able to dress for the right occasion. I used to be able to dance the right dance to match the music, and to choose the right tie to match the suit and to tie the right knot. I became an expert at tying and untying knots.

But now I seem to have lost that part of my mind. I have a difficult time just knowing how to stand and walk. I have a difficult time moving my arm to allow my hand to scratch an itch on my forehead. I have a difficult time knowing where to go to find inner peace and a sense of well-being.

I found myself one day reduced to the basics of life. My nerves became raw, my emotions became hypersensitive, my mind became limp, unable to rise to meet the daily challenge of the treadmill. I found myself unable to think in straight lines, unable to structure my thoughts to fit into department store patterns and the monthly billing cycles. I found myself out of control.

But then a strange thing happened. I was able to take a deep breath for the first time since I was a child. I felt such a relief at being on the outside, and I felt such a revulsion at what was inside the mainstream that I knew I couldn't go back. It was at this time that I also recognized that something new had been born inside me, and after a while I realized how wonderful it was, this new infant soul of mine, but also how scary it was. I realized how easily it could be destroyed. I vowed to not let it be destroyed so it could grow. I imagined a flower or a tree growing in an arid desert land. I'm sure there is other similar new growth trying to stay alive out there. I just don't think it can be done in the mainstream slave life. I may not make it, but I feel like I have a better chance of surviving out here in the streets. So I'm very happy that I let myself become the way I've become. I'm very happy that I lost control.

Before my breakdown my life was enclosed in clouds of advertisements, newspaper images, lottery games at the checkout counters, shopping, sales and a few daily home chores. I didn't even notice the homeless. The little I saw or read about them was like having to deal with annoying gnats that buzzed about my head, mostly invisible but persistent.

It's not that I wasn't capable of caring—it was that my ability to care had been so long apathized—is that a word? Anesthetized? My creativity and caring was anesthetized, taken away from me by the experience of my own dull, conditioned behavior. Sure, I had work. I was successful, but I wasn't living a life that was me, that satisfied what was really inside me. Inside, my needs were like plants that needed the sun but instead were placed in a back shady corner of a garden. My caring and creativity wilted and I couldn't bother about the homeless or the starving children or the disabled or anyone else as far as that goes.

Now I am alone and homeless. But I have begun to notice things. And I think that I could begin to care again. That feeling still seems such a long way off. Now I just feel angry at the mainstream and its masters and slaves. I feel like ranting and raving at injustice and ignorance and arrogance, and I do rant and rave in my journal.

My anger is based on the fact that I know that there could be more. Things could be different. I think all of us, the slaves and the outcasts have the capacity to be decent. We have the capacity to live together in cooperative and loving ways. I believe we have the potential of reaching this next step in the evolution of consciousness. I think enough people have reached that higher level to allow the creation of a more humane society. I know that people of the older generation, born in the forties and early fifties, have the secret of bringing society to a higher level of positive living for everyone, but so many of them have not lived up to their potentials. But other younger generations have not done well, either. It seems like a spell has been put on us by corporate magicians. Decent people who would be willing to help the less fortunate have been reduced to upscale slaves who have nice shiny homes, cars, clothes and children, and are letting the precious secrets that they have remain locked in the back of their minds, while society as a whole deteriorates and more and more people of this nation and the world are not able to have access to the basics of life, food, shelter, medical care and opportunity to develop one's potential and share love and friendship with others.

In this atmosphere all I can do is try to protect the new side of myself and hope that one day there is an awakening and resolve to participate in civic activism by enough people to make a difference. I have no urge to reenter society. I couldn't even if I wanted to. I couldn't sustain the effort. I've been there and I don't want to go back and do the bullshit things I would have to start doing again.

I didn't just get burned out at a job. I got scorched out on the wildfires of America's obsession with accumulation and privilege at the expense of the common good. This false hope for excessive wealth and unrestrained individuality and freedom causes people to run themselves to death trying to get up to the great white light of the rich and privileged. The propaganda is that material wealth will allow us to enter a new class, the ruling class. But I didn't get there. Instead my American Dream was punctured and flattened, and my psyche fell apart. Now I don't want to get back into the race. I don't want to be a slave. I don't want to reach for something that might make me feel good inside my house while outside people are starving, skies are hazy, trees are dying, and hospitals are rationing medical care. Why would I want to achieve a dream at the expense of other people? Almost every business success, every promotion, every celebration today in America is at the expense of someone else. As long as America accepts the fact that it's okay for some people to make it rich while some people starve then the American dream is not worthwhile. Why do I want to reenter such a society? I'd just as soon stay out in the cold and hope for a miracle of change, a miracle of love.

I know I'm being harsh even though I feel I'm justified in my anger. I've decided that when I start to feeling this way I don't want to dwell on my anger. I have to either act or to change my focus. If I can't think of any worthwhile way to channel this anger I may just go over to the Treasure Market and put in a few hours of hard work. Besides I could use a good meal tonight.

~~ TESTING THE BUTCHER

I didn't want to but on the way to the Treasure Market suddenly I decided to stop in front of the Butcher's store to see if Ransack really had dealt with him. I hid my pack near Casey's Cafe, then walked to the Butcher's Block. I slowly walked to the store entrance and stood right in front of the glass window and looked inside. Without my pack I knew that I could take off quickly and outrun the Butcher if I had to.

I could see the Butcher cutting meat behind a counter. Another butcher was also working behind the counter. The Butcher—my attacker—looked up and saw me. It was all I could do to keep standing there. He stared at me for a moment, then slowly came around the counter and stood in front of me on the other side of the glass. He still had his meat cleaver in his hand. He began to smile at me, like he knew something I didn't, like he didn't have to chase me away and it didn't matter. He didn't seem like someone who had been beaten and forced to quit his violent ways. Yet he didn't attack me. I have to remind myself that this was a good thing—a very good thing, and not try to imagine the worst. He walked back to his table and continued cutting his meat and I walked away, feeling relieved but uneasy. The Butcher didn't attack me. I have to keep reminding myself of that. But what was that smile about?

~~ THE UNEXPECTED JOYS OF A HOT SHOWER AT THE TREASURE MARKET

When I arrived at Esola's this afternoon, Justine was waiting on a couple at one end of the front room. I waved at her and went back to the work room and started cleaning some mirrors and bedroom sets that had just been delivered.

About a half hour later Esola came into the work room. She looked at me for a few seconds, then told me I needed a shower. Even with this direct statement it was hard to feel offended because she expressed it so caringly. A little apologetically I answered that I hadn't realized I looked so bad. She smiled and replied, "Not bad. Just sweaty and dirty." I felt somewhat better. She asked me to follow, then turned and walked away without waiting for my response.

I'm really not ashamed of my appearance. I've accepted it as one of the casualties of being on the street. Appearance. Style. I'm so sick of all the phony and expensive costumes the mainstream people feel that they have to wear to be accepted by others. I realize birds and other species display their colorful appearance for purposes of attraction in courtship rituals, but they don't pay for it with high interest credit cards. Nor do they have to buy new clothes each season so another huge amount of money has to be charged again. It's so obvious that the masses have been pulled into a tighter, well-groomed herd by the forces behind fashion designers.

Quite frankly I didn't have all these thoughts and feelings at the time I was following Esola through the store. I followed her to another one of the backrooms on the first floor which serves as a kitchen area. One door in this room is an outside entrance. Another door leads to a large wash room, where fabric and clothes that don't need dry cleaning are washed and dried.

But Esola led me through another door into a room I had never been in before. It was a small bedroom sparsely furnished with a double bed, and a dresser. Adjoining this room was a bathroom.

"There's a shower and a bath tub in there. Feel free to use it whenever you want," Esola said. "Clean towels are kept in the cabinet by the shower."

Then she took my right hand and put a key in it. "Gibson, I trust you. I have a good feeling about you. I'm giving you a key to that backdoor in the kitchen so you can come here whenever you need to take a shower. I have also discussed something else with Justine. In the past we have rented this room cheap to someone who was willing to serve as a security guard. We'd like to offer you this room free of charge if you could serve that purpose for us. You don't have to stay up at night. We have alarms. We just want someone to be on the premises to handle emergencies. Don't answer me now about this, Gibson. Take your shower, and we can talk about it later."

I told Esola I'd like to take a shower, but I didn't want to take the key. But she wouldn't let me give it back to her. She insisted that I just think about it. "Gibson, like I told you, I have this feeling about you. I think you are destined to be an important man. You have strength. You have, I don't know, something special. Besides, Gibson, you're the only one who will drink wine and dance with me." She jabbed me in the side and laughed. Then she turned to me and said in mock seriousness, "Gibson I know you will not misuse that key. In Greece, we hunt down men who betray us and cut their balls off." I felt and looked shocked. She laughed again, and said, "I'm not serious, Gibson. I'm just trying to sound, what you call…macho. I would never do anything to harm a man's balls. I don't believe in destroying such treasures of the world." And she left laughing.

I stood there for a moment shaking my head, but feeling amused at Esola's dramatic humor.

I decided I would go back to work first and take a shower afterwards. I had to sand down some table and chairs, so I knew I'd need a shower after I finished. I felt good. One of the things that bothered me about being on the street was that I couldn't take a shower or bath very often. I knew I wouldn't take her offer to sleep here. That would be devastating to my present purpose, my new creative soul. I couldn't do it. It would be getting too close to the mainstream, just too close. I think I might already be too close, working here at Esola's, but somehow I don't feel threatened as yet. I feel ok. I think Esola and Justine are letting me be who I need to be now. Justine leaves me alone. And Esola? I don't know about this business of her thinking I'm destined to be someone important and all that bullshit. But I enjoy being around her. She has a zest for life, and she's funny both in how bluntly and spontaneously she talks.

I finished my work and went to take a shower. Just as I was stepping out of the shower, the door opened and Justine came into the bathroom. I could tell she was surprised as she stood staring at me. I quickly stepped back into the shower. When I looked back out she was gone.

I felt very self-conscious. I don't know why. As I dried myself and dressed, I planned on how I could leave the store quickly without anyone seeing me. However, as I walked out of the bathroom into the small bedroom, I saw Justine sitting on the edge of the bed. She had been waiting for me to come out. "Gibson, I'm sorry I barged into the bathroom. I forgot that Mama was going to tell you that you could use it to take a shower.

"That's ok," I said. I stood there, still feeling naked even though I had all my clothes on.

"You look very nice," she said.

"I think I look the same, except I have a shower and I'm a little cleaner," I responded.

"Well, I think that makes a difference," she said, looking at me with such... thoroughness. I don't know how to explain it. I felt like I was in a spotlight, and she was just sitting there on the side of the bed, trying to decide what to do about me. "I have to say that it was such a surprise when I opened the bathroom door and I saw you step out of the shower. I was surprised in more ways than one. You have a very nice body. I've not been able to tell with the kind of clothes that you wear."

"I don't know what to say. I feel a little awkward."

We stared at each other for a moment, and I began to feel even more awkward. It must have showed. Justine smiled and said, "Why feel awkward? It's just a compliment. You have a nice body. Why not feel good about it?"

Out of desperation to get back to a safe subject, I remembered the key in my pocket. I pulled the key out and said, "Justine, I don't think I want to take this key. I appreciate being able to use the shower after work, but I don't want to sleep here. I don't want to come here when the store is closed."

She stood up from the bed and walked over to me. It was all I could do to keep from stepping back from her. "Mama really likes you, Gibson. She trusts you. I've learned to go along with Mama's serious intuitions. I like you too. Please keep the key for a while. You don't have to use it if you don't want to. Let's just see what happens. But I do hope I see you here more often."

I nodded and said thanks. She stood for a moment, only a few feet away from me. I smelled an earthy perfume. Even now I shudder when I think of how lovely she was. And how scary it all was. Somehow I put the key back in my pocket, and was able to walk around her and leave the room. Now I'm left with a strange mixture of emotions. Part of me feels like I'm floating, completely content. Another side feels heavy with this foreboding feeling, like a dark cloud building and hanging above me in the sky. I don't know. The image of Justine sitting on the side of the bed. Then standing before me, so close. Is she the cause of the contentment or the foreboding feeling? Or both? All I know is that she got closer to me than I feel comfortable with. I have to keep reminding myself that she is in a relationship and I am not relationship material right now. I don't think she meant anything. It's me, it's my loneliness and desperation for touch and emotional sharing that lets me imagine she would want to be with me in a romantic way. I just need to move on now. My stomach's screaming for food. And I think I'll walk the streets after I eat. Maybe I'll be able to drive this loneliness and these demons out of my system.

March 17 ~~ THE COSTUME PARTY

I seldom walk around downtown at night, but I did last night. Vacant buildings, festive restaurants and nightclubs each have their uncomfortable effects on me. Downtown streets at night are filled with the slaves who can afford to explore their dark sides. Against the neon glow and bright lights, the people who come out on the town appear like ghosts, spirits who can't remain dead, who crawl out of their suburbia or remodeled town¬house graves and try to resurrect themselves. They dress themselves in fancy clothes disguising their deathly condition.

I know they're just trying to have a good time. They reach out to the black booze and sparkling tonic water, and only to find shadows they can't hold on to, shadows that never seem quite right, never quite satisfying. Last night I was drawn to this type of social desperation because I felt so desperately lonely myself. Like some powerful magnetic pull from the center of downtown, perhaps the Holy Skyscraper, was trying to get me to rejoin the slave life. I felt restless and alone.

As I was walking by a nightclub, I noticed a long, sleek white limousine pull up and park. Three couples dressed in costumes got out and hurried inside. A costume party. I was fascinated. I walked across the street and sat against a building to watch more people arrive dressed in their costumes. Some came outfitted in fancy clothes, dresses or suits, wearing elaborate masks. Others wore more complete costumes. I saw a frog, a magician, a military man, a cave man, two or three witches. I saw someone dressed as a hot dog in a bun. I saw someone dressed as a gypsy. I saw a few people dressed as Charlie Chaplin-like bums.

At one point three women came walking down the street, all three dressed in tight black sweaters and pants. Two were dark haired, the other was blonde with a pony-tail. The tight clothes they wore highlighted their shapeliness. I didn't think they were going to the nightclub at first. They didn't seem to be in costume. I noticed how eerily frozen and expressionless their faces were. They were beautiful faces but profoundly sober. Then I realized with the help of the club's lights that they were wearing life-like white masks. The blonde woman fascinated me the most. She had such an attractive face for one that wasn't real. Her blonde pony-tail swaying back and forth in movement with her lively body sharply contrasted with the smooth seriousness of her mask.

When they turned and went into the night club, I jumped up and felt like following them inside. I stopped myself and turned away. I admonished myself, trying to gain control of my emotions. Maybe it hadn't been such a good idea to stop and watch these people. It's just that being alone feels so painful.

Perhaps it was because I was so emotionally needy or emotionally unstable—or perhaps I needed something to get my mind off my emotions period! Whatever it was, I decided I would try to crash the costume party. I had the brilliant idea I could go in there as if I were a homeless man in costume. No one in there would know the difference between a real homeless person and one playing a role. I still had some money in my pocket to pay a cover charge and maybe buy a drink. So what if there wouldn't be enough left to buy tomorrow's meal. I had to do this. I had to see the blonde woman again with her strikingly beautiful immobile white face.

I walked to the nearest alley and hid my pack in a garbage bin. I found a piece of cardboard, and wrote on it, "I'm homeless and haven't had a martini since lunch. Would somebody please help me out?" I figured most of the people in there were martini-type people since their costumes seemed so expensive. I thought they'd think my sign was clever, and it would keep them from looking at me too closely.

I took some string out of my pack and tied it to the cardboard so I could hang it around my neck. I felt ready for this bold but probably stupid action I was about to take. I walked across the street. As I approached the door of the club, I tried to adjust my posture so that I would look more mainstream. I stood straight, pulled my shoulders back and tried to walk with a stride of self-assurance. I knew it would contrast with my appearance, but I didn't want to appear too down-trodden. I guess a part of me still was worried some people wouldn't believe I was in costume. I had fantasies of them shouting at me and telling me to go back out into the street where I belonged.

But I pulled it off. They took my money and let me in. When I first walked into the club, all I could see was flashing lights and the stage area where a band in costume was playing. I stood for a moment by the door waiting for my eyes to adjust, and listened to the band play some lively electro-rock dance music. They weren't bad. They had a woman singer who had a good voice. She sang with such intense emotion, with soul. She was dressed in a skimpy, tight yellow-and-black tiger outfit which showed off her long legs and full breasts. She wore a cat's mask with long golden whiskers.

Many people were dancing but I was able immediately to see who I came into the club to see, and perhaps meet. The three women with their skin-tight white face masks were near the stage dancing, sometimes with each other as partners, to the rock music. The blonde woman was taller than the rest. I watched them as they moved their arms, shoulders, their bodies in beats to the fast rhythms, their faces remaining still. It was eerie, but somehow the blonde woman's face was like a magnet pulling me. I wanted to dance with her.

I thought about how not too long ago I was a spectator to another dance, a performance by the Thai dancer that seemed otherworldly to me. I wasn't able to break into that world, but somehow tonight I could enter this world. This was just a night club, although I have to admit being here was as strange for me as being in the bushes watching the Thai woman dance. But these people were at a social event. They expected to intermingle. Intrusions were permitted. At least I hoped so.

I was attracted to the fact that I would probably never see that woman's real face capable of expressing her emotions. Her mask gave me a feeling of protection.

My view was suddenly blocked by a gorilla. I looked into its huge, ugly face, and was surprised to hear a woman's voice say, "I'll buy you a martini, if you'll buy me a banana daiquiri. I think your sign is so clever."

I couldn't help but laugh. This gorilla had a sense of humor. I said to her, "I'm sorry but I'm playing the role of a homeless man all the way. I don't have any money on me. I decided I'd experiment and see whether or not I'd leave here tonight drunk or sober." I have to admit it's not easy talking to someone in a gorilla costume, even knowing it's really a woman. Especially knowing it's really a woman.

"Well, good luck in your experiment," she said. "I may be back later." The gorilla took off and I automatically looked back at the women in their expressionless masks dancing. I walked further into the room. It was multi-leveled, and I was on the mid-level where a long bar stretched almost the width of the room. The dance floor was sunken in the middle of the room with the stage at one end. In a semi-circle around the dance floor were tables on two or three levels above the main floor.

I walked around to the left, closest to where the women were dancing. I was halfway to them when a green lizard with a loud male's voice asked me to join his table of people. I said that I couldn't, that I didn't have any money. I told them that I had just come into the club to keep myself warm. They all laughed and the lizard said that I could drink some of their beer. I noticed there were a few pitchers of beer on the table.

The lizard stood up to make room for me. At the table were two female punk rockers, a nun, a sorcerer with a tall pointed hat, a Bush Jr. look-alike, and the lizard. He was motioning to the waitress for an extra glass. Just then I saw one of the masked women, not the blonde, leave the dance floor and walk towards the table next to the one where these people were sitting. I instantly decided to take the lizard up on their offer.

I sat down and watched the masked blonde woman sit down, pull her mask up just a little and take a sip of her drink. I couldn't see what her face really looked like. The other two women were still dancing.

While the lizard poured me a drink, Bush Jr. said that he thought my costume was creative, but he really didn't believe there were homeless people. Everyone around the table laughed. I laughed too, and said I wasn't homeless, just in between town houses.

The nun looked at me and said, "You down-played your costume. I like that. Unlike some people's costumes." She looked around the table. They protested loudly. She looked back at me. For the first time I noticed her makeup. She had painted a red cross on each cheek, and her eyes were blue and sparkly.

"Tell us about yourself," one of the punk-rocker women said. "What are you in real life."

"I prefer to remain in my role tonight," I said. "So let me just say I've been on the streets for over six months. I sleep under the freeways near the fields by the Burnside Bridge. I haven't been with a woman the whole time I've been on the street."

Everyone was silent, staring at me. I held up my glass of beer and laughed. "Come on," I said. "This is a costume party. Get into your roles. Don't be so serious. Let's toast to being who we are not tonight."

They all laughed with me and picked up their glasses to join in the toast. Eventually they lost interest in me, and only the lizard and one of the punk-rocker women continued to engage me in their conversations. The lizard was an accountant, and the punk rocker worked in an insurance company. They were friendly and kept buying me beer. I was getting drunk quickly. All during the conversations I kept checking on the blonde with her pony tail and her white expressionless face. From time to time she would lower her head and lift up her mask for just a moment, but in a manner that prevented me from seeing what her face looked like.

When the band took a break the two other women joined her. I was trying to get enough courage together to join them, but before I could, the band started playing again. As if on cue all three got up to dance.

I watched them a little while longer, and finally felt I was ready to do something. I excused myself from the table, and walked onto the dance floor. I walked up to the blonde woman and asked her to dance. I felt strange talking to this porcelain white face. Up close the face seemed harder, a bit meaner, less soft than it did from a distance. She looked at me, then looked at the others. I smiled at her and started dancing. She shrugged her shoulders and started dancing with me.

It felt good dancing with her. I realized this was all I wanted to do. To make a connection of some kind. While I was dancing I didn't care what happened next. I just wanted to dance with this woman who had such an effect on my emotions. Here was a woman whose face I couldn't see and someone I knew nothing about. Yet it felt great to be dancing with her.

Then the dance ended, and all three women walked off of the dance floor towards their table. None of them said anything to me or to each other. I stood on the dance floor watching them and then the music started again. I felt like the good feelings had just been ripped away by their sudden departure. I couldn't let it end like this. I'd gone this far. I had already acted in ways that weren't normal for me. Not that I'm shy, but being on the street lends itself to being unsocial, and here I was playing a role, crashing a costume party, drinking with strangers, and dancing with a blonde, mannequin-faced woman.

I walked off the dance floor straight to their table, then sat down next to the blonde. "I wanted to say thank you for the dance, but you left too quickly. I really like your masks. Did you make them yourselves, did you buy them or what?"

They looked at each other, and didn't say anything for a few moments. Finally, one of the dark-haired women spoke, her voice muffled by the mask. "We'd like to be alone if you don't mind."

"Well, that's a typical reaction to a homeless man," I said, trying to think of a way to break through to them. "Nobody likes to be around us poor folks. Because I'm homeless and without a dime, everyone treats me like a leper."

The dark-haired woman spoke again, "Look, we can see you're dressed as a homeless guy, but it's just a role, and we're still not interested. We like being by ourselves."

"It's not a role, Ms. Un-Friendly Face. I am homeless and I followed you all in here because I felt a little lonely, and very intrigued by your masks, especially yours." I turned and looked at the blonde woman. I had gotten drunk and was expressing my frustrations more boldly than I would have if I'd been sober. At that moment I had enough of being the outcast. I wasn't thinking straight. "And I thought it'd feel good to dance with you. Strange, now I can see how appropriate your masks are, void of feeling, frozen, unfriendly. They leave me cold. Thanks for the dance."

As I started to get up the blonde woman laid her hand on my arm and asked me to wait. The dark-haired women protested, but she told them to go dance, and she'd join them in a moment. After they left, she turned to me, and asked if I were really homeless.

I nodded my head. She stared at me for a moment. I told her it was very strange communicating with a face that didn't move.

She didn't respond to that, but said, "We're not trying to be insensitive, but we came here to be together. The woman who spoke to you is my lover. I apologize for her, she was jealous. My other friend wants to be with us tonight because her lover just left her. We're just not the right threesome for you to be with."

"We don't have to be lovers to dance, do we?"

"No, but I prefer to dance with my lover tonight."

All my anger had dissipated at this point. I was still infatuated with the beautiful blonde, but I said, "Well, I appreciate you talking with me and dancing with me. I'm sorry I bothered you." I paused, took a long look at her, then said, "I actually do like how you look. Very stunning."

I got up from the table and started walking to the door. I was feeling a bit sad, but satisfied because she had talked with me. I meant what I had said to her. I felt a tap on my shoulder. I was elated for a moment thinking it was her, but I turned to face the gorilla quite close to me. My elation dropped rapidly until I heard her say she'd like to make a new deal with me. She'd buy me a drink if I'd dance with her. I said sure.

She bought me a drink, and we danced a few dances. Then this man in a loin cloth who looked like Tarzan came up to her and they went off together. I left the club, found my pack, and even though I was drunk I still felt like walking.

~~ JEROME SCARES ME

When I crossed the Burnside Bridge I thought about going to the Campfire. I was feeling high from my bold adventures and wanted to continue being around people. I started toward a street that ran underneath the bridge. When I turned the corner around the next building I ran right into Jerome. I jumped back frightened. We stood looking at each other for a moment. I had this scary sensation rush through my body. I could see Jerome's hunting knife in the scabbard underneath his opened jacket.

Finally I said, "You scared the shit out of me, Jerome. I was heading toward the fields and I guess I just wasn't looking when I walked around the corner. Jeez, I'm sorry I ran into you like that. I hope that you …"

Before I could finish my frightened rambling, Jerome scowled, turned around and walked away into the darkness in the direction where I was heading. I still felt a chilly tension in my chest. I decided I didn't want to walk into the darkness with Jerome in there somewhere. I turned around and walked in the opposite direction. I walked east toward Grand Avenue, which is usually busy. I realized unhappily that my fear of Jerome was limiting where I walked in the darkness. I wondered if I'd have the courage to try to talk with him again to find out if he really has something against me. Maybe I look like somebody he hated as a kid.

As I got to the street I turned and thought I saw someone following me again. It was hard to see, but Jerome is hard to see. I got to Grand Avenue and hurriedly turned right. I walked quickly to the next corner and turned left. I zig-zagged around for a while and then sat underneath a street light on the corner here by Casey's Cafe and wrote for a while in my journal.

Shit, I don't want to be frightened of Jerome. I'm going to have to try and find out more about him. I need to find out if he's really following me. I don't see why he would be. I don't even really know him. Of course, I don't know the Butcher, either.

Jerome's a street person like me so why should he want to follow me and harass me? True, I'm not like him. Perhaps his violent past has warped his thinking. Maybe he thinks I'm a terrorist and need to be killed. Why hasn't he already done it then? This line of thinking just sent shivers up my spine. Thinking about this is doing me no good. I'm just going to have to go up to Jerome soon—when it's light out and there are a lot of people around, including Ransack—and ask him why he's following me and why he scowled at me.

And I had such a good evening before running into Jerome. I felt a little safer when I was sitting outside Casey's even though it was closed. It was still familiar. I suppose if I'm going to get killed I'd rather it be in a familiar place.

Before I went to sleep I thought about what happened earlier this evening. I made contact with two women, a lesbian mannequin and a gorilla, but they were nice and at least they were feminine in their own ways, and they were people—I mean underneath their masks, they were people. And before I decided to go around into the alley way behind Casey's to sleep, I thought about my brief experience earlier in the evening with Justine and I felt happy.

March 18 ~~ QUEEN AVARICE BEYOND THE FIELD OF GOLD

I have to admit that since I've had Delores's doll, I have been having better dreams. At least not horrific nightmares, even if sometimes the dreams are unsettling and confusing. In a dream last night I was walking in a field of golden wheat, and I felt so content and happy. I could see a large mansion in the distance beyond the wheat field and beyond a green manicured lawn. I saw a woman come out onto a balcony, and I knew it was Queen Avarice. She was waving for me to come to her.

I started walking through the field of golden wheat but I suddenly realized that the stalks of wheat were really stalks of gold, tall golden rods glistening in the sun. At first this fascinated and excited me, until I realized that I could not walk through the field, the golden rods were so close together and surrounded me. I couldn't move. I began to feel panicky. I looked up to where Queen Avarice had been standing on the balcony to ask for help, but she had gone back inside. I realized that I would die alone in this field of gold, and at that moment I woke up filled with anxiety and confusion.

Why am I dreaming of Queen Avarice? I know I have no interest in relating to her in any manner. She represents everything I'm trying to get away from. What side of me is trying to undermine my true purpose. It disturbs me that I must still be attached to the extreme materialistic, greedy life style she represents.

Anyway, I've got to return this doll to Delores. I've stopped by the family shelters a few times, but haven't found Carlos and his family. I'll keep looking.

~~ FOLLOWING QUEEN AVARICE

This morning I slept later than I usually do, so I missed going to the Holy Skyscraper to watch for Queen Avarice and the other members of her royal capitalist order. I've created such a grand fantasy around them—but I believe fantasy rooted in reality. Despite my strange dream with Queen Avarice last night, or perhaps because of this dream, I decided to do my observance from my safe place across the street during the lunch hour, hoping I'd at least see Queen Avarice and perhaps Lord Lucre go to lunch. I was lucky because shortly after I arrived Queen Avarice came out of the Holy Skyscraper by herself and started walking toward the center of the downtown.

Without hesitating I jumped up and followed her, careful not to get too close. After a few blocks she turned a corner and halfway down that block she went into a deli. I walked up to the edge of the deli and looked in. She was standing in line in front of a counter. I reached into my pocket to make sure that I had enough money for a coffee or a snack. I struggled with myself for a while but I eventually decided that I wouldn't go into the deli even though I realized this might be the perfect opportunity to actually meet Queen Avarice. I was able to convince myself again that it's better that I don't meet someone like her, and I remain one of the multitude of peons in poverty that is beyond her royal awareness. Even if she does notice me she'd probably think of me as the bum that I am. She'd probably pity me, if she is capable of that kind of feeling.

I waited for a few moments outside the deli, standing by a street pole. I had a good view inside the deli and I was able to see that she sat alone eating. It seemed so weird that I would even entertain the idea of meeting her. What's insane about this notion is why would I want to meet her unless it would lead to some kind of meaningful interaction or relationship? But that kind of relationship could never occur unless I was a master in the slave society, some corporate manager or shareholder. Otherwise what difference would it make if I met her?

I guess I carry around some idealistic notion that people like her have a part of them that would care about others, a part that would be able to see beyond appearances. Another part of myself says I'm a fool to have these positive notions of people like Queen Avarice and Lord Lucre. I know that I'm doing the same thing I am accusing her of doing, not being willing to see beyond appearances. At least I'm struggling with my preconceived feelings. I wonder if there are any people like her, who have so much money and power, who wrestle with these kinds of feelings.

I'm using her beauty for my own purposes without her permission but I'm not disturbing her or bothering her. I walked away, realizing that I would never want to invade Queen Avarice's privacy. But why am I so focused on her? It's irrational. I could never be a slave again, and never a master. Being a regional sales manager certainly did not mean I was in the master class. And now I realize I would probably never have been able to reach the level of financial royalty where she exists. The people in this class live in faraway places or high up in corporate penthouses. Most people have to be born into the privileged financial class, but to be transformed into royalty, a middle- or lower-class person would have to suddenly have so much money that winning a lottery wouldn't even do it. And fame. You'd have to have some kind of celebrity status to be transformed into a royalty.

~~ CAUGHT LIKE A FLY

I just saw Billy Buzz caught behind glass doors of a fancy office building, caught like a fly behind a window. How he got in there I don't know. I was walking downtown around SW Taylor and 5th Avenue when I saw Billy in the foyer of a building trying to get out. Apparently, he couldn't remember where the glass door was. He kept walking toward the glass window with his hand out in front of him and when the glass wouldn't give way, his arm did and he would smash up against the glass, bumping his head, his nose. He looked both pathetic and silly.

The glass door of the building was just to the right of him but he kept going to the left. He seemed totally drugged out. A few people had begun to gather on the street outside. I ran across the street and led Billy outside. I took him down the street and sat him down on a transit bench. I asked him where Livid was and he shrugged his shoulders. She was around here somewhere, he said.

I decided to leave him there and go on my way. I can't go around taking care of everyone living on the street needing help. I can barely attend to my own needs. I think what is bothering me is that I might be more like Billy than I want to accept—when I go into my trances, my reveries. Yet he is worse off than me because he can only exist with drugs, his awareness of himself, of this reality and perhaps other realities, blotted out. There are so many people who exist on the street in such an anesthetized manner.

March 19 ~~ RETURNING THE DREAM DOLL

I ran into Jeremiah today and he was talking to me about this mother and her two children he ran across in one of the shelters. He said the little girl was sick with a bad cold and if it got any worse, she'd have to be taken to a hospital. Jeremiah said he helped to find the little girl some medicine to take. At one point he said that the father was a Hispanic who was working somewhere out of the city.

I interrupted Jeremiah and asked him where the shelter was. I knew that had to be Delores who was sick, and her mother and brother. Jeremiah told me the shelter where they were, and I took off to see them. When I arrived they were still there. Delores was sleeping but Laura came down into the front room to talk with me. She looked worn and worried. She said that she thinks she will have to take Delores to the hospital.

She looked at me with tears in her eyes and said that she and Carlos temporarily split up so that she and the kids could get some financial help from welfare. He's in Eastern Oregon trying to find work. She said that he doesn't know Delores is so sick. I talked with Laura for a while and before I left, I gave her the doll to give Delores. Laura said she had made this doll for Delores and when she lost it her daughter cried for days. She said that maybe it is a good sign that Delores will get better.

I'm going to miss that doll but I think it served its purpose. I think it softened up Fallacious for a little while but I have no doubt he is planning a whole series of horrendous dream movies for me. One day I hope my new soul will be able to control him. Anyway, I'm glad I found Delores but I'm not happy she's sick. I'll have to check on her in a few days.

March 20 ~~ WAILING SIRENS

Early morning before dawn. The sirens of police cars and an ambulance woke me up last night. I hear sirens often in this city, but these alarming sounds are far enough away from me that I can ignore them. Tonight these sirens woke me up as they became louder and louder, and closer and closer to where I was sleeping. As I woke I saw the flashing lights against the building across the street. An image flashed through my mind of a figure standing over a sleeping man in an alley with a raised knife.

Shaking, I stood up and as if in a dream, I slowly gathered my stuff together and walked out onto the sidewalk in front of the alley where I had been sleeping. I looked to my left, and in the next block, I could see police cars with lights still flashing, and an ambulance. A few people were standing around outside the police barriers.

I walked closer to the police barriers, and stood with the people. I could not see what was going on, but the barriers were in front of the entrance to an alley.

Someone next to me said that he heard one of the police officers say another homeless man had been murdered.

"Why don't they go into the shelters," a woman near me said. "Why do they have to sleep out here on the street. It's not safe and I don't like how the neighborhood looks with them sleeping in doorways and alleys."

I looked at the woman who had spoken these words, and I was surprised that I did not feel angry at that moment. I think I was in shock and probably felt like I was still in a horrible dream. I had been feeling a deep despair that another homeless human being had been killed, and for some reason this woman's words had no effect on me. I remember looking at the woman, and then back toward the alley. I saw a police officer point in our direction, and one of them started to walk over to us. I quickly walked away. I did not have any information that would be helpful and I didn't want to be questioned by the police.

This murder happened so close to where I was sleeping. How does the murderer choose his victims? Randomly. I don't always take care to hide when I make my place to sleep, and I just don't think I will always find a place that will be completely hidden. I can't keep myself totally safe out here on the street, but I'm not going into shelters or back into mainstream life. I am determined to survive somehow. I'm too tired and numb to write more, but I know I will not be able to sleep anymore tonight.

~~ RANSACK'S DISPLAY OF VIOLENCE

Just about a half hour ago—around 10:00 p.m.—I was walking over by Lloyd's Shopping Center. All the shops were closed. I was across the street from one of the parking garages with the street level parking visually open to the street. A few cars were still parked inside.

I heard the yelling before I could see where it was coming from. I saw two men standing in front of another man, and the men were gesturing wildly and yelling at the other man. I walked ahead further to get a better view of the other man, and to my surprise it was Ransack. I couldn't see any of the men that well, but even in the dim lights of the parking garage I couldn't mistake Ransack with his flowing light hair, beard and mustache. I had just passed a telephone pole and decided to backtrack a few steps so that I wouldn't be seen while I watched. I think my curiosity is one of the things that keep me alive but it might also kill me one day.

I couldn't tell what they were arguing about, but all of a sudden Ransack punched one of the men in the jaw and he staggered back. The other man started to attack Ransack, who in a flash brought his leg up and kicked the man in his stomach. Then Ransack hit him on the side of the head, knocking him down. The first man who had been hit had regained his balance and jumped on Ransack. What I witnessed in the next few minutes scared the shit out of me. I watched Ransack literally mutilate these other two guys. He didn't just defend himself. I knew that he had almost immobilized them with his first few punches, but he went further. He grabbed one man's arm, and bent it back until it broke. The man screamed as he fell to the concrete. Then Ransack kicked him a few times. When that happened, the other man started running but Ransack chased him, caught up with him, and beat him until he was unconscious. When I saw him start to beat the man I turned away. I stood leaning against the telephone pole, feeling dazed, feeling disgusted with Ransack, with myself, with what I had seen.

Ransack really is a vicious bastard. No matter how I thought about it I couldn't justify the type of violence he had just displayed. But Ransack has always been out front about who he is, and what he does. It's one thing to listen to his stories though—to hear him create a scene of violence with words. It's another thing to see him mercilessly continue to beat two men even after they had already been beaten.

What is my relationship to Ransack? I have no relationship. I asked him to help me before I knew how horrible he really is. Now he says I owe him something. Oh shit, I don't want to get more involved with him. Not after what I've just seen.

March 21 ~~ SOMETHING STRANGE IS HAPPENING AT THE BUTCHER'S STORE

The first day of spring. What does this mean? It's a rainy, chilly day. I guess I should be happy that winter is over. Warmer weather should make my life a little more comfortable. I won't have to wrap myself in as many old blankets when I go to sleep. How come I can't get excited? Maybe because it's still rainy. Maybe because the dark clouds over this city have nothing to do with the weather patterns. I blame Fallacious for creating my inner fantasies and dreams with overcast, ominous atmospheres. I think he feels that as long as so many street people are suffering why should others enjoy life so much. With Fallacious darkening my vision and no changes in sight to make things better for us street people, the spring and summer represent just two more seasons full of long hungry and scary days.

Last night after seeing Ransack beating up those two men I saw something else that unsettled me. I was hanging out in front of Casey's Café. Carissa wasn't working. It felt warm as I stood looking into the café. I wished that I had enough money to go in and buy a hamburger and a milkshake. Or a chili dog. Anyway, I was standing on the corner fantasizing, and I looked at the clock behind the counter in the café and saw it was almost 11:00 pm.

I felt a little lost. Whenever I let myself fantasize about food, it usually takes a lot out of me. Probably thanks to Fallacious my imagination soars out of control, then all of a sudden, I crash land and I'm totally drained for a while.

I was in this drained state when I stepped away from the window of Casey's Café. I looked listlessly around. I didn't have the energy right at that moment to keep walking. I usually don't like to sit on street corners unless I'm really exhausted because I draw too much attention to myself. If a street person is sitting on a street corner, especially at this time of night, he's just a sitting duck for the police. The police will generally leave us alone if they see us walking. They delude themselves into thinking that we have a place to go and that's where we're walking. Of course, the police wish that all of the homeless and street people would just keep walking to oblivion, to some invisible land so that they don't have to deal with us.

Anyway, I was just exhausted, so I decided to risk sitting down on the street corner. The warmth of the café lights made me feel a little better. I was looking across the street at the large parking lot extending across the block behind Al's Meat Market. The store was dark except for one dim light over a doorway. It wasn't just the light that caught my attention, but I could see four or five men standing outside the door. I thought I could see the lights of their cigarettes. Then I noticed a car pull up, and two more men got out and joined the others.

This was curious. Were they night-shift workers? Probably. Except one of them seemed to have a bottle, and was passing it around. If they were workers, they were making sure they weren't going to be productive that night. At one point someone in the building opened the door beneath the dim light, and all the men went inside. I then saw that the light above the door was switched off.

During the next half hour while I sat there on the street corner, four more cars pulled up, and at least ten more men went into the building. My curiosity was aroused. Who were these people? Why did someone turn the light out? Maybe nobody turned it out. Maybe it just burnt out. Sure. Just as everyone was going in. I began to think that they didn't want to draw attention to themselves. I began to think they were doing something horrible in that building. A vision flashed through my mind of the Butcher and these men planning who would be the next homeless person they were going to murder that night. A vicious vigilante mob.

With that last thought I leaned over and gently knocked my head a few times gently against the street-light pole. I had to control my imagination. Fallacious must be trying to get me to see things that don't exist—must be trying to get me paranoid, as if I wasn't already haunted by enough scary fantasies.

Try as I could, though, I couldn't control my imagination or my curiosity. I had to get a closer look to see what was going on. I got up and started walking down the street in the direction of the building the men had filed into. I walked along the edge of the parking lot until I was almost to the back of Al's store, the butcher's store. Then I took a deep breath and starting walking across the parking lot so that I would eventually be even with the door.

I hadn't taken more than ten steps before I saw movement in one of the cars, and I froze. It looked like the glow of a cigarette, and I realized that if these men were doing something horrible, then they certainly wouldn't just leave the back of the store unguarded.

Someone was in a car waiting for me to come closer.

Then I thought I heard a car door open, and I turned and ran. I looked back. Looking back over my shoulder, I thought I saw two men standing by the car, but they weren't coming after me. I ran past the café and didn't stop running until I was three or four streets away. Finally I ducked into an ally, and I hid under some huge bushes that bordered a building.

After lying still for a while, I eventually unrolled my sleeping bag and went to sleep for the evening. I dreamed about the Butcher standing over homeless people who were sleeping in a dark alley. I saw he carried his butcher's knife, and I knew he was looking for me. I was hiding in a corner of the alley, and I knew he would eventually find me. Just when he saw me and started toward me I woke up. I missed Delores' doll and wished I had it tucked next to my dreams.

March 22 ~~ WALTER TAKES ME TO SEE THE SPACE ALIENS

Earlier today I was walking north Burnside Street, a few blocks west of the river, and I spotted Walter down the block. He was standing near the street, just staring into sky. I walked closer to him. I could see his face alternating back and forth between a serene look with a slight smile and a worried, even fearful, expression. I looked up in the sky in the direction he was looking, wondering if he were seeing something I couldn't see. As I watched Walter, despite how crazy Walter seems, I felt an affinity and a kinship with him.

I finally approached him and said hello. He looked at me for almost a minute, it seemed, and then said, "Gibson, you're the only person that I've told about the aliens."

"About the aliens?" I asked, thinking that it might be fortunate for Walter that I was the only person he told, otherwise he might have already been committed. Ok. Ok. I can't write that without also writing that I do believe him a little bit. I would like it to be true. And I guess I do believe in UFOs and aliens from outer space or other dimensions. I admit it. It's just that Walter is a goddamn wino. How can anybody believe him? Well, I guess I now sort of do. Especially after what he just showed me.

Walter said to me, "Gibson, I know you don't believe me. I've thought about that often. If you are willing to come with me, I can prove it. I can take you to where I think the aliens are staying. I can't guarantee that today or tonight you will see the scary buggers, but if you are willing to come with me and wait around, then sooner or later you will see all the proof you need."

"But Walter, I don't understand why you think they are so scary?"

"We have to assume the worst. If we don't know, we have to assume that they came here to take over our American way of life, and that we are at risk of losing our precious freedoms."

I almost laughed. What freedoms are we at risk of losing? The freedom to starve? The freedom to buy a gallon of cheap wine every night and drink it until we're oblivious to the pain of living on the street?

Walter continued, and I was surprised at his next words of wisdom. "I can only go by what our own civilization has done in the past. Every time a more civilized society has entered a less civilized society, the more civilized society has plundered and raped the people of the less civilized society. So I can only go by what I know of history."

I couldn't think of any argument to what he was saying, so I just agreed to go with him to see where he thinks they are staying. But now that I am thinking more about what he said, I wonder what makes a society more or less civilized. It seems that Walter thinks it's the ability to dominate another society, but I know a more civilized society would not try to dominate another society, and definitely would not condone plundering and raping people of any society.

Before we started off, he grabbed my shoulders, looked me square in the eyes, and said, "You will be risking your life, Gibson, but I feel that somehow one of us will make it through to warn the world when it is time."

As I walked with him, I had a thought that if space aliens were hiding among us, when would be the right time to warn the world? I mean, if you knew life forms from another planet were lurking around, wouldn't that be the right time to tell someone? But then I thought to myself, who would I trust to tell anyway? I wouldn't want to tell our militaristic government because all they would do is try to capture or bomb the aliens. Our imperialistic government is probably the major reason Walter is so goddamn paranoid.

I followed Walter further southwest, and finally he stopped across the street from a five-story brick apartment building. He pointed to it and said, "That's where they meet. I'm not saying that we'll see anything tonight, but I followed one of the aliens I saw in the alley that first time here, and he went into the apartment. I tried to get into the building, but all the doors and windows on the ground floor were locked-up tighter than a stingy old coot. I came back here across the street, and I noticed a glow in the corner window up there on the third floor. The glow lasted about ten minutes, then stopped. I've seen that glow often when I've come here. Something's going on in there, but I can't prove it yet."

"I'll wait around with you for a while, Walter, and see if I can see anything," I told him. I sat down on the sidewalk and leaned against the building we had been standing by. It was in the middle of the afternoon, and I guess I was sleepy, because after an hour or so, I dozed off. When I woke up, Walter was not around. I didn't think I had slept all that long. I stood up and searched up and down the nearby streets, but I couldn't find Walter.

I had just come to the spot across where Walter thought the aliens live, trying to figure out what to do, when I saw someone come out of the building. He was wearing a black suit and top hat, like Walter had described. I watched the man walk to a limousine. He wore dark glasses which preventing anyone from seeing his eyes. Something about the way he walked did seem strange to me. His walk appeared lilting, almost as though he was floating on air. I shook my head at this outlandish thought, and looked closer at this man's legs to make sure he was indeed walking on concrete and not floating on air.

I waited for the car to pull away from the curb, but it didn't. All of a sudden, the back window lit up in a glow, as if someone had turned on a spotlight inside the car. The intense glow lasted for probably a minute or so before it went out. The limousine then pulled away from the curb and was driven down the street.

I felt this chill travel up my spine, and then I quickly walked away. There must be a reasonable explanation for that intense glow inside the limousine. Maybe he was testing out some camera equipment. Maybe—I don't know. I just can't believe what strange things I've seen living on the streets. No wonder the slaves stay in their binding chains within their secure, safe houses. If you break the chains and start looking around, you might see more than you can handle. I'm not sure what I just saw, but even if they are space aliens for some reason I don't feel scared. I feel excited! I have a feeling that they would be here to help us, not dominate us. I don't understand any of this right now. So what if I can't often tell between reality and fantasy. At least this is a little more suspenseful and even enjoyable than what Fallacious usually throws into my mind. I'll try to roll with these out-of-this-world, visionary punches.

I am concerned about Walter though. I hope he is all right. Where in the hell would he have gone off to?

March 27 ~~ QUEEN AVARICE AND THE GOLDEN UMBRELLA

Last night Queen Avarice was in one of my dreams again. It was a sunny day, and I was sitting with her at a table on the patio outside the Holy Skyscraper. She looked different than how she usually looks. She had a sad expression on her face, and then looked at me and said, "Gibson, I feel sad that you think of me in such harsh, negative terms. I care about you and I want you to return to an above normal, well-paid lifestyle. With your MBA and your previous work experience, you have excellent qualifications. I can give you a job here in our firm. The job will have prestige, and you will make the kind of money that I know you have always wanted to make. You can work near me, and we can go often to excellent restaurants. You can ride with me in the royal limousine."

As we were talking I noticed that dark clouds were forming in the sky all around the Holy Skyscraper, and I was beginning to feel uneasy. Queen Avarice looked up at the clouds, and said that it would hail soon. As a cold wind began to swirl around us, she snapped her fingers and someone came running out of the Holy Skyscraper and held a golden umbrella above her to protect her in case it hailed.

"Gibson, you need to make a decision to let me help you return to above-normal life. There is another golden umbrella waiting for you, and if you don't hurry, you will get wet, or worse, you will get hurt. Hail stones from the sky are becoming larger and harder…we don't know why, and we don't care…as long as we can afford to protect ourselves. Will you let me protect you?"

I couldn't move. I couldn't say yes, and I knew that soon hailstones would start falling on me. I looked around for cover, but for some reason I just sat there in front of Queen Avarice, knowing that I would get hurt if I didn't accept her offer, or at least run for some other cover. She held my gaze with her eyes, and then I began to feel the pain of hailstones falling on my head and body. As the hailstones fell on me, I knew I would not be able to last very long. I realized I had no choice but to accept her offer or die. Fortunately, I woke up.

I just don't understand why I am dreaming of Queen Avarice. I know. I do know. There is some part of me that still wants to go back into society so that I can achieve the "above normal life," as she said. That part of me remains hidden from my daily thoughts, waiting to undermine me. I just have to find a way to not let this happen.

It seems like every time I dream of Queen Avarice, I have to go to the Holy Skyscraper, which I did this morning. When I saw Queen Avarice come across the street toward the Holy Skyscraper, I felt this uncontrollable urge to run over and introduce myself to her. Before I could control this dangerous impulse, I jumped up and ran across the street toward her as she walked across the plaza. But as I got closer to her, thank god I suddenly stopped. Again, all this was without any conscious decision-making on my part. Everything was just happening, like in one of my goddamn dreams. What actually did happen was that I suddenly saw a glow of golden light surround Queen Avarice and I knew that I would not be able to pierce that light in my current condition of poverty. I stood there watching her walk through the large tinted-glass door into the Holy Skyscraper, feeling even more confused about why I would even want to pierce the golden light and meet someone like Queen Avarice. I walked away feeling angry at myself for not having more control over my strange impulses.

March 29 ~~ DEAD ZONES

I hate waking up before 4:00 or 5:00 a.m., but sometimes I'm too cold or restless to sleep. Or I have to take a piss. I have to get up out of my bed on the street, in an alley, under a bush, under a loading dock, whatever. But the city is still dead. Very few places are open. All I can do is just wander around, or stand in doorways, shivering, feeling miserable, waiting for this dead time zone to pass. I feel most like a zombie during this time of day.

My first goal each day is to sleep at least until 6:00 or 7:00 am, even though I never know what time it is anyway. I can sort of sense certain times of day.

Sometimes I meet my goal. Sometimes I don't. I think of sleep as a Dream Zone, where I have to fear Fallacious because I can't consciously battle him. At least not yet. Maybe someday. I think of the daytime hours, my space of mind, between the Dead Zone and the following night's Dream Zone in different ways. Sometimes it's the Struggle Zone. Sometime it's the Hungry Zone. Sometimes it's Lonely Zone. Sometimes it's a Lost Zone. At times, Fallacious comes into these zones, too, and torments me.

Every once in a while, when I'm in the Dead Zone I see a jogger invade this land of the half-dead, half-alive. I don't know what a jogger represents. Joggers are so incongruous to me. I'm sure jogging is good for the body but is it good to jog on concrete, forcing oneself to breathe deeper and deeper, faster and faster, breathing all the shit from cars and buses and factories? I don't know. Maybe joggers are mutants, their bodies already having changed to allow them to breathe poisonous air rather than clean air. Maybe that's why joggers belong in this torturous dead time zone.

Even when the buses start running, it's still a long time before the city really becomes alive, opens up in a way that street people like myself can gain some kind of warmth, substance, energy, food, a place to use the toilet.

I usually never ride buses or the Max transit, but when I do it's during the early mornings or late at night. I ride from the Eastside to Beaverton, way on the west side, and back. But I try not to do this too often. This is one of the mornings I just had to ride the Max transit. I woke up at first feeling relieved that I wasn't hacked to death during the night. Then I felt depressed at how early it was so I decided I needed to take the transit. Maybe get myself in a better mood. I've already been to Beaverton and am heading back downtown. I'm sitting behind two men with briefcases in their laps, both of them reading the Wall Street Journal. Every once in a while, one of them nudges the other and points to something in the paper. They both shake their heads, but say nothing. They look like they might be accountants of the royalty class. They wouldn't ride mass transit if they were royalty.

This morning I'm struck by how sour everyone looks. I mean, everyone looks like they hate everyone else on the bus, they hate where they are going, and they hate the Max. I can understand their sour dispositions, but it's just very unusual to see it all concentrated in one spot.

A young woman carrying a baby, maybe nine or ten months old, just got onto the transit. The baby is smiling. That's different. She has a lot of black hair, rich blue eyes, and she's looking around at everyone, smiling. The young mother sits down beside an older woman, who had been staring straight ahead with a deep frown molded onto her face.

I watched as the baby looked at the old woman, and smiled and cooed. At first the old woman ignored the baby, but then, she finally turned and smiled, a small reluctant smile that seemed to require so much effort. Then she turned back stared, straight ahead again, but at least she was not frowning.

During the rest of the transit ride, I was delightfully entertained as this baby's smile invaded the spaces of various other grumpy bus riders, forced them out of their frustrations, and got them to smile. For brief moments I glimpsed expressions of caring from these seemingly soulless people, and it gave me hope. And lately I have been in desperate need of hope.

March 31 ~~ UNREAL DREAMS OF ROMANCE

Last night I dreamed that Justine was standing outside the front door of the treasure market calling to me. I was standing across the street and she was asking me to come into the store with her. I stood there for a time captured by her beauty. I remember that her long hair was as black as the night sky, but seemed to shine as it flowed over her shoulders. I remember focusing on her dark penetrating eyes and I felt like she could see inside of me. I saw her smile and her eyes softened and made me feel like walking across the street to her.

Then I remember hearing the screeching of the night dragons. Justine called to me to quickly come inside the store before they came, but somehow, I knew that I would not be allowed to cross the street. And I was afraid that the night dragons would attack and burn Justine's store even if I could cross the street and get inside with her. I turned and ran away, and then found myself in my familiar night-dragon dream. Fallacious must have a sadistic side to keep torturing me with this same nightmare over and over again.

I walked around for a while, and then sat down to write some more. The images of Justine remained in my mind. In real life, she is so receptive and has been willing to engage me directly despite the barriers that I put up to keep my distance, to protect myself. She just seems to be able to flow through these barriers, and I feel she does try to see who I really am. Even if I am not showing her who I really am.

Justine is a strong woman who asks directly for what she wants. I've seen her be caring and soft, and yet turn around and be as firm as she needs to be. She seems to be able to deal with finances and sales quotas as adeptly as she can deal with the simple, sincere emotional interchanges between two people. She is the type of woman who knows how to be assertive and yet keep a sensitivity that seems to indicate whatever is being done is never more important than the feelings of the people involved.

Quite frankly I don't know why she is being nice to me because I feel like I've fallen off the edge of life's continuum into a vacuum. I don't know where or what I am. My life is not my own. I am no longer just a man. I am a protector, a caregiver to my new soul. Yet I still have the feelings of a man. I dream of one day finding someone like Justine with whom I can share my life with. Even though I know so little about Justine, I dream about her. And I find that I am writing about her more. I suppose there is no harm in this as long as I don't allow myself to be swept away by feelings for her. When I get to this place in my thoughts and feelings, it's helpful that I know she is already in a relationship. I feel all right about having her as a friend. This seems what I really need.

But right now, I have to get up and get moving. I think I'll stay downtown and watch the slaves struggle though their day and then later catch sight of them desperately going home. It might make me feel a little better and it might help me get my mind off Justine.

~~ THE BURNSIDE SHELTER

The Burnside Shelter for single men sits right next to the Burnside Bridge across the river from downtown. At any given time homeless whites, blacks, Hispanics, many drunk or drugged, sit or lie on the sidewalk on either side of the bridge, like trolls—ragged, dirty, wounded, grotesque. Their presence makes the Burnside Bridge appear to be the downtown gateway to the homeless population of the city. Yet the bridge is also always full of traffic. Drivers speed by, probably giving no more notice to the grotesque figures on the bridge than they do to the beautiful Willamette River below.

I walk the Burnside Bridge almost every day. I am one of the homeless but I do not belong to the Burnside Bridge group. For whatever reason I feel I have more control of my misfortune. I have more control of how the dirt and poverty affect me. I will not rejoin society but I won't succumb to the sludge of the gutter. I won't destroy my developing, vulnerable creative soul with alcohol or drugs.

Shelters seem like what refugee camps would be like with hungry, desperate people crowded together in spaces that are too small. No privacy. Not enough good food to go around. Feelings of fear, anger, bitterness, defeat all mingle together to create a psychic atmosphere that drags me down.

I know that most of the shelter managers are decent, but I just can't take being inside the shelter for too long. Herding homeless people into shelters is a convenient way for society to try and hide the people that are being rejected and not cared for. Shelters are reminders that the good life is out of reach. Grungy oppressive walls. Antiseptic odors not quite covering the rancid smells of urine, sickness and sweat.

I know that shelters help some homeless people. Some people who just cannot survive on the street. Children and women. Families. I support shelters for this reason, but in general I would only go into a shelter if I were extremely ill or it was extremely cold outside.

Whenever I think of homeless shelters I think of shaky hulls of men, women and children with glassy looks in their eyes or sad, sullen faces, wondering what went wrong, how did they end up here? Where is the cozy home? Shelter people often are still trying to keep their grasp onto the edges of society. They don't want to fall totally away from society. They are sad they don't belong. They feel defeated because they mostly feel that they should have their role in the mainstream slave life. The parents feel humiliated. The children feel rejected. Shelters are for people who believe that society really wants them. I have no such illusion, and I don't want to expose my new self to such emotional pain. I would rather shiver through the night in the cold.

~~ RAUL

I was walking across the street from the Burnside Shelter coming back from the downtown when a young Hispanic boy standing outside the shelter caught my attention. He looked about 13 or 14 years old and was so thin he looked like a wire figure. But he was tall, unusually tall for his age. His clothes hung on him like a scarecrow, except that image didn't really fit because he wore old, faded red tennis shoes and was bouncing a basketball.

Four young, black men stood about ten feet away from this Hispanic boy.

One of the black men yelled, "Hey man, bet you wish you were black so you could really play basketball."

The Hispanic looked over at the black man, and then began a display of ball handling that was truly astounding. He dribbled between his legs, passed the ball up over his back, caught it and dribbled some more. The black men stood staring at him. The Hispanic began spinning the basketball on the middle finger of his right hand. "I can play basketball better than you motherfuckers. You can stick this up your black asses." Then he took off running down the street and turned a corner with the four black men chasing him.

I ran across the street and into the shelter to find one of the shelter managers. When I found him, I told him that four black men were chasing a young Hispanic boy. He looked at me like he was thinking, "What the fuck do you expect me to do?"

"Aren't you going to do anything about it?" I asked. "That boy could get hurt."

He continued to check off something on his clipboard. "That boy can take care of himself. Raul is always trying to get people to chase him. I think it's his way of keeping himself busy. It's unlikely he will be caught. He has never been caught before. And I'd rather him play his obnoxious games with other street kids than burglarize people's homes, you know what I mean? But thanks for your concern." And he walked away.

As I left, I couldn't help thinking how terrible things were when a shelter manager could only hope to keep a young teenager busy, no matter what it was, so that perhaps they wouldn't have time to break the law. Keep these poor people from bothering the masters and slaves at all costs.

~~ FADING AWAY ON THE GRAND DRAGON BOAT

The darkness of the night has surrounded my mind. Earlier this evening I faded out. I remember visualizing myself riding on the magnificent, ancient Grand Dragon boat up toward the blackness of space. I remember standing on the deck outside the entrance to the large pagoda cabin. I walked to the door and tried to open it, but it was locked. I put my hand on the solid, hardwood door and tried to imagine what was beyond it in the cabin room. I felt I must find out what was inside the room. I walked to the left and tried to look through a window, but all I could see was darkness. I tried to see through the darkness. Suddenly I thought I saw someone or something move, but that was the last image I could remember.

I eventually came out of my trance, and felt like walking toward the river. As I walked I reflected on the image of movement I thought I saw in the cabin. Maybe I just imagined it. I don't know what this vision means, but I felt good that at least I remember more of being on the ship—I wish I knew where it went when I faded out. If I could get inside the main cabin of the boat, maybe I could find out some answers to these questions.

I have found a place to sleep for the night. Hopefully a safe place.

April 2 ~~ CARISSA ASKS ME VERY PERSONAL QUESTIONS

I met with Carissa again today. She was waiting at the park when I arrived, and she had her pen in hand ready to write in her notebook. It was another warm day, so we sat at a picnic table where we could enjoy the sun. I looked around but I didn't see the Bag Lady anywhere.

Carissa's first question to me was, "How do you keep yourself clean. I mean where do you wash up, take a bath, or shower?"

"That's a very personal question," I said, teasing her.

She creased her eyebrows and thought about it for a moment. "I don't think so," she said. "I think it is a perfectly natural question. One thing that turns so many people off about the homeless is how dirty they look. So many smell of urine or vomit or both. I'm not saying you look that way or smell that way. As a matter of fact, you don't, which surprises me. But how can you stand to live in stinky clothes all the time?"

"OK. OK. I agree, it's a perfectly natural question. When I was first forced out onto the street, I found it very difficult to keep clean. The only places I could wash up were in some public washrooms, but the owners of these places tend to monitor them more than they used to. I went to the shelters often. When I have the money, I go to laundromats to wash my clothes, and actually I do that quite often now. I try to keep clean clothes on. You have to understand that not all homeless people are in such a terrible condition that they can't keep clean. I don't like to be in dirty clothes. I've learned to wear clothes a little longer than I used to, and at times I let my clothes and myself get dirtier than I want. Lately, I've been able to take a shower at a place where I work every once in a while. Keeping clean is a problem but it goes with the territory, so to speak. If you don't have a place to live then you're not going to be able to do the basic things you need to do for yourself, like cook, eat, keep clean, keep healthy."

Carissa took notes as I talked. She seemed so serious, sincere and intent on being thorough with her project. I had to admire that. I also figured that everything I said she was applying to her and her family in case they became homeless. So I added, "Now when families become homeless there seems to be more resources available to them. More access to different kinds of living spaces not just at shelters. Places like at churches, even some people's homes and so I think homeless families have more access to cooking and cleaning facilities." I knew this wasn't totally true but in a few cases it is. "Where do you go when you have to …"

I could tell she was having a difficult time finishing what I think she was trying to ask, so I finished the sentence for her, "… when I have to go to the toilet?"

She nodded, and straightened her glasses nervously.

"Most of the time I can find a public building or facility where I can go, but sometimes they won't let me in, and I just have to find an out of the way place."

"Don't you feel bad that you are creating unsanitary conditions by doing that?"

"Carissa, you talk as if we're in a civilized state of being. We're the outcasts. We are unsanitary in the very nature of our existence. We've been thrown out into the streets. We have nothing, but we still have to eat and …piss."

She sat up straight, preparing to challenge me. "Excuse me, Gibson. You talk about being thrown out onto the street. Isn't it your responsibility that you are on the street. Isn't it partly your choice that you are on the street? I mean, you are what my teachers refer to as an 'able-bodied man'. Why can't you work? Why can't you come in from the street, get a job, get a place to live so you don't have to do unsanitary things?"

I felt a slight tinge of irritation, but as I looked at Carissa I could see a tentativeness behind her bravado. I realized my irritation was not at her, but of the uninformed, insensitive ideas that were being taught her.

"For most people it's not all that easy to get jobs that pay well enough to support a family. The term 'able-bodied man' doesn't take into account a lot of things, Carissa. You have to be careful about buying into that able-bodied bullshit. Able-bodied for what? For minimum wage jobs? For jobs where you sell your soul and break your back so a few others can make huge salaries while you make a small wage that barely pays the rent and doesn't even allow you to go to the doctor or the dentist as much as you might need to prevent illnesses or disease? Most people who stay at these terrible jobs live in a rut, and have been lobotomized by whatever material securities they think they have. It's not just that these people are bad or wrong in what they are doing, it's that they have been damaged by the illusion of the American Dream.

"The higher paying jobs are usually for white men who know the right people or who come from the right families. Other people in general, minorities, women, people who want to do human service or creative things—most of these people don't have real opportunities to contribute to society in meaningful ways.

"I lost my job and my house partly due to this crazy economy we have in the states, and partly due to my psychological breakdown. Now that I am becoming more rational, I am choosing to remain on the street because I don't feel like I want to be a part of an unjust, degrading horrible system that will enslave me again. Now some people think that I am emotionally unstable, crazy, which may be true, but I can only do what I feel is right."

I looked at Carissa, as she continued to write in her notebook. Finally, I said, "I didn't mean to go on a tirade. It just that I think that your question is based upon a type of propaganda that actually misinforms the public and turns them away from finding right solutions."

"What are the solutions? How do we change this?"

"I don't know if I have the energy to go into that right now. I don't really have it all thought out. The only thing I know is that people have to care that they are being controlled by a select few who don't really have the general population's well-being in mind. People have to want to break away from a slave system and to really believe that they can do that. Most importantly, people have to care about others. I believe that our resources and technology could be channeled toward providing houses, food, medical care, training and a guaranteed income for everyone, and that the taxes for the wealthy and large corporations should be increased to pay for these things."

Carissa said that she needs to think about what I just said, do some research, and then she would talk with me more about my thoughts later. Then she said she needed more specifics about where I do my laundry and which shelters I go to for showers. She asked me where I got my clothes. I told her that most of the clothes I have now I owned when I was a slave. I told her that I find a few things that have been thrown away and that places like Goodwill and the Salvation Army have some good bargains, except that some things are more expensive than I would have thought.

Eventually she put her pen away. "Don't forget, Gibson, I'd like to spend time following you around one day. And I'd want to give you some money so you can get something to eat." She started to open her purse.

"No, no, Carissa. Maybe next time we could meet at a café somewhere, and you could buy me a sandwich or something. I have a few bucks right now."

"Are you sure?" she asked.

I nodded. She asks tough questions, but she is a nice girl. I wish more people would be like her.

Now that Carissa is gone, I am sitting at this park bench writing in my journal. I can't stop thinking of her questions. Where do I take a piss? Why can't I meet up to my able-bodied responsibilities? Again, Carissa doesn't bother me, it's answering her questions and trying to explain and discuss my homeless condition that gets my emotions fired up. It brings up in me all sorts of resentments about our uncaring capitalistic system.

I think I'll go back up to the Thai dancer's house. I've been thinking about her a lot the last few days. This afternoon just seems right. It's warmer than usual, and it hasn't been raining for a few days.

April 4 ~~ A PERFORMANCE I DID NOT WANT TO SEE

By the time I got to the Thai house it was late afternoon. I went back to the alley. I found the path and crept through the shrubbery until I found my hiding place behind the bush. Nobody was in the backyard. I sat down and waited for a while. At first all I could hear was the delicate clinking of the wind chimes that hung by the back porch.

Then I heard the back door open, and a balding, grey-haired, Asian man came out of the house. He wore an elaborate robe with blue and gold colors followed by four younger Asian men, dressed in black suits and ties. The younger men had short black hair and wore dark sun glasses.

The older man led the others to the center of the backyard, then turned and looked at them. The first of the younger men took off his jacket, shirt, and tie.

He laid a small rug down on the grass, then knelt down on the rug and bowed forward before the older man until his head touched the ground. Then the older man pulled out a long sword from a scabbard under his robe. In his other hand he held what looked like a leather strap.

I looked around nervously. Shit, what was going on here? A movement in one of the second-story windows caught my eye. It was in a different window than the one where I had seen someone the first time I came here. I couldn't make out who was looking out the window.

I looked back just as the old man was raising the sword above his head. He brought it down sharply just inches in front of the young man's neck. I had winced and looked away. When I looked back the old man was bringing the leather strap down hard on the back of the man. The old man must have hit the younger man ten or fifteen times, then each of the other younger men hit the man another three or four times. After the last man finished, the old man took the strap. He picked up the sword in the other hand, and then led the other men back into the house. The man who had been beaten stayed in his position.

Nothing happened for a long time. I was afraid to move, but then finally two women came out of the house, one carrying a bowl and the other carrying towels. I recognized the woman carrying the bowl as the one who had danced the last time I was here. I thought she looked over my way once as she walked to the man, but mostly she kept her head down. The woman carrying the towels wiped the blood off of the man's back, and afterward the two women helped him get to his feet and walk back to the house.

I stayed where I was for a little while longer, but finally I left. I felt terrible. I had wanted to see a beautiful woman dancing, but instead I saw a man brutally beaten. I feel badly for that man. I try to focus on the beautiful and the serene, but I can't seem to get away from violence.

April 5 ~~ RANSACK DEMANDS REPAYMENT

For weeks I've been dreading finding out what I would have to pay back Ransack for his help with the Butcher. Today I found out what he wants me to do, and it has filled me with foreboding. I was walking on the bike path that runs along the river, and I came across Ransack sitting on a bench. He asked me to sit down by him so he could tell me what I owed him.

"I was just thinking about you, Gibson," Ransack said, clapping me on the back. "And here you just walk right up to me. That must mean that what I've been thinking is the right thing to do. I've noticed how you're always carrying a notebook around and often you're writing in it. And I've thought to myself, you might be writing about this fuckin' street life, and maybe one day you might get what you're writing down published. And then, I thought, well shit, that means that if you write about me, then I'll be in the book you get published, and I'll become famous. Or at least I'll become immortal to some degree. So I've decided that I want to get with you as often as I can and tell you about my life. Tell you stories about my life as a secret agent in the secret agencies of our government. Gibson, I could tell you enough spy stories to keep you busy writing best sellers the rest of your life."

"But I'm not interested in writing spy stories or even getting published. And I doubt even if I did publish something that it would be a best seller," I responded emphatically.

Ransack laughed and shook his head, and then said, "Gibson, don't you believe in destiny? I know that each person has a destiny. You may not believe this, but I know for a fact that destiny is being created for each one of us in huge U.S. government facilities underneath the whole state of New Mexico and part of west Texas. Most people think they are free to choose what kind of life they want to lead, but that's wishful thinking. The government has developed a life plan for each individual born in the U.S. I looked at your file. I know you are going to be best-selling writer."

I looked at him in disbelief. I began to wonder whether or not I was sitting beside a true paranoid psychopath who lived in a violent imaginary world of his own?

But then Ransack said, "I'm only half-serious here, Gibson. What I'm really trying to say is that you might not have any control over what you do in the future. For example, right now I'm taking control over part of what you do, part of what you write. I'm demanding this in repayment for helping you get the Butcher off your back. And I'm also helping you to create your destiny."

I couldn't believe what I was hearing. I felt angry but then as I looked into

Ransack's eyes again I decided that I needed to be careful so I just repressed my feelings and gripped my pen a little tighter than I usually do. I said, "If you tell me about yourself, I'll write it down, but I can't say I'll do anything else with it. I sure as hell can't guarantee that I'll make you famous. I don't consider myself related to the things that make a person famous or infamous. That's a part of another realm. I'm an outcast from that realm."

"You'd be surprised how easy it is to move back and forth between realms, as you call these different parts of society. I call them circles of power. The working and middle classes could have power, but they have given most of it away to small circles of government and business people who are so fuckin' powerful it's sometimes frightening to even me. Down here in the streets, the homeless and outcasts, like you, are totally powerless. But since you know me, I will be giving you some access to power as long as you write a book about me."

"But I don't want to be famous, or have access to that kind of power," I tried to object.

"Listen, Gibson, it doesn't matter to me what you want or don't want," Ransack growled, exhibiting a side of himself that reaffirmed my need to be more careful around him. "What I want is all that matters in this situation, and I want to tell someone my story, and you're a good place to start. If you can't do anything with it, I'll eventually tell someone else. Only if I have to do that it will make me very unhappy"—he emphasized the word "unhappy" in a very unappealing way—"I want you to at least try to listen to me and write down exactly what I tell you."

I agreed to listen to Ransack because something inside my gut told me that if I wanted to live very much longer I should do exactly what he requested. I didn't know if he really was a killer, like he said he was, but I decided not to take any chances. I didn't know if he had been a real secret agent or not, but if he had been a real secret agent, I rationalized that listening to him would be like reading a good spy novel. That's all. I knew that I would not be trying to get anything published, but I didn't want to emphasize this anymore to him.

Ransack wanted to start immediately, and he said he wanted to tell me about his early life, and what led to him becoming a part of the secret armed forces. So I sat back on the bench by the river, and started to take notes about his story.

"I grew up in the Southwest—Arizona, Nevada, New Mexico, West Texas. My father was a laborer, working on ranches and construction jobs. I can only remember being with my father. I can't remember having a mother. I remember different women who were with my father for brief periods of time. I mostly remember growing up around campfires on ranches or construction sites. Which is perhaps why it comes natural for me to hang out around the fires we build here by the river.

"I learned to ride a horse before I could walk, and I learned to operate a backhoe before I could drive. I killed my first man when I was sixteen years old. I don't even remember why the hell I did it. That doesn't matter. What matters is, I remember how I felt. In control. Just so fuckin' powerful." He had been gesturing with his hands, and then he stopped talking for a few seconds, as he had been overtaken by the power he had been describing. Then he sat back and continued in a more even voice, "I was in jails and detention homes for a few years. Then one day I was visited by this man who had an air of strength and purpose about him. He wore a khaki shirt and pants, and carried a thin brief case. He said that he belonged to an organization that was looking for willing young men to join a special force that would be trained to fight communists in South America. He said that this special army would not be sanctioned by the United States government and would be operating independently of the US armed forces. I obviously wanted to get out of the detention home, and the idea of fighting and killing communists appealed to me. So I joined them.

"I was taken, along with about fifty other recruits, to somewhere in Panama. After six months of grueling training I was among thirty who were handpicked to be a part of this special force. Everything came so easy to me, especially killing. Also setting up traps for the enemy and avoiding traps set by the enemy. At times we were given objectives to locate headquarters in the jungle and to find sensitive documents. This was always so easy for me and I developed a reputation of being sort of wild—on the edge of being out of control—but still always remaining in control, like a trained lion. Except that I had more opportunity to act the way I wanted, to tear up another person if I needed to."

As Ransack talked about how he had always felt detached about killing but rather thought of it as special skill, I began to feel uneasy. I guess up until this time, I had chosen not to think all that much about the killing side of him. Here was this guy sitting beside me who was saying that to him killing another human being was like stepping on an ant. One thought that went through my mind was how Ransack's actions and beliefs were opposite from everything that I believed in. I didn't like the slaves of society, but after all, they're human, and couldn't help it if they had been brainwashed into believing that it was good to work to make a few rich at the expense of everyone else.

And the masters. I just don't believe that killing them is the answer. They are human, too, and maybe someday they might be able to learn to care. OK, so part of me is a foolish idealist, but I believe that even the masters and royalty have the potential to care. I'll have to try to figure out if something is wrong with me for believing that, especially in the state I'm in.

I tried to think about how Ransack said that he has changed and was trying to do good for others. That didn't make me think more highly of Ransack, but it did make it a little easier for me to be near him.

Ransack continued: "For a while our special forces were used to raid Marxist rebel camps. Then after about a year or so of this jungle shit fighting, five of us were brought back to the states and that's when I knew for sure that we weren't just a part of some mercenary group, but that we were connected to the government in some way. It wasn't until later that I learned who was directing us. Even the President knew we existed, but I don't think he knew everything we did.

"I belonged to a group of cold-blooded mercenaries sanctioned by secret agencies in the government. My home base was Washington, D.C., but I operated all over the states and throughout other countries. My main chores involved retrieving documents and materials that our government wanted and doing a lot of killing, all in the name of national security. I left the work because even though the killing was easy, it was just too easy for me to be killed, and I got tired of living in a way that took so much effort to stay alive. I was shot and stabbed so often that to me it was like catching a cold, and I eventually decided that I had to change my work so that I wouldn't have to experience so much pain."

"But I thought you said that you left this type of work because you got tired of killing other people."

"Well, that's true too, I guess," Ransack said, as if he were annoyed to be reminded of something he would just as soon forget. Then he laughed a little and said, "At least it makes me seem like a better person, a changed person, to any moral asshole who would be upset that I have killed so many people and that I don't mind killing. I mean, I think people are obsessed with life too much. For most people life is the shits. What's there to enjoy? Quite frankly, I sometimes think of myself as a liberator."

"The people you kill probably don't view you as a liberator."

"Of course not, but what the fuck do they know? They don't know anything. If people don't know enough to even guard themselves against the likes of me, then what the fuck. Why should they live? They don't know the difference between what is good and bad."

"Come on, Ransack, you don't kill people to liberate them."

Ransack looked at me for a moment without answering. Then he said, "I kill people who in some way deserve to be killed because they are in the way of an interest that I have, or an interest that someone I am working for has. That's all."

"I have to tell you that I think you are wrong. I think killing a person to achieve any goal, other than self-defense, is wrong."

Ransack laughed and clapped me on the back again. I wish he wouldn't do that, goddamn him.

He said, "That's ok, Gibson. It's attitudes like yours that made my job so easy. Most people are squeamish about killing, which means they can't protect themselves from being killed, or worse, captured, tortured, controlled. Listen, Gibson, I have to get going. I just needed to get started here. We'll get into things in more depth later. Make sure you get down all I've told you."

"I can't promise that I'll be like a tape recorder," I told him, even though I know that I'm pretty good at remembering conversations very accurately and have a lot of time these days to write down what I hear and see. Except when I go into trances. "By the way, aren't you concerned that I might tell someone else about you, and that would lead to you being found by the secret government or whatever?"

And you know what he said? He said, "What the hell. I'm not worried about that. If I find out that you've been telling others about me—and be assured that it would come back to me—then I'd just kill you and probably publish your journals myself." Then he laughed again and said, "Don't worry. I'm sure you won't be talking about me to anyone else. Just keep those journals safe and secret."

My god, what have I gotten myself into? What have I gotten myself into? Maybe I should suddenly get a writer's block, and tell Ransack that I can never write another word again? No, I can't do that. My journal somehow is providing nutrients to my developing creative soul. My writing keeps my mind from disintegrating. I would probably die anyway if I stopped writing in my journal. Maybe more painfully than if Ransack killed me. So I just have to be careful about Ransack. I have to write carefully, and keep my mouth shut. As long as he thinks I will make him famous, he'll keep me alive.

April 6 ~~ TAROT READING FROM ESOLA

Today at the Treasure Market Esola was sitting at the kitchen table doing her tarot reading. I've seen her do this often, and she's explained to me that it's her way of consulting the higher spiritual powers regarding how the state of the universe relates to her and her loved ones. She has asked me often to let her do just a simple tarot reading for me. Today I agreed.

She excitedly asked me to sit across from her at the table. Then she asked me to breathe deeply and clear my mind. As if I had control of my mind. But I did breathe deeply. She asked me to cut the cards. Then she laid out just four cards, one to her right, one directly across from it, one midpoint above the two, one midpoint below the first two. She said the card to her left indicates my immediate future, the card to her right, my immediate past. The card below indicates personal concerns. The card above represents influences from the outside world.

"This is amazing," Esola exclaimed. "The card on your right tells you where you have come from. It's the four of pentacles which pictures a man clinging to his material possessions. It indicates a man in love with earthly power. But it is reversed, so that it means a loss of what he has. The card to your right provides information on where you are going, your possible future. It is the two of swords reversed which pictures a blindfolded woman with two swords resting on her shoulders. It means that you will find release from a situation that is in a stalemate or release from indecision. Caution against dealing with rogues. The card below tells you what inner resources you can rely on to meet your challenges. It's the five of pentacles, a destitute couple pass under a lighted window. This relates to your homelessness, material trouble, loneliness. The card above tells you the conditions of the outer world that can affect your situation. It is one of the Major Arcana. The Tower. It pictures the crown of materialism being struck by lightning, falling from the tower. This card indicates conflict, unforeseen catastrophe. It indicates a condition where existing ways of life are overthrown, old notions upset. But the lightning also indicates possible brilliant, momentary glimpses of the truth."

I kept staring at the tall tower in flames having been struck by lightning. Then I looked slowly at the other cards. I finally said, "Doesn't seem like very pleasant images here. It seems like it's trying to tell me my life has fallen into the gutter. I already knew that."

"Gibson, Gibson, don't take things so literally," Esola said with dramatic exasperation. "Sure, it indicates that you are going through difficult times, but there is a positive indication here."

"Only one?"

She stared at the cards. "No, a few good things. There's a release from a stalemate, from indecision. I think it has to do with receiving that enlightenment, that special charge from above."

"Are you talking about being hit by lightning? That's supposed to be positive? That kind of enlightenment would fry my brain."

Esola gathered the cards back into the deck. "Well, it's only one Tarot Reading. We'll do it again in the next few days and see if things get better for you."

"I don't think my situation is going to change in a few days, Esola. This reading could last for my lifetime. "

She smiled. "Come on Gibson, things never stay the same. Everything changes."

"Esola, after that reading I think I need a glass of your wine. Is that ok with you?"

"You have to ask if that's ok?" She stood up from the table. "Besides, every good tarot reading ends with a glass of wine."

"I never knew that."

She laughed. "It's my own special gypsy touch to an age-old ritual."

"I can see why though. You need to get drunk to blot out the bad news."

She laughed, obviously not wanting to let me depress her day. "Gibson, Gibson. Just look for that glimpse of truth. That's all you need. That's all the cards say you need, anyway."

I went with Esola into the kitchen and we drank some wine and eventually I forgot all about the tarot reading until just a little while ago when I started writing about it. Now the strange thing is that I can't get out of my mind one of her statements, "Be careful of rogues." What does that mean? Anyway, all of the images in those cards seemed so dark. It's like Fallacious has had a hand in shuffling that deck.

April 7 ~~ SOAKING WET

No matter how careful I try to be in making my bed in dry places, there are times when I get soaking wet, and when I get soaking wet, I get chilled to the bone, and if I don't get dry and warm quickly, I start shivering. Only it's not easy to get dry. I have to find a place where I can change my clothes, a place both out of sight of people and where it is somewhat protected from the rain.

Getting the chill out of my body is more difficult.

Today I got soaking wet about 5:30 am. When I went to bed last night it was drizzling but I thought I was safe with my cover; however, when I woke up at 5:30, the drizzle must have turned into rain, and I was soaked.

I had put my backpack underneath some plastic so the rest of my clothes were dry. But I was still in the dead zone. Maybe that was good. Not a lot of people out. I got up and walked the streets trying to find an out-of-the way spot to change into my dry clothes. I thought about going over to Esola's but instantly and forcefully rejected the idea. I cannot let myself weaken.

It took me a miserable 20 minutes but I was able to find an enclosed parking garage behind a restaurant. Shivering, I stripped my clothes off, and just as I was completely naked a car pulled into the parking garage at the far end. I quickly hid behind a post. But I had to leave the pack with my clothes leaning against a wall a few feet away, in full view of the driver of the car.

I crouched behind the huge concrete pillar, naked and shivering, and thought to myself that this day was not starting all that well. I tried to laugh at my understatement, but I focused again on the car that had driven further into the parking garage toward where I was hiding. Then I heard the car stop and the car doors open. It seemed like two or three people were getting out the car, talking and laughing.

I heard the clicking of heels on concrete, and the voices of probably three women. I realized I could be arrested for indecent exposure. God I felt cold. I thought for sure that these women could hear my teeth chattering.

The clicking sound stopped. They had not walked that far. I peeked around the pillar, and had a side view of the three women leaning against the car smoking cigarettes. I could not see them too well in the dim lighting of the garage. All wore different types of warm coats, so if they wanted, they could stay out here in the garage forever, or at least until I froze to death.

Shit. I couldn't take this much longer. Other cars could come in at any time. I decided to take a chance, and slowly stepped out from behind the pillar. Very, very slowly I reached across the open space, as I held my breath, and grabbed my bag. I kept my eye on the women. They just stayed there, leaning against the cars. They seemed to be in a lively conversation.

When I pulled the backpack behind the pillar, I closed my eyes and slowly let out my breath. But I didn't hesitate for long. I needed to get some clothes on. As quietly as I could, and as quickly, and without stepping out from behind the pillar, I managed to put dry clothes on. I also had a warm sweater that I put on. When I finished I peeked again out from behind the pillar. Goddamn it, they were still there talking and smoking cigarettes. What were they, chain smokers?

I was dry but I was still shivering, and I knew that I had to get someplace warm. I decided to just get up and walk out even though I would have to walk right past them.

I got up and put my pack on, and started on my way. I took a few steps and they all turned to look at me. It was then that I realized they were transvestites. They didn't say anything at first, but just kept staring at me, two of them continuing to smoke cigarettes. I felt curious, perhaps confused, on guard, and I had forgotten how cold I was. Just as I walked past them, one of them said in a deep masculine voice, "You shouldn't have been so shy." She/he threw her/his cigarette on the concrete floor, smiled at me, and all three, with their heels clicking, walked to the door near where they had parked, unlocked it and went inside.

I shook my head, and thought to myself, "The goddamn nerve of city people. Nothing's embarrassing to anyone anymore. Nothing is as it seems in this city. How would I have known people I thought were women were really men who would have enjoyed seeing me get dressed in front of them?" I walked away shivering again, feeling relieved, but pissed off. And I'm still pissed. I don't know why I'm so irritated. I'm sitting here in a Laundromat drying my clothes, sitting as close to one the big hot dryers as I can. Some of the other people here are looking at me kind of funny, but fuck them. I've stopped shivering, and I've got to stop worrying so much about what other people think.

~~ LIVID AND BILLY BUZZ

I came across Livid and Billy in the park near Burnside about half hour ago. Livid was sitting against a tree, and Billy was lying down with his head in her lap. He is in that position a lot, with or without Livid's lap.

I was walking by her when she looked up and said, "Billy misses his family. I can't believe it. They were so horrible to him."

I decided to sit down and talk with her for a while. "Livid, shouldn't you encourage Billy to go somewhere to get help? To a drug rehab program?"

"I'm not encouraging Billy to do anything here in the U.S. I am saving my money so that I can marry Billy and take him back to Amsterdam with me. Billy will get the kind of help he needs in Amsterdam."

"I thought that you liked it here in the U.S."

"I did at first. I still do a little. I'd like to be able to come and go. Being in the U.S. has made me appreciate my country more. The U.S. has no heart and feeling. It is supposed to be this great place that has more freedoms than other places in the world. I just see that people here are freer to starve and live off the street. Freer to be murdered and raped. In Amsterdam, people are taken care of. Billy would get the help he needs to get him off drugs."

"Billy may not make it too much longer in his condition," I said, looking down at his pale complexion.

"I know. I know. That's why I am doing double duty. The only reason I can work such long hours is so we can get to Amsterdam."

Livid talked for a while about what she misses in Amsterdam and Holland. When I left, I wondered if she would really be able to take Billy to Amsterdam. I'm sure that Billy could get some help here in the US but maybe not. People like Billy have become expendable, funds for so many social programs have been cut. I hope she succeeds at what she's trying to do, for her sake as well as Billy's.

Before I left them Livid asked if I'd heard about the killing of the homeless men and women. I said that I have been keeping track of these killings, and that it is very frightening.

"It's horrible!" she responded. "You know, Gibson, I have this feeling that something bad is going to happen to us—Billy and me. I feel like I'm running against time to get out of America before this bad thing happens. I'm getting more afraid that one of my tricks will become violent, or no matter how careful I am, I will get AIDS. Now this crazy killer will become one of my fears."

"Why don't you get off the street, try to get a regular job?"

"Because I'm good at this. And I can make a lot more money in a shorter period of time than any other job I could do."

I ended my conversation with her by saying that while it may be true about her ability to make money faster, the dangers and the position she is putting herself in surely outweighs the benefits she is getting. I just wish she could find a way to go back to Amsterdam with or without Billy.

April 9 ~~ CHARLES AND LOUISE

Another Dead Zone morning. I'm tempted to go find a 24-hour donut shop or café but going to those places is like going from the Dead Zone into a Dead Space where I fear florescent lights and cockroach spray are contaminating my new soul. Maybe it's a little warmer in these Dead Spaces but I can't always eat what they call food. The phrase pops into my mind, "Beggars can't be choosers." But I'm not a beggar and I will insist on being choosy, especially when it comes to protecting my new soul.

When I woke this morning in the Dead Zone, I tried to go back to sleep, but couldn't. I got up and stumbled around the industrial section, unable and a bit unwilling to get my bearings, not caring whether I went one way or the other. It was in dead-zoned-out condition that I came across Charlie and Louise walking toward me.

Louise was pushing a store cart full of clothes and whatever. Charlie walked beside her with a vacant stare. I thought that we'd just pass each other since at this time of the morning the ability to speak seems way out of reach.

But Louise spoke to me! She asked me if I wanted to share some tea with them. At first I couldn't grasp what she was asking. Share tea with them? She pulled aside a cloth on the top of her pile in the cart, and lifted out a gallon can that appeared shiny and clean on the outside.

"It's English Breakfast tea and it's warm, so make up your mind quick now," Louise said. Charlie stood beside her, still not acknowledging me. He looked worse than I felt. I noticed that he was holding some Styrofoam cups in his right hand.

"Where'd you get the tea, Louise?" I asked. I mean, warm tea sounded so good, but I had to have some caution here.

"We was walkin' by the Lutheran Church up there a ways," she pointed in some direction. I think it was east. I usually know my directions pretty well, but I get confused sometimes. "The pastor was just openin' the doors, and he turned to us and asked if we wanted something warm to drink." She laughed showing her stained and rotten teeth. "I started to say 'Shit yeah,' but I stopped myself, and just said real sweet like, 'We'd love somethin' warm to drink.' Charlie here was just standin' there, hung over, not sayin' nothing. But the pastor took us inside. He said they had to make a lot of tea and coffee for some early morning meetin' they were having, and after he made the tea in this big pot, he grabbed this can, and poured it full." She held the can out for me to see. She pulled the plastic cover off the can, and wonderful, warm, mildly bitter aroma of the tea rushed into my nose. The inside of the can looked clean.

"Do ya want some or doncha?" she asked.

I told her I'd love some. She handed me the can, and took the Styrofoam cups from Charlie, and set three of them in a row on the side walk. Then she told me to pour. After I poured the three cups, she took the can back, and put the lid on it and put it back into her cart. We sat down on the side of the curb and sipped our tea, and waited for the caffeine to bring us back alive.

I was surprised to see that the tea made Charlie mentally rebound so fast. Charlie sat in his faded green jacket hood. He was shorter than Louise. His face always showed a stubble of a grey beard, and his grey hair had thinned to almost being bald.

All of a sudden he said, "I'm fuckin' sick and tired of this city. Louise, let's go somewhere else. Let's go to New Orleans."

"Charlie, I told ya I ain't travelin' no more. I'm through with travelin'. Go on to New Orleans if ya want."

"Damnit, Louise, you know I can't leave you. You have to come with me, baby. I know you'd come with me if I went. You've always come with me. Don't you remember that New Orleans is where we said we'd always go back to die."

Charlie turned to me and said, "New Orleans was where I first met Louise, and it's where we fell in love. We stayed in a room in the French Quarter above a bar where someone was singing a Cajun song, just for our love it seemed to us at the time. Remember, Louise? And do you remember we vowed then to return there when we finished our traveling, to die in the city where we met?"

"Charlie, are you thinkin' of dyin' on me now? Is that why you want to go back to New Orleans? You think I'm dyin'? I don't feel good but I don't think I'm dyin'. Shit," she said and sipped more of her tea.

"How long you two been together?" I asked.

Louise shrugged, and Charlie said he couldn't remember how long, but he knows they've traveled all around the states more than a few times. He said they like the West Coast cities, except for LA. He said the cities of East are hard on street people.

"That's why we came out here, but we love New Orleans." He turned to Louise. "Didn't we just have the best time in New Orleans?"

Louise finally smiled and nodded her head. "We did have some good times in New Orleans, Charlie. But I just don't feel up to travelin' anymore. Maybe later in the summer I might feel better, but not now."

Charlie shook his head. "OK, honey. Maybe later in the summer."

The tea had warmed me just like their love for each other, and made me feel like joining life again. Made me feel like I could take my morning journey over the bridges of the river to the Holy Skyscraper. I thanked the two of them, and went on my way, thankful that I had been able to escape another Dead Zone.

April 10 ~~ SHAPE-SHIFTING WOMEN IN MY DREAMS

Last night I dreamed of Sally Waters. We were sitting on a park bench. I was writing in my journal, and Sally asked me if I ever wrote about her.

"A few times," I said. "And I wrote nice things about you."

I looked down at my journal, and when I looked back up, Sally had become Kristen. She said, "Oh come on, Gibson, I'm sure you haven't written nice things about me. I left you and we really didn't love each other."

"But I did write nice things about you," I said, looking back down at the journal. I looked up and Kristen had changed to Queen Avarice. She said, "I don't care what you've written about me. I don't think it matters what you write in your journal. It's a waste of time. You should be pursuing a different dream—with me in the Holy Skyscraper."

Then suddenly Queen Avarice morphed into the bag lady, and she pulled out a long, curved hunting knife, stood up, and yelled, "I'm gonna make sure you never write another goddamn thing in that journal about me or anything else."

She raised the knife up above me, and started to bring it down. I woke up with a gasp.

I looked around and realized with relief that it had been a dream. I was sleeping behind Casey's and the cold of night and the hardness of the alley all seemed just fine. That was a weird dream.

~~ QUEEN AVARICE LOSES HER BLUE SCARF

Even after I had that unsettling dream, I still decided to go across the river to the Holy Skyscraper. I watched Queen Avarice walk across the street, but instead of entering the Holy Skyscraper she kept walking. I jumped up and started to follow her. My first thought was that maybe I'd get to meet her. Then I instantly got angry with myself. I really don't want to meet her.

She was wearing a long, bright red coat and a beautiful blue scarf tied around her neck. And her walk! She walked like she was parading on a red carpet before her awed subjects whom she rules, whom she can hypnotize with the movement of her body, whom she can control with a nod of her head.

She first stopped at a fancy and expensive clothes boutique. I waited down the street, pacing back and forth. When she left the store, she carried a few bags, and I noticed that she'd had taken the scarf off her neck and had tied it to her purse. Then an amazing and unsettling thing happened after about a block. I noticed that the scarf had slipped off the purse and it had fallen to the sidewalk. I ran forward quickly and grabbed it before anyone else did.

As I held it in my hand I first became lost in its sweet smell and the silk's soft texture. Then I found myself in a dilemma. I knew that I should give the scarf back to her, but this would mean coming face to face with her. How could I go from fantasy to reality so abruptly? What would it do to me at this stage of my instability. But I knew it wasn't right just keeping it—then I realized that I better do something because I might attract unwanted attention just standing out in the middle of the sidewalk holding onto a woman's scarf.

By this time she was in the next block. I ran to catch up with her. I didn't know if I had the courage to actually give her back the scarf, but I had to try. The light was red when I got to the corner. From where I stood I could see that she had stopped and was standing outside of a shop looking in a window. Her blonde hair was being lightly blown by the wind.

I waited for the light to turn green, half-impatiently, half hoping it would never turn green. Finally it did turn green, but by the time I walked across the street, Queen Avarice had walked further down the block. I tried to stop my thoughts, held tightly to the scarf, and walked toward her. When I was ten feet from her, my heart was beating faster than a runaway train, and I thought an electric storm had invaded my emotions. Now I was just a few feet away from her. I started to call her name, Queen Avarice, but stopped myself realizing that wasn't her real name. Shit, how stupid of me. That almost put me back miles from my goal, but somehow I pushed forward, and when I caught up to her, I was just about to touch her shoulder near her beautiful blonde hair. I reached forward, but out of nowhere some teenage asshole rushed in between us, and ran into me, knocking me down. "Sorry, Dude," he yelled, but he kept going. I briefly looked at him as he ran down the block. When I turned back Queen Avarice was gone. I jumped up and ran down the sidewalk a little ways but I couldn't see her. She couldn't have gotten that far. I went back to where I was knocked down, and I stood there, confused, holding the scarf.

It was then I noticed that I was standing in front of a beauty salon. She must have gone in there. I went closer to the window, trying not to be too obvious, and sure enough I could see her following someone back into another area.

I walked down the block, and leaned against a pole of a traffic light. I was so close to her. I was just about to touch her. It must not have been meant to be. That's what Esola would say. Somehow I was being protected. If I would have touched her, maybe she would have disappeared right before my eyes. Maybe I would have been electrocuted. Maybe I'm involved in a curse—another curse. I thought of the bag lady. Am I doomed to remain in a strange fantasy relationship with her, and actually never meet her, never talk to her, never find out who she really is?

I looked at the scarf and became aware again of its wonderful silky texture. I knew a little more about her now. I knew one type of perfume that she wears. I put the scarf in my pocket, and waited for her to leave the beauty salon. She was in the beauty salon for hours, it seemed. I obviously didn't have anything else of importance to do.

I almost missed her when she came out of the beauty salon. I wasn't looking at the beauty salon, but I noticed someone leaving out of the corner of my eye. I didn't think it was her, though, because the woman had short hair. I looked more closely at her, and realized it was Queen Avarice. She had cut her hair. All I could tell was that her hair had been cropped short along the nape and the back of her neck. I wondered if she was going through some major life change. Do royalty go through life changes?

I followed behind her as she walked back to the Holy Skyscraper and entered the building. I walked up to the entrance, and almost entered the building, but at the last moment I turned away. I couldn't go inside, even just to the lobby to give the scarf to an information clerk.

I walked away. After a few blocks I stopped and put the scarf in my backpack. One day I'm sure I will find a way to return it to her.

~~ THROWING IMAGINARY ROCKS AT GLASS WINDOWS

I have to be careful about these strange, aggressive urges I've been feeling lately. I'm fantasizing more and more about throwing rocks through windows. I remember I first felt this impulse when I was standing across from the Butcher's Block, looking at the window of Al's Custom Meat store.

Earlier today before leaving the Holy Skyscraper, my sense of awe was replaced by feelings of anger. Ever since this morning I've felt irritable. This building seems encased entirely by glass. Fallacious quickly flashed an image of me standing out on the street hurling rocks at the Holy Skyscraper, breaking window after window. I know it's a fantasy to think it could happen because glass windows these days are so damn durable rocks wouldn't break them.

I know I was really angry at myself, at my lack of courage to enter the building. Sometimes in my anger I become sacrilegious and call that building across the street the Holy Skyraper. I see it as a huge erect prick raping the skies, raping the slaves, raping the earth. There are so many skyrapers around the city but none as powerful and huge as the Holy Skyraper. But then I chastise myself for being so obscene and irreverent. I ask myself, how can a beautiful building like that be as vile as I imagine it to be. Doesn't the sky want to be blessed by its presence?

Such power and promise are why the slaves allow themselves to be taken advantage of. But I've freed myself from most of its lure. As angry as I become, I'm still drawn to its power, its promise. I still often have to come here and look at the building. Maybe one day I won't have to.

April 11 ~~ JEREMIAH AND THE CHRIST CHILD

Every time I run into Jeremiah lately he seems to have only two things on his mind. Searching for the Christ child and the terrible plight of homeless children. He's crazy but he's doing what he can to help the children. I have to give him credit for that.

Today he told me his latest experience in his search for the Christ child: "A few weeks ago I was attending this one church service and I witnessed this young boy who looked like an angel, I swear to God. I was sitting up in the balcony right up front on the side so I could see the boy sitting down on the first row. I could tell there was something special about his expression, the way he conducted himself. When the congregation sang I'm sure I could I could hear his angelic voice through all the others. That was three weeks ago. I watched for the last three Sundays but just last Sunday and this Sunday I saw him use a rubber band to shoot a paper wad or something at another kid. And then I knew that he was not Christ."

"He's only a kid," I said. "You think Christ never did anything like that?"

"Christ would be wise beyond his years. The Christ child would never shoot a paper wad at someone in church. He would know better."

"Maybe the other boy was sinning and it was Christ's way of stopping him." I had to keep myself from smiling.

"No I can tell. I'll be able to tell," Jeremiah said, obviously dejected.

"Could I ask you something without you getting offended?"

Jeremiah nodded and then I asked him if he ever had doubts that the Christ child had been born again in Portland.

"I have doubts all the time. All the time. Gibson, I never used to be able to stand kids. I don't really even like children that much even now. They are just selfish little beings. The homeless children are usually different, though. The homeless children haven't been spoiled rotten. Some may have become mean, and are breaking the law, but I don't think it's their fault. And I know the Christ child will be different. He will bless us, the street people, and somehow will restore us back into our rightful place in society. I want to be the first to recognize the Christ child. I want to be the first one there. Once he's recognized things will be better for us."

I didn't try to challenge Jeremiah anymore. He has a right to his fantasy and who's to say it might not be real. I wouldn't mind being blessed and restored to my rightful place in society. It would have to be a different society than it is now for that to happen. I'm not sure what my rightful place in society would be. I would assume if this all happens Christ would know. My only concern is that I don't consider myself a Christian.

Therefore Christ may challenge me to convert and I'd just have to tell him that I might believe in his spiritual path, but I also believe in a lot of other spiritual paths. I don't know which path I'm following, but I believe in spiritual dimensions, perhaps even spiritual beings. I just don't believe in one almighty God. My spiritual thoughts are open-ended. I sometimes visualize the leaders of all the religions that humans have developed through history sitting around a big table somewhere in the universe discussing the best way to solve the problems on earth. My difficulty with all these religions on earth is that most of them think they are the ones who are right and the rest of the humans are wrong. Somehow what little I know about Jesus, I believe my spiritual visions would be OK with him.

But, hell, I won't have to worry about this. The Christ child has not been reborn. I'm almost sure of it. Almost.

~~ ANOTHER HOMELESS MURDER

I've been making a point of finding a discarded newspaper every few days and reading it to see if any more homeless murders had been committed. Last night another one of us was murdered. Goddamnit. Just like before. Hacked to death in his sleep. This time in a downtown alley. A note was attached to the body, "Unable to survive, not worth keeping alive. The survival of the fittest keeps our nation strong."

This random killing of street people is horrible. The police can't stop it. The killer could strike anywhere. I suppose this fanatic could be called "The Charles Darwin Killer," except that sounds too legitimate, too acceptable, like all he's doing is putting into practice a well-accepted theory. I know a lot of slaves do feel the homeless are inferior. I don't think many would actually support killing to get us off the streets, at least not yet. But I don't think most people are really going to care enough. I mean really deeply care... rather than having a fleeting thought like, "Shit happens in this world. What can anybody do about it?"

What can anyone do about it? What can I do about it? In some ways I'm just as guilty as the mainstream slaves about not doing anything to stop things like this from happening. But I do care. I just don't know what I can do. I thought about the advertising man who wanted to video me for a public announcement on TV. So it's not that I don't know what I can do. It's more that I don't know what I am capable of doing. I understand the difference even if I still feel guilty.

~~ CARISSA ASKS ME HOW I WOULD SOLVE THE HOMELESS PROBLEM

Earlier today I met Carissa at this café near Union and Morrison, and she bought me a chili dog and fries for lunch, and interviewed me as I ate. By the time I met her I was able to allow the depressed and angry feelings about the homeless killings flow through me. I know there is so much other injustice and murder of innocent people around the world, I can't let this particular fanatic's violence continue to ruin what little joy I feel each day.

I welcomed spending time with Carissa to get my mind off these troubling thoughts. However, her first question was: "What do you think could help resolve the homeless condition?"

"The complete dismantling of the military-industrial complex," I said with a full mouth of food.

Carissa asked what I had said. I waited until I had finished chewing my food, then said more clearly, "Dismantle the military industrial complex. You know what that is?"

"Yeah, I know what that is. It just seems so... extreme." You have some chili on your cheek."

"What are you, my mother?" She looked up, concerned that she had upset me, then she saw me smiling and smiled too.

"No, I'm just not used to hanging around a weird, radical street person, I guess. I don't know what to expect from you sometimes."

"What did you expect me to say... buy more cheap houses for people, send more food to the shelters, provide more training. Training for minimum wage jobs? Carissa, I think American houses are death chambers, built with toxic materials, imprisoning people to high mortgages, and dulling people's ability to develop into good human beings. What do people do in these houses? They forget about the world? They hook themselves up to TVs, computers, iPads, smart phones, TV dinners, microwaves, and zone out. I have no hope for a system that locks people into low-paying jobs, and yet encourages them to buy, buy, buy. Carissa, our nation is broken. Not broke, like some corporate criminals would like us to believe. Broken. Our way of life is totally corrupt, serving the welfare of a small group of rich people."

"You sound like you hate the U.S.," she said.

"You know what's funny, Carissa. I'm not really anti-American. I love many aspects of the United States, our great nation and land."

"You do? Or are you just being sarcastic?"

"No, no, I'm not. I think America has accomplished a lot and that all people have the potential to develop their caring and compassionate sides—even Americans. I just think most Americans have been conditioned and brainwashed for too long by leaders who have powerful tools at their disposal. Americans should have done and should be doing a lot more for others and for the world. I don't see any compassion, any willingness for people to learn from their mistakes, to demand more."

"I need to ask you a question, then, Gibson. What are you doing? Aren't you hiding in the streets just as the other Americans are hiding in their homes?" I thought about how her question related to exactly what I was struggling with earlier in the day, and it makes me feel that our ideas and feelings must float up into the some invisible space around us and connect with others who may be on the same wave length—we are connected with the minds and feelings of others regardless how separate we think we are.

I must have been staring into space. Carissa waved her hand in front of me, "Gibson, Gibson, are you there." As I came back to focus on her, she shook her head. I'm glad you came back, Gibson. I need you to answer my question."

I focused on her again, and said, "Carissa, how old are you anyway? Are you some reporter disguised as a sixteen-year-old? Who's feeding you these questions?"

"No, I don't need anyone to feed me questions." She seemed offended. "Please just answer the question. I bought you a chili dog!"

"You are a tough one." I thought for a moment. "Carissa, you're right to challenge me, but I think you're missing something. At first, I didn't choose to be a homeless person." She raised her eyebrows, but I continued. "I was forced into my homeless condition. I worked for years. I fulfilled my responsibilities, paid the mortgage, everything.

"It's only been since I was forced onto the streets that I came to realize the horrors of the mainstream slave system that's got most people by their souls. Not that everything is bad about the American way of life—but it's been allowed to run wild without any true guidance as to what its limits should be, or how we could do things better. I see the only thing that is keeping us from creating a more caring and compassionate society is the corporate interest groups. The large group of mostly white Americans who live a slave-like existence won't stand up for their rights, as well as other people's rights. I guess I'm not strong enough to do anything else right now except protect what little I have left of worth in me."

"What is that? What do you have left in you?"

"I can't go into that right now, Carissa. Ask me another question."

"Gibson, how come you keep telling me you don't want to answer my questions just when I feel I'm getting somewhere. Just when I think I'm getting to key issues?"

"I don't think they are the key issues. I'm trying to draw the line between talking about homelessness and about more personal, private things. Everybody has things they don't want to talk about."

Carissa reluctantly said she understood, and after another half hour or so, we got up and she paid. She thanked me again for talking with her.

Some of her questions do get under my skin. Ah well, I can't isolate myself from everyone. I'm realizing that part of living on the street is surviving not only the barbs but the hooks that people throw at you to try to pull you back into the regular brainwashed state of existence. Carissa means well. She is a nice girl. She has a toughness about her, but there is also a sadness. I sense a deep hurt in her. Despite that, she seems caring, and that's the most important thing. Even when she tries to challenge me, she seems caring. I told her I would meet with her again sometime soon. She wants to go around with me for part of the late afternoon and evening. I wonder how that will be.

April 16 ~~ RELUCTANT NIGHT AT THE SHELTER

The last few days I've had a deep cough in my chest so I went to a shelter. One of the rare few times I've been at a shelter. But I needed a cot.

When I go to shelters I feel like I'm in a concentration camp. Faces drawn. People in slouched positions sitting on cots. Kids screaming. Parents yelling.

The way I was feeling tonight it seems like I was visiting a motel to have a luxurious warm sleep rather than having to sleep out in the cold on the street. My bed partners are a mass of strangers—most of them unknown to me, unknown to the world, people linked to each other through poverty.

It's difficult to be modest here. You lose the privacy you have when you are in a shelter. You lose your physical privacy and I suppose it's up to you whether or not you lose your inner privacy. Of course, I sleep in the men's section of the shelter. There is a women's section and a family section.

I was sitting in the lobby drinking some tea before I went to sleep. A couple who looked a little older than me sat nearby and introduced themselves. Their names were Larry and Beth. They were new to the streets. Both were overweight, but were well-groomed. Beth was crying because it turns out she and Larry had just been evicted from their apartment. He had lost his job and couldn't find another one. She hadn't been working. Apparently, she gets a little money from social security for a psychological condition, but it is not enough for them to live on.

They asked me questions about the shelter and I told them they'd have to ask one of the staff. I explained that I was not a shelter person, and they seemed shocked that I could just live on the streets. "We could never do that," Larry said.

Larry spent most of the 15 minutes or so I was sitting by them trying unsuccessfully to console Beth. After I finished my tea, I said goodbye and retired to my cot in the men's sleeping area. The man sleeping next to me seemed to have nightmares most of the night and talked and cried in his sleep. Even though he kept me awake most of the night, at least the room was warm, and this morning I feel a little better. I may need to stay in the shelter one more night but I'm going to try to get another cot in another area away from this man who seems to be fighting demons in his sleep. If I'm going to be in a shelter at least I should get a good night's sleep.

April 20 ~~ CHALLENGES FROM ESOLA AND JUSTINE

A little before closing time today at the Treasure Market, Esola and Justine came into the work room where I was cleaning some ceramic and glass vases. They began questioning me about why I didn't come to work at the store more often, and they wouldn't let up. Esola kept asking me, "Why don't you get back into life? What's the matter with you?"

"I can only do what I can do," I kept answering. I didn't want to try explaining myself.

At one point Justine asked, "Why can't you do more? I know you like it here."

I didn't answer right away. So many things went through my mind. I could say, "It's just a job for a few bucks to help me have a good meal every once in a while." But I couldn't say that. I realized that I was feeling the need to minimize how much being in the Treasure Market with them really meant to me. They both were silent, staring at me, waiting for my answer. They had done a lot for me. I didn't want to seem ungrateful. I admitted to them that I did enjoy working at the store and I admitted that I enjoyed my relationship with them. I told them that I had things to work out that I couldn't explain, and that I had to spend a lot of time alone right now.

Since it was closing time, they invited me into the kitchen where they brought out a tray of cheeses, meats and raw vegetables. Esola opened a bottle of wine. She said lightly, "Sit down here, Gibson. We have to talk about your future some more. We can't do that without some good wine and something to snack on. We have to resolve this. You can't just continue to be a homeless person. I know you have something important to do in life."

I took at glass of wine that she had poured, and said, "If I have something important to do, I'll just have to do it on the street."

Esola shook her head, "No, you have to come in from the streets. I just know that you have to. You know, Gibson, maybe we should consult an astrologer about how and when you could best get your life together."

I told her that even though my life was in shambles I felt more together now and satisfied than with any of the alternatives I could think of. And I told her I didn't believe in astrology. I was surprised then that Justine asked me what I knew about astrology. I can always debate with Esola. It's more difficult for me keep on solid ground with Justine.

"Only what's in the newspaper," I admitted. "And when I worked at the department store I would glance at the books written about my astrological sign. Everything I've read seems so general, like it could apply to everyone."

"You don't really know anything about astrology then," Justine said firmly but in a nice way. How can she be so nice even as she is telling you that you have no clue about something? "It's a lot more complex and meaningful than what's in the newspapers. Why don't you let us get your chart done by an astrologer we know? She could come here and talk to you about it. Then you could decide for yourself if astrology has any meaning for you."

I found myself saying, "Sure, that would be just fine." I seem to agree so easily to things Justine says or wants. I have to watch this tendency more carefully in the future and try to resist it. I did tell Justine that I am suspect about conventional explanations of how the world works—something seems to be missing, many of the prevalent viewpoints seem so one-sided. I know such a generalized statement was probably my feeble attempt to stubbornly maintain control of a discussion about something, like astrology, that is so out of the ordinary.

Justine asked me if I believe in what I write in my journals. I said that I didn't think of my writing as explanations of how the world works. I told them that I thought of my writing as a way of living with myself.

Justine wrote down my birth date, place of birth and what I could remember of my birth time. My mother told me I was born about half an hour past noon. Justine said that would do, but that the exact time would be better. I looked at Esola and said that sometimes I think my birth and early life was a past life since they seemed so vague in my mind. She said that she knew what I meant. She believes that through our lives we are meant to be open to change, and sometimes that means becoming a totally different person.

Then Esola asked me why I was on the street. I guess they really were serious about trying to figure me out. I said that I had suffered a psychological breakdown. She responded by saying that my psychological breakdown was in the past, what's wrong with me now? I told her that I must still be broken down. Justine said that they were just concerned about me and wanted me to feel all right about becoming more a part of the store.

By that time I was feeling very relaxed around them, less guarded, less defensive, despite their probing. I like both of them very much. I was still careful not to say anything about my newborn self, my infant creative soul. I have never told anyone about my infant creative soul. I've always known that to talk about it would risk its destruction.

Esola at one point asked me if I missed being with a woman. I looked quickly at Justine, who at first looked back at her mother with eyebrows raised. Then she looked at me, waiting for my response. "That's kind of personal, isn't it?" I said, trying to evade the question. I was feeling pretty good at the time with the wine, so the question didn't bother me as much as it probably should have. As much as it does now. How could she have asked me that question, especially in front of Justine? Of course I miss sharing life with someone I love.

Anyway, I looked at both of them and said as straight-faced and sincerely as I could, "No, I don't miss being with a woman. Women do nothing but destroy a man's creativity." Of course I don't believe this, but I thought it would be better to joke about the issue rather than get into a serious discussion, and what could be a rather painful and even embarrassing, discussion.

"Bullshit," Esola shouted.

Justine just shook her head. "You don't really believe that Gibson."

Esola continued, "If you believe what you just said, you don't know your true feelings. You don't recognize that men need women to bring their creativity alive."

"OK. OK. I'm just joking, Esola. The truth is that the street life doesn't encourage getting into a relationship like that," I said. "When you have to scrounge around for food and a warm place to sleep, then you don't have anything left over for love. At least I don't." I knew that I was partly telling the truth and partly lying.

Esola wouldn't buy it. "Gibson, I've been poor before in my life, and I've still been able to love. It's the love that has gotten me through the worse times."

"It seems like you're different than me then."

"In some ways I'm different. But in that way we're all the same. Men and women alike need love, need to share with someone else, especially during the hard times." She looked at her daughter. "Justine, what do you think?"

"I'm just listening, Mama. I'm just listening."

She seemed to me to be doing more than just listening. She was looking at me with that look that lately has been piercing my emotions with some kind of an electric charge. I tried to bring to my mind the image of a cattle prod, but I had to admit that what I felt was very pleasant, not at all uncomfortable. I decided, though, to try hanging on to the image of the cattle prod. I figured it might help me from returning to the cattle herd just for love. I had to remain a stray animal even if I was lonely all of the time.

At that point I held up the wine, and said, "No matter what you two are trying to corner me into, I still want to say that I really appreciate everything you've done for me, and I want to offer a toast to tell both of you that you are very special, and that I will put up with all the harassment you want to dish out as long as you remain as lovely as you are."

They looked at each other, trying to decide whether to acknowledge the toast. Finally they laughed, and clinked their glasses against mine. It was at that moment that I felt a relief. I had survived another difficult encounter.

Maybe I shouldn't go to work at the Treasure Market for a while, though.

Right now I still feel a little drunk, and I did enjoy sharing the wine and cheese and talking with them. I hope I find a good place to sleep rather quickly.

April 22 ~~ LOST CLOTHES AND DISTURBING DREAMS

Today I'm feeling particularly despondent. Last night was horrible. It was like the universe was punishing me for feeling so good. For flirting with regular relationships. When I quit writing for the evening, I went looking for a place to sleep. I thought that I had found a little nook between two buildings, but when I tried to make my bed, I began to smell this terrible odor. It had the terrible smell of rotten eggs. It seemed that someone had used this space to dump something that didn't smell right…so I gathered my things and went in search for another place.

I knew that it wasn't all that far down to the river, and I was on the industrial side, but then it started raining. I mean, I'm used to rain, but I wasn't in the mood to be caught in it. On my way down to the river, I had to take a long detour because first I saw a gang I wanted to avoid, and then I saw some cops. It seemed to take forever to get to the industrial section, and then when I did, all the good places to sleep were already taken. It took a long time to find a ledge to sleep under that was out of sight and out of the rain. But then, just when I had fallen asleep, a bunch of rowdy and drunken street people got into some kind a fight just around the corner from where I was. I knew that the cops would come, or if the gang discovered me, I would probably be beaten up. Sure enough right after thinking that a couple of the gang members came around the corner. I crawled away as quietly as I could and luckily they didn't see me.

Only in my hurry to get away, I left the blanket I was sleeping in and one of my bags in which I kept most of my clothes. Hiding in a doorway I watched from the distance as they picked up my bag looked in and took it back around the corner with them. That was the last I would see of those clothes, I realized, feeling really dejected. I also had one of my journals in the bag. I usually keep my journals in my backpack. The lost journal was more upsetting to me than my bag of clothes, until the coldness of the night reminded me of how little I have to keep me warm.

Most of those clothes I had brought with me when I had been forced out onto the street. It had taken me a few months to collect the other clothes. With my sleeping plastic and blanket gone, I realized that I could not sleep lying down unless I could find a vacant hot air vent. I walked over to the closest hospital, but all the good vents were already taken. Anyway, some of the vents are built slanting diagonally, indicating an obvious insensitivity to the needs of the homeless on the part of the management and architects of these medical buildings. I sometimes make these exaggerated connections to try to laugh at something that makes me mad. I walked around for two or three hours before I found a warm spot by a condominium.

My sleep for the rest of the night was brief and fitful. I dreamed again of being out in front of the Treasure Market and I could see Justine alone inside. As I went inside the store to talk with her, I saw her go into another room. As I went from room to room, I kept getting a glimpse of her going into the next room. I was getting frustrated, and kept trying to go faster and faster to catch her. Finally, I caught up to her, and turned her around, but it was Queen Avarice. She was laughing, and she said "We are sisters. You can't have one of us without the other. Do you want us or not? We won't wait forever. But you have to come in from the street, clean up and agree to always do what we say with no questions asked. I'm your Queen. I want you to obey me."

I woke up feeling disgusted and dismayed. Justine and Queen Avarice together in a dream. How did that happen? What is Fallacious trying to do to me?. It was past dawn; the sky was dreary and depressing and I was wet and cold. I knew I wouldn't be able to go back to sleep, but I didn't want to get up. I felt like the universe was piling too many things onto me. I'm having too many things to deal with, and I'm just not up to it. Let me be hungry and cold, if I have to be, but other than these unpleasant conditions, give me a break. I'm tired of having to constantly worry about getting attacked or killed, or about keeping myself from returning to the slave world. Now I have to deal with confusing dreams with Queen Avarice and Justine. And I'm cold and wet. What else can go wrong?

I'm kind of in a daze, half asleep since I woke up. My first chore is to find some more clothes and sleeping gear. I'm not looking forward to this task. I'm not good at completing tasks these days. I can't keep myself going in one direction long enough. I can't keep my mind on one thing. But enough complaining. My day's work is cut out for me.

~~ SEARCHING FOR MORE CLOTHES AND SLEEPING GEAR

After I wrote that last bit earlier in the day some amazing things occurred. I feel a lot better now, a lot more prepared as the cold and heatless night approached.

Early this morning I was completely wiped out—shivering—discouraged. I could barely put one foot in front of the other, but somehow, I managed to start looking in garbage bins and trash cans, searching for old clothes.

The very first dumpster I looked in I found a torn, black woolen blanket, which lifted my spirits a little. I wrapped it around me, and felt warmer and much, much better. I looked through the same dumpster for a long time, but I didn't find anything else. I was in a semi-residential part of the city, still east of the river, but a little further south than the area I usually hang out in. I was trying to decide which way to go.

I decided to walk down alleys to find garbage containers kept behind houses in this Southeast area of town. Many of these houses had been remodeled and looked upscale.

There I was minding my own business more or less (even if I was trespassing at the edge of a private property)—looking through someone's garbage container—looking through things someone had already thrown away, discarded for some sanitation company to come and pick up.

Then suddenly I hear this man's voice say, "What on earth are you doing?"

I look up from the garbage container I was rummaging through and saw this well-dressed young man in a white shirt and tie, short haircut, looking like some kind of well-paid corporate prince, standing on his back porch looking at me.

"I'm cold," I said. "I'm just looking for something to keep me warm." In this situation I felt honesty was the best tack, honesty with a little bit of simple, straight-forward expression of discomfort to try to hook his pity. This man looked like he might be the kind that was used to reading abbreviated stock reports, and not one to listen to lengthy monologues.

He looked at me for a long time without saying anything.

I decided to take the offensive. "I'm sorry to trespass on your property. I'll leave and I won't come back." I can be pretty mealy-mouthed if I want to be. I learned this a long time ago sucking up to other sales managers in my work to try to get the raises or promotions I wanted. Sometimes it worked, other times it didn't. I started backing away.

"Wait." That's all he said, but I stopped. He seemed to be talking more to himself rather than making a command. I waited and prepared myself to take off running in case he pulled out a gun or something. Ok, Ok, so that seems a little dramatic. But after what's been happening to me, I was getting really paranoid. And you can never tell about the weirdoes living supposedly respectable lives.

But this man astounded me by finally saying to me, "I have some old clothes in the house. And I think an old sleeping bag. Come on in, and I'll give you something warm to eat while I get these clothes and sleeping bag for you." He turned to go back inside. I heard him add over his shoulder, "It'll save me from having to go to Goodwill."

I stared at the man with his conservative, expensive clothes, and wondered what I should do. I thought for a moment that he may be trying to lure me into a trap, but I decided that I had to get control of my paranoia. This guy seemed decent enough, seemed concerned. But I could see the headlines, "Homeless Trespasser Shot Dead." I wondered if I was being set up.

The man stood at the doorway waiting for me. When I hadn't moved for a few moments, he said, "I'm getting cold. I'm going inside to get warm."

Now it was my turn to stop him from leaving. I asked him why he wanted to help me. He turned and looked at me, frowning and shaking his head. "Good god, are you that frightened of other people?" he asked. "What is this world coming to? I just want to help you. I've been fortunate in my life and I don't usually get an opportunity to help someone in need in such a direct manner. Look, come on in. Don't be frightened. I just want to give you a few things."

I followed him into his kitchen. He motioned for me to sit on one of the stools at a counter that separated the kitchen from the dining area. As he poured me some coffee, he said he was fixing himself some eggs and toast and wanted to know if I wanted any. I nodded. While he cooked, I looked around. I looked at the dark wood dining room table in the adjoining room with a huge chandelier above. I could see the living room from where I sat. I could see a plush, black leather couch. He had large, colorful abstract paintings on the walls of the dining room and living room. Spanish guitar music was being played on a digital music system, and it sounded like the musician was in the same room with us. His house was rather luxurious, and I began to wonder what the hell I was doing there.

As he made breakfast he began telling me about himself. He told me he was an attorney. He was about 45 years old, and he said that he had either gone to school or worked steadily for his whole life, or at least for as long as he could remember. As he handed me the plate of eggs and toast, he said he had recently undergone a major crisis in his life. His wife had just left him. He said that since she had left him about a week ago, he has been going through a painful period of soul-searching, questioning his life-style, his values, his purpose in life. I thought to myself that I knew there had to be a reason for this display of generosity.

"I know something about life crises," I told him. "I used to have a house—though not as expensive as yours. And I used to have a wife. We were getting ready to start a family. Now I don't have anything." I didn't tell him about my psychological breakdown, or my infant creative soul.

He looked really concerned and asked me what happened. I told him that I'd rather not go into it. I told him that I was still trying to figure things out.

"That's what I am trying to do now," he responded. "One thing I've realized is how selfish I am. I've been so focused on my career that I wasn't responsive to my wife. I know that now. And I've realized that I haven't done anything to help others, to really help solve some of the social problems we're facing. It's like I've suddenly awakened and realized how insensitive I've been, not just to my wife but to everyone."

I ate my eggs and listened to him describe the evils that he thinks he is guilty of, and how he wishes he could be different. I wondered why he wasn't having a psychological breakdown like I did. I figured that he had too much money to afford the kind of breakdown I had, and besides, he probably works in the Holy Skyscraper, or someplace like it, so life crises may not be as devastating to him as it was in my case. When I lost all of my financial resources, I also lost the opportunities to even make career and life style changes. Now I'm trying to let this new part of myself grow out here on the streets where poverty, indifference and violence so easily destroys the will and the ability to live.

At one point he said, "So maybe it takes a jolt like this to make me grow, to become a better person. I'm dealing with some personal issues that affect how I relate to people, but I'm also trying to figure out what I can do to help the world become a better place to live. I keep asking myself, how can I help? From your perspective what do you think would be something that someone like me could do to help the homeless?"

I suddenly realized that he was asking me a question. I had just taken a big bite of the toast, and I froze. I must have looked funny. He laughed and said, "Keep eating—you can answer my question when you finish that bite."

When I finished what I was eating, I took a sip of coffee, and then said, "Let me get this straight. Your wife left you, and suddenly you want to help the world? You want to devote your life to social causes?"

"Of course that's only one part of what I want to change in myself. One of the tensions between Lisa - my wife - and myself, was that I was so conservative, and she had become more progressive. She was becoming much more socially conscious, and has even become an activist for some environmental causes. Then she really became galvanized around women's rights, equal pay and the plight of women and children in developing nations around the world. I not only ignored these issues, I put her down for wasting her time on them. When she left me she said that not only had I ignored her, I had ignored the concerns of the world. She said that she could not live the life style that we were living. I want to show her that I can change. But I'm just beginning to search for what I can do."

I took another sip of coffee and, looked at the back door, and wondered if I should make a run for it. I'm not a counselor or a social worker. I had to admit, though, that the warmth of the kitchen and the coffee felt good. I decided to stick it out. So I said, "I don't know how anyone can help solve the problems we're facing today. I feel like the people who have the power have become more and more powerful, and have control of the economy, the media, the politicians, the justice system, and the military. I think an elitist and wealthy group, mostly men, have gained control of the media, which then controls the thinking of the average American who doesn't have time to see through the bullshit."

The young lawyer was listening intently. He nodded and said, "What are your ideas about how to change things?"

"I really don't know. Look, you asked me how you can help. I don't know how well-to-do professionals can help unless they are willing to start from scratch and go out into the streets to join with the people who either have never had anything or who have lost everything."

"So you don't think we can understand unless we experience what it's like to be destitute?"

"I don't know what it's going to take to make people care. You're a lawyer. Try to figure out how else you can make people more caring, sensitive, willing to help others. Everyone wants their share of the American pie no matter what harm is done to others. So many Americans are disconnected from how their actions and choices cause destruction and death throughout the world."

I stopped, dumbfounded at myself. Ken was staring at me. "Wow!" he said, "I haven't heard a good tirade like that for a long time. Except on progressive radio, which I am listening to more these days."

I felt a little awkward, and said, "Listen, I have to get going."

"Yeah, sure—here, let me get you some of those clothes I told you about." He left the room and came back in a few minutes with a pile of clothes. He had three or four shirts, two of them flannel. He had a few pair of wool socks and a couple of grey sweatshirts. He also came through with the sleeping bag he had talked about. This was quite a haul. As a result of his charity, I had gained back almost all the clothes and sleeping gear I had lost. Actually, I had better sleeping gear. I thanked him, and as I was leaving, he said, "I'm sorry that I can't do more for you. I also feel like I need to say that I won't be able to do anything more for you. Please don't come back for further hand-outs. I know this may sound contradictory, but I don't want to be asked to give money or things to people every time I turn around. I want to spend my time helping in other ways. But you have given me great deal to think about. Thank you."

As I walked down the back steps, I thought to myself, "What does he think I would be doing? Coming to his door begging all the time?"

Oh well, after what he gave me, I can't be too critical. Besides everyone is trying to protect themselves today, including me. Especially me.

~~ LIVID'S OFFER

"Are you lonely tonight, Gibson?"

Livid said that to me tonight at the Campfire. Billy was passed out lying in the weeds on the other side of the Campfire. I had been lying against my backpack, staring into the fire, my mind faded out, vacant. I didn't know who had spoken these words at first, whether it was someone from one of Fallacious' films or someone from my past. The words had visually hung in my mind as if written on a large billboard: ARE YOU LONELY TONIGHT, GIBSON?" Needling and mocking me.

Then I realized that someone had actually asked me this question. My mind returned to the Campfire reality. I looked up and saw that Livid was sitting beside me. Fifteen-year old Livid. Or was she only 15 years old? Or was she 21 or 31? Hell, I don't know, but I had to admit she looked rather sexy to me at that moment.

"Are you offering me sex, Livid?" I asked, trying to seem light.

"Would you accept if I was?"

"Of course I wouldn't. I don't approve of someone your age, or any age actually, doing what you're doing."

"I told you that I'm 21. I just look young for my age. Anyway, you Americans are so hard to understand sometimes. Everybody is so different. Sex doesn't have anything to do with age. I wasn't offering you sex anyway. I came over here to thank you for your concerns about Billy and me."

"I am concerned about the both of you. It's difficult to see you struggling so much at your ages."

"We'll make it! Together we'll make it. Especially if we can get back to Holland." She said with bravado. "Anyway I just wanted to thank you. I didn't mean to invade your loneliness."

"I think you mean, my aloneness or privacy. But anyway, that's ok. I appreciate you thanking me…and your concerns."

She smiled and went back over to Billy.

April 24 ~~ CARISSA VISITS THE WRONG SHELTER

When Carissa started her interview this afternoon, she asked me what I did all day, how I spent my time. I told her I just walk around and try to keep out of trouble. I told her I write in my journal. I try to find cheap food to eat. Sometimes I look for things people throw away. I observe things. I listen to things. I listen to people talking. I eavesdrop. I sometimes interact with some people who live on the street and others who live regular lives. I have certain places I like to walk to each day and certain places where I like to hang out. I work at a second-hand furniture store sometimes. But I told her that mostly I just try to keep warm and keep writing in my journal.

As I talked, I noticed she wrote notes, but did not seem to really be listening. She finally put her pen down and looked at me and said, "Yesterday I went to a shelter downtown on Burnside Avenue and it was so awful. I couldn't believe the conditions those people are living in. It made me feel so…frightened. We may have to live in those shelters. I could not do that. That would be more than I could take. I could never stay there."

"You went to the wrong shelter, Carissa," I said quickly, trying to relieve her anxiety. "That one is mostly for single men. You should go to one of the family shelters."

"I will. But I feel so bad about what I saw. I think it is horrible for people to have to live in those conditions."

So do I. So do I. I hope that Carissa and her family are able to keep their house. I can sympathize with her mother going to pieces after her husband died. I don't think anyone plans on falling apart. I just wish our great nation hadn't taken down so many of the safety nets. Somehow I feel that Carissa will survive, though. She seems to be a fighter, and she has a lot of determination. Unfortunately, just like Livid, I think Carissa is being forced to grow up a lot quicker than she should. Teenage years are for having fun, being a little irresponsible and wild. But Carissa has had to take the responsibility of her whole family, it seems. I wish she didn't have to be struggling so for their survival.

Oh well, I think I will go over to work at Esola's for a little while. I might be getting too dependent on having a few dollars in my pocket.

~~ HOMELESS MAN DYING ON THE STREET

Almost every day I experience some kind of discomfort from being in my homeless condition but somehow I have been able to endure these discomforts and have not become really physically ill. To stay healthy is one of my main concerns. I don't mind the diarrhea, the nausea, and the occasional cold and sore throat. I just don't want these symptoms to become worse. I need to stay healthy enough to move around, to survive, to protect my new soul.

Since I don't take drugs or drink enough to blind myself to my condition I cannot live in my urine and shit like many of my unfortunate fellow homeless people do. I am determined to stay alert, alive and healthy, even if means being more acutely aware of the pain and the discomforts of this unprivileged lifestyle.

I'm a little shaken right now. Earlier today I came across a homeless man who was lying on the sidewalk. He had spit up some blood which lay splattered on the concrete by his mouth. I knelt beside him, and tried to get him to talk to me. He was conscious but delirious. I looked around for help but there were no other pedestrians around. This was just east of the industrial section and it was on a side street.

I left the man lying there and ran back down the block to an office building. I ran inside and into a room where four or five men and women were sitting behind their desks and in front of computers. The women had white blouses on and the men had on white shirts and ties. They all looked up at me when I ran inside the room.

"There's a man lying on the sidewalk hurt," I yelled. None of them said anything or hardly even moved. I didn't know if I were getting through to these robots. It looked to me like they were trying various software programs out in their heads to try to figure out the right goddamn response to make.

"A man is dying out there on the side walk. Will someone please call 911?"

One of the men finally jumped up and ran outside. Then he came back into the room with a disgusted look on his face. He said in an offended tone of voice, "Janet, call and tell them that a derelict has passed out on the sidewalk down the street from our office."

I felt like yelling at the man, at all of them, "Excuse us for dying in front of your businesses."

But I ran back outside and waited until the ambulance came and took the man away.

One thing for sure. We won't crawl away and die. The people of this society who are clutching onto their houses and their TVs better get used to seeing a lot of people becoming ill and dying on the streets of the cities and small towns. More and more of us homeless men, women and children are being created each day, and we won't hide from you. We won't just crawl away. If you're not going to care for us, then you'll have to watch us die.

~~ WHY ISN'T JUSTINE MARRIED?

Esola complained today of Justine not marrying. She was sitting at a white table in the workroom watching me clean some mirrors and sorting out some window lace.

"Justine's a beautiful woman, don't you agree?" she asked.

"Of course I do."

"Then why isn't she married. It's not right that a woman her age with her beauty is not married."

"She is seeing someone, isn't she?" I said, and felt strange I was defending her relationship with that egocentric actor.

But Esola said with extreme exasperation, "That man she is seeing is not a man, he's just a boy. She can do better than him. He's good looking and knows it. He's so brooding and moody and flies off the handle at any little thing. Justine shouldn't be wasting time on him."

"Aren't we all a little moody? I certainly know I am," I said. "I never know what I'm going to feel from moment to moment."

"You're not like he is. He displays his moodiness as dramatically as possible so that everyone around him has to notice. If you are around him for two minutes you would know he's an actor."

"I guess I do try to keep my moods to myself," I said. "And I have noticed Chris seems to be very demanding and edgy."

"I don't know what she sees in him," Esola said, shaking her head. "But I've learned not to say anything about Justine's love life."

"How did you learn that?"

Esola laughed. "We had a good argument one time. A loud argument. I remember it so well. But in the end, she won. I let her win, of course. I remembered how I hated my mother telling me who I should marry. I remember that my mamma and papa didn't like the man I married, and oh, how wrong they were."

She became lost for a moment in her memories. Then she abruptly remembered what she had been talking about. "Maybe it was a mistake to allow her to take over the store. She's had only a few steady boyfriends since she began managing the store. I just want Justine to be happy. And I know that having a good man is what happiness is all about, no matter what the modern women say. Love is what it's all about."

"I think modern women say love is important, too. They just also say that women shouldn't have to be a servant to be in a relationship."

"They don't know what they're talking about. Women can get what they want if they know how. They always have been able to outsmart men by not trying to battle them on their territory. Let the men be masters of the work world. Let women rule all the rest of life. Modern women try to compete with men in areas where they will lose. Women are giving up the areas where they can use their special strengths. This is the wisdom of the ages, Gibson. Modern women are losing touch with this wisdom."

I finished separating the window lace. "Well, I don't know. It seems that women are just as capable of being strong and effective as men in all areas of life."

"Nobody can have it all. It's is a sad state of affairs. Women are losing what is really important. I see it in Justine. She is alone so much of the time. She doesn't have anyone to share life with. I know she sees Chris but the two of them don't really spend all that much time together. I don't have anyone to share life with either, but I haven't given up by any means." Then she laughed with a mischievous look, she said, "If you see a good-looking old man, send him over to the store, will you Gibson?"

I mainly just listened to Esola after that. Before my mental breakdown I thought more like her, maybe not as definite as her. I guess I didn't really think much one way or the other about women's rights. I did accept that my wife wanted to develop her career before she had children. At the same time, she did most of the housework and cooking, so I now understand how much more than I she really did on a daily basis. She didn't have much free time. We both were sort of workaholics.

Now I feel women shouldn't be trapped in a role of someone else's making, just like I don't want to be trapped in a role or a job of someone else's making. I want to be able to choose more about how I want to contribute to society. I think women have the same needs. So I disagree with Esola, but I won't make a big deal out of it. I can't expect her generation to change. It's our generation and the generations coming now that have to change. I know I won't be able to come in from the streets until things change. I know that now I'm too weak to come in from the streets and fight for the things I believe in. I fear I would lose.

I don't really see what Esola is worried about. It seems to me that Justine somehow is able to remain working in society and still keep the special creative and lovely sides of herself alive. She seems to be happy and successful. But I'm not really around her all that much, so I really don't know how happy she is. Actually, I don't want to really know that Justine is unhappy. As a matter of fact it bothered me when Esola started talking about how she misses being without a man. I don't want her to be lonely either. I know how terrible it is to feel that way. But I don't want to get my mind on my loneliness now.

April 25 ~~ CHARLIE WANTS TO LIVE AND DIE IN NEW ORLEANS

I was standing by the edge of the freeway field today and Louise came up to me crying. She said to me, "Charlie keeps telling me he's dyin'. He says he's gonna leave Portland with or without me and go back to New Orleans. He wants to die in New Orleans. I want to be with him but I don't want to be left alone in New Orleans. I can't be left alone in New Orleans. I don't want to live in the south again. Will you talk with him for me.?"

I started to ask, "Why me? What can I say? What can I do?" But I said, "Sure." I remembered the tea that she had shared with me that chilly winter morning, and I did feel an affinity for Charlie. I miss some aspects of New Orleans, too.

Charlie was resting, sitting with his back against a wire mesh fence surrounding a manufacturing plant of some type. I walked over to him while Louise stayed back where she was.

"Charlie, Louise tells me you think you're dying."

"What she's really telling you is that she doesn't want to come to New Orleans with me. Ain't that right, son?"

"That's right."

Charlie reached in his pocket and pulled out a harmonica. "New Orleans is where I first learned to play this thing. New Orleans is a place where you can hear good music and you can dance in the streets any time of day and on any day of the year. It's where I have my best memories. It's where I met Louise."

"She said that she doesn't want to go back to the south."

"I know that, and if I weren't dyin', I wouldn't ask her."

"How do you know you're dying? Have you gone to a doctor?"

"No, but I just know. I can't explain it, son. My time's comin' up. I've always wanted to die in New Orleans where I could have a parade to help my spirit dance away from this world."

He stopped talking, put the harmonica to his lips and began playing some bluesy sad song. Then he played something with an upbeat tempo. Louise came over while he was playing and sat beside him. During one of his songs she sang as he played. She had a rich full voice. After one of his songs, Charlie turned to her and said, "I'll stick around until after the summer, then I might go. If I'm still alive. You'd better help me stay alive."

She smiled, and said, "I'll keep you alive. Haven't I been doing it since we first met?"

"I can't argue a bit with that," he said, hugging her, and started playing again. I eventually left them alone. Why can't I fall in love with a woman on the street? Maybe I need to go to New Orleans. No, I have a different purpose now than finding someone to share my life.

I just got bummed out walking by this shelter house and saw a family, a mother and father with their six children all sitting on the steps. The father was leaning against the front post of the old Victorian house that had been turned into the shelter. He was medium-height, wore jeans and a work shirt, and had short brown hair, but his shoulders were slumped forward and he just seemed to be staring out at nothing in particular. Two of the children were playing a game with each other. The boy and girl both looked about five or six years old. A girl a few years older than them sat to their right, reading. On the next step up, two older boys sat, both staring at nothing in particular, just like their father. On the porch step the mother and what looked like the oldest daughter sat.

Anyone who has been around homeless families for very long and seen the look in their eyes cannot feel good about the priorities of this country. I see so many families now, and so many young children on the street that I feel sad and angered. I don't know what to say. My feelings are mixed. I could look to these homeless families as the hope for the future. I would think that having experienced such injustices that they would fight for justice, but one cannot underestimate the power of the corporations in controlling these people's minds.

The children of these families. Those who survive will become the slaves of tomorrow, the soldier of war, the computer operators, the number crunchers, the wearers of the latest fashion, the owners of the biggest cars they can afford.

But now when these families are on the street and desperate, I can relate to something human in them. Something human is exposed and spills out with their despair. I can relate.

April 26 ~~ TAKING ANOTHER CHANCE TO SEE THAI WOMAN DANCE

All afternoon yesterday, I thought about the Thai Dancer but my fears of being caught by the men in the house helped me to decide I should not go back. Despite my apprehensions and resolve, as the evening darkened the sky, I found myself walking toward the northwest side of the river, toward the Thai Dancer's house. My mind seems to be captured by the exotic and mesmerizing image of her dancing, and this has more power over me than the fear of being caught and beaten by those men I saw. What was it that I saw—some kind of ritual discipline? I wonder what they would do to me if they caught me watching the young woman dance? I'm usually so cautious and strive not to put myself into dangerous situations. The dance was so magical, though…

It was near sunset when I arrived at the Thai House, and as I walked along the hedge to the alley, I listened for music, but I couldn't hear anything. I found my path and made my way to my hiding place. Nobody was in the backyard, and I couldn't see any movement in the house.

I waited. I figured that something would happen sooner or later. It had the last few times. I kept watching the windows to see if I could see anyone, but I kept hidden behind the bush. I didn't want the old man or his sons or whomever they are to see me.

At one point I thought I noticed movement in one of the windows where I had seen someone the last time I was there. Whoever it was stood looking out of the window for a few minutes, then left. I waited about ten more minutes. The evening was warm, and it hadn't rained during the day. I felt very comfortable in my little hiding place.

Finally, the back door opened and the Thai woman whom I had been waiting for came outside. She was wearing a different type of costume. She wore a long skirt with a mixture of designs in dark reds, yellows, and oranges, and the upper half of her body was bare except for the gold strip of cloth covering her breasts. She also wore a head dress, but I could see her lovely face.

She had put her music on and had come out into the yard where she had danced before. She stood still for the longest while, staring in my direction. I stared back, and found myself lost, literally lost in time. When she began to slowly move, I realized that I had already thought she had been dancing, with her eyes. She had captured my total attention.

She danced and danced. As the evening passed I felt like I had been given some kind of pleasant drug. The nerves in the back of my neck were tingling, and my body began to feel so languid. I didn't care what was happening to me.

Now I wonder what the hell was happening. But actually I don't really care. Whatever power she has I love it, I thoroughly enjoy it, and that's all that really matters.

Each time she finished one dance, and before she began another, she would stand in her place in some kind of meditation looking in my direction as if she were staring at me. I knew that she knew I was watching her, but I still remained hidden, sitting behind the bush.

This time I was determined to not go to sleep, but as strange as it seems now to me, after a while, after she had danced into the evening, and had lit the lantern, I eventually became drowsy and fell asleep. As she danced, and as I stared at her undulating movements, one minute I was watching her, the next minute I was asleep, sound asleep.

I woke up the next morning right before dawn. As before, a glass bracelet was hanging from the bush, a red glass bracelet with symbols that I could not understand painted on it.

I stumbled out of my hiding place, not a very good hiding place, it seems, and headed downtown.

As I walked, I noticed that I felt good, really good. I seemed to have so much energy. I was amazed at how good I felt. As the day has gone on, I still feel this way. I feel like someone has replaced my generator, and I feel happy to be alive, like I have something to do. All I can say is that she has a powerful dance. What have I stumbled on?

~~ JEROME MIGHT BE FOLLOWING ME

I've been walking around for about an hour trying to find a place to sleep on this side of the river, and right now I'm sitting one block from the downtown Hilton because I think Jerome is following me. Why Jerome would be following me is the question. I have no idea why I would be frightened if he were following me, other than the fact that he won't talk to me. He growls as he sharpens his knives. He's been trained to kill. He's six-foot-five or six and probably weighs over two hundred pounds with no body fat that I can see. Why would I be frightened of Jerome?

I hope I'm wrong about him following me but the bright lights of the hotel sure appeal to me right now.

About an hour ago I thought I saw Jerome a couple blocks behind me. Jerome usually wears a black knit cap on his head and a green army jacket, and since the guy I saw was so huge I thought it had to be him. I decided to wait around and say hello to him to see if I could get him to talk to me. But when I looked back, he wasn't there. I could've sworn I'd seen him. Shaking my head, I continued walking in the direction I had been going. A few blocks away I turned the corner, looked back and could have sworn I saw him again, the same distance behind me. When I looked back, he stepped out of my vision into an alley or entrance way of a building. I couldn't tell.

I started heading toward Broadway where I knew there would be a lot of traffic and hotels and lights. I saw him a couple more times, but he always stepped out of my sight when I turned around. Even if it wasn't Jerome, which I'm sure it was, it was somebody—and I don't like it. I've generally tried to keep a low profile and I imagine I'm invisible a lot. That may sound silly but so far it's kept me from being attacked more often than I have.

I'm getting really tired now though. I've been hanging around the Hilton for about half-an-hour. Just a few blocks west are some places to sleep. I going to take my chances but I'll try to stay in the lighted areas as long as I can.

April 28 ~~ THE GRAND DRAGON BOAT AT THE TREASURE MARKET

Today when I was working at the Treasure Market, Esola came into the room where I was working carrying a replica of a Chinese boat that looked exactly like the one I had imagined so often before I faded out.

Esola said to me, "I thought you might want to see this. We are fortunate to find something so rare. But I think you know that."

Stunned, I looked at the dragon boat and Esola for a few seconds, then managed to ask, "How would I know anything about that kind of boat."

It seemed that it was Esola's turn to be silent for a few seconds. Then she said, "I don't know, I just had the thought you would find this special. Isn't it a beautiful hand-carved replica? So grand! This culture understands the importance of beauty."

"Right now, I'm caught up in how incredible this boat is. The designs on the hull are so intricate. The pagoda-shaped cabin on the deck seems mysterious. It makes me wonder what goes on inside."

"What do you think is happening inside?" Esola asked.

"I would like to know," I said, staring at the pagoda-shaped cabins in the same way I do when I'm in a trance, though I wasn't going into a trance at that moment with Esola standing by me.

She said, "Use your imagination, or your psychic abilities. That's what they are there for, Gibson. I know you are more psychic and imaginative than you let on."

"I don't know what you are talking about, Esola."

"Well, what can I say? It looks like you will just have to keep staring at this cabin from the outside until you wake up." She wasn't saying this in a mean way. She actually smiled at me as she turned to walk away with the boat.

Another mystery for me to figure out.

April 29 ~~ THE HOMELESS CONTINUE TO BE MURDERED

I had a lousy sleep last night. I kept waking up at every sound of someone walking by or talking. Then I realized if Jerome wanted to harm or kill me, I probably wouldn't even hear him coming. As a matter of fact, I was surprised he even let me see him follow me. I talked myself into believing that it wasn't Jerome and that I had imagined someone was following me. I believed it and fell asleep and slept for a few hours more until dawn, but now that I'm awake and more coherent, I feel worried that someone like Jerome might be following me. If it is him, I can't imagine any good reason why he would follow me. I have to believe he's not following. I have to believe that, because I don't think I could cope with having to deal with someone like him tracking me, trying to kill me.

As I walked toward the Holy Skyscraper, Fallacious tried to flash images before my mind of the Butcher attacking me with a huge meat cutting knife as I sleep peacefully under a bush in the park. I was a little confused. I had been thinking about Jerome attacking me so it would have made more sense if Fallacious would have flashed images of a black special forces military man harming me rather than the Butcher. Then I had to admit that I have become so paranoid—scared of everyone. Well, everyone who carries or uses a knife.

There was another murder of a homeless man last night. Same style, hacked brutally. This murder also occurred near downtown. I just read about it in the newspaper. My nights have not been the same since this started but what can I do. I don't want to leave the city. And I don't want to come in from the streets even if I could. I'm a homeless person reading about someone going around killing homeless people. I'm like a frequent flyer who's sitting in an airplane reading about an increase in plane crashes. What can I do? I can't jump out of the plane. Some things you just have to leave in the hands of whoever is messing around with the universe.

I can't go around getting myself so anxious that I wouldn't be able to sleep because I could have another psychological breakdown. I want to continue taking my chances out here on the street. The odds are that I won't be hacked up while I am sleeping but I know I have to be careful about my sleeping places.

April 30 ~~ TWILIGHT BY THE RIVER

Twilight. I've been sitting beside this river for so long today that I've forgotten when and where I'm supposed to be going next. Right now I feel like I'm part of this river. With many different currents all flowing in one direction. I don't want to be forced to flow in only one direction. I want choices. Choices may be the only thing of any value I have left.

My mind continues to have almost no boundaries these days of where and when it goes. I just seem to become a part of things outside myself without any control. Sometimes it's okay, but most often its disconcerting because I feel like I'm losing what little awareness I have of myself, and I get frightened knowing if I let my mind go further it might be gone forever. So I struggle. Like now. I focus on some discomfort to bring myself back to this reality. Like now—I'm thirsty. I need a water fountain to satisfy my thirst and to keep me anchored in myself.

I feel better. I found a fountain in this river park in the downtown area where I'm trying to enjoy the twilight. The Willamette River sparkles with silver and red. I'm awed by the number of bridges extending over the rivers in Portland, like highways to faraway lands. I almost always feel alive and excited being near the river at this time of day.

Now, despite the twilight, I feel so damn emotional, morose, sad, self-pitying, lonely. I want to find a place where there's a feeling of love and acceptance and sharing. In moments like this I know why people put up with meaningless jobs, bankrupt relationships, unhealthy compensating routines and habits—it's because they belong—they at least feel secure.

What do I have? At least I have my inner integrity, even if outwardly I'm seen as a bum and a failure. I'm living, getting sick, getting cold, often hungry, getting sores on my skin. But it's all on my own terms.

I don't know if I would have been able to leave the security of the mainstream slave life if I hadn't been laid off, if my wife hadn't left me, if I hadn't had a psychological breakdown. When a memory fragment of being comfortable in my home invades my mind and catches me off guard I can feel so down, so lost. I can rebound quickly but the feeling of loss remains. I wish I didn't have to remain out here on the street. I wish things were different. I wish going back to a home didn't mean reentering the slave life, didn't mean turning my back on the poor and my infant creative soul. But I am sure, no matter how sad I feel, that I'll never go back.

Despite the pain I feel at times I am still trying to pull memories from the back of my mind—memories that allow me to say at least I've lived some worthwhile moments before my breakdown. But I have a difficult time coming up with memories that can validate my life. What have been my accomplishments? A nine-to-five job with minimal training and promotions as my only career accomplishments. Non-communicative, alienated family relationships. Pushing aside my own personal creative drive. It's all my fault, but how can you grow roses in concrete without first breaking the concrete? I have shattered the concrete around me to pieces and yet the roses haven't had time to grow. I keep looking back to find something to hold on to in this desolate space while waiting for my roses to grow.

Memories. Lately the only memory I dredge up is of an old shed by a bayou. I walk up to it on a hot sunny day, sweat pouring down my back. I'm just wearing blue jeans and old tennis shoes. I'm fourteen years old. I know that inside the shed is an old water jug, and some memories. I can't open the door at first, and when I do, all I can remember is myself walking into darkness. I can't feel the quenching of my thirst or see any other memories.

I've had other memories, but they're so few. It's like my mind says, "Just forget it and try to make the best of the rest of your life." I say to myself that I'm willing to do that. I'm willing to go on, but don't I have anything worthwhile to remember? My mind doesn't answer. At least I haven't yet been able to get an answer. I am willing to go on, but I need to remember something worthwhile from my past. I'll keep trying to look until my eyes get accustomed to seeing in the darkness.

So now what? Twilight is over. I can barely see to write, and now with the beautiful sunset passed, I do feel the cold winds more. I see the night lights all over the city and they have a certain beauty. But now all I can think about is being careful. I have to find a safe, out-of-the-way place to sleep before I get caught, beaten up, stabbed, and killed. And I thought when I became a street person all I had to worry about was the wind, rain, cold and lack of food.

OK, I think I've frightened myself enough. I've frightened myself out of my twilight reverie. I'm going back down into the real world to face the night.

May 2 ~~ THE BAG LADY ATTEMPTS TO MURDER ME AGAIN

I opened my eyes this morning to the bag lady standing over me with a huge knife in her hand, her arm raised, a crazed look in her eyes. I acted instantly, raising my legs toward my chest, the sleeping bag and all still hanging on them, and I kicked at her midsection. She had been bringing the knife down, but it tore into the covers and somehow missed my leg. My kick knocked her on her back. As she screamed obscenities and tried to get up, I kicked off my sleeping bag, grabbed my pack and bag, and before I ran out of the alley, I knocked her back down with a swipe of my bag.

I can't even be philosophical about this anymore. I'm just in shock. I keep coming so close to leaving this life of mine, and somehow I just manage to escape. Maybe I should write a bunch of nice things about the bag lady in a notebook, and give it to her. Yes, maybe that would do some good. I've got to do something about her. I don't want to have to worry about another person killing me in my sleep.

Maybe the Bag Lady really is the homeless killer. She might be, but I think that she only has it in for me. Just me.

Now I feel angry. I should go back and...what? Beat her up? I can't do that. Take her knives away? She'd just find more even if I could take them away. What can I do? I guess all I can do is try to stay away from her, and hide better when I'm sleeping. I feel more helpless and dejected now than angry. I seem so at the mercy of the whims of Fate. I just don't want to die right now. Not before my creative soul grows up.

~~ JUSTINE TALKS ABOUT HER LOVE RELATIONSHIP

Today while I worked at the Treasure Market, I could hear Justine arguing over the telephone with her boyfriend. "No, I can't see you tonight. Chris, I told you that I want to go to this performance alone tonight. We can see each other tomorrow...I told you I am going alone. I'm not going with anyone else and I don't have plans to see anyone else. You know that I can't determine who I might run into...I'm hanging up now. I can't talk to you anymore about this."

Justine hung up the phone, and clenched her hands into fists, shaking her head. "Ohhh, he's so frustrating!" Then she looked at her watch and walked into the next room.

I remember thinking, "Why does she put up with this guy anyway?"

A few minutes later Justine came into the workroom, still angry and fuming, and started complaining to me about her boyfriend.

"Chris is so unstable, so emotionally unstable. So dramatically emotionally unstable. He's so sensitive he's insensitive. Any little criticism or disagreement can throw him into a frenzy. Most of the evening last night I had to deal with him being upset that I didn't come see his dress rehearsal for a new play of his. I just couldn't do it. I had to stay late at the store to see some out-of-town customers. I told him that, but he said he thought I just didn't want to come."

I didn't know what to say. Actually, I didn't think she wanted me to say anything. I'm sure she just wanted someone to listen. And sympathize. I did sympathize. It wasn't difficult to sympathize with Justine. I'm sure she wouldn't have become so angry without a good reason. But I have to admit that for a moment while she was pacing back and forth complaining about Chris, I lost track of what she was saying. I was thinking about how real and beautiful Justine is, just too real, too much flesh and blood, too much here and now. Here she was standing right in front of me sharing her deep feelings. I could have actually reached out and touched her, but that thought brought me crashing back to reality. What good would it do? What harm would it do?

I finally told Justine that Chris seems like a real jerk and asked her why she continued to put up with him. She stopped pacing and stood still for a moment, thinking. Then she said, "I don't know. Actually I do. He has some pleasurable sides. He can be warm and loving. We share some of the same interests. He likes to go to the same restaurants I like to go to. He didn't use to be so possessive. We both know that we probably won't stay together forever. When we first met, he didn't pull these kinds of tantrums. But lately he's just getting more unstable. I don't know what I'm going to do."

"Sounds like a strange relationship to me. Maybe your mother is right."

She turned to me, and I realized I had made a mistake. "What did she say? Did she say that she didn't like Christopher?"

I put my hand to my mouth and shook my head. "I didn't say anything about your mother. Did I say anything about your mother?"

Justine frowned at me for moment. Then she threw up her hands and turned away as she said it was okay. She knew how her mother felt. She said she actually preferred her mother talking to me about her relationship with Chris than to her.

Then, a few minutes later, she admitted that her mother was probably right about Chris. She said that unfortunately her mother seems to feel that marriage is the only outcome for relationships these days.

She said, "I've never been married, much to the consternation of my mother, as you well know. I went through a period when I thought I just didn't know how to pick the right men. But now I know that I have a different way of relating. I don't know if I can explain it. I don't worry about the concept of 'forever'. Yet I feel I'm romantic. I have been with a number of men, but I don't feel I am promiscuous. I believe in commitment. A commitment that comes from the soul, from two souls, minds, emotions, bonding and responding honestly with each other. It might lead to a partnership. It might not." She stopped talking and staring at nothing in particular. I wondered if she were thinking, "I can't believe I am telling all of this to Gibson, a homeless man whom I barely know." But actually she looked back at me and said, "Does all this confuse you…because sometimes I get confused. I believe that relationships should be built on mutual attraction and needs that come from each person's heart, not from some outer structure."

I surprised myself by responding to her. I said, "I've been married, and now I'm not. Right now I don't think I'll ever get married again."

Justine kept looking at me, but now it seemed she was focusing on me. "Gibson, I didn't know you had been married. Of course, I don't know hardly anything about you."

"I like to keep things to myself."

She smiled for the first time. "Well, that's certainly obvious. But have you noticed, Gibson, that you are beginning to share a little more of yourself despite your attempts at secrecy? Have you noticed? I bet soon we'll know everything about you and I'm looking forward to that."

Before I could respond she thanked me for letting her vent her feelings. Then she walked back into the front room, sat down at her desk and started looking through some papers. I went back to my work, mulling over what she had said. She was just teasing because I haven't really shared that much about myself with her. But I'll have to make sure what she said really doesn't happen.

It's been an hour or so after I left the Treasure Market and I can't quit thinking of Justine.

Justine treats me with respect. She even says she's fascinated by me. She calls me "The Homeless Journal Writer." She shares her feelings with me as if we've known each other for years and years.

Justine, I'm trying to see you only as an employer. I can relate to you as being a good boss, maybe even a good person. I can't relate to you as being an attractive female. That would cause my emotions to flip—I catch glimpses, despite myself, of your delicate beauty, of your long neck and chin in profile as you talk on the telephone. I catch glimpses of your lovely dark eyes as you talk to your customers. I catch glimpses of your delightful expressions of wonderment as you unpack your "treasures." And my emotions get caught in these glimpses. I become unable to free myself from the thoughts of you as woman I would like to hold close to me.

These images are all part of your feminine world that I am battling to ignore. You are more than nice to me and in some ways that makes it more difficult. It would be easier if you treated me with formality. I am appreciative that you don't treat me with cold calculation, but I would prefer that you treat me just as an employee. And even more, not as a writer. I wish I could say these things to Justine. I know that I see Justine as a beautiful woman rather than in her encasing as an employer. I try to think of Justine as a benevolent employer. When I become caught by her beauty I try to picture her in an old photograph hanging on the wall of the store, or as a sculpture, a beautiful work of art but not a real flesh and feeling woman with the potential to love.

She said yesterday that she finds it easy to talk with me. I'm a good listener, she says, and somehow I make her trust me. So she says that she feels like she can share things with me that she doesn't usually share with people. She asked me if that was OK?

As I looked into her soft eyes I said yes, that she could tell me what she wanted to, but I was thinking, as long as I don't have to betray myself.

There was something about Justine that made me feel instantly bonded to her when I first met her. As a woman. I think she is attractive, more than attractive. The fact that she is a beautiful, caring and warm woman has everything to do with my feelings. Even though I will not acknowledge it. I can't afford to acknowledge it to anyone. I can't afford to.

She offered to employ me and pay me a few dollars for my work with no strings attached. It was an opportunity to work in an environment that was both familiar and fantastic. The Treasure Market. As a department store sales manager for many years I had work in a sales atmosphere but the atmosphere of the Treasure Market is different. The objects in this store have been created with love and artistry unknown and unseen in most American department stores. Each dark wood chair, each candle holder, each glass item has a history, a story. Justine is the keeper of these treasures.

Lately, with Justine, I'm feeling more relaxed and noticeably less nervous being around her. It's only after I leave that I feel nervous about how I've been feeling. I don't know. It's so complex. I can't quite figure out why I am feeling these things now when so long I didn't.

Maybe I don't have to explain it. So far I've been successful here at diverting my emotions from being focused on Justine. That's what I have to keep doing if I'm going to keep from being drawn into a relationship when I'm not ready.

~~ QUESTIONED BY THE POLICE

I was stopped by the police a few minutes ago. They said they were questioning street people asking for information about the latest homeless men killed. They were trying to uncover any information that might help them in their investigation. They showed me pictures of the men who had been killed and I didn't recognize any of them. I wasn't much help to them. I have no idea who could be doing the killings. When they left me, they told me that I should be staying in a shelter, and that I should stay off the streets at night.

I nodded but didn't say anything. I'm not going to run and hide in a shelter no matter how bad it gets out here in the streets. That's what the goddamn serial killer wants. I'm not going to let him win.

Actually, I do have an idea of who is killing other street people like me. It's an intuition, but I keep thinking I'm right. I think it is the Butcher. Even if it's not the Butcher, in my mind he is the symbol of the killer.

~~ LOOKING INSIDE THE PAGODA CABIN OF THE GRAND DRAGON BOAT

Tonight I watched the Grand Dragon Boat with the glowing amber sails fly away above the city light into the sky. I visualized myself on the deck again standing in front of the door. I walked to the door and again found it was locked. I tried to push the door open, but it would not budge. I looked at the heavy dark wood of the door, and felt the essence of its solidness.

I walked to the window on my left, and looked inside expecting to see nothing, expecting to see darkness that my vision could not penetrate. Instead, I saw a candle lit on a long wooden table. The candle light allowed me to see books, stacks of papers next to drawing instruments—a compass, straightedge ruler and pens. I tried to see other parts of the room, but the darkness would not allow me.

I looked back at the table, and felt drawn to inspecting the papers and books more closely. I thought I heard someone cough, and quickly looked around the room again to see who was in the room—but I could still not see through the darkness. Then my awareness faded away until I woke from my trance.

I realized I'm seeing and remembering more of these visions. I now feel determined to study the papers on the long, wooden table and to penetrate the darkness of the room to find out who is in the room. Maybe then I will be able to find answers to where else my mind goes during these visions.

I thought about the Grand Dragon boat at the Treasure Market. I want to study it more closely soon.

May 4 ~~ WALTER GIVES ME SOMETHING TO HIDE

Sunny spring morning. Spent some time in front of The Holy Skyscraper. I didn't see Queen Avarice today. I felt disappointed but finally got up and started walking toward Burnside Street. I decided not to go east, down to the hardcore wino section by the river, but instead to go toward the northwest.

Before reaching Burnside I ran into Walter. He was sitting by a fountain, mumbling to himself, and didn't see me until I nudged him on the shoulder. He jumped and frantically pulled himself away from me until he saw who I was.

Walter just stared at me for a moment and then said, "You really scared me, man. I thought they were coming after me."

"Who would be coming after you, Walter?" I asked, even though I knew who he meant.

"The aliens," he whispered. "The aliens who know that I know."

When I didn't say anything, he grabbed my arm and asked me to sit beside him. Then he took something out of his shirt pocket and held it clenched in his fist. He grabbed my hand closest to him and put what he had into my palm and closed my hand around it.

"Don't look at it now," he said. "I know they are after this, but they won't know you have it. One of them dropped it before going into one of their meetings. I picked it up and hid behind a car parked on the street. When he noticed that he had dropped it, he and a bunch of others of his kind came out to the street and started looking around. They were very angry and upset, and I was afraid that they would notice me. I decided they would eventually find me, so I started running. One of them noticed me and yelled to the others, and some of them started chasing me. I managed to find a hiding place in the basement of a building, so I was able to get away from them. But I'm afraid they know who I am, and it's just a matter of time before they find me."

"What do you want me to do with this? What is it?" It felt like some kind of small, metal object.

"Just keep it for a few days. Hide it. They won't know you have it. I'll get it back from you when it's safe."

"Look, Walter... what if these people are not aliens, and what if they believe that you stole this... whatever it is?" I held up my closed fist. He pushed my hand down with both of his hands and looked around. "You could be charged with theft and maybe I could."

"No, no—you got to believe me, goddamnit," he said frantically. The thing about Walter, I realized, was that even though what he was talking about was definitely crazy, I had to admit he was still more coherent than he usually has been, even if he was also quite agitated. But then he continued, "These are aliens, and they may be a danger to our world. They may be planning to take over the world. I know people won't believe me. I know I need to get proof. Maybe what I found will be just that object you are holding in your hand. But I'm afraid to keep it with me in case they find me. They don't know about you. I don't think. It will be safe with you."

"Walter, what if these aliens are all-knowing, and now know that I have this object?" It would be just my luck. Not that I believed Walter, but I figured I'd bring it up anyway.

"They can't be all-knowing—they haven't found me yet, have they? Anyway, Gibson, we all have to take some risks," Walter said. "We could be fighting for the survival of our precious way of life."

"What way of life?" I asked. "Our homeless way of life. The American slave way of life. Let them take it over." I held my closed fist for him to take back the object he had given me.

"You don't know what you're talking about," Walter said. "Their way of life may be ten times worse."

"It could be ten times better."

Walter started shaking his head. "No, no. You don't understand. These are horrible beings. They believe in torture and destroying people's minds and souls. Do you think it would be better to live under an alien rule where your mind is controlled by some alien drug or machine so that your body has to obey their every command?"

"Well, sure, I guess our homeless life would be better than having to exist in those conditions, but I don't know. But how do you know these aliens, if they are aliens, are so horrible?"

"I think we have to assume the worst. To remain safe. Please, Gibson, just keep what I've given you for a while. I'm going to go now because I don't think it's safe for you to be seen with me."

After Walter left, I opened my hand and looked at the object. It was a black metal ring that held a large dark glass-like stone. I held it up, and the stone seemed be a dark blue color. I looked closely at the strange metal band and saw inscriptions of some type. I didn't recognize the symbols. I noticed that the metal band had a reddish tint to it.

I suddenly realized how out in the open I was holding the ring, and I quickly put it in my shirt pocket, looking around to see if anyone was watching me. All the pedestrians seemed to be just walking by as preoccupied and oblivious to world around them as usual.

Shit, what was I thinking? Was I thinking that some space alien would be after me? I laughed to myself and got up and started walking toward Burnside again.

I decided not to go up to visit the Thai dancer again tonight. I knew I just wasn't in the mood to appreciate an evening of music and dance. I didn't know what I was in the mood for. The city was laid out for me, but I was shut out of so much. No sense thinking along those lines. I am choosing to be on the outside. I have to be on the outside, and I have to accept this street life for what it is. I realize now that I also felt troubled by having this ring and what Walter was telling me.

At the time I didn't feel like writing either. So I just walked. I walked for most of the afternoon. As evening approached, I found something to eat at a park in the southwest side of downtown. I saw that someone had just thrown away some food after their picnic. By the time I finished my leftover meal in the park, it was getting dark, and I decided to just go find a place to rest.

It was later when I was sitting in the shadows of a doorway to a retail store closed for the evening that I remembered the ring. I reached into my pocket and pulled it out. I looked at the stone closely again. At first I couldn't see much. I leaned over and held the ring up so that the street light could fall onto the stone.

Suddenly I began to see sparkles dancing around in the blue, like tiny stars. In some spots the dark blue seemed to change to a lighter blue. I looked more closely, and began to feel like I was falling into a watery space. It seemed that my mind was becoming liquid.

I don't know how long I was in that state of consciousness. The flashing light of a patrol car startled me, and I huddled back into the doorway. I sat very still, a bit stunned by what I had just experienced. I wondered if Fallacious was doing something to my mind again. The patrol car stopped in front of a building the next block down, and I could see that the patrolmen had gotten out to look at something. I decided it was best that I leave.

I put the ring away and got up to go. Not long after, I found this spot by a building with an air vent that will be my bed for the night. I have been sitting here writing about Walter and the ring. I will look at the ring closer in the daylight hours. I am having a hard-enough time keeping my mind clear these last few months, and I guess I must be very vulnerable to suggestions.

Nighttime is not the best time for me to rely on myself to do clear thinking or to look at what might be an alien ring.

May 5 ~~ AN UNEXPECTED JOURNEY TO ANOTHER WORLD

I'd been trying all day to avoid thinking about this ring I have in my pocket, but earlier this afternoon I finally decided that I needed to look at the dark blue stone again, only this time, to be safe, I decided to do it during the day, in broad day light.

I walked to a small park nearby in the northeast section, south of Burnside street. It was about one o'clock and there were only a few people around. Kids were still in school and the weather was a little overcast, but the light of the day was still bright enough. I walked to one of the picnic tables, sat down, took a deep breath, and pulled the ring out of my pocket.

I leaned back against the table, held the ring up close to me, and looked into the dark blue stone. For a moment nothing happened. But as I kept staring, the dark blue began to surround me, and it was when I began to see lights sparkling and flashing in the dark voids that I vaguely realized I was losing awareness of my surroundings. I somehow managed to lower the ring from my sight, and the light of the day came crashing back to my consciousness.

I was amazed. What was this ring all about? Was this an example of my mind's tendency to fade out? I took another deep breath, moved my shoulders around, and stretched my neck from side to side. I actually felt pretty good. I wasn't feeling any kind of fear. I was feeling more surprised, but I also felt drawn, intensely drawn, to look into the dark blue stone again. I thought to myself, what on earth could happen to me? Here I am sitting on a park picnic table bench. It's just a ring, just a blue stone. But it was exciting. It did seem to have an effect on my mind. An effect that seemed both relaxing and stimulating at the same time. So I asked myself, why not look at it again? Then I thought, how many times am I going to ask that question before I get on with it and look at the goddamn stone again? I tried to laugh at myself as I realized that I was just putting it off.

I leaned back against the table again and stared into the stone. After a while I felt myself being drawn into its space. As I became surrounded by the darkness, I again saw lights sparkling and flashing. They seemed so far away, like stars in a night sky. Then I remember that I began to feel the sensation that I was moving, traveling through the dark space because I began to see lights move in their position in relation to me, and after a while I began to see them flash by me.

I felt exhilarated, excited, totally at ease. I remember that I imagined myself with a smile on my face, and at one point I started laughing. I felt the laughter erupt pleasurably from deep inside me, and it felt so fulfilling. It was like my total body was laughing, and I was feeling so good about everything in the world, everything in the universe.

Eventually I saw a large round shape in the distance. As I moved closer to it, I realized that my movement seemed to be slowing down, slowing down, slowing down. I seemed to be falling right into that round shape, but I somehow knew everything was going to be all right. It was like my consciousness was a zoom lens zeroing in on something. I was being drawn to a large inhabited place with buildings of all different shapes and sizes, but the buildings all seemed linked together, and as I came closer, I realized that rivers and trees and mountains were intertwined within the expanse of buildings in what seemed like a natural landscape.

I continued to flow closer and began to focus on what looked like a large plaza. Only one person stood in the plaza. He looked like a man, but I could not see him clearly, and suddenly my motion stopped.

Once again, I began to slowly drift closer, and for a brief moment I saw that he was smiling at me and waving, waving for me to come closer, come closer, and that's all I remember.

I woke up a few minutes ago with a start. I jumped up and realized that I had fallen asleep on the park bench. The ring had fallen out of my hand and lay on the ground. I stared around me. It was almost dark. A few people were in the park, children were playing on the swings. Some men were playing basketball. A couple was walking their German Shepherd.

I reached down and picked up the ring, and I felt I had to write about what I had experienced right now, before any time had passed. I feel so good. I feel so good. I don't know what the hell this ring is all about. And I don't even care if it's all in my mind. I don't care if it was a psychotic hallucination. It just feels so good!

Maybe Walter is not so crazy after all, but the question that's in my mind is why is he so frightened? Maybe he just doesn't know. Maybe he didn't look closely at the ring before giving it to me. But then again maybe I'm being fooled. Maybe I'm fooling myself. This is just too much. I put the ring back in my pocket, and now I'm hungry. I'm really hungry. I have to think about all of this. I have to find Walter and find out more about these space aliens he thinks he has discovered.

May 6 ~~ FINDING NAOMI'S RED PURSE AND UNEXPECTED AWARDS

Yesterday early in the evening I was sitting on a bus-stop bench downtown on Washington and 6th Street to rest for a few minutes, and I noticed a red suede purse was tucked in the crack between the seat and the back of the bench. Nobody was sitting on the bench, which is why I sat down there in the first place. I left the purse sitting on the bench for a few minutes and looked around to see if someone nearby would be coming to retrieve it. It would be just my luck that I'd pick up the purse and some screechy woman who had been looking in a shop window would rush back to the bench and scream that I was robbing her.

My curiosity finally got the better of me, so I reached over, picked up the purse, and looked inside. I found a small handgun, which, despite my shaky hands, I carefully determined was loaded. I found a wallet with credit cards—Visa, American Express, charge cards for a number of department stores. No money, except a little change, which was a relief so that my honesty would not be tempted in my present state of hunger. I found an address book full of names and phone numbers, and I found a tag on the inside on the purse on which had been written, "If anyone finds this notify me at immediately, and I will give you a reward you won't forget." A telephone number was written at the bottom of the tag, and below that was a signature of "Naomi."

I called the number and Naomi answered. I told her I found her purse, and I heard her scream over the phone, "Thank god! Thank god!" She asked me to bring it right over. After she gave me her address, she told me which busses to take. I said that I would be there as soon as I could. I didn't ask her if she would be giving me a reward for bringing her purse back to her, but I figured, what the hell. I'd get a free bus ride and would be doing a good deed. Besides, I had always tried to discount good fortune until I knew it really was going to be good fortune. I had always found life to be so undependable that I didn't like getting my hopes up. I hated to be this way. I wished I could say that I am a hopeful person, that I believe in good luck, that I believe in people, but I have always felt the tools of persuasion used by the rich royalty were too strong and most slaves' resolve to become thinking, caring humans was too weak. I still believe this way a little, but I have to say that I have just experienced a big ray of sunshine and hope, and it has done my heart good.

I used the change in Naomi's purse and bought a transit ticket. I followed her directions, and eventually I stood in front of a tall condo, rather fancy looking, with balconies, a water fountain in front of the curved driveway, and a doorman inside the entrance. I walked up and told the doorman I wanted to see Naomi. He looked at me with a frown on his face and shook his head as he picked up the telephone. As he talked with her I could tell that he was a bit surprised at how enthusiastic she must have sounded. The arrogant bastard. I can't stand the rich and famous Masters looking down on us who have nothing, but I especially get upset when their servants also think they are so much better than we are.

He showed me the elevator to use, and I waited patiently in the elevator as it climbed to her floor. It was unusual and at first a little uncomfortable for me to be surrounded by the elevator mirrors and to be forced to look at myself from a variety of angles. I looked a little scroungy. Quite a bit scroungy. My face looked clean, sort of. I had a black streak right below my left ear, extending under my cheek. I couldn't remember how I got that. I tried to rub it off, but that only made it worse. I was wearing a long black wool coat that the attorney had given me, which didn't look too bad, but my old black shoes were scuffed and muddy. They really gave me away. My blue jeans and brown button shirt were also old and faded. By the time the elevator got to the right floor I had to admit I looked more than a little scroungy. I tried to tell myself that I looked presentable in a rugged, down-to-earth way. I could have just come back from a camping trip to South America or Africa.

I walked out into the hallway and was stunned by the elegance of the chandeliers, the carpet, the dark wood tables, and huge plants. I made my way along the hallway looking at the paintings that hung on the walls wondering where I had been transported to. I finally found her apartment, and rang the bell.

I didn't know what I expected, but the woman who opened the door was like something out of Vogue or one of those other women's magazines. She stood there for a moment looking me up and down. I probably would have been self-conscious, except that I think that I was also looking her up and down. She was wearing some kind of sparkly, black, see-through blouse, no bra. Tight black pants. No shoes. The first thing I noticed about her face, besides her fiery short red hair, was the expression of her eyes. She was one of the most beautiful women I have ever seen.

"You have my purse?" she finally asked.

I reached in my pack, pulled it out and gave it to her. It was like I had handed someone a million dollars or a long-lost treasure. She took the purse, closed her eyes and held it to her chest like she was thanking some higher being. She opened her eyes and smiled a warm, thankful smile at me. Her eyes became so happy. She took my hand and asked me to come in. She closed the door and then I followed her through the foyer into her living room, which seemed like the sitting room of some exotic palace in Africa. The room was decorated with dark reds and purples, browns and yellows, with plenty of large green plants sitting in brass or brightly colored clay pots. The room looked like a fiery sunset in a place where a desert and jungle met. A mirror extended the length and width of the living room wall opposite us. We could see each other standing, talking. I found myself looking back and forth between the mirror image of us and the real her, still a little disconcerted at having to deal with the multiple reflections and images of my surroundings. Besides, I had never before seen so much of myself in such a short period of time.

The two sofas in her living room were huge and plush, brown, with red and purple pillows. A camel-colored rug stretched in front of the couches. Adjoining the living room was a dining room with a glass window that served as a wall and looked out over the city.

After looking through her purse she turned to me and said that she wanted to give me a reward. I smiled at her, thinking that ten or twenty dollars would allow me to have a nice breakfast tomorrow and maybe buy a better pair of shoes at the Salvation Army.

She looked at me with a slight smile and a mischievous expression, and said, "Your choice. Five hundred dollars or the best fuck you've ever had."

I must have looked like I had gone into shock, because she reached out and touched my arm and said, "Are you okay?"

I managed to tell her I was okay, it was just that I hadn't expected either that amount of money or…that choice. I looked at her to see if she would start laughing at me and then tell me it was all a joke, but instead she said that this offer would not seem so unusual if I knew more about her and if I knew how valuable the address book in her purse was to her.

I nodded as she spoke, but inside my feeling of shock was giving way to a tremendous dilemma. I thought to myself that $500 is a hell of a lot of money for anybody, but especially for someone in my condition. Yet I have been without money for so long anyway. $500 might disrupt my rhythm, might corrupt me, make me regress, take me back to the edge of society and then leave me hanging. Yet I could do a lot with $500 dollars. Get my teeth cleaned and fixed. Buy that good pair of shoes.

I looked at her and realized she had been standing there staring at me, waiting for my answer. I looked at her image in the mirror and was struck by how beautiful and sexy she was. It had been a long time since I had felt the touch of a woman, made love to a woman. I turned back and smiled at her and said, "This is a hell of a difficult decision to make. Mind if I sit down and think about it."

"Sure. Go ahead. Make yourself comfortable. Take all the time you want."

She sat in a chair across from me. "You know I usually charge most of my customers $500 just to do a hand job, but as I said, I'm really thankful for what you did. You brought me back my list of customers. I was really stupid to take it out of my condo, but I was afraid I was going to be raided, and I had to leave in a hurry. Thank god, the tipoff was wrong, but I wasn't thinking straight, and I just left my purse at that bus stop. I don't usually ride buses either, and that could have been the problem. I was just out of my usual routine and really worried. But everything is all right now. You are such a sweet man to bring this back to me."

I looked at myself again in the mirror. I seemed so out of place and I had this perplexed expression on my face. Suddenly everything about the whole situation seemed funny to me. Why was I taking it so seriously? I looked down at the rug, smiling to myself and thinking that I should just choose one or the other and get on with it. Instead I looked at her and said, "How about $300 and just an average fuck?" I don't know where that idea came from.

Naomi laughed and thought for a moment before she answered. Then she said, "Maybe. Let me consider it. I tell you what, while I'm thinking it over, why don't you go clean yourself up. No matter what decision I make, you look like you could use a shower."

How come every time I get anywhere near the slave world the first thing a person does is tell me to take a shower? Is a shower the initiation ritual to slave life? Do you have to be squeaky clean to be able to participate in mainstream life? On the other hand, I do enjoy showers, the warm water running over my body. I really didn't want to make showers a negative symbol of the world's tendency toward sterile lifelessness. So I agreed.

The bathroom was spectacular. It had a huge sunken bathtub, a large shower stall with benches, a sauna, and a massage table. The tile on the floor was white but the fixtures were black and gold-plated. She showed me into the bathroom, handed me a towel and razor, and left. I noticed she didn't close the door. I stood there thinking about that for a few seconds. I finally left the door open and started taking off my clothes.

I shaved and then walked to the shower stall, which was almost as big as the rest of the bathroom. I stepped inside and closed the door. While I showered I thought of my counter offer, and before I was through I had changed my mind numerous times. Take the money. Take the fuck. Oh god, what a choice. I not only thought she was extremely attractive, I just liked her. I know that I didn't know her all that well, and given her profession I may not be seeing the real her, but it seemed to me that she was being real. And I liked what I was seeing. Her body, her damn sexy body, but also how she was. She seemed so spontaneous, so warm.

As I dried myself with a large, soft towel, I could hear music in the background, a sensual jazz instrumental. It was nice. It was definitely getting me in the mood for something. After I finished drying myself, I turned to find that my clothes were not there. I looked in the closet and drawers, but found only towels and toilet articles. I wrapped the towel around me and walked into the hallway leading to the living room. As I neared the living room, I noticed that the lights had been turned off and on the walls I could see the flickering shadows from what I figured were candle flames.

When I turned the corner into the living room, Naomi sat at the round dining room table with a clear glass top. Behind her the night lights of the city sparkled. Two tall candles were lit and standing in elegant candle-holders on the table. She also had two wine glasses on the table. And she was completely naked. She had created a breathtaking scene.

"Please join me for a glass of wine," she said, holding her glass up.

I stood for a moment just enjoying how beautiful and sexy she looked. I wished I had a picture of this. It would be a work of art. Her curvaceous, luscious body with her red hair, and her generous, playful expression would be the focal points of this art piece. At least I know that I will have that image as a part of my eternal memory somewhere in my mind.

I finally remembered that she had asked if I wanted to share a glass of wine with her. "I would like very much to share a glass of wine with you," I said, and started across the living room.

"You don't need that towel covering your body, unless it makes you feel more comfortable," she said.

"I guess you're right," I agreed, and let the towel drop. "It's just that I am not used to being this uninhibited."

"You don't look so uninhibited," she said as she looked at my erection. "Besides, inhibitions are the cause of all of society's illnesses. Did you know that?"

"No, I didn't, but right now I think I would almost agree with anything you say."

"With almost anything I would say? I wonder what you would disagree with me about. That makes me curious." We looked at each other for a while, and sipped our wine.

Finally, she set her wine glass down, and said, "I've thought about your counter offer to my proposal about the choice of rewards. I've decided to not agree to the counter offer. I'm not into negotiating this reward. You have to choose one or the other." I noticed that she had an envelope of money sitting by her glass of wine.

I remember thinking that she had a deep undercurrent of power and resolve that she seemed to be able to just bring to the surface of her idyllic face with no forewarning. I looked into her eyes and without as much as a glimmer of hesitation I told her to put the money away.

She smiled, took the envelope and tossed it on the kitchen counter to her right and behind her. "I think you have to be more than just horny to turn down $500. I think you have to be a romantic, which means you must find me attractive, and I am excited by that. I try to make all of my customers feel special, but many men don't know how to respond to true romance or emotion. Most of the men I deal with don't have time for romance. It might be nice to spend time with someone who can appreciate romance and has the time."

"I do have time," I said. "That's about all I have, but I have plenty of it."

Naomi did take her time, and we spent most of the night together. I have never been with such an uninhibited, sensual, and sexual woman. Perhaps my life is complete now. Perhaps I can die knowing that I have experienced the most complete satisfaction that this life has to offer.

As I think back about it now, I realize that this experience with Naomi was like my street life in that it had nothing to do with day-to-day slave reality that most people experience. It was like walking into a movie, a long passionate movie that climaxed in pure sexual pleasure and sharing and then…the movie ended, and I walked out, knowing that someone else would be playing there the next night, knowing that I could never be able to go back there and see the same movie, or get the same experience. I had nothing to hold onto but the memory of this beautiful lovemaking and the sharing. And as I walked out I did know that I would remember what I had experienced, what we had shared. Thinking back now, I feel like maybe she healed me a little bit. I don't know, it sounds crazy to me, but I feel so much better about people, about life, about everything. I have a little more hope that things might one day be different for me. Perhaps I could get the same experience with someone else. Perhaps the world could become a better place to live.

Leaving this encounter with these expectations is probably the one aspect about being with Naomi that could cause me trouble in the future. But it was fulfilling and it was fun, and I liked being close to someone else. Even if it was just for a night. It feels to me like Naomi and I shared more than just a fuck, and I like that feeling even if it may not be true. It felt like we reached a place of loving where I have been shut off from for most of my life. Shut off by all the hypocritical and unnatural rules and regulations of our uptight society. Shut off by my buying into these rules at an age when I couldn't have known any better, but somehow did. I knew deep down that the path I was following was not the path for me, but I didn't know how I could do things differently.

I told her some of these things during our time together. Naomi listened and I felt that she understood what I was saying. At one point she asked me how I could stand living the way I do, out on the street, with nothing but what I carry around in my bags. She said it would seem awfully lonely to her. I told her I didn't have a choice, and explained my breakdown to her. I didn't tell her about what I was carrying around inside of me, what I was protecting. I just said that I considered living on the street to be better than the slave life I had to endure just to have a place to sleep in with four walls and a roof.

"I sort of know what you mean," she said. "I come from a wealthy family out east. I've never been without money, but when I was quite young, I had terrible disagreements with everyone in my family, and I ran away. I couldn't stand what they wanted me to be, and they wouldn't listen to what I wanted to be. I certainly didn't plan on being a high-priced call girl at the time. But at least now I'm here doing something I enjoy, and making money for myself. So you don't have to live on the street to be yourself."

"I do. At least for now. But Naomi, how can you sell your body to men?"

"I don't just sell my body to men," she said smiling. "Quite a few women come to me, too."

"OK, then how can you sell your body to anyone."

"I don't like doing this all the time and I don't want to do this forever but I believe I do a valuable service for people. I don't go in for any violent sexual crap. If a man wants to do that, I throw him out. Men are the only ones so far who want to be violent. As crazy as this might seem, I really do try to reach out to my customers. I try to give them a little more than just a good fuck, even though giving a good fuck does a great deal of good for people."

"Come on, Naomi. People who come to you aren't thinking of anything but getting laid, having an orgasm."

"More people than you realize want more than that. They have an idea in their mind that they just want sex, but they don't argue with me when I give them more. People want to be touched. They want someone to think they are special without any conditions. Who doesn't want this, and why shouldn't I get paid for doing this? I don't think I'm just selling my body, or maybe I wouldn't be doing it. Or maybe I still would." She smiled.

"If it's true what you're saying I think you'd be unusual."

"That's why I get paid a lot. And I tend to have regular customers who come to me from all over the world. But let me tell you a secret. Since you are a street person you might appreciate what I am about to tell you. I decided a while ago that I needed to give something back to the community; I needed to give to charity. So I give a lot of free fucks to people who can't afford me."

I laughed, which was a mistake. An expression of hurt flashed across her face and she told me that this meant something to her.

But I told her it sounded funny. Free fucks for charity.

She smiled then and shook her head. "It really is important to me though. And I have quite a few people I see who are disabled, and who could never afford me and who have never experienced sexual expression before I've been with them. You just can't imagine the loneliness some of the severely disabled feel." Tears came into her eyes.

I reached out to her and pulled her close to me. "I have never really thought about that, the sexual needs of someone who is disabled. It's amazing to me how much we're programmed to think in certain ways. You may also have a special talent of shattering people's programmed thinking. You sure have shattered mine, and I thought my programmed thinking not only had already been shattered, but that all the pieces had dissolved. Anyway, I think what you are doing is special."

I slept for a few hours in her bed, the first bed I had slept in for months. Then she woke me up and asked me to leave. She said she would like to see me again, but she was moving to Paris as soon as she could. She said that even though she wasn't raided, she didn't want to take any chances. She said that most of her paying customers have the money to come see her in Paris anyway.

Sometime after I left her, I found that she had put the envelope with $500 in my pack and she had written the following note to me: "I think you could use this money, and from the beginning I intended to offer you both, but it seemed like a good idea at the time to make it a choice. No matter what you had chosen I would have given you the other, too. It made me feel good that you made the choice you did, and it made me feel good being with you. I hope you survive your street life and can get to a place where you can live life comfortably. You are a nice man. Love, Naomi."

May 7 ~~ GETTING RID OF A SOURCE OF CORRUPTION & GREED

I just spent a tiny portion of the $500 on a good meal. I think I'll buy me a good pair of shoes. Then I could donate the rest to a homeless shelter. Even if I don't want to stay in shelters, they do help a lot of women and children. Money like this could damage what is really important in me but is still so weak. I have to live on the street, even though I wish I had a choice. I wish our society was the type that would encourage each person's specialness rather than trying to fit everyone into a role that crushes uniqueness. Our society is corrupt like acid burning out the layers of spontaneity and then burning deep down into the soul of each person, burning each person's special spirit. Only a few can survive. I am determined to survive. I have just met another survivor, and I feel hopeful today. I do not feel so lonely.

Anyway, I finally decided to give the rest of the money to Charlie and Louise. It's not all that much, but maybe they could use it to go back to New Orleans, or at least make their life a little better here. Maybe he could afford to see a doctor. I think there is a free clinic I can go to, get my teeth cleaned.

I found Louise where they usually hang out near the freeway fields, and she was so surprised and thankful. She said that perhaps she might be willing to reconsider going back to New Orleans. With a huge smile on her face she said she wanted to find Charlie and show him the money.

~~ ESOLA AND JUSTINE NOTICED A CHANGE IN ME

I just went back to the Treasure Market to finish a job I had started a few days ago at Esola's, and damned if she didn't say that she noticed I was changed in some way. I seemed less uptight to her, less self-contained. I looked at her, shook my head, and said "What are you talking about, Esola? Nothing has changed."

Damned if she didn't then say, "You look like you have been with a woman."

I looked over at Justine, who had glanced up from her papers at that comment, and was looking at me. She raised her eyebrows in a questioning manner and smiled.

I turned back to Esola. "How could you tell if I had been with a woman? No, I haven't been with a woman."

"Come on, Gibson," Esola responded. "That's nothing to be ashamed about. You need to have a little fun in life. You need to join life a little."

"Leave him alone, Mama," Justine said, still smiling at me. "Some things should be private."

They both went back to work as I continued to deny that I had been with a woman. I realize now that if Justine would not have been there, I might just have admitted to Esola that she was right -¬that I had been with a woman last night and it was wonderful. But for some reason I felt uncomfortable saying that in front of Justine. Damn Esola's psychic abilities.

~~ DOES ESOLA HAVE PSYCHIC ABILITIES?

A few hours later I was still working in the backroom, watching Justine doing her work in the main room, and I felt this urge to go talk with her. I realized that I felt like still being with a woman, talking with a woman and Justine is someone who I can talk with, even if there is nothing romantic between us. Justine makes me feel comfortable.

I sat my cleaning rag down, and walked into the main room, trying to think of something to talk about. Esola came to mind.

"Justine, I have something I want to ask you," I said. She looked up from the papers she was working on at her desk. She seemed so open and willing to give her whole attention to me. "Is your mother psychic?"

Justine smiled, and looked away for a moment, as if trying to decide. She finally said, "Sometimes I think she is. She has had amazing premonitions. It's like she has access to some pool of knowing that transcends place and time. She can read people amazingly well. When I was younger I would get angry at her and tell her that I didn't want to hear her psychic feelings about my new friends, especially my boyfriends. It's one thing to have a mother who is always pressuring you to marry—it's another thing to have a mother who says that she can tell what a person is like after she first meets them. It takes all the mystery out of discovering who a new person is.

"After I got a little older, I realized that it didn't have to take the mystery out of meeting a new person. I learned from someone else that psychic perceptions are still only potentials. That nothing is written in stone in future time. That all future realities can be changed depending on the consciousness of the individual. I liked that explanation. It helped me accept my mother's special abilities."

"I don't know what to think," I said. "I guess I have always felt that it is possible for someone to be psychic, but I never really met anyone, except kooks who said they were psychic."

"Are you saying my mother is a kook?" she teased.

"No, no. She may be the first person I've met who truly is a psychic. And not a kook."

"Well, be careful. The knowledge that she can give you carries a lot of responsibilities."

"What do you mean?"

"The more you know about yourself. About your potentials. About the future, the more you have a responsibility to not misuse that knowledge."

"Who's going to be the judge," I said, feeling a little uneasy.

She laughed and said, "Esola. She is really hooked onto you. She really believes you have an important destiny."

"Oh, god," I said. "I enjoy Esola, but I just can't meet up to her expectations."

"Just enjoy her and forget about her expectations. I have learned to do that, mostly. But let me ask you something, Gibson. Do you ever show anyone what you write in your journals?"

"No, I don't. I consider what I write very private."

"You mean you are not writing stories or poems or plays?"

"No, definitely not. I just write about what I do each day, and I try to record my thoughts and feelings about things, that's all."

"Private journals can be very powerful expressions. I can understand that when a person writes a journal or a diary that they might at first need for it to be private. But then, especially if the person is a writer, I guess I think that what goes on in a person's private thoughts can be very meaningful to others. It seems like such writings could help others understand conditions and experiences that they would not otherwise be able to understand. Do you know what I mean?"

"I do understand what you mean. But my writings are just very personal and I think I need to keep them private right now.

"If you do ever write something, like a description or a poem or something, I'd love to read it. That is, if you wouldn't mind me reading it."

"No, I wouldn't mind," I said, wondering why was I agreeing to something that I have no intention of doing. I have no intention of writing a poem or story or anything for others, but I guess if I did write something like that, I'd be willing to show it to Justine.

"By the way, Gibson. I talked to the astrologer and she will have your chart done probably in a week or two. She's been really backed up, and she's doing this one as a favor to us."

"That's great, I guess." I said.

"I understand you may not be that excited about it now, but I think you will get something out of it."

"I'll take your word for it. I am a bit curious."

"I am, too." Justine tilted her head, looked at me and studied me for a moment.

"Maybe we will be able to learn some secrets about our mystery employee."

"I have no mysteries," I said, feeling torn between wanting to protect myself and wanting to respond to something in Justine's expression. I began to feel a little disoriented. "Well, I guess I better get back to work so I can finish this project." I turned toward the backroom.

"Gibson," Justine said. I stopped and turned back. "You know this is the first time you've just come up and talked with me. You do seem so much more relaxed and willing to share a little of yourself. I hope you do it more."

I nodded and went back to work, feeling emotionally satisfied. Being in her presence gave me another emotional boost. Only now that I am alone, back down in the old industrial section, and have allowed myself to experience some sharing, and have felt so good, I have to also allow myself to get back to my street reality—to go through the drenching of self-pity and depression so that I get back to my normal lonely self. I have to remain alone, but damn it feels good being around a lovely woman.

One thing I do feel is more alive. Somehow I don't feel as depressed as I thought I would. I don't feel like I am going to go right out and get into a relationship, but having been with Naomi, and just my brief talk with Justine has made me feel alive, more capable of sharing intimately with a soul mate. I don't know what I'm going to do with this new feeling of aliveness, but I have it. Now I'm just going to have to wait and see if I do get more depressed than I've ever felt before. When you get too high up, you run the risk of falling down far and hard.

May 10 ~~ RANSACK'S SCARY SAGA

Earlier today I was sitting with Ransack by the river looking over at the tall buildings of the downtown. I had run across Ransack while walking up near Burnside Street and Sandy Avenue, and he asked if I had time to talk. I knew it wasn't really a question and I knew he didn't want us to talk, but for me to listen to him and to write down more of his story. I figured, what the hell, it would pass the time. I had nothing else on my schedule. Except to stay alive.

"Believe it or not I had never been to Portland before I quit the special forces," Ransack told me. "I had been to and through Seattle often and to and through San Francisco, but never to Portland, Oregon. I don't know why? Just a fluke. Others of the gang had been here. So I wanted to check this city out after I quit because it was one of the locations that was outside my personal history.

"The instant I got here I knew that it was the right place for me to stay. It didn't have the kinds of things I was used to, the hardened, scrappy street people or the run-down areas of chaos, like you find in D.C., New York, Chicago.

I recognized that Portland did have a kind of urban freshness and naïveté that could easily be taken advantage of and manipulated for my survival. I mean, Portland is so upscale clean, it almost made me puke at first. I thought, where's the trash? Where's the street violence that can erupt from racism? Then I realized that I could still use this atmosphere for my advantage. People trust so much more here in Portland than in the cities in the east or in LA. And the gangs are so unsophisticated, almost soft, unless they come from these other places.

"Even though everything seemed so peaceful I knew there was still some violence here. Situations of destruction, outbursts of frustrations, drug-related and cult-related robberies, mutilations and deaths—all these wonderful human behaviors were here underneath the pretty urban renewal facades, and I knew I could use these behaviors and the chaotic, disruptive situations they caused to disguise whatever activities I needed to do for my survival, just like I had always used when I was working for the Special Forces."

"But I have to admit, I have come to enjoy Portland and the surrounding areas, like the coast and the mountains. But what I was really surprised about was how close Portland is to Eastern Oregon which kind of reminds me of the sparse and arid lands of the Southwest where I grew up. I know it may sound out of character a person like me would be able to enjoy Portland.

"I don't know what the phrase, 'out of character' means these days," I said. "I think so many conflicting points of view and realities exist in this world that I don't think we can help but become mutated in our minds, mutated in our characters."

"Mutated in our minds ..." Ransack repeated, looking thoughtfully at the wide Willamette River. Then he looked at me, smiling, and said, "I like that. That helps me explain a lot of my weird thinking. I'm just mutated in my mind as a result of my upbringing and the training I received in the jungles of Panama. I like that."

Mutations of the mind. I don't like it but what can I do about it? Maybe try to take control of the mutations and create something positive. Ransack certainly isn't a positive mutation, and I realized how difficult it is becoming for me to listen to him. I suddenly felt this need to get up and get away from him. I looked at him and told him that I just remembered that I had told my employer that I would help move some furniture today. I didn't want to tell him where I worked. I told him that I would try to find him later.

Ransack grabbed my arm and said, "Wait a minute. I haven't told you the story I wanted to tell you. Your employer can wait, can't he?"

It wasn't really a question. Again, the look in his eyes made me sit down quickly. "Yes, I suppose my employer can wait," I said.

And I waited. Waited for him to begin his story but he just sat there staring at me. I couldn't figure out why and I was becoming more and more uneasy. I thought that maybe I had crossed some line, and he was about to pounce on me. At that moment Fallacious made Ransack appear before me as the lion he had described himself as being. I have never sat that close to a lion and I was really getting myself psyched up to jump up and try to run away.

But he finally spoke, "Aren't you going to open your notebook?"

I realized that I had just been sitting there with my journal closed and he wanted me ready to write before he was going to begin his story. When I was ready with my journal and pen in hand, he sat back on the bench and seemed to relax. He finally started the story he wanted to tell me,

"Those first days in Portland were difficult, but eventually I began to set up my daily survival routines. You know, I don't spend all my time in the freeway fields.

"I was only in Portland a month before I met this beautiful, forty-year old woman who was married to a rich rancher just on the other side of Mount Hood. When I met her she had come into Portland for the weekend and was staying at one of the fancy downtown hotels. I was on the street by the hotel late one afternoon, I saw these two punks standing by a Mercedes. I knew what they were going to try to do before they did it. They were going to try to strip the lock and steal the car. I walked up to them and knocked their fuckin' heads together. I took away their lock-stripping tool and broke one of their little fingers, just one little painful finger each, just to try to discourage them from further criminal activity, and I sent them on their way, howling and crying. Pitiful examples of the male gender."

I didn't look up from my journal. I didn't want to acknowledge the account of his cruelty. And I couldn't quite understand how Ransack defines criminal activity or who should be allowed to do it or what makes criminal activity justified.

He continued, "There I was, standing by this light blue Mercedes, admiring it, thinking, shit, I might even like to steal it myself. It had been so long since I had driven a Mercedes. About this time, Ellen Steele—that's her name—Ellen came out of the hotel and walked to the car. She saw me staring at it and asked me what I was doing standing there looking at her car. The instant I saw her I knew I that we would be fucking later that night. I could see wildness in her eyes. I looked at her tall, well-shaped body and at her wavy sandy hair falling down below her shoulders, longer than my hair. I looked into the wildness in her eyes and I told her that I just saved her Mercedes from being stolen by a couple of punks and felt like I deserved being bought dinner. I handed her the lock stripping tool.

"She took the lock stripping tool, then took her car keys out of her purse, and opened the passenger door to the Mercedes. Finally, she said to me, 'I was just wondering how to entertain myself tonight. I'm very much looking forward to hearing how you saved my Mercedes. I like heroes. I like tough men. I can't find enough of them.'

"Sure enough, we ended up fucking all night. During the next few months, each time she came to Portland I'd stay with her. Everything was going just fine. But one day she asked me to come to the ranch with her. She explained she told her husband, Bill Steele, that she had met a man who knew a lot about training horses and who she'd like to introduce to him. Apparently Bill had been looking for someone to train some of his wild horses. And Ellen told me that she wanted me to be able to come around the ranch from time to time when she couldn't get into Portland. She said that her husband was twenty-five years older than her and let her do anything that she wanted just to keep her around.

"She was right. That very day she drove me out to the ranch and introduced me to her husband. She told him that I had just moved up to Portland from New Mexico where I had trained horses for ranchers in the area. She talked him into hiring me to break his wild horses whenever I had the time. I told him that I could come out to the ranch every week or so and he told me that if I wanted to stay overnight I could sleep in a room in one of his guest houses. He didn't seem to care what I was doing in Portland or how I had met his wife or anything. He just seemed to want to get the arrangements over as quickly as possible and get on with what he had to do.

"Let me tell you, Gibson, Bill Steele was a cruel man. It takes a cruel man to know a cruel man, but at least most of my cruelty—nd I say most, because I know that I am not perfect—" he laughed, and nudged me. I tried to smile. "No, I'm certainly not perfect...anyway, most of my cruelty has been done for a good cause. For our country and for the power brokers behind our government. And I've usually tried to be quick when I had to kill, unless I had to get some information from someone, but that's another matter."

I thought to myself, "Yes that's another matter. Torture...Another matter altogether. You bastard."

"Bill Steele's cruelty seemed to be for no purpose. He hired Hispanics, most of them illegal aliens to work on his ranch, and he treated them with such cruelty that it even got under my skin. He'd hire them, starve them, not give them the proper medical care, and work them long and hard. When some of them would just drop dead from exhaustion or sickness or starvation, he would have a doctor come out and legitimize the deaths, and then he would have them buried somewhere on his land.

"But I had a good thing going there. He was gone often, and I had a full run of his stables and his bedroom. It was very nice. But I became more and more pissed off at the way he was treating his workers. I mean, I'm not a saint, but I don't like to see people hurt or killed without a purpose. I just don't get off on hurting people just to hurt them. And I have never been a racist. Again I'm not trying to paint myself as a saint, but since I'm telling you my story, I might as well emphasize some of the good parts of me.

"Every time I was around this bastard though, he'd talk about his cheap labor and complain about the government trying to limit his ability to hire illegal aliens. He complained that there are not enough white Americans willing to do the real work, the hard work, the shit work, and that employers like him needed the poor Mexicans and Asians, who were willing to work for almost nothing.

"Well, you know, Gibson, I just got to hate this guy. I don't know why it bothered me so much that he was cruel to his cheap labor. I certainly wasn't jealous of him. I still can't figure out why he bothered me so much. Maybe you can sort that one out when you get to know me better.

"Anyway, I thought about killing the bastard out right, but I felt like it would raise too many questions. One day, though, I was working in the barn, replacing some rotten boards in one of the stalls and I heard Bill yelling obscenities at someone. I looked out of the stall in between the boards, and saw Bill chasing a young Hispanic man. I saw the poor young man run toward the doors of the barn but when he got there, he found that they had been chained shut. He turned around, and crouched with his back against the doors, frightened, not knowing what to do.

"Bill had stopped running, and was strutting toward him carrying a bull whip. I watched as he swung the tip of the bull whip at the man, and with a crack, caught him on the side of his face. The man screamed, as he grabbed his face and fell to his knees. Bill swung the whip around again and with another crack, caught the man on neck below his ear. The man screamed again, and still on his knees, fell back against the doors.

"This was just too much for me to take. I couldn't stand there and let this bastard whip this poor man. He probably had just stolen some food for his starving family. Whatever he had done I felt that he didn't deserve to be whipped. So I walked out of the stall, walked up behind Bill, grabbed his head with my hands and snapped his neck. It happened quickly, perhaps too quickly. I should have let him experience a little pain. The young man just stayed on his knees, shocked, staring at his dead employer.

"Now I knew that there would be a problem for me if I let the only witness to this murder live, so for the sake of all the other Hispanics and for my own protection, I killed the young Hispanic, too, so he couldn't identify me."

Shocked, I jumped up and yelled, "What?"

Ransack laughed and said, "No, No, Gibson, I didn't really kill the Hispanic. I just wanted to see if you were listening. Hey, it's good that you are able to tell the difference between a good killing and a bad killing. If there is a moral to this story that could be it. Don't be so quick to judge a killer. He might be killing for a good reason. Now sit back down. Take it easy." I slowly sat back down. "You know, during my training I was taught that good killing is the backbone of law and order and a successful government's foreign policy. But anyway, I didn't tell you this story for the goddamn moral. I'm almost finished. Keep writing.

I began writing again as he continued his story. "Everyone around the area knew how horrible Bill Steele had been so the police figured that some Hispanic had killed him, but they didn't know which one since all of the Hispanics hated Bill so much. Ellen used some of her financial influence and smoothed things over with the police so that there wouldn't be a huge investigation. Of course, she wanted to avoid problems with the illegal aliens working on the ranch.

"By the way I never told Ellen that I had killed her husband but I think she suspected it. It didn't really matter to her. She saw marriage as a business arrangement anyway. As a matter of fact, she went right out and within a few months married another older man, a banker, who is worth millions. But she still wants to see me from time to time. She says I bring out that wildness I see in her eyes. And I like the arrangement because I can ride horses whenever I want to…and her." He sniggered and nudged me before he continued. I just kept writing. "Sometimes I wonder if it's Ellen or her horses that keeps me involved with her.

"I wanted to tell you this story so you could have a well-rounded picture of me. Since I've left the secret government forces, I think I am learning to enjoy other things in life even though I have to resort to using my old skills from time to time. My relationship with Ellen is the most regular one I've ever had. And I have access to her ranch without all the hassles of owning or running it. What more can a retired man ask for?"

And that was his story. How he seduced a woman, killed her cruel husband and says that he is now living a well-rounded, normal life. I don't know if he killed the Hispanic or not. He probably did, goddamn him. I have to figure a way to get Ransack to lose interest in me.

~~ TRYING TO CONFRONT JEROME

It's later in the day. I've sitting by a warehouse a few blocks away from where Ransack had told me his story. I happened to look up, and I saw Jerome about a half block away, just standing there staring at me. He turned and started walking away. What's going on here? I need to find out. Why is he always following me? I decided to find out.

After I wrote that last sentence, I closed my journal, put it away, jumped up and ran after Jerome. As I got close to him I called his name. He didn't turn around. I finally caught up with him and began walking beside him. I tried to sound as friendly as I could, "Hey, Jerome, I'd like to talk with you for a few minutes. Do you mind?" I was breathing fast partly from my spurt of running, but I think partly because I was standing so close to Jerome. He was huge, and the expression on his face seemed to indicate he was gritting his teeth. His eyes stared straight ahead.

Without looking at me he said, "Talk."

Where was I going to start? I cleared my throat. "You know, Jerome, it seems like I have seen you around so much. I think I see you and then when I try to find you to say hello, you're gone. Lately, have you noticed how often we seem to be in the same places?

"I haven't noticed," was all he said. "Excuse me, I have something I have to do." He turned and walked in a different direction from me.

I stopped and stared at him. At least he spoke to me, but I felt so helpless. This guy is so powerful. He wouldn't even have to use his knife to kill me if he wanted, he could just break me apart. Well, it was a start. Maybe the next time I'll have the courage just to ask if he's following me. I don't see why he really would be following me, but I know I've seen him in back of me all over this city. I don't like it. On the other hand, do I really want to know if he is planning to kill me? I know, the next time I see him, I'll ask him if I bother him in any way. That would be more honest. Maybe I'll tell him that I'm afraid he is following me and wants to do something horrible to me. Maybe I'll just do that. Maybe.

May 11 ~~ HOWARD AND SUSAN

Late yesterday afternoon I met a couple in their late forties who are living out of their old Dodge van that was parked on one of the side streets near the industrial section. As I was walking by, they asked me a question about how strict the cops are in this city. I told them there's been rumors that the cops are going to become stricter about not letting homeless people hang around the downtown areas, but right now they're generally leaving us alone.

Their names were Howard and Susan and they had been living in Sacramento when Susan became ill with a heart condition that required surgery. Their insurance didn't cover all the costs and when complications developed, they had to sell their house to be able to afford the medical payments. She had to quit her job as a bookkeeper for a small business. Howard said that he'd been working as a counter salesman in a building materials store but it didn't have good benefits. They said that they were fortunate to have their old Dodge van, and they got in it, left Sacramento and started for Seattle where Susan had a brother who might be able to get Howard a job as a carpenter.

"I can't believe that this has happened," he said. He had pulled some folding lawn chairs out of the van and invited me to sit with them. They had a cooler with some soda pop in it. They gave me one and I sat down. Susan seemed to have difficulty breathing and said she had to stay lying down in their bed most of the time.

"It is terrible what happened to you, I said. "Something like this happened to me about a year ago. But it had more to do with my mind than my body. I was fired, then seemed to lose the ability to do what I'd been doing for sixteen years and I lost everything."

"I'm sorry," Howard said shaking his head. Then he leaned forward and whispered. I don't know how long Susan can live if we don't continue medical treatment for her."

"What are you going to do?"

"Rob a bank. Make counterfeit money. Hell, I don't know. I can't believe it's happening. It's like I'm in a nightmare."

"I feel like I'm in the same nightmare. I wish I had some answers."

"You know, I've worked hard all my life and so has Susan. We've paid our taxes and tried to be good citizens. But it just seems like we've been forgotten."

"Forsaken. We are expendable, Howard. If we can't provide cheap slave labor, then we're just a corporate burden.

Howard shook his head and said, "Maybe what you are saying is not an exaggeration."

Susan started coughing. He went inside then came out about five minutes later. "Susan is going to need to get some sleep, so I'm going to have to ask you to leave."

I wished them the best of luck on their journey to Seattle and went on my way. More broken-down pieces of human machinery that's being discarded.

May 12 ~~ IMAGES OF JUSTINE AND THE TREASURE MARKET

I'm sitting on the sidewalk leaning against a building on one of the back streets near the Burnside Bridge. It's a warm afternoon. I feel comfortable. Images of Justine keep drifting in my mind.

—I walked into one of the rooms at the Treasure Market, and I smelled the musk scent of the perfume that Justine wears. I walked into one of the adjacent rooms, no Justine. Another adjacent room, no smell. Another adjacent room, the smell of musk even stronger. I continued through that room, and there was Justine, in the next room, taking inventory, writing on a clipboard, as beautiful as ever. Before I could walk away she looked up and smiled at me. I smiled at her and quickly returned to the workroom.

—Justine's face is beautiful and part of the beauty is her mercurial changes of expression when she is in dialogue. She uses her whole body, her whole self to convey the words and emotions she is feeling.

Other times I have seen a calmer receptive mood where she listens, she takes in, reflects. Like an animated surface of the ocean inlet on a calm day, still, and yet conveying power underneath the calm receptive surface.

—Sometimes I would see Justine working in blue jeans and a plaid shirt. Then I wouldn't see her for a while, and she would walk into the room wearing a business suit, or a dress. She must have a place in the store where she changes clothes, but I don't know where it is.

—I remember hearing Justine humming and singing to herself while working at her counter. She seemed so content. I got caught in her voice, her mood, and found that I had just been standing in the workroom ten or fifteen minutes not doing anything but listening to her. I reluctantly went back to work but I could still hear her singing off and on and I felt drawn to her. When I recognized what I was feeling I left the Treasure Market for the day. I have to protect myself from myself, and it's not easy when my total being gets caught up in something so nice.

—Another time Justine was putting small glass statuettes in a tall glass cabinet one morning. It had been a slow morning. One of the sales people was showing a customer some furniture in another part of the store. Justine had put on some music and as she went back and forth from the counter where she had placed the small statuettes to the glass cabinet she moved rhythmically to the music. The way she moved her body was delightful. She moved her hips and her shoulders, rhythmically, sensually.

—Justine talked with me today about how she has a serious, practical side and a creative, artistic side, and how she has a need for independence and yet a need for romance and commitment. "I know I am fortunate having so many opportunities that many other women do not have. Yet I feel torn a lot of the time. I dream of having babies. I sometimes feel like I want to be behind a stove and an ironing board all day. At other times I think that's a crazy urge. I love my independence. I feel lucky being able to take over and run this store. It's a lot of work, but it does give me some freedom with time that I wouldn't ordinarily have. At least at this time I am keeping all my different sides satisfied and am having fun doing it."

~~ RAUL, THE EVIL STREET URCHIN

Earlier today when I was writing images of Justine in my journal, I suddenly became very tired and I just wanted to sleep. I closed my eyes and must have dozed off. Then through my light sleep I began to hear a bouncing sound, something slapping the pavement. I barely had the energy to open my eyes but when I did, I saw Raul standing before me bouncing his basketball. He was staring at me with a grin on his face.

"You'd rather sleep man, or watch a pro play basketball?" he asked.

"Sleep," I managed to say. I had a foreboding feeling.

Suddenly he threw the basketball at the building right next to my head. The loud slap of the rubber hurt my ears and made me jump. "Wake up man. It's not a time to sleep," Raul yelled, laughing.

My first impulse was to jump up and grab the bastard. But I remembered how he likes to be chased. And then I thought that maybe he was doing this to me because he thinks I am a drunk and too out of it to respond. An idea came to me. I closed my eyes, shook my head like I was disgusted and leaned back heavily against the wall like I was too drunk to move. Then I opened my eyes again and got ready.

He was bouncing the ball in front of me. He had been ready to run away but now I saw that he had relaxed, still grinning. He came closer to me and this time when he tried to bounce the ball next to my head, I was able to grab it. I jumped up with the ball and said to him, "Now you lost your ball, you little punk. If you keep messing with people like you're doing you may lose more than your basketball. Some people on the street would rather just take you out than have to put up with your nuisance."

But Raul was not listening to me. His whole demeanor changed. He took on a hurt, desperate look and started repeating over and over again, "Please don't take my ball away from me. Please mister don't take my ball away from me. It's all I have. Please mister. I'm sorry. I'm sorry." He reached for the ball, and by god, he even started crying. This really took me by surprise. Every time I had seen this kid before he was being such a cocky asshole.

After a few minutes of his pleading I decided to give him back his basketball. What the hell, I thought. I'm not going to change his life just by taking his basketball away from him. I handed him the basketball. He started wiping the tears from his eyes and stepped back a little ways from me. Then suddenly he threw the basketball as hard as he could at my crotch. As I doubled over in pain he scrambled for the ball and yelled as he ran away, "You mother fucker, never touch my basketball again."

I stood on the sidewalk, hunched over, watching Raul run away. Eventually the pain subsided and I was able to breathe again. I moved to the side of the building, lay down and put my head on my backpack and went to sleep. I decided the less I think about Raul the better. Let the prick have his basketball.

May 14 ~~ CARISSA'S PROBING QUESTIONS

Carissa's first question today was, "Do you feel lonely?"

I'm beginning to hate that concept. When does a person reach a state of being where he has no desire to be with other human beings? I guess that happens when one devotes oneself to certain spiritual pursuits, which I haven't. I know I'm caught between my desire for love and my aversion to the required attachments to slave life that goes with it.

I took a deep breath and tried to channel my thoughts into a very matter-of-fact answer. "Yes I feel lonely, but that's my life right now. I'm not a magician. I can't just create any reality I want. I don't have anything. I'm not completely together in my mind. I drift off. I wouldn't be a good person to be around."

"I don't know," she said smiling. "I know a lot of adults who just drift off, who are totally not there, but who seem to live normal lives."

"The difference is that they are still tied to day-to-day responsibilities that keep them from drifting off too far and always brings them back to their safe and secure homes. I don't know where I drift off to, and it's not just a matter of drifting off. It's also that I don't really have any secure place to come back to. I like to think that I'm drifting off to somewhere special, to some wonderful alternate reality that I'm exploring. But I might be wrong. The point is I'm just not a fit person for a relationship."

"I think you're okay to be around."

"Thank you, Carissa, but our little interviews don't really last that long. You don't get to see how strange I can get. And grumpy. Things bother me a lot, and I'm not pleasant to be around when I get really bothered."

"I've seen how grumpy you can get. And weird. And dishonest."

"Now wait a minute, I can accept the grumpy and weird, but dishonest? I'm always totally honest with you."

"Sure. Sure, Gibson. Can you tell me that you have never lied to me, or not told me the total truth? Can you swear that you have always been totally honest in answering my questions?"

I thought for a minute. "I'm sure I have. I can't always remember, but I'm sure I have." I raised my eyebrows and shoulders to emphasize my innocence.

She pointed her finger at me, "See. Saying you can't remember. That's so dishonest."

"It's not dishonest. It's evasive…do you know what that means?" I teased.

She didn't answer, but looked at me with an expression that seemed to say, "Do I have to put up with this?"

I continued, trying to defend myself, "Honest, I can't always remember things. That's part of my problem. You may be right, but I have no way of knowing. Listen, I'll try to watch out for my evasiveness from now on." I was partly having fun with Carissa about this, but I was also being serious. I don't remember so much. Sometimes when I look back in my journal, I'm really surprised not only about what I've written, but what has happened to me. Sometimes I wonder if I make things up about my life.

"Sure. Sure, Gibson. I'll just have to make sure not to let you get away with not telling me the whole truth. I need to know everything about you."

"You can't know everything about a person. Even a normal person has secrets, things they want or need to keep private."

"Do you have a lot of secrets?" Carissa stared at me intensely.

"Yes, I'm sure I do, and I am not even sure what they all are yet. I figure that if I can't even remember things about myself then I must really have a need to keep them private."

Carissa looked down and wrote something in her notebook.

"What did you write?"

She looked up and smiled sweetly, "I'm sorry, Gibson. I never let anyone read my notes."

I laughed. "OK, OK, you got me...so we will both keep some things secret or private."

I started to say that this project won't be lasting that long, but I decided to not respond to the issue any further. I do like Carissa and I think that I'm more honest with her than I am with most people, perhaps even more than Esola and Justine. Of course, Esola has her psychic abilities which is really scary sometimes. Carissa, though, feeds me breakfast sometimes and is pleasant to be around. I like her curiosity, her tenacity in the face of so many difficulties, and just her basic niceness and warmth. I hope she doesn't lose those qualities. But whether or not I will ever be able to trust her enough to share some of my deeper thoughts and feelings remains to be seen.

May 15 ~~ USING WORK TO REPRESS DESIRE

I heard Chris come into the store yelling about something. Fortunately, I was upstairs, and I didn't have to deal with him. I heard Justine arguing with him, and finally he left. I had the urge of going downstairs and asking if she was all right, but I realized that would be too personal.

I turned my attention back to the cabinet I was sanding and preparing to stain. There's nothing like hands-on toil to repress concern—and desire.

May 16 ~~ HOMELESS KILLINGS CONTINUE

Oh shit, another homeless man was murdered last night. The headline in today's Oregonian blared, "HOMELESS SLASHER KILLS AGAIN"

Reading about another killing makes me feel outraged again. It's still difficult for me to separate the killing of homeless people by some maniac, from the apathy of most Americans. What do I expect Americans to do? I expect them to demand changes, to stand up for what's right for everyone, not just for a few.

I don't know who is killing the homeless people here in this city, but I know who are allowing the poor and homeless in America and across the world to suffer and become ill and die. Americans. The supposedly great Americans who are so good at looking the other way.

Hell, why am I going on like this. It's because I have to let it go and get on with my job of finding a safe place to sleep at night. I can't be as free as I have been to sleep anywhere I want. I probably should sleep at the Campfire more often, except that I still need to be alone most of the time. I'll just have to take the risks. I've gotten this far, and I feel that I've experienced some breakthroughs. I can't let a little fear of being stabbed and hacked to death in my sleep make me come in from the streets.

Now, when I read about this killer, I just have to acknowledge it, let the anger or depression come, and try to move on. I can't dwell on how horrible and frightening this is. If something happens to me, then it will. I just have to move on. I'm going to do a lot of walking today.

May 17 ~~ THINKING ABOUT TRYING TO MEET THE THAI DANCER

I woke up this morning thinking about the Thai dancer. I felt like going to see her perform again, but I have another play tonight and I can't risk getting zapped out and falling asleep all night like I usually do.

It seems that lately I've been experiencing a lot of things out of the ordinary. I am living beyond the ordinary, so what the hell. I only want to allow myself to experience this wonderful event at special times. It's just like with the ring. I realize that things so powerful cannot be taken lightly—not be indulged in. Why do I also think this Thai woman's dance is like a drug? Because I feel it? I feel drugged. Or at least I feel like when I watch her dance I enter a different reality.

Maybe I should go up to the house in broad daylight and knock on her door, introduce myself, and tell her how much I have appreciated her dancing. Maybe this could be the first step in getting to know her. Why not? I don't really think she is a part of this slave society. All those people in that house must be so new to America that they can't be fully indoctrinated, so maybe it's worth getting to know her. Why not? I've been able to sleep with a high-class call girl and travel the universe with a ring. Why can't I meet a beautiful Thai dancer and get to know her better?

For one reason, it could ruin the magical quality of the situation. She's been dancing for me, knowing I'm there observing her, and maybe she wants to keep it that way. There's only one way that I'm going to be able to find out. I'm going to have to just go up there and knock on the door. I'm going to walk over there right now and do it before I think about it too much more and change my mind.

~~ VISITING THE HOUSE WHERE THE THAI DANCER LIVES

It's later in the afternoon. I am very far away from the Thai house. My attempt to meet the Thai dancer was not a success. Yet I feel good about trying. I just hope that I didn't ruin any further chance of seeing her again in our usual way.

When I got to the house I walked up to the door and knocked on it. I didn't hesitate once. I knew if I stopped, even to catch my breath, I would probably not go through with it. I stood waiting for a while, and then I knocked again. While I waited, I went over in my mind again what I wanted to say. How I wanted to ask to meet the Thai dancer without giving away that I was sneaking back behind the house spying on her.

Finally the door opened. It was one of the Thai men I had seen in the backyard. He was very well dressed in a dark blue silk shirt and black pants. He also had a very stern expression on his face.

"Excuse me, I live around here, and every once in a while, I've heard some beautiful music in the backyard as I walked by, and I just wondered if you or someone could tell me what kind of music was being played. Maybe you could tell me the name of the music so that I could buy it." Looking into the eyes of this man I made a decision that I would not even mention anything about the dancing.

He shook his head and said in a gruff voice, "I don't know anything about what music that could be."

I could hear some commotion behind him and I thought I saw someone moving in the hall way. "Perhaps someone else in the house might have played the music. Would you mind if I asked? I wouldn't be so forward but I want to buy this music for my mother, who loves all types of Asian music."

He shook his head again and said, "Sorry. Can't help you." Then he shut the door in my face.

I turned and left. I can't believe it. I can't believe that I had the courage to even go up to the house. I guess I can believe that man wouldn't want to talk with me, given what I had seen in the backyard that one time. But at least I tried. At least I tried.

May 19 ~~ A CURE FOR JUSTINE'S TENSIONS

Earlier today at the Treasure Market, I was cleaning a dining room table and chairs, and moving them into one of the display areas. Justine's boyfriend came into the room, and asked where Justine was. His tone was very arrogant.

I looked up and said, "How should I know? I'm not paid to keep track of her for you."

Now what made me say that? I don't know. I'm usually not that bold. He looked at me as if he were going to pounce on me and beat me to a pulp. He actually started to walk toward me.

Fortunately, Justine called his name from another room. He reluctantly turned and walked away with a scowl on his face.

I have to be more careful of my statements to Chris. I don't want to make him an enemy.

Later, Justine walked into the backroom, looking unusually tired, and her face showed a great deal of tension, her lips set tightly, eyebrows creased. But she still looked lovely.

She sat in a chair beside me, and said, "Damnit, Gibson. I can't do it all. Sometimes I wonder why I let Mama talk me into managing this store. I should have done like my little sister did, say no, and start traveling."

I realized that it wasn't the store, but probably something that happened with Chris that made her upset. "Is there a particular problem right now?"

"Everything is the problem. Everything! I am expected to oversee everything around here and make sure the store makes money. Then I'm trying to direct a play. I'm trying to keep that side of my life going because that means so much to me. And then my relationship with Chris. I wonder if I really have time for a relationship, especially with someone like Chris. He's such a baby sometimes."

"Why do you put up with him?" So far my responses seemed easy to come up with. I was pleased that she was telling me these things, even though she seemed so down. I did feel badly for her, and I sincerely was hoping I could help her feel better somehow.

"I don't know, Gibson," she said, getting up, and beginning to pace back and forth. "I guess I do too. It's a fiery relationship. It's exciting, when it's good. I just don't think I can put up with his selfish tantrums very much anymore. I have too much to do. I don't have the time to deal with his emotional tirades. He has become so loud and dramatic. He demands so much attention. It's not just a matter of holding and nurturing someone who feels down. It's so much more with him"

"I have a temporary solution to your problems, Justine," I said.

"You do?" She looked at me, surprised and with anticipation.

"You need to come with me and let me buy you an ice cream sundae. Ice cream sundaes are good antidotes when you have a case of being tied up in knots. Especially when you go for a sundae right in the middle of the work day. Just walk out of the store with me. Let one of your sales people take over the store, and we can just walk down the street, and enjoy a sundae."

She smiled at me, "You're crazy, Gibson. You sound just like my mother. She says just dance a little."

"Does it work?" I asked.

"Sometimes it does? Okay, let's go. I'll let you buy me a sundae."

"On one condition, though," I said.

"What's that?" She looked at me curiously.

"You need to pay me first for the work I will be doing today. And don't say anything. I want to buy you this sundae. I appreciate your allowing me to work here the way you do. Letting me come in when I want to. Letting me use the shower. I just don't like seeing you feel so down."

"Okay, Gibson. I won't try to talk you out of buying me a sundae. I'll go get your pay, and tell Jan that we're going, and I'll meet you at the entrance."

We had such a great time. Justine's spirits seemed to lift when we got out of the store. She talked about what it was like growing up with her mama and papa. She said they traveled a lot, and they took her and her sister with them. She said she has gone to Europe often, and loves traveling. I told her that I have never really travelled, except when I moved up from Louisiana. As we ate our sundaes she described her favorite places in Europe. I was mesmerized not only about what she was describing but how she looked. She seemed to radiate with such happiness in remembering the travels she has been on. Her mood did seem to change dramatically and it felt good to see her feeling better.

At one point I asked, "Justine, why do you do this type of work? Is it just because of your mother?"

"Not just because of my mother. I enjoy finding treasures. I see myself as a treasure hunter. Gibson, I like finding treasures hidden in dust and dirt—treasures overlooked. I like discovering them, bringing them here and restoring them, magically bringing them back to life. I feel it's like setting them free from a curse that has made them unappreciated, ignored, hidden from view.

"Sometimes it only involves cleaning them up, dusting them off, and using a little cleaner on the mirror or glass. Other times it involves more work. Scraping off the surface dirt. Brushing, sanding off layers and layers of coating.

"After the restoration is completed and the treasure is placed in the store, I love to see people come and discover it."

On the way back to the store she said she realized that she just has to find a way of taking a break sometimes. She said that after she finishes this play that she is working on, she might step back from theater for a little while. And she said that she might try to hire a manager. She didn't say anything about Chris, and I didn't ask her about him, even though I was tempted.

When we got back to the shop she thanked me for taking her to get a sundae. She didn't know that I was feeling inside like a young teenager, with my heart racing. I went back to work and could barely concentrate.

Now I'm sitting in a doorway of a closed office building, trying to keep out of the drizzle, and I'm writing in my journal by the street lamp light. I'm feeling lonelier than I usually do. I am feeling like I have fallen into a crack between mainstream life and the street life, and I know that my desire to be with a woman who I love has caused this crack. Love is my worst enemy at this time. I can't let it get to me. I can't let Justine get to me. I just have to be able to enjoy her from a distance, like I enjoy Queen Avarice. It's easy with Queen Avarice because she doesn't know me. It's not so easy with Justine. Why can't I stay more aloof from her, damnit? Why did I ask her out for ice cream? Why can't I act like I don't know how to speak English? Well, I just have to think of this as just another challenge, just like the cold and rain are challenges, the lack of food and shelter are challenges, and the tendency of my mind to drift often into other realities are challenges. Justine has become just another challenge.

May 21 ~~ RANSACK CONTINUES HIS DEMAND FOR A LITERARY REPAYMENT

Just finished another session with Ransack. Each time it's like entering a three-dimensional horror/spy flick. The story is about spying and killing, but the feeling I get is horror.

Ransack told me today, "I have fought with a demonic passion to remain alive. I was trained at a young age to be a killer, to destroy the enemy. Killing is like drinking water to me. At one point in my career I would have destroyed all of civilization if I had been told to do so by my superiors.

"There are other things than killing and destroying the enemy that I like. I like telling stories. I like to teach. I like to share my experiences with others who are naive, gullible, who are like children in a pit of snakes. I don't think anyone can do anything much about what is happening in the world today—and what has already happened in the U.S., but I want people to know how gullible and stupid they've been and still are. I want them to know that they are being brainwashed and hypnotized.

"But hell, most Americans have a good life. A good lie. They don't care one way or the other that they are part of a bigger lie. As long they can keep their possessions. So shit, why should I care what they know. But I do. I want Americans to know what they are condoning by their apathy and blind patriotism. I want them to know they've given a green light to death squads to go around the globe killing other people who won't fall in step with the American way.

"By being so apathetic, quite a few Americans don't realize they are supporting blood-thirsty bastards who don't mind slicing throats and ripping out guts in the name of the American flag. I've seen it, man. I've done it. Have you ever seen a man who's just been stabbed in his stomach? For real? Not in the movies?" He didn't seem to care that I was shaking my head. "It's something that pictures can't capture, even moving pictures. There's a smell of panic, and a sound of death that goes along with the desperate sight of a man grasping, clawing at his stomach as he attempts to hold his life in."

He finally looked at me. "Am I depressing you? Upsetting you?"

"It's horrible what you are talking about," I said.

"Killing ain't pleasant man."

"Then why do you do it."

"Because I do it well. And a lot of the people I kill deserve to be killed. But I try to do it humanely. If I don't have to torture the person then I do it quickly."

"I'm upset at the society we're living in, but I'm not going around killing others."

Ransack laughed derisively at me. "You're pitiful, Gibson. Why don't you stand up and fight for the way of life that you really want?"

"I can ask you the same question."

"I'm fighting the goddamn system more than you are. Besides I don't give a damn about fighting the system. It's too powerful to fight. I just want to survive and have a little fun now that I'm retired."

"I don't see that. I see you're hiding out just like me."

"Well, my friend, you don't see everything."

"Tell me what I don't see ..." I can't believe I said that. I was just dueling with him and forgot the larger picture. I didn't really want him to tell me anything.

"In time I will tell you everything—everything that is important."

Ransack then proceeded to tell me a story about how he and his group foiled a plot to assassinate Castro about 15 years ago. He said that the government has wanted Castro to remain in power so that the threat of communism in Central and South America would remain real enough that Congress would give money to the right-wing rebels in various South American countries. He said that many of these rebel groups were just fronts for CIA drug-laundering operations, which used the money raised to fund operations world-wide that the US government wouldn't fund. He also said that the money from drug operations also kept a lot of people in office in the US, and ended up in a few powerful people's bank accounts.

I didn't know what to believe or if I even cared. What's the difference between the CIA illegally making money off drugs and all the financial scams that are going on in the U.S. by our elected leaders? The fact is that a few people are making a lot of money for the interest of the few while the rest of the world is either starving or struggling and sacrificing their souls just to keep a home.

Fortunately, Ransack said he had something he had arranged to do, and our meeting abruptly ended. How much more will I have to put up with him? Why can't he just take off to South America or wherever he wants to hide next?

~~ THE BAG LADY'S STRANGE DISAPPEARANCE

Late afternoon. I had just crossed the Burnside Bridge into the downtown area and I almost ran into the bag lady coming around the corner. The look on her face was that of a wild animal. She gaped open her mouth holding a few jagged teeth, and she let out a horrible scream. She had already stuck her hand into one of her bags and was pulling out this long knife.

I turned and ran back toward the bridge. As I started down the concrete steps leading under the bridge, I saw that she was running after me, even though, thank god, she wasn't really all that speedy.

"Ya bin writin' bad things about me, and I'm gonna get ya. I'm gonna stick ya good. I'm gonna cut off ya writin' hand," she was yelling.

I reached the bottom of the steps, and turned under the bridge. Just then I heard her let out a yelp and yell, "Let go of me, ya son of a ..." Then all I heard was the usual street noise.

I turned back and crept slowly toward the steps. I peeked around the corner but didn't see her. I started slowly climbing, and when I almost reached the top I found her knife lying on one of the steps. I picked it up, feeling kind of spooky, as if I were dealing with some supernatural force that could make people disappear.

I walked up onto the street, and went up to a drunk who was lying on the street a few feet from the steps. I tried to ask him if he had seen anything, but he was too far gone. I looked around for someone else who may have seen something. But there was nobody else for about a block or two. What could have happened to the bag lady? I want her to stop trying to kill me, but I didn't want her killed. I feel like I'm going crazy. I'm afraid that I'm already crazy. No, I'm not crazy. I have to stop believing that something's wrong with me. That's the only way I'll be able to figure out these strange things that have been happening to me.

May 22 ~~ POSSIBLE HELP FOR BILLY BUZZ

After thinking about it for a while, I went to the shelter on Burnside, and got information about a drug rehab program that could help Billy Buzz. I don't know why I did this. I'm trying not to get involved in other people's problems. I must put all my focus on myself if I'm going to survive out here on the street. But it breaks my heart to see Billy Buzz so strung out and Liv having to do what she does to support both of them.

The shelter manager gave me the name of an intake counselor at one of the programs nearby the shelter. Later that afternoon I found Livid and Billy Buzz near the freeway fields, and I took Livid aside. I gave her the name of the intake counselor and said that she needs to get Billy into a program. She said that she would try, but that she didn't think he would do it. I said that I was worried about how long he would survive with his drug addiction, and she agreed. She said that she almost had enough money to take both of them back to Amsterdam. I told her again that she shouldn't be doing what she is doing and that she should go back to Amsterdam and get an education. Then, if Billy Buzz went into a drug program, she could one day come back for him, or he could come to her.

She listened politely, but I knew she wouldn't take my advice. I think that something happens to us when we've been abused or damaged that makes us wild and perhaps untamable. I know that's not good, but I understand it.

At least I'm trying to help Billy. Maybe it will make a difference. It makes a difference to me that I did try no matter what. I do care about others. I do want to try to do what I can to help others. I just don't feel confident or capable that I can do much more than very simple things right now to help others.

May 23 ~~ THE BLOWOUT BETWEEN JUSTINE AND CHRIS

Today I noticed that Justine was a little preoccupied. She seemed bothered again by something. She couldn't sit still. I was putting some round table-tops on their center stands in the work room, and every time I looked up, I could see Justine pacing around the counter. She came into the room where I was working a couple of times, and then just turned around, like she had forgotten what she had come in for, and walked back to her desk. Both times she just stood there for a long time before getting on to another task.

Eventually I asked her if something was bothering her. She said that she was worrying about the play she was working on. She said Chris had the lead in the play, which probably was a mistake since she was directing it, but that she had received a telephone call from him earlier that morning. She said he was very upset about how certain other cast members were behaving. He did not think they were being serious enough. Justine said that Chris was a great actor but that he couldn't keep his emotions in control, and it was really going to put a bind on things if he broke down. She said that the opening night was less than a week away.

I had never seen her worried like that. It made me want to do something to help her. But I didn't know what I could do. I felt a painful kind of helplessness. All I could do was say that I hope everything worked out. She smiled at me and said thanks. I think I'm feeling more than sister love for Justine, but damnit, I have to keep reminding myself she's in a relationship even if it's not going well for her, and she's my employer. I have to be realistic. And protective of myself. That's the real issue. I have to be protective. I can't give up my purpose.

But then the big event happened. I went back to work, and she went to work. She said that talking about it that little bit had helped her. Just getting it out. She said that she had been so upset that she had felt like screaming, and she said she probably would have right then if customers weren't in the store.

About an hour later Chris came into the store, and I heard him start to yell at Justine. Something about how could she expect him to do something he didn't feel was right? And why wasn't she making as many demands on the other cast members as she did on him?

I looked up from my work. Chris was just laying it right out there in front of Justine, in front of everyone in the store.

I noticed that Justine was trying to calm him down. There was an older couple at the other end of the store, and I could see that they had turned around to look at who was yelling. I could also see that Justine was not able to control this loud mouth. I'm not one to get involved in fights, but I figured this was different. He was really getting off on causing a scene. I put my cleaning rag down and walked up to the counter where he was standing. I said to him that he was disturbing people in the store and told him that he should leave.

He looked at me like I was dirt. He slowly curled his upper lip, and said I had no business telling him to leave. He had something to settle with Justine. She then told him that she would rather discuss it with him that night at rehearsal. He looked at her, and then at me. He started walking back and forth, yelling that he couldn't believe he was being kicked out of her store. He said he wanted to resolve this thing now. I think he must have figured that if he kept up the attack now, rather than wait until the rehearsal, he would stand a better chance of getting her to do things his way. But maybe he wasn't capable of thinking. I was beginning to be an expert at judging when people don't have control over their emotions, and I could tell that he definitely had that crazed look. I got caught up in his emotional intensity and started toward him shouting, "If you don't leave I will throw you out."

Thinking back on this outburst, I realize that I really am crazy. I can't even stay in touch with what I am capable of. Maybe I could throw this guy out, but I have never been in a physical fight in my life. I have made it a point of avoiding at all costs getting in the middle of other people's fights, especially when the participants are men who look stronger than me. I figure, let them punch each other out. It's my nightmare fantasy that I'd try to break up a fight, and guys would start pounding away on me. But this was only one guy. On the other hand, he did look strong and I didn't even know the best way to grab him to throw him out of the store.

I could vaguely hear Justine yelling something in back of me. Chris started backing up toward the door. Just when he got to the door, he picked up a plate off a shelf and hurled it at me. I saw this blue and white china plate heading for my face, and I tried to duck. The edge of the plate missed me, but the flat side of it cracked against my skull and crashed to the floor shattering.

For a moment I was dazed. I looked up and saw that Chris had exited. Then I felt Justine standing by me, asking if I was okay. She led me to a couch and told me to lie down. She sat beside me on the couch, took my head in her hands, and inspected where the plate had hit me. It wasn't really hurting anyway, and I began to focus on how pleasant Justine's touch felt. Then I saw she was crying and I asked if she was all right.

"I'm okay," she said. "It's just so upsetting to me for Chris to be that way. Thank you so much for helping me get that crazy idiot to leave."

"Do you think that I made things worse?"

"No, I don't think he was going to leave until he got his way." Then as she wiped away her tears, she started smiling, "I have to admit that I was surprised that you would try to throw him out of the store."

I laughed a little. "Oh my god, what was I thinking. I've never been in a fight in my life. But fortunately he wasn't that brave. What an ass, throwing that plate at me as he ran out of the store."

Still smiling, Justine said, "If you hadn't stepped in, he may have tried to break something larger, like me. You could have saved my life, Gibson. You deserve a kiss." She leaned over and she kissed me on my cheek. She became serious and said, "But please don't try to get up. Stay still for a while. Your head was banged pretty hard."

Justine stood up and sighed. "Now, things are really in a mess with this play. I'm not going to let him perform after what he's done. I do have an understudy, but then I don't have anyone to take the understudy's place as a stagehand."

Then she slowly looked at me. "Gibson, would you help me out and be the stage hand for my play?"

I felt both pleased and anxious. I wanted to help Justine, but I didn't think I could make a commitment like that. I found myself in one of those situations with her again in which I couldn't say anything.

"Listen, Gibson, I wouldn't ask you if I didn't need you desperately. I really need you. It's only for three weekends, two nights each weekend."

"Aw, come on, Justine, that's so many times I would need to be some place at a particular time. Even if I could somehow make it there when I needed to be, I don't know if I could really do what you'd require of me."

"You could do it, Gibson. I know you could handle the things you'd need to do as a stagehand. It's just moving some sets, creating some special effects, turning lights on and off at certain times.

"It sounds complicated to me. Doing things on schedule and at certain times on a regular basis, I think, is beyond me right now. I just can't commit to anything so demanding. I'll go crazy. I'll have a relapse. I'll ..."

I could tell that she was thinking that she shouldn't have asked me, and that perhaps it would be too much for me. She was looking down with a defeated expression on her face.

I sat up on the couch and said, "Look, Justine. Maybe I could try the first weekend performance, and then you could find someone else to do the rest. That will give you time to prepare for next weekend's performance."

The darkness in her expression lifted and she smiled and said "Thank you, Gibson. Thank you." She ran to the telephone, saying that she had to call the understudy to tell him that he had to prepare for the lead role.

Sometimes real life seems like sticky paper to me. I'm almost free and then something pulls at me, pulls me back. I'm not very happy about this stagehand thing. I am happy that Justine's happy. Who is Justine? Just another woman I'm in love with. Foolishly in love with. At least with Queen Avarice its pure fantasy and I don't have expectations that I have to try to fulfill. Even though I'm obsessed with Queen Avarice, I don't like what I am imagining she represents. With Justine it's beginning to be real interaction. I have to keep thinking that she's a sister, not a lover. That way I won't get into more trouble than I already am. She's such a wonderful sister. As I stared at her beautiful butt in her tight blue jeans as she talked on the telephone, I shook my head, thinking,

"Sister, hell."

I thought for a moment that maybe I should stop working at the store, but I knew I couldn't do that. I'm hooked. But somehow I have to keep myself from becoming a love-struck fool. It could never work. I'm a hopeless, homeless outcast. I have to keep it this way. As long as I keep my resolve that I can't rejoin the slave life and as long as Justine doesn't put any pressure on me to rejoin it, then I can continue working at the store. I can continue to relate to her and Esola. I can help her on out on this play. Helping her out on this play doesn't mean I'm returning to slave life. Now that that's clear in my mind, why don't I feel better? I think it's that I'm not doing very well at being the outcast observer.

I keep getting involved in the things I'm observing, and I have no business getting involved until my new creative self grows up. I don't want to destroy the good things that are growing just because I foolishly get involved in things I shouldn't. Like love and aliens and exotic dancers and plays and murders. At least I have been able to keep my distance from Queen Avarice, but she's from a high class. She is royalty. She almost doesn't count. And the way I'm acting, I'm not sure I'll be able to keep my distance from her all that long.

It's been a few hours since that blow-out at the store, and I have about an hour before I'm supposed to be at the theater. At least it's on this side of the river, not too far away from the store. I'm nervous and, I have to admit, a little excited. I also feel a little tired and my head hurts. I think I'm just going to sit here on the sidewalk against this building and rest until I have to go. There's not too many people walking around here, so I don't think I'll be bothered.

~~ MY RETURN TO THE THEATER

I stood outside the theater for an infinitely long half hour until Justine arrived. She took me inside and introduced me to the cast and then asked me to look around the stage while she talked with them to explain what had happened.

I stood at one side of the stage and gazed up at the tall curtains, at the catwalks above, and at the lights hanging everywhere. I had this strange feeling that I was in a sacred place, a sort of temple where powerful rituals took place, where magic occurred, where wonderful things were created and offered to the world. I felt again like I was returning to a familiar place, and the feeling was more than pleasant, more than exciting.

I walked around the backstage and found the control box for the light. I didn't understand a damn thing about it, but I found it. Finally, Justine came and showed me around and explained what I was supposed to do during the play. She went over it once and said that we would go through the play tonight a couple of times and would do the same the next night. There was one other stage hand.

I had a horrible time at first concentrating on what I had to do. I kept getting involved in the play and would then miss the cue. I could tell Justine was getting frustrated and that made me frustrated, and I know she knew it. At one point she told the cast to take a fifteen-minute break and asked me to go for a walk with her. During the walk she put her arm through my arm, walked closely to me and talked. She just talked to me and told me how difficult it must be for me to come into this play and learn things so quickly, but she told me how much it meant to her, and that whatever happened it would be okay. It was just a play. She asked me what was happening to me, and I told her that I just kept getting involved in the play, kept getting lost in the dialogue, and then I would forget what I was doing.

"Maybe the play is better than I think," she said, smiling. "But we have to find a way for you to stay detached and focused." She thought for a few moments. "I think I have the answer. I'm going to give you a set of earphones to wear. They are thin and light, and they'll be attached to a receiver where I can talk with you. During the rehearsals I'll tell you what to do when. I'll talk with you during the play, and if need be I'll do it during the actual performances, but I think by that time you'll be able to stay detached. How does that seem to you?"

"Well, it should work. I mean, you will be right there in my head. Even if I do drift off, I think that I would always respond to your voice." I like the idea. I like being connected to her that way, even though I know I still have to get myself to stay focused so I can do the play on my own.

We went back to the theater, and we tried it the way she suggested. It worked fine. It was kind of fun, and after the rehearsal I felt really energized. It's a wonderful feeling to be a part of a group like that where everyone is working together yet expressing themselves in their individual ways. I felt immersed in creativity and it felt like I was getting nutrients that I have been missing all of my life. I didn't tell Justine, but after this rehearsal, I think I want to stay with the play for the rest of its performances.

May 24 ~~ DRAMATIC INVOLVEMENT

I made a suggestion to Justine and the other actors about the play that they had created as a group. One character in the play is a man of wealth and power who loses everything and eventually kills himself. I suggested that they shouldn't have him kill himself. I suggested that they should end with him alive, but having to face a life of struggle without all the means he has had available to him. I thought that it would be more powerful for the imagination of the audience. With him standing alone outside the huge expensive house where he had once lived, performing a monologue about material loss. He hasn't gotten beyond his material loss. I thought that it might hit the upscale theater goers who might identify with him just a little, and maybe force them to think about what would happen to them if they lost all of their access to money and power, credit cards and family fortunes. What would they do if they didn't have game rooms with pool tables and second homes in Florida, smart phones and iPods, maids and lawn keepers? What if they didn't have the money to go out to gourmet restaurants whenever they wanted? Would they kill themselves? I don't know. But without the death scene, I thought the emphasis would be on this guy having to face a life of struggling and scrimping financially, and that this might get more under the skin of the audience.

I explained my idea first to Justine, and to my shock she immediately called the other actors around and asked me to explain it to them. I had a difficult time speaking at first, but she helped out, and once I saw they were interested, I was able to get more into it. Finally, they accepted the idea. I was amazed and I'm still feeling…useful, no creative. It just feels good being able to contribute to the drama.

May 25 ~~ CARISSA SEARCHES FOR A FRIEND'S FATHER

Carissa started her interview today by asking me, "Do you know many homeless men who have left children behind?"

"That's a strange question. I really don't know the personal lives of many homeless men. I'm sure there are some who have left children behind."

Carissa then took out a picture of a man and showed it to me. He was a handsome man about my age, with dark hair. "Have you ever seen this man? It's the father of a school friend of mine. His family doesn't know where he is. He apparently is homeless, and an alcoholic."

I took the picture and looked at it. "No, I don't think I have seen him before. Are you helping your friend look for her father?"

Carissa took the photograph back from me. "I told her that I'd ask a few people. I felt that since I'm doing this project anyway and talking with a number of homeless people that it wouldn't be a problem for me to ask around about him."

"If I see someone who looks like him, I'll let you know."

Carissa thanked me and we finished our interview for the day. She's a good-hearted girl. I was impressed that she was taking the time to help her friend try to find her father. I didn't tell her that I thought it would be rather unlikely that she would find him.

~~ JUSTINE'S CONCERNS

I put in a few hours at the Treasure Market earlier this afternoon. Justine came up to me and said, "Something seems to be bothering you today, Gibson. Is it something you can share with me?"

"Another homeless man was murdered last night."

"I know. It's so awful. I worry about you. I hope you are being careful."

"I'm trying to be as careful as I can. He kills people while they are sleeping. There's not much I can do except try to make sure I'm well-hidden."

"Do you feel okay about doing the play tomorrow night?"

"Yes I do."

"I really appreciate you helping me. I won't ask you again to sleep in the room here at the store. I guess all I can do is hope you take care of yourself. Not because of the play. I just want you to be all right."

"Thanks, Justine. Nothing's going to happen to me." I smiled. "I found a magic potion in one of the vases I unpacked for you, and it makes me invisible.

I use it when I go to sleep."

"Then maybe I have nothing to worry about. I hope you have plenty of that magic to keep you safe."

It was so nice joking and laughing with her. Before she went back to her desk she reached out and touched my arm gently and told me she'd see me later that night at the final dress rehearsal. That simple touch now remains larger than life in my mind. I think I'll take advantage of this sensual memory, despite how brief it was, to carry into a reverie that hopefully will last until the rehearsal. My mind and emotions are involved in a state of war with the negative forces in life. My reveries allow me to retreat to a safe place, allow me to regenerate myself, allow my new soul to grow outside the contaminations of day-to-day slave society.

May 30 ~~ THE NIGHT OF THE PLAY

Tonight's the play, and I'm nervous as hell. I did sleep better than I thought I would last night, but I woke up before dawn. I didn't use the earphones for last night's rehearsal and I'm not using them tonight. I have to know when to turn the lights on and off and how to move sets between scenes without making too much noise. I have to work fast. I have to blow a whistle in the second act right on cue, and shake some rattles at another time. Shit. Why did I agree to do this? Maybe I just won't show. No, I'll be there. I can't let Justine down. And I have to admit, once I got to the theater and was shown what to do, I enjoyed the rehearsals these last few nights.

Justine is so charismatic and beautiful as a director and actress. She flows in and out of her role with so much ease. I could tell that everyone looks up to her, respects her. I've even felt that a few of the other actors are in love with her, and I've felt a tinge of jealousy. But what right do I have to feel jealous? Where is that feeling coming from anyway? Feelings like that surprise me. I shouldn't have those feelings. Even if these feelings are normal, I'm not in a normal condition right now. I have to keep reminding myself of my abnormality. I think there must be something wrong with that. Something abnormal. I'm smiling as I write this.

Anyway, I have to get ready for the play, which first means I have to make sure I'm in the vicinity of the theater when I'm supposed to be there, and somehow I have to keep track of time. Damn, this is so scary.

~~ I BECAME THE PLAY

Simply amazing!

That's how I feel. I can't express the feeling any other way right now. I feel like I just floated up and consciously reached those stars in the night sky I keep imagining. I've been on such a satisfying creative experience. Perhaps if I were rational it would seem kind of silly. It was just a short little play.

But the emotional intensity was overwhelming. The immediate gratification, the immediate response from the audience. I have never experienced anything like this. I felt so joined with the other actors and with the audience. I lost all self-consciousness. I became the play. And it is just now, as I am sitting alone in this all-night café, drinking coffee, that reality has come crashing back down on me. It's like what I imagine a hallucinogenic drug experience or a peak spiritual moment might feel like.

Fantastic!

And to think that this was just opening night. I remember when I arrived backstage. I was sullen, nervous, edgy. But then Justine saw me, ran up to me, threw her arms around me, and said how much she appreciated me being there. From that point on I was in a different world. I felt excited, alive, at one with the beautiful part of the universe. Now that I've found it, I don't want to leave it.

However, I have to realize it's probably all an illusion. I look around this all-night café. I see a bunch of lonely and frustrated, alienated people. People like me who have nowhere else to go, probably nobody to go home to. If they have a home. Hollow people. Sad people who have never experienced the beautiful part of the universe. I know I am projecting my fears onto these other people. Many of them are probably happy and some might be in love.

I have to bring back the memories of this play to fight my fears and depression. A part of me wonders what's been done to me. Am I letting myself be tricked again? I can't let myself be tricked again. I worry about indulging in my feelings. I have my infant creative spirit to think of. But then maybe I have to acknowledge that what I just experienced in the theater certainly is good for my own young creative spirit. I have to allow it to experience this beautiful part of the universe I have just discovered.

I will let Justine know tomorrow that I will finish out the play as a stage hand. I'm caught in this beautiful dramatic web. I can't deny it. I hope I'm not making a mistake. I hope it's for the best.

Now I just want to go find some warm place to sleep, to close my eyes and relive the moments I have just experienced.

~~ RESISTING THE LURE OF THE RING

I was just looking through my pockets trying to find some money to pay for a cup of coffee, and I touched Walter's ring. The alien ring. I have this urge to go somewhere in the darkness and look into the stone again. I feel so up—why not keep going? Why not travel again to wherever this ring makes my mind go? It was a good feeling. Like being a part of the play. No, I don't feel like I want to do it now. I don't want to mix pleasures. I just want to enjoy the creative and social experience I've been through. It's a part of this world, one of the few parts of the slave society I've felt good about. Actually, it's not really a part of slave society. Such creative expression like that is beyond the shackles of everyday, mindless work.

The ring is a link to another world. Whether or not it's real, I don't know. I don't care. I've ceased worrying about whether my mind, or Fallacious in my mind, helps me see other realities, ones that actually exist or imaginative realities. As long as I experience them as being real, they're real. Maybe one day I'll be able to tell the difference, and that might mean that my creative soul has grown up enough to take over and run my life. But anyway, the ring is a link to another world, and right now I want to enjoy my new link to this world. I just feel so good about being a part of this play.

Right now though, I better pay my bill before I get kicked out. The waitress has been looking at me suspiciously. I don't want to cause trouble tonight. I'm in too good of a mood.

May 31 ~~ CAPTURED, TIED AND GAGGED

It's early morning once again, and I'm sitting in another all-night café drinking a cup of coffee, feeling like I've been in both a wonderful dream and a frightening nightmare. A wonderful dream that turned into a horrible nightmare, then turned back into an OK dream—at least into an OK resolution. I've got to stop taking chances. Hell no, I don't! After this I've decided that taking chances is one of the few things I have left to keep myself alive. I will try to keep myself hidden as much as I can, but I will still keep taking chances.

Yesterday before sunset I returned to my hiding place behind the Thai House, but found nobody in the backyard. I waited again, and soon I saw someone eventually look out of a window. Then, as before, the beautiful dancer dressed in an exotic costume came out into the backyard, put on music, and began dancing for me. I know for sure now that she was dancing for me.

She did everything as before. After each dance and before starting another dance she would maintain a still, meditative position, sometimes with her arms crossed in front of her, sometimes with her arms down by her side, and she would stare straight at me, at where I was hiding, as if in a trance. Then, after a few moments she would start another dance.

Darkness had come, and she had lit her lantern. As usual I was feeling that the world was slowing down, that time was stopping. My awareness had been captured and my mind was gradually losing consciousness. All of a sudden I was jarred out of my trance by movement at the back door of the house. I turned my head to look and saw something horrible. I saw three men run out of the house, yelling, and head directly toward where I was hiding. For just a second my mind could not register what was happening, could not believe that they knew I was there. Then it was too late for me to get away. It probably would have been too late even if I had reacted immediately. These men could definitely move faster than I could.

I was just standing up when they were upon me. One of them grabbed me, and the other one hit the side of my head with the side of his hand, which felt like a brick. I lost consciousness. Right before I was hit, I think I remember the woman screaming. But who knows? It could have been me screaming.

When I awoke I was in a large kitchen. I was sitting in a straight-back chair with my hands tied behind me. I had a gag in my mouth. Across the table the old Thai man sat looking at me, drinking what looked like tea, and smoking a hand-rolled cigarette. Two younger Thai men sat on his left, two others sat on his right.

My eyes riveted on the sword that was sitting on the table in front of the old man.

After what seemed like forever, the old man finally nodded, and one of the younger men came over to me and loosened my gag. The old man spoke in his language, and one of the younger men translated what he said. The old man wanted to know who I was. Who was I working for, and why was I spying on his house? What was I trying to find out? He repeated the question, "Who was I working for?"

I told him that I was just a homeless man who slept in the shrubbery in the alley by his house. I decided definitely not to say that I came to watch the young woman dance. They might think that was worse than spying on them.

Then the man who had answered the door when I had come earlier said that I told him that I had lived nearby. He said I was lying about who I was.

The old man shook his head and stared at me for at least five minutes. Then he slammed his fist down on the table-top. He spoke again and then got up and quickly left the room. The four young men stood, and the translator told me they would give me until tomorrow morning to answer truthfully the questions that were asked of me. If I did not tell them what they wanted to know, they would make me talk.

I started to yell to them that I was telling the truth, but the gag was put back in my mouth, and they left the room. I was alone in the kitchen feeling as scared and helpless as I had ever felt in my life. Everything had happened so fast. I had just been a spectator, and now I was pulled into their lives, and was accused of being their enemy, a threat to them, a spy.

The next few hours were close to the most excruciatingly long and painful hours that I have ever spent in my life. The only time that was more painful was when I was having my psychological breakdown. At that time I experienced an intense emotional pain, losing my wife and eventually when I started losing all my material possessions.

Goddamnit, I tried to remain on the outside. I tried to just mind my own business. I didn't come into their yard. I remained hidden in the bushes near the outside of their property. What more do they want? What more does anybody want? I can't stop looking at things. I can't stop enjoying life. I can't imprison myself in a shelter and remain weighted down in that squalor. I just want to go about the city, not harming anyone, just enjoying a few of life's pleasures. I know they think I was invading their privacy. I wasn't invading their privacy, I was invading her privacy, but I know that she didn't mind. She actually was inviting me to her performance. She was performing and I was her audience. She wasn't doing anything obscene or anything that she should be embarrassed about.

Sitting there tied to the chair my thoughts flew frantically around. I thought about the possibility of being tortured. I tried to justify what I had been doing. I tried to think of a way to escape. I looked often at the sword on the table only a few feet away from me. I tried to bend my head forward, but one of the ropes was tied around my neck so that if I bent forward too far I would choke myself. I tried to rock the chair, but I couldn't move it. It was either fastened to the floor or else I was really weak. I didn't think I was that weak.

At one point I heard a sound behind me, and I thought, oh shit, they aren't going to wait until tomorrow morning. Then I saw someone move around to the front of me, and I cringed until I saw that it was the young woman who was the dancer. I almost didn't recognize her. She wore blue jeans and a white blouse, and her hair was tied back in a pony tail.

She motioned for me not to talk. She took the gag out of my mouth and before I could say anything, she put her hand to my mouth and motioned again for me not to talk. I nodded. She picked up the sword and cut my ropes. She took my hand and led me over to the door that led to the rest of the house. Beside my backpack and bag were two suitcases. She picked up my pack and handed it to me. When I had put it on she picked up one of the suitcases and motioned for me to pick the other one up. I did, and then followed her out the back door. We didn't go directly across the backyard, but followed the hedge until we got to the shrubbery near my hiding place. We walked through the pathway, along the alley, and down the street away from the house.

After a few blocks, I finally spoke and thanked her for setting me free. She said that it was the least she could do. She said she felt partly responsible because she knew that I had been watching her and looked forward to those times I came so that she could dance for me.

"You are a beautiful dancer," I told her. She smiled and lowered her head.

"But let me ask you something. The way you dance, it almost seems magical. It had the power to put me into a trance. It hypnotized me, and each time I fell into the most peaceful sleep I have ever had."

She giggled. She said that if I fell asleep, I must have been bored. "No, no, I wasn't bored," I told her. "Far from it. It was magical, intricate, flowing, lovely, certainly not boring."

She looked at me with a pleased expression. "When I was five my father sent me to a school north of Bangkok where I was taught ancient traditions and practices. I cannot talk very much about these things, but I can say that we were taught that people limit their ability to enter into more powerful, peaceful, spiritual, enjoyable realms by their thoughts. We were taught how to help ourselves and others get beyond these limitations of our minds. I am pleased that you experienced enjoyment and peacefulness from watching me dance. But now I must ask that you help me find a taxi cab."

I was at first jarred by her shift of focus. I realized that just in that short moment I had become totally engrossed in her explanation. I finally said, "Sure, I'll help you find a cab, but do you mind if I ask what's happening. What are you doing?"

"I'm leaving my family. Mainly I am leaving my father. His old ways have become too abusive."

"No shit," I said.

She smiled again. "No shit...I haven't heard that expression for a long time. In Bangkok, I had many American friends, children of American soldiers and businessmen. They had a lot of such expressions."

"How long have you been here in the states?"

"Just over a year, but since we moved here, we have been under a cloud of the past. My father keeps us imprisoned. It is worse than when we were in

Bangkok. He fears we will be corrupted by America."

"He might be right."

She hung her head for a moment as we walked along the sidewalk. We had seen no taxi, and I had told her we needed to walk to a busier street. She looked up at me and said, "I have already been corrupted by America, if it means wanting the freedom to do what I want to do, what I need to do...for me, not for my father or for the old traditions."

"I have to admit that I believe in that kind of American corruption, as long as it's corrupting old and outdated ways, but I guess I think true American freedom has been taken from most of us by American men who are like your father."

"I don't know what you are saying. I just know that I have not had any true freedom, especially since coming to America, and I could not stay in that house any longer."

"Where are you going?" I asked her.

"I have a place to go. I have an American friend whom I met in Bangkok. She'll let me stay with her until I can figure out what to do. I have some money that I took from my father. Some of it I earned anyway, but he took all of what we earned."

I told her that I understood what she was doing, that she was breaking away from an environment that would destroy who she really was. I told her that I tried to stay in an unhealthy environment, and that it was only after a breakdown that I got away. I told her to be careful that she doesn't buy too much into the American society and that she might need her special powers to keep the best of her from being destroyed. "Many Americans don't value anything they can't put in their microwave or on their credit cards."

"I will be careful," she said. "But you be careful, too. I hate to tell you this, but my father may blame you for taking me away."

"Oh, great, this is all I need."

"I wrote my father a note telling him that you had nothing to do with my leaving." She looked up with such sincerity and concern. "But I don't know if they will believe me. I am sorry. I hope they will forget about you after a while. They may try to find you."

My god, I hadn't thought of that possibility. Just what I needed. Someone else wanting to kill me.

We walked along without talking for a while. I finally turned to her and told her that I would miss her dancing, that I wished I could see her dance again. She smiled and said that maybe someday I would. She wrote her name down on a piece of paper. She told me that she could not tell me where she was going, but she believed that if I had her name, and if I really wanted to see her again, that I would. She told me that I should not lose that paper with her name on it, or the chances of us meeting again would be lessened. And I believe her. I don't question that at all. I've put that paper in the same place I keep my journal, one of the few possessions that I want to hang on to.

Before we found her a taxi, I asked her if her father would have really tortured and killed me. She said she didn't know. She didn't think that he would have killed me, but he probably would have tortured me some. "Tortured me some!" I exclaimed. "What kind of person is he?"

"He is a person I am leaving," she said. "But he is also my father, and I still feel bonded to him. I think that my father and my brothers are perhaps involved in illegal or dangerous things. I think their paths have taken a wrong turn, and I am leaving them to follow my own path. I am sorry you came across us, but at least you are safe now."

We found a taxi shortly afterwards, and she left. As I watched her drive away, I realized that my feelings of relief at being saved from torture had given a way to the pleasure of talking with her, and I felt sad that our encounter was so short. Now that I am writing about this, my sadness has eased away. I feel my life has been enriched by that brief encounter, and I feel strangely happy right now. Life is indeed wonderful. I'm a little groggy. I haven't slept all night, but I feel satisfied. I guess what all this is teaching me is that I can experience closeness and intimacy with someone even for just a brief moment, and that can be enough. I am learning that I don't have to own another person's time to be able to experience moments that are special enough to give me a lifetime of pleasure.

But now I do need to find a place where I can sleep at least a few hours even though it's during the day. I guess that I have to stay away from the northwest for a while, perhaps for the rest of my life. I hope her family doesn't come looking for me. But right now, no matter what happens, knowing that she is off on her own and knowing that maybe I helped a little to make it possible for her to break away makes me willing to take the risk of her family coming after me. That's the way I'm feeling right now, though I hope I still feel that way if they corner me in an alley one night.

June 6 ~~ SECOND WEEKEND OF THE PLAY

The second weekend of the play is over. It was wonderful. Just like last weekend. We performed the play three times during these last three days, Friday and Saturday nights and Sunday afternoon. I felt full of life during these last three days, and I haven't even written in my journal, but I don't feel upset about that. As a matter of fact, it felt comfortable to have it around me, and comfortable that I didn't feel like writing in it. Friday night after the play I walked around for a while feeling good, thinking of the performance and of Justine. Then I found a place to sleep and slept soundly until 10:00 or 11:00 the next morning, which is very unusual for me. I had enough money to buy a big breakfast, and I sat there in the café reading newspapers and drinking coffee for a couple of hours. Nobody bothered me. Nobody tried to hurry me out. Then I walked around, downtown and back. I found a place to rest in the industrial section near the Burnside Bridge and, surprisingly, fell asleep again. I woke up worrying that I had missed the play, but I had plenty of time. Saturday's performance went well again, except that I noticed how each performance is a little different. The actors tend to deviate a little from the script either by accident or design, and I noticed how on certain nights certain actors are more expressive, are "on" more than on other nights. But in general, they were all pretty even, and the small variances I noticed didn't affect my responsibilities.

I slept well that night again, and followed the same routine as I had on the morning before, except that I only had money for a cup of coffee. But that was okay. I was able to snatch a roll and some fruit that were left at the next table before the waiter came. I read the Sunday newspaper and just took my time again. After my coffee I walked around until I had to go to the play.

One more weekend to go. I feel so good to be a part of this play. I know that it's important to me. I'm just a stagehand, but I feel that being exposed to this creative expression is giving my new self a boost. I feel like I've been given some special creative nutrients that will stimulate the growth of my new self ten times what would be normal. And it feels right. I don't feel overextended or in a rush or nervous. I just feel right.

However, now that I have another week before the next performances, I'm beginning to feel my usual anxiety return. I haven't dreamed of the night dragons since the play started, and I haven't worried about someone following me the last three days. I haven't thought of the murders of homeless people or the Butcher. I haven't even really thought of Queen Avarice or the Thai Dancer or even Walter's ring for the last few days, but now all of these parts of my world are rushing back into my consciousness, and I feel like I'm reentering my mixed-up existence on the edges of the slave life.

I feel like the play is a part of some new existence that I haven't yet been able to bring fully into focus. But it's there. At least now I know it's waiting there for me. Somewhere in my future.

It's late at night now, and I've been trying to sleep for a while. I keep getting pulled between pleasant images of the play and frightening images of someone stabbing a homeless person as he sleeps. It seems like Fallacious is back in control again, goddamnit. Get out of my mind, Fallacious. Let me sleep. As I write these sentences, I imagine yelling at him. But I also imagine him just laughing at me as he searches for another scary or unsettling film to put on my inner projector.

June 7 ~~ RANSACK'S MYSTERIOUS ACTIVITIES

Earlier this morning I saw Ransack come out of a building not too far away from the Holy Skyscraper. It was a building that even has a similar appearance as the Holy Skyscraper, but is more ominous with tall, dark glass windows on the street level that seem to forbid the general public slaves from even trying to figure out or even think about what goes on inside.

I saw Ransack walk out of this building with two other men, both of whom wore black suits and dark sunglasses. Quite a contrast, Ransack with his blonde beard and faded beige leather frilled jacket walking like a celebrity between two mean-looking body guards. I didn't think they were body guards though.

The two bearers of darkness stood by a black limousine. I saw them hand Ransack an envelope before they got into the limo. As the limo drove off, Ransack walked away. This little scene has given me something more to think about. Like what the fuck am I doing hanging around this guy? Sure, some things about him are intriguing, until I get to the violence, mutilation and killing parts. It's not just those things by themselves but it's also the fact that he likes doing them. I hope he is really trying to do things for the good of people. I hope at least that much is true about him.

I've been able to avoid Ransack lately. I have started a separate notebook full of his stories so that I don't have to contaminate my own writings. It's not that what he's telling me is so new. It's what everybody knows about secret mercenaries, sort of, but it's scary to have the details of violence and uncontrolled espionage described first-hand, so graphically. I'm not reading about this in a book or seeing it in a movie. There still may be a chance that he's making a lot of it up, but I've become more convinced that he really has been a secret agent. I'm still not planning on really doing anything with the stories he's telling me and I hope I can continue to avoid him. I have this terrible feeling that he can find me anytime he wants.

~~ LIVID'S DESPERATE GOAL TO HELP BILLY BUZZ

I ran into Livid a few days ago and she said that she almost had enough money saved to take Billy to Amsterdam. She said she was so excited to be close to leaving the U.S. "It's been hard work to satisfy uptight American men. American men do not seem to be taught how to love a woman. They are rough. They drink so much they vomit all the time. Or pass out. I thought, when I first came here, that if I were careful, I could pick the right kind of men and weed out bad ones. But most American men just seem frustrated and they take their frustrations out on me and they think paying me enough will make it all right.

"When I get to Amsterdam I'm going to go back to school and become something like a nurse so I can take care of Billy the rest of his life."

At least Livid is working for something. At least she has dreams.

I asked if she was able to get Billy to the drug rehab program I told her about. She said that she tried, but he wouldn't go. She said she even contacted the program, but they referred her to State Vocational Rehabilitation, and then when she called that agency they told her he would have to come in for an eligibility evaluation, and that since their funding was cut, it would take a month or so to even see if he is eligible for their services. Livid said she asked about other resources, and she was told that all the community service non-profits are limited in what they can provide now due to the budget cuts and reduction in donations.

"I just can't stand it anymore," Livid said. "This country just doesn't care about its people, especially its poor people. I can't wait to get back to Holland."

"I don't know what to say, Livid. This is just not a good place for the poor or the working class—or even the middle class - to live right now. I'm glad you are going back to Holland, and I know you will succeed in finishing school and making a life for yourself that will satisfy you. And I hope Billy somehow gets help soon."

What else could I say? I don't think Billy will make it much longer if he doesn't get help. Budget cuts and lack of donations. All because the rich don't want to contribute to the common good, and as a nation we value greed and war over caring for each other and the precious earth that sustains us.

~~ MY MYSTERIOUS PROTECTOR

Earlier tonight I was wandering around the Southeast residential Ladd district where the streets are laid out both diagonally and with circular centers. It's a nice area to walk through because there is little traffic, and the houses have an old-world character, some of them two- or three-story Victorian.

The alleys tend to be long, since the streets are so weird and are also a little longer than normal city streets. I had just turned up one alley so see if I could find a good place to sleep when I thought I saw two or three figures duck behind a fence at the far end of the alley. I wondered if I had really seen something. Were they just flickering shadows caused by some movement of traffic in the street at the far end of the alley? Could Fallacious be trying to project another one of his horror films in front of my psyche?

I thought about turning around and getting out of the alley as fast as I could. I was feeling disappointed that this residential alley might be just as dangerous as the alleys in other parts of the city. But another part of myself urged me to walk on down the alley to challenge Fate. I wanted to make Fate, or Fallacious, or whoever was trying to scare the shit out of me, back down.

Surely, I had imagined seeing these people. If they were going to attack me, why wouldn't they just come storming down the alley and attack me? I didn't want to be frightened in this area. It's one of my special refuges. I also didn't want to give this area up. I was standing there battling with myself when I thought I heard some muffled cries coming from the other end of the alley where I had seen the shadows.

I instantly remembered the incident a few weeks ago when someone may have saved me from a gang. I had this feeling that someone was just saving me again. I don't know who or what was being my guardian, but I suddenly felt confident to walk down the long alley.

When I reached the point where I saw someone duck behind a fence, what I saw first caused me to jump back and almost start running and yelling down the alley. Two Asian men—I think they were from the Thai house—were lying unconscious on the ground behind the fence. A knife was lying on the ground by one of them. What in the hell happened to them?

I suddenly remembered that I thought I had seen someone go to the other side of the alley, and I quickly turned around. I saw two feet protruding out from under a bush.

Immediately I walked away. So three of the Thai men had been waiting for me. But someone else had somehow intervened, and all three are now unconscious. I assumed they were just knocked out. I didn't see any blood on the ones by the fence, but of course I didn't look all that closely. I didn't want to think that they had been killed.

Who's protecting me? Could it be Ransack? Ransack would have the skills to incapacitate these three men with what seemed like so little effort. Should I be thankful that Ransack is looking out for me? But he's a killer. I don't know what to think about this. I don't like danger. I don't like pain. I don't like violence or killing or spilled blood. If there is anyone controlling the universe, just let me be. Please let me be!

June 8 ~~ QUEEN AVARICE SLUMMING AT A DELI

Today Queen Avarice went to a deli not too far from the Holy Skyscraper. I had a few bucks in my pocket, and I decided to go in, too, and buy something to eat. I didn't think I looked too bad. I had showered and shaved yesterday afternoon at Esola's. My clothes weren't in the latest fashion, but what the hell? Who can tell what's really in fashion these days?

While I waited in line to order, I noticed that Queen Avarice was sitting alone at a small table. I ordered a half sandwich, took a number, and looked for a table where I could sit. I noticed that there was a table right beside Queen Avarice. I couldn't decide if I should go over there or not. I couldn't decide about sitting at a table next to Queen Avarice. I was nervous that something would happen, a chance meeting I wouldn't be prepared for.

I looked around and realized that there were no other tables where I could sit. Another example of destiny, or perhaps of a quirky, divine crap shoot. As I walked toward the table, I noticed that she was reading a magazine. I sat down, but didn't look up. I immediately felt awkward. Here I was sitting right next to someone rich and perhaps famous, royalty slumming it in a downtown deli, and I had nothing to occupy me. While I waited for my food, I just sat there looking straight ahead, but staring peripherally at her.

Out of the corner of my eye I noticed that she looked up and turned her head toward me, but I couldn't tell if she was really looking at me or at the counter. All it would take would be for me to turn her way and smile. But I could no more move my neck to turn my head than I could walk upside down on the ceiling.

I sat there thinking about how this was my chance. Why can't I just do something? I didn't feel it was right though. As much as I wanted to break my illusion of her, I didn't want it to be at the expense of my new creative soul. I'm not understanding this strange obsession I have with Queen Avarice, but something inside of me is keeping me from making a fool of myself, or worse betraying me. This awareness does make me feel better about myself.

I noticed that she looked at her watch, and then I saw her wave at somebody. I looked in the direction she was waving and saw Mr. Unnaturally Handsome. Goddamnit. He came over to her table and sat with her.

I heard her say that she had ordered for him. I felt a sense of relief that things were unfolding like this. I had the impulse to just get up and leave, but I had spent my last money on half a sandwich and I really was hungry. So I stayed, and I tried to listen to what they were saying, but they had their heads close to each other and were talking softly, so I could only hear fragments:

"I can't wait until..." he said.

"Jeff, I have something to tell you..." she said. Then she said something to him I couldn't hear.

He looked at her as if he couldn't believe what she was saying, "You can't mean that!" he finally said.

Something was happening here and he didn't like it.

"No, no. You can't do this," he continued in an angry tone of voice. He reached out and grabbed her arm.

"Just watch me," she said defiantly, pulling her arm out of his grasp. Then she got up and walked out of the deli. He stood up and watched her. Then he sat back down, put his head in his hands, and moaned. I looked over at him. He looked up and saw me staring, and said "What the fuck are you looking at, buddy?"

"Nothing. I just wondered if you were okay, or if you were having some kind of medical problem."

"I'm all right. Just mind your own goddamn business."

Chastised by one of the privileged beings. But it didn't look like he was doing so well himself. He even sounded a little like a frustrated slave. Ah well, it's amazing how quickly things change. It seemed like Queen Avarice had dumped this guy.

My sandwich was brought, and I ate it, feeling pleased, but...why? Why did I care that Queen Avarice had broken up with some other man?

June 9 ~~ QUEEN AVARICE BUYS ME A STEAK DINNER

I dreamed of Queen Avarice again last night. As much as I consciously try to discredit her in my waking conscious state, when I go to sleep, she slips into my dreams. I'm really upset with myself—or Fallacious—or whoever is to blame.

Last night I was following her into a fancy restaurant. She was wearing the most beautiful blue sequined full-length dress. When we entered, a maître de came up to me and said that I needed to be wearing a jacket or he couldn't let me come in. He gave me a white dinner jacket with an emblem of a Cadillac convertible on the back.

"I don't want to wear this jacket," I protested. "I don't believe in driving cars anymore, and even if I did, I wouldn't own a Cadillac even if I could afford it."

Queen Avarice looked at me sweetly and said "Oh, Gibson, it is just for tonight. Don't be so silly. You'd look even more handsome than you are"

I put the jacket on—I guess to avoid a scene, or—I don't know why. But I next remember sitting with her at the table getting ready to order. I looked at the entrées on the menu, and was astounded to see the prices. A sirloin steak was $10,000.00. The appetizers ranged from $1000 to $3000.

"These prices are outrageous," I said.

Queen Avarice said, "Gibson, when you accept the top level position we are offering you and you see the income you will be receiving, you will understand that you'll be able to afford anything you might want to buy—no matter what the cost."

"But I don't have any money now," I said to her. "I don't even have a credit card."

Queen Avarice again smiled sweetly at me, and reached across the table to put her warm hand on mine. "Don't worry Gibson. I'll take care of this dinner tonight. Just enjoy your meal."

The next thing I knew a big sirloin steak was in front of me, and I was enjoying each bite. The meat was so tender and juicy. Then I remember looking up from the plate of meat and baked potato and steamed vegetables, and looking out of the large glass window of the restaurant. To my horror, a row of gaunt and emaciated homeless men, women and children were standing just on the other side of the glass windows just staring at me. I instantly knew I was betraying all of these people. Worse, I felt I was betraying myself. But I looked down at sirloin steak, and realized I wanted very much to finish eating this steak. It tasted so wonderful. But when I reached for the fork and knife, I had to look up at the faces of the homeless people standing on the other side of the large windows. I became frozen and then I realized that other people in the restaurant were beginning to notice me. Why were they noticing me, I wondered? Do they know that I am homeless and should be standing on the other side of the window?

Would someone attack me and throw me back out on the street. I tried to look at Queen Avarice, but she was no longer sitting in front of me. I woke up feeling afraid.

It doesn't make sense that I keep dreaming of Queen Avarice. She can't be sweet and caring. And I don't want to work in the Holy Skyscraper. I don't want to be involved in that type of life anymore, that type of life where money is worshipped and anyone who does not have money is not worth anything.

The sirloin steak seems so real, and taste lingers in my mouth. But the images of the gaunt homeless men, women and children also haunt my thoughts.

June 11 ~~ CARISSA SHADOWS ME

Today was the day I agreed to let Carissa accompany me for the afternoon and early evening. I decided not to take her to the Holy Skyscraper because it's too personal. I don't know whether the Holy Skyscraper represents for me a profound spiritual battle or a continuation of my psychotic breakdown, but I do know it is too personal to share with anyone else right now.

We met at our usual meeting place in the park. The weather was pretty nice, blue skies with some cloudiness. We left the park and walked west toward the river. We were about a block from the Butcher's store before I realized that if we stayed in the same direction we were walking, we would have to pass by his store front. I decided to change directions. I didn't want the Butcher to see Carissa with me. As we continued walking toward the river, I showed her some of the alleys I had slept in, alleys with overgrown bushes, or old, rundown garages in the backs of houses or residences. She was amazed at how many of these places there are.

We crossed Martin Luther King and Grand Avenues and got to the industrial and old warehouse section of town. I showed her some of the abandoned buildings that I sleep in, and some of the areas underneath the loading platforms that provide good shelter from the rain. We looked through a few garbage bins and came up with some large cardboard pieces and some large cardboard boxes that were big enough for a man to sleep in. She took pictures of all this and asked me dozens of questions about if I'm allowed to sleep in these places without getting hassled, who hassles me, and so on.

As the evening approached, we went looking for something to eat. I took her to a few restaurants where I have been able to find edible leftovers that have been thrown out. We found a few heads of lettuce, some half-eaten bread, and even half a sandwich. I offered her some, and she reluctantly ate with me. She said it tasted okay, but it was just the idea of where we got it that bothered her.

Finally, we headed off toward the Freeway Fields. When we got to the fields, Billy Buzz was there with Livid. I introduced them to Carissa, and she asked them a few questions. Livid answered her questions, but Billy typically was so drugged out that he couldn't talk clearly. Carissa finally gave up on talking with him, but they both agreed to let her take a picture of them.

When we ran across Ransack, he wouldn't let Carissa take his picture. He took me aside and said that it wouldn't be safe for him to have his picture taken, and he didn't want her to write about him in her report either. I agreed, and steered Carissa away from him.

Carissa's basic reaction to the Freeway Fields was that it was a horrible place. We got there before sunset, and she was able to see all the litter and trash, including the drug paraphernalia. As we walked through the fields, she stayed close to me at first, but then she started going off on her own, talking and interviewing various people. Most of the people answered her questions. A few were rude to her, but nobody created any serious problems.

As she interviewed people, she showed them the picture of her friend's father. Only one person said that the man in the photograph seemed familiar but he couldn't remember where he had seen him before.

As I walked her back to Casey's for her late evening shift, she was extremely quiet. I was surprised that she didn't ask me any questions.

"Are you okay?" I asked her.

She nodded. "Just a little overwhelmed by it all. It's one thing to read about homelessness but to see these terrible conditions…It's really sad to me. And scary."

I knew why she was scared about her family becoming homeless.

Carissa looked at me and said, "You don't seem to be as bad off as so many of the others."

"I experience the same discomforts," I assured her. "But I just haven't totally been reduced to a gutter life. There are many homeless people who aren't the usual winos and drugged out people that are so visible on the street. There are many homeless people who are just normal everyday people who are locked out of jobs that will provide them enough income for them to have homes. I'm not like these people either. I experienced a psychological breakdown, and I have a psychological aversion to mainstream life. Of course, I don't know if this means I am psychologically impaired or if I have achieved a level of psychological sanity and well-being that won't let me return to the mainstream, unhealthy way of life. Maybe one day I will find out the answer to that. But to get back to your question, I still experience the coldness, the wetness, the hunger and the loneliness of the street, even though I don't always look a total mess."

She listened, and when I was through, she sighed. Her mind seemed miles away.

"Are you bothered that you couldn't find anyone who has seen your friend's father?" I asked.

"A little. I wanted to help her. I wish I could have found someone who has seen him. Of course, I'm also bothered in general about the horrible conditions I've seen."

"Now remember, Carissa. If your family becomes homeless, you won't have to exist in places I've shown you. There are shelters where you can go."

"I know. There are just so many things that are bothering me right now." She thanked me for letting her come with me and then said she had to get to her job at Casey's Cafe. As I watched her walk away, I was struck by how emotionally overwhelmed she seemed. I will have to check with her over the next few days to make sure she bounces back to her usual feisty self.

June 13 ~~ THE ENDING OF THE PLAY

The play ended last night, and I feel proud of my ability to stay with this project to the end, and yet now I feel empty. I wish it could have gone on forever. To be a part of such a display of creative emotion just felt fantastic.

They had a cast party after the play. Justine wanted me to go, but I couldn't. Despite how wonderful I feel, I can't go to the cast party. I feel a familiar fear. Not a fear of being social. I'm not shy. It's a fear of being destroyed. I feel protective. I feel the need to avoid putting myself in a vulnerable place. Especially now. Being involved in this play seems to have brought me closer than ever before to understanding what role I can assume as I try to relate to and make a contribution that might help improve an unjust society. Yet I'm still not strong enough to join the mainstream and expect that my new creative self will be able to continue to develop.

Everyone has left, and I'm sitting on the outside steps of the theater. Justine was the last to leave for the cast party. She said she wished I would come with her to the party, but she didn't try to pressure me. She hugged me before she left, and it was a long, electrifying hug…at least it felt that way for me.

Justine has been spending more time with me the last few times I have worked at the store. She's been asking me more questions about myself. I like it. I like the attention. I'm sure she has been showing her appreciation for the help I have given her in the play. She probably doesn't realize how much it has meant to me.

These sweet moments Justine spends with me stimulate my emotions and my fantasies tremendously. When I was about fourteen years old, the few times I was taken to church I remember how the full, vibrating, harmonious sounds of the church organ, the choir, and the people singing and how pleasant and sensual it was. These feelings and sensations were not the results of the attainment of spiritual heights, but rather were the results of being overwhelmed with yearnings that the music just stimulated further. I was usually in love or infatuated with some pretty girl sitting close by. Here I am more than twenty years later still yearning for love, for the experience of being swept off my feet by a woman who feels swept off her feet by me. By the real me, not the mainstream me.

Being involved in the play and experiencing Justine's attention certainly seems to arouse my romantic feelings and my sexual desires. But then afterwards, when I am alone in the streets, I can feel confused and frightened as hell. Attractive avenues that promise to lead me to meaningful relationships with others seem to be opening up to me, but I'm afraid if I start down them, they will close up, trap me forever in meaningless dead ends, and never let me go.

June 14 ~~ TRYING TO RESIST INVOLVEMENTS

Another dawn. I think of the day ahead, and I know I will be participating in the usual unplanned outsider activities in my life. While I was lying in my sleeping bag after waking up, I realized that the line between being an observer and being a participant in what I am observing has been constantly shifting and quite often has become difficult to keep firmly in place for me. I surprise and annoy myself at times for wanting to cross over and to participate in what I am observing because I know that's when problems begin. I have to resist involvement. For now, at least.

I did get involved in that play. I realize that during the play I exhibited a great deal of control to make sure I was ready for each performance. For example, I didn't look at Walter's ring during the weeks I was involved in the play. I didn't want to take a chance of not being able to come out of a trance the ring pulls me into and missing a performance of the play. I just have this feeling that if I looked into the ring's stone again I might actually be pulled further into that place I travel to and might not be able to get away. Now that the play is over, I may take the chance. Maybe. What I experience when I look into the ring scares me quite a bit, but also attracts me. The experience has not been unpleasant; as a matter of fact, it has been exhilarating.

I will walk over to the Holy Skyscraper and watch the privileged walk through the expensive patio into the building. Then I'll just take the day as it comes. Justine flashed into my mind. Maybe I will work a little at the Treasure Market today.

~~ ESOLA'S SAD MOOD

I did go to work at the Treasure Market earlier today. Esola was in such a sad mood. She went on and on about how she had no purpose in life. I found her sitting in one of the upstairs back rooms by herself in the late afternoon. She was sitting at a huge round table staring into space, and it seemed that she had been crying.

"Esola, what's the matter?" I asked.

"I have no purpose in life anymore," she said, shaking her head. "Not since my husband died. I don't like this life alone. I am too old to find a new man."

"Nonsense, Esola. You are a beautiful, lively woman. Many men would love you."

She shook her head. "No, Gibson. I'm too old. My beauty is gone. There are too many mirrors in this shop. I don't like what they show back to me."

"Esola, mirrors don't really tell the truth. The whole truth. I try not to look into mirrors anymore because they don't show what is important in me. Parts of me that most people can't see."

Esola looked at me and seemed to see me for the first time. What I said seemed to mean something to her.

"I know you're right, Gibson. I of all people know you're right because I can see what is hidden in people. Mirrors don't usually reflect this inner self. They don't tell the whole truth. You are right. But unfortunately, most men can't see the whole truth either. Most of them only look at the surfaces."

"But you're not interested in those kinds of men, are you? You're interested in finding that special man," I said. "Besides, Esola, you have a major purpose in life. You have the purpose of enlivening people's lives. Of getting people to dance a little bit, or at least keeping them on their toes."

She laughed and wiped the tears away from her eyes. She reached out and took my hand. "Thank you, Gibson, for trying to get me out of this mood I'm. You have succeeded a little. For that I thank you. I know I have some purpose in life. It's just that sometimes I walk around this huge store and remember my husband. I imagine him, and I miss him so much. I feel so lonely. You know, he wasn't even so nice all the time, but he was there, with me. We went through a lot, and now I'm without him. And I haven't been able to feel as alive."

"Esola, you seem so alive. You have so many interests. You have so many friends. Whenever you are here, you're either visiting with someone you know, or you're doing something with your tarot cards and other strange things you fool with, or you're cooking something wonderful."

"Yes, I do all of those things, but sometimes I'm just going through the actions, the motions, and I'm not feeling as good as I should. It's that there is no man, Gibson. No man in my life. I need a man."

"Well, go out and find a man," I said.

She laughed her delightful, throaty laugh. She said that, yes, she should go out and just find a man. Yes. Then she turned to me and said that she knew what she needed to do. "I need to travel. That's what's missing. I haven't taken a trip for so long. I need to start traveling again. Especially in Europe. That's where the men are. European men think that what they want is the young women, but I can show them that the older woman is better." She slapped the table. "Yes, I am going to plan a trip. I will consult my cards and my chart to see when the best time for me to travel is. And I will start planning. Oh, I'm so excited, Gibson. Thank you for talking to me. Gibson, you have such a gift." She looked at me with the look she gets when she is going to start in with her metaphysical advice. I interrupted her and told her that I was glad she was feeling better, but that I had to get to work.

"So do I," she said. "So do I. But wait, Gibson. I have arranged a meeting next week with the astrologer who has done your chart. I'll remind you when you come next week, and we can set a more exact time."

I said okay, and left her to return to work. I have to admit I am a little curious, but I'm also very skeptical. Very skeptical. Maybe not as skeptical as I would have been when I was a slave, but still skeptical. I have no doubt that strange realities exist that I have no rational explanation for. I have no real sense of rationality anyway. But astrology? It seems like looking at fortune cookies. So general, so meaningless. But because Justine and Esola want me to go through with this chart reading, I will do it, and I will try to be open.

June 18 ~~ SUCH A WASTE

I was working a rush job at Esola's Treasure House when Justine came back in the workroom and said she wanted to help make sure we finished sanding the table so it could be painted the next day. I could tell she was tired, probably from working round-the-clock with the play and managing the store.

"Justine, I can finish this. You probably have more important things to do… or you could just rest. You've been doing so much lately."

"I appreciate that, and I know I'm tired, but I think I need to do some physical work right now." She grabbed a sanding block and started in before I could say anything else. We worked in silence for a while. From time to time I would look up from my work and see the thin film of sand spreading over her black hair, which she had pinned up. She worked with her usual intensity, even though I did see her yawn a few times. From time to time I would look at her body and become a little distracted. Rounded hips. Strong hands, long, thin fingers. I tried not to look at her breasts, but then again I figured, what the hell. I don't have anybody to be with. It doesn't hurt to enjoy the beauty of a woman and to do a little fantasizing.

After a while I decided I had to begin talking with her to get my mind free from the sexual urges I was feeling. I asked her if she felt the play had been successful. She had been kneeling down working on one of the legs of the table. She stood up, picked up a rag off the work bench, and wiped her face before answering. She said that she was extremely pleased about how the play went and that she had been getting a lot of good feedback from other people in the theater community. She said that she was glad it was over, though and that she was going to enjoy the extra time she has before beginning another project. She said that she was surprised how exhausted she'd been feeling, and knew she needed a break.

For the rest of the afternoon we talked and joked as we worked. The time went by faster than it had earlier. I worked a couple of hours longer than I usually do. With Justine working side by side with me, it was a special occasion.

After we finished, I went to take a shower while Justine washed up at the kitchen sink. When I walked into the kitchen after the shower, I found that Justine had put plates of cut-up raw vegetables, cheeses, meats and bread out on the table and had opened a bottle of red wine. She handed me a glass of wine and said, "You know, I find it easy to talk with you, Gibson. I feel comfortable with you."

I took the glass of wine and said, "Thank you. I'm happy I make you feel comfortable." I didn't know what else to say, so I looked down at the table.

"Now don't get embarrassed," she said. "Here, I want to toast your expert help with putting on this play. We could not have done it without you." We clicked our glasses together and sipped our wine. Then she said, "Let's eat. I want you to tell me about your street life."

I first tried to tell her that I didn't know what to tell her about my street life, but she wouldn't let me get away with that. She asked me questions, some of them similar to Carissa's, about where I slept, how I kept warm? Didn't I feel angry about how nobody is helping the homeless? As we talked, we ate and drank. Before we knew it, we had almost finished the bottle of wine and before I knew it Justine opened another bottle. She said that she hasn't drunk that much in years, but she felt like drinking tonight. She said that she really hadn't celebrated the ending of the play in the proper way since not everyone involved in the play made it to the cast party.

"Are you talking about me?" I asked.

"Yes," she said. "So here I am drinking more than I should tonight just to celebrate with you."

"I feel honored," and I did profoundly feel honored.

As the wine started getting to me, I talked more and more about my life on the street, and I had the urge to tell her about the new self I was trying to develop, but I didn't. Somehow I stopped myself and I don't know how. I was feeling so wonderful. I did admit to her that I didn't feel I could cope with regular life right now, and that I was using my journal writing as a way of working through my problems.

I began to notice that that Justine was getting a little drunk herself. Her words were slurring a little, and she was yawning more often. At one point she looked at me and said, "You know what I'm thinking of doing, Gibson?" I shook my head. "I'm thinking of running away. I'm thinking that I might first disappear in the streets, hiding among the transients, just like you did—then eventually I might hitch a ride to the East Coast, buy a cheap ticket to Europe, find a small village somewhere in Spain, and then hide out some more. Just stay hidden so only a few people would know where I am. What do you think? If I ran away, would you show me where to hide here in Portland?"

I sat my glass of wine down. "Why would you want to run away? You're kidding, aren't you?"

"Why would I be kidding? You ran away. Why can't I?" She stared at me with a most unsettling intensity, waiting for me to respond. I couldn't tell if she was serious or not. She looked very serious.

"I didn't just run away. I had a breakdown."

"Maybe I'm having a breakdown. A dramatic breakdown." She said as she raised her right arm in a sweeping gesture. "Here's to dramatic breakdowns, Gibson." She raised her glass.

I asked her if she was drunk, and she said, "Well, hell, I hope so. Aren't you?" She looked at me suspiciously. Then she started giggling, and I couldn't help but laughing, too.

"See, you're drunk, too."

"Yes, yes, I am. I admit it."

We stopped laughing but kept staring at each other. I wanted to reach out and touch her. I wanted to make love to her.

Just as I had those thoughts, she put her right elbow on the table and her hand to right cheek as if she were holding up her head. She said in a dreamy kind of voice, "You look so good after you take a shower. You're a handsome man. But what are you doing with it, Gibson? What are you going to do with it?" Then she laid her head down on the table and continued talking, "Such a waste. Such a waste." Then she stopped talking and her breathing became more rhythmic.

I got up from the table and walked over beside her. She had her eyes closed. Her right arm stretched across the table, her left hand resting by her empty wine glass. I reached out and gently shook her. She didn't respond, and I knew then that she had passed out. We did have more than the usual wine. I definitely felt it, but since she was so exhausted, the wine put her to sleep. I carefully pulled her chair back, picked her up, and carried her to the bed in the adjacent room. After laying her in the bed, I found a blanket and laid it on top of her.

I decided to stay and sleep in the chair near her bed because I didn't want her to wake up alone in the building. After a while I finally fell asleep. I woke at dawn, and she was still sleeping. I fell asleep again, and next time I awoke, she was gone. She had written a short note: "I have to run to make an appointment. I'm a little hung over, but it was worth it. Thanks for finally celebrating with me, and thanks for putting me to bed. Your friend, Justine."

I put this note away in a special place in my pack. Now I have to get some distance. I have to walk around a lot and get immersed in my outcast reality. I am an outcast, and I have to stay reminded of it. But I can't quite lose that image of how she looked at me with her lovely dark eyes as she told me how handsome I look after I take a shower. "Such a waste," she said. Am I wasting my life? I hope not. I hope I'll know the right time for me come in from the streets.

Before she passed out, I could feel the emotional connection between us. If I could have just reached out to her. Well, I did reach out to her, but just not physically. So what am I feeling frustrated about? I know exactly what I am feeling frustrated about, but I have to let it go. I can't think of what could have happened. I have to enjoy what did happen. I spent a delightful afternoon and night with Justine, working, eating, drinking and talking, and she passed out and I put her to bed. What more could I want?

~~ CARISSA SHARES INFORMATION ABOUT THE HOMELESS KILLERS

Now I'm even surer of who is killing the homeless, but I don't know how to prove it. Yesterday after Carissa got off work, she came up to where I was sitting outside Casey's Café. She said that she wanted to tell me something that she saw in Al's Meat Store earlier that afternoon. She looked around as though someone might be listening to us, and when she was satisfied that nobody was eavesdropping or could hear her, she whispered. "During the noon rush, I was sent to Al's to pick up a some hot dogs and ground beef to carry us over until the main meat delivery from Al's later this week. I have to do this from time to time in emergency situations. Since they know me at Al's, one of the other meat cutters sent me down in the basement to the refrigerator to get the packages that I needed. When I went downstairs, I noticed that nobody was in Al's office and I opened the door and peeked in. I was shocked to see that on the wall behind his desk, he has pasted newspaper articles of the killings of the homeless. I was nervous about being caught, but I did try to count the articles, and it seemed like there more than ten of these articles—how many homeless have been murdered?"

"Ten homeless victims that we know of," I said. I know that this doesn't prove that the Butcher is killing homeless people, but it's disturbing and at least proves that must be obsessed with these killings. But that's not a crime.

Carissa continued, "I wanted to tell you what I saw because I know you think the Butcher might have something to do with the killings of homeless people."

"Carissa, I appreciate you telling me. Don't tell anyone else, because I don't want you to get into trouble, and please don't take any more chances like that. I wish you didn't have to go to Al's Meat Shop anymore."

She seemed pleased at my expression of concern. "Don't worry, Gibson. They don't send me there that often. And I didn't stay looking into his office that long."

Later, when I got to the library, I read in the newspaper about the eleventh homeless killing. I was sitting among the newspapers and magazines in the section of the building with the ceilings that curve in arches. I sometimes get lost in those arches—sometimes for an hour or so.

Anyway, as I was reading the newspaper article about the killing, I kept thinking about who would do such a thing. Who would come up on a defenseless, sleeping, homeless street person and start hacking him to death? The image that kept coming to my mind was that of the Butcher, with his red face and blood-stained apron, standing over a sleeping man, swinging his meat hatchet down. I stopped the image before the hatchet hit the man. That would be too horrible to even imagine.

I shook my head to try to get rid of the image, but the thought of the Butcher as the killer persisted, especially after what Carissa had just shared with me. I tried to imagine another crazed person doing the killing, but the image of the Butcher just wouldn't go away. It would be too much of a coincidence that the Butcher would be the killer, but then it would just be another example of meaningful coincidence that occurs in all of our lives.

I thought Ransack had already dealt with the Butcher, and I even tested that he had. I have stood in front of his store a number of times, but he has not come out to attack me. Maybe the Butcher started secretly attacking homeless people and killing them since he wasn't able to continue to harass them openly. I shook my head again. It didn't seem such a far-fetched notion. I thought again about the night that I saw all those men sneaking into the back of the Butcher's shop, and I wondered if on the night of that meeting a homeless man was killed. Perhaps these men were a part of some vigilante group whose aim is to rid the city of bums and street people.

My rational mind tries to tell me that it would be too obvious, but I still had no trouble believing that the Butcher could be behind the killings. I've continued to see images of the Butcher as the killer in my dreams and visions. It could be that I truly am psychic and my mind is actually seeing what is happening across time and distance. I wish I knew for sure. I wish I could prove my suspicions one way or the other.

I looked back in my journal and identified the date I saw the men going into the Butcher's store. Then I went to the reference desk, and got the copy of the following day's newspaper. I was stunned to find that on the next day after I saw that meeting, the newspaper reported another homeless man had been killed.

I sat in the library in a daze for quite a while. The idea scared the hell out of me. I still sleep a lot in the areas near the Butcher's store. I was excited but also scared. Fallacious may be laughing at my fantasies, but it could be real. I may be onto something that could save a lot of homeless people, including myself.

~~ WHAT SHOULD I DO WITH THIS INFORMATION?

It's two or three hours later. I'm sitting on the steps leading up the Burnside Bridge, getting my energy to cross it, and I still feel a little blown away by the connection between the killing and the night I saw all those men behind the Butcher's shop—and also the newspaper articles about the killings pasted up on the wall behind his desk. But I also realize that most people would think I'm full of shit if I accused him of killing homeless people. It feels strange to think that I might know who is killing the homeless people but that I might not get anyone to believe me.

I think I should start by telling Ransack about this connection and see what he thinks. He's more prepared to deal with this kind of thing than I am. If half of what he says is true, he is our town specialist on secret groups and what to do about them. I know I'm leaving myself open to another session with Ransack but I feel that this is too important for me to worry about my petty likes and dislikes.

~~ TELLING RANSACK ABOUT MY SUSPICIONS

I was at the edge of the Freeway Fields this evening when I finally found Ransack. I asked if I could talk with him a few minutes, and I told him about the connection that I had made. After I finished, he stared at me for a few minutes before responding. I saw that his eyes narrowed as he looked at me. He has a goddamn intense stare.

He finally said that he couldn't believe the Butcher is smart enough to organize a secret group of men. He said these guys are probably playing poker or watching porno movies at night. He said that it would be more their style. He said that he would have nothing more to do with it, and he said that I should leave it alone, too. He said that he thinks the Butcher is abiding by his promise, but if the Butcher catches me snooping around, he might go on a rampage again. He repeated his advice to me, leave it alone. And he walked away.

Maybe Ransack is right. The Butcher can't be doing this, and what the hell am I doing, trying to play the sleuth or the hero? I'm not either one. I'm going to take Ransack's advice and try to let it go. Besides, if I can't convince Ransack, what chance would I have of convincing anyone else?

~~ FEAR OF BEING FOLLOWED

Someone has been following me all night. I could just feel it, and a couple of times when I turned around I could see someone duck into a doorway or around a corner of a building. I tried to tell myself that I was just being paranoid, and maybe I was. But paranoia hasn't been my style of craziness, or at least hasn't been up to now. But shit, what I've been through these last few months on the street could make anyone paranoid.

Why would someone be following me anyway? I mean someone other than the bag lady, the Thai woman's brothers, an alien looking for his ring, the homeless killer, the Butcher (if they are different), Justine's old boyfriend, one of the many gangs of this city or someone who just doesn't like my looks? Yes, who could be following me?

I just came into to this 24-hour diner on Grand Avenue down from the Lloyd Center and have spent my last few dollars on a cup of coffee and an apple pie a la mode. Maybe this treat will make me feel better. But how long can I stay in here? I'm even surprised that I was served. I guess I don't look too bad tonight or maybe the waitress needs glasses. I guess I will try to stay in lighted areas for the rest of the night.

June 20 ~~ COULD I HAVE BEEN A WARRIOR IN MY PAST LIFE?

I was working at the Treasure Market today when Esola comes up and tells me she thinks I might have been a warrior in one of my past lives for some powerful African tribe. She seems serious but in her dramatic way, as if she were expressing some monumental discovery. She says that I had killed many men and fought many battles and saved many people's lives. I told Esola that I had a tremendous aversion to physical violence of any kind. She waved her hand and said in this lifetime I am developing other sides of myself but that my warrior side is inside me waiting for the right time to show its force.

I have become used to humoring these metaphysical pronouncements of Esola but now that I'm living on the street, I wish what she said is true. I wish I could remember some of my old fighting skills in case I need them.

I was talking with Justine a little while later and she asked me if I would try writing something that she could read. She had come into the workroom for no other reason than to talk to me. She has been doing this a lot since the play has ended and I like it. I shouldn't like it but I do. I feel this pleasant excitement when I'm around her.

"You mean like a poem or story or something?" I asked.

"Maybe just a description of something or of how you are feeling. Maybe just a dialogue."

"I don't know, Justine. I don't know if I'm that kind of writer."

"I bet that you are, Gibson. You just need some encouragement, or as Esola would say, maybe a kick in the butt. You're wasting your time, Gibson. I know that you have talents you're not using."

I was surprised at how so suddenly she switched from just a normal conversation to an admonishment. But she had said it with such caring I couldn't get defensive. I just said, "Are you going to kick me in my butt?"

"Maybe I will," she responded and ran around the counter. Before she got to me, she stopped and looked around to see if any of the customers were in the sales room. Satisfied that nobody else was around she tried to get near enough to be where she could kick my butt. But her hesitation allowed me to dodge away from her. We were both laughing. Finally she grabbed my arm to stop me and said that maybe she couldn't kick me in the butt today but she will if I don't start writing. She continued to hold my arm. We stopped laughing as we looked at each, then I turned and walked away from her touch, back to my work bench. I said, "I can see I will have to watch my rear from now on."

I told her maybe one day I'd be able to write something for her, but as usual, now that I am away from the store I don't know when I'll be able to pull it off. It doesn't feel right, but maybe I'll give it some time.

What would I write? If I were writing to Justine I would try to write something poetic. But if I were writing for mainstream people, I think I'd try to write something to wake them up to their lack of caring. I'd try to write something that would stimulate their compassion. But then what? So what if they started caring more and their compassion were stimulated? What do I think they should do with all their caring and compassion? They could take some risks for others. They could stop hiding behind their material securities. They could realize that if we're ever going to make the government more responsive to the everyday people, control the corporate royalty and allow everyone to truly have their basic needs met, then more mainstream Americans would have to come out into the streets and get involved in taking our society back from the financial elite.

It's amazing to me how long I have written in my journal and never even considered for a moment that I would write something for someone else to read, and then just in a moment of lightness, Justine has got me to seriously think about writing something for her and for others. Except now that I've let this fantasy flourish in my mind for a few minutes I feel uneasy again. I don't know if my new soul is ready.

~~ SPACE TRAVEL

Tonight I felt I had to look at the ring again. I decided that if the same thing happened to me that did last time I looked at it, and if I was able to return to my body, then I would show the ring to somebody else. I have not been able to find Walter anyway.

I decided it didn't matter if I did it in daytime or nighttime, but I realized that if I passed out, I should be in a little more isolated place so that I would not run the risk of attracting attention or having the ring stolen from me. I waited until it was near midnight. I found a perfect place to sleep under the loading docks of an old warehouse. I lay my sleeping bag down and crawled into the space. I leaned back against the building and took the ring out. It was almost completely dark, but I didn't think it would matter. I raised my knees up, and rested my fore-arms on them so that I held the ring right in front of me. I felt comfortable, and I just waited.

Soon I was experiencing the same sensations as before, and, as before, it was one of the most exhilarating experiences I have ever had. As the array of lights floated past me, this time I noticed that they were constantly changing colors, and I enjoyed the display immensely. The planet appeared before me as it had before, and I floated down toward it, and eventually toward the plaza.

This time there were two people standing in the plaza, a man and a woman. This time I came closer. I could see that the man was trying to talk to me, but I couldn't hear him. I continued getting closer until it seemed like I was hovering only a few feet from them.

Suddenly, I heard him say, "Don't be afraid. We're not dangerous. Don't be afraid. It's important that you listen carefully to us. You have found one of our communicators. You must take the communicator, the ring, back to where you found it. You cannot yet safely use what we have to offer your species. Please understand that we do not wish you harm. But I'm afraid harm will come to your species if our lost communicator becomes known to others of your species who are in power. You are not able to talk to me now. You will be returning soon. I hope you have understood me. I hope you do what I say."

He did not say anything else. He just stood there looking at me, seeming very concerned. I felt myself begin to float away from them. Then I lost awareness.

When I awoke, I didn't know what time it was. It was still dark. I felt around to get my bearings and assured myself that I was under the loading dock. I gathered my belongings and walked to a place with a little more light. When I walked by a store I noticed that it was about 4:00 a.m.

I sat down and again wrote about this experience, and now I'm deciding what to do about it. I think I will take this to Esola. Even as I write this, I know it seems crazy to take this ring to Esola. But she is the only person I know who seems to have an understanding of things beyond the ordinary. And then I'll find Walter. Somehow I'll find Walter, and I'll take this ring back.

I'm totally convinced that I must return the ring. It's so weird. I have no selfish urge to keep it. I may change my mind. But right now, I feel that there is a danger in not taking it back. Only I also feel that I must share it with someone, and Esola is the only person who I feel is open enough to truly accept what I will be telling her.

June 21 ~~ GIVING ESOLA THE RING & RECEIVING HER GUIDANCE

I found Esola today sitting in the kitchen looking at a travel magazine. She looked up when I walked into the room, and after saying hello she started telling me that travel magazines have so much garbage in them. She said that if all people see when they travel is what they show in travel magazines, then they might as well stay at home because they're not getting the true flavor of the country.

"Then why are you looking at the travel magazine?" I asked.

She smiled and said, "To give me something more to complain about."

"It's nice to see you smile for a change. I haven't seen you smile for so long."

"I can't get out of this mood I'm in. I think I need a change. I'm fed up with the rut I'm in. My whole life I have hated being in ruts. I have hated staying in one place too long. And I have hated being without a man. All these things are true in my life right now, so you can't expect me to be in a good mood. At least I'm not in a nasty mood, which I could be."

"That's true," I responded. "Please don't get in a nasty mood. I don't know if this building would be left standing."

She smiled and reached out and pushed my shoulder. "I'm not all that bad," she said.

"Esola I have something to show you. You're the only person I know who might be open enough and knowledgeable enough to give me some advice." I could see that she seemed to perk up. I took the ring out of my pocket and gave it to her. "I know this may sound crazy to you, but I believe that this ring belongs to aliens from another planet or perhaps somewhere other than what we know as reality. I don't know, but I think you are the only person who would not think I'm crazy. So I'd like you to look at this ring."

She took the ring and studied it carefully for a while. Then she asked me to tell her about the ring. I told her about Walter and what he told me about the aliens. I told her how I got the ring and I described the experiences that I had looking into the ring. As I talked with her I could tell that she was becoming more and more excited.

After I finished, she said, "Gibson, you have had a wonderful experience. You have had the opportunity to see beings from another planet, or perhaps another dimension."

"What if it was just all in my imagination? There's a part of myself that likes to create hallucinations to confuse me."

She laughed for the first time in weeks it seemed, and said, "I don't think it's a hallucination. For one thing, I have never seen a ring like this. For another, I'm not a skeptic. The scientists who don't want to believe in wonders and possibilities that can't be seen or measured, let them be skeptics! I believe in all possibilities, and I know there are things that exist that you and I can't see. This ring and the visit from the aliens could be of great benefit to our civilization. Our whole world could be expanded by knowing that another life form actually exists. Peoples' views will broaden. Perhaps people of this world will be forced to break away from their insistence that only one way of living, one belief system, is the right way. Also, Gibson, just think of the new worlds that will be opened up for travel and exploration."

"I'll bet you will be on the first spaceship."

"We may not need a spaceship," she said, looking at the ring.

"But we have to give the ring back. They say we aren't ready."

"They're probably right. It's not necessarily right to give this ring to the government, but maybe these beings could benefit themselves from contacting certain types of people who are more developed and who truly have concern and compassion for all life forms. I want to try to talk with them and convince them to start communicating with a few of us. Anyway, I would like to keep the ring for a few days. See if you can find Walter and bring him here. By the way, how old is Walter?"

"I don't know. I have to admit that he's been looking younger and younger since he's been spying on the aliens. He quit drinking and he just looks better." Then I looked at Esola with a sly expression. "Esola are you trying to solve all your problems at one time?"

"Why not, Gibson? Why not? You have made my day, Gibson," she said, jumping up from the table and throwing her arms in the air.

"But we have to give the ring back."

"I know we do. And we will. Soon."

I started to leave, but Esola called after me. "Gibson, have you been able to find out what's in the pagoda cabin of that Grand Dragon boat?"

Surprised, I turned back to look at Esola. "No. I still have visions of myself on a boat like that, but I can never see inside."

"Take control of those visions, Gibson. I know you can. I know you are able to see inside if you focus. I suggest you spend time meditating on the boat we have here at the store. It may help you take more control of your mind."

I told her I might do it, and left the Treasure Market. I have been sitting outside, leaning against the building, writing in my journal. For the first time, I am feeling positive that I can take control of my mind and maybe even develop my mental abilities in ways I could never before imagine. I realized that I should try what she suggested. I shouldn't leave. I turned and went back inside.

~~ INSIDE THE PAGODA CABIN OF THE GRAND DRAGON BOAT

I walked into the room at the Treasure Market where the Grand Dragon Boat was displayed, pulled up a chair and sat next to it. I thought about what Esola had said to me. I wanted to see what was on the table and in other parts of the room inside the pagoda. I felt as though it would give me an understanding of what had happened to my mind since my breakdown. I felt that when I faded out, I actually was traveling somewhere, and I believed the reoccurring visions of the dragon boat flying into the night sky held the secret to my destinations.

I stared at the dragon boat, and began to breathe deeply and rhythmically. I focused my attention on the door to the pagoda cabin, and imagined myself standing in front of the door reaching out to open it. I became aware of myself standing in front of the dark wood door, and when I tried to push it open, it gave way. The door slowly swung open. I walked into the room, and saw that the candle was lit on the long wooden table. I walked over to the table, and stood before it. I could see the books, the stacks of paper and map drawing instruments. I could also see a series of nine large square-shaped maps spread out side by side on the table.

In the center was a map of the earth. All around it were eight other maps of places I could not recognize, except one of the other maps seemed to display our solar system. There were three other maps that seem to be of galaxies, and then the other four maps seemed to be of landscapes and oceans similar, but different from earth. I noticed that someone had drawn concentric, overlapping circles that crossed through adjacent maps, and lines had been drawn from areas on some circles to areas of other circles, and these lines crossed through and connected different maps. I realized that someone was obviously plotting journeys to faraway places, and the phrase, "faraway dimensions" came to mind.

Suddenly, I heard someone cough gently behind me. I turned to look, but I could not see through the darkness. I reached back behind me, and took the candleholder. I then held the candle in front of me, and walked into the darkness. After a few steps I could see faintly the figure of a man sitting in a chair near the wall of the room. I walked further until I could see him more clearly. He had long flowing black hair.

I could not tell how old he was, but when he spoke, his voice seemed both wise and vibrant. "You have taken the first step of many long journeys you are destined to take," he said. "I will be able to teach you how to consciously take these journeys to other galaxies and dimensions so that you do not lose yourself. If you learn what I can teach, you can be one of the messengers who will enlighten some of the peoples of your homeland. You are not ready now to consciously travel where you need to go. You are not ready to endure the challenges you will face in these other places. You are not ready to effectively convey what you will see in your journeys to others in your reality. Hopefully you will be ready soon."

When I came out of this trance, I went to my backpack and took out my journal so I could record this experience. I am amazed that I could remember every detail.

I am amazed that I was able to see though the darkness. Maybe I am not crazy after all. Maybe my mind can travel beyond rational thought, beyond the limits of space and time. If this is so, the question I now have is, how can I become ready?

I must first need to believe in myself and that I have these powers. I have to continue to focus on consciously remembering where my mind goes when I fade out. And perhaps more importantly, I have to stay grounded and involved in the world I'm living in. I need to do that with compassion and love. Esola has helped me with her laughter and wisdom, and Justine has helped me with her love and acceptance.

June 22 ~~ VISITING THE HIDEOUT OF THE BEINGS FROM ANOTHER WORLD

Even though I had given Esola the ring, I still couldn't get it out of my mind. I decided that I had to find Walter and figured that the only place he might be was at the apartment building where he thought the aliens were hanging out. I had just finished my watch at the Holy Skyscraper, so I wasn't that far away from the area of town where the apartment building was located.

When I arrived there I couldn't find Walter. I decided to stay around for a while and sat down in the same spot where I'd sat the last time I was there. I looked up at the third-floor window, only this time I had more anticipation about seeing something. What I saw when I looked into the ring the last time still seemed so real. I knew that I had seen some things that made me believe that there were aliens in that third-floor room.

Just then I saw a bright light shine from behind the shades of the window. It was so sudden, I quickly stood up from the sidewalk. I ran over to the front door of the building but it was locked. I ran around to the back of the building. I saw a man getting out of his car and heading for the backdoor. I jumped behind some tall bushes a few feet from the door. I thought that maybe I'd be able to grab the door in time.

The man was awkwardly carrying some packages, which gave me an idea. He dropped one of the packages and as he stooped to pick it up I came out from behind the bushes and walked away from the backdoor. I then started walking toward the backdoor just as the man was continuing his walk. We arrived at the door about the same time and I began searching through my jackets. He was doing the same, and again dropped one of his packages. I picked one up, and said, "Here let me help you." He thanked me. I asked if I could help carry his packages up for him. He said that he should be okay once he got the door open. With me holding a couple of his packages he unlocked the door, and as went inside, I handed him the rest of his packages. He walked on to an elevator.

I could see a stairway going up, and after waiting for the man to get into the elevator, I started up the stairs. I came out on the third floor and walked down the hall to where I was sure the apartment would be. I knocked on the door.

The door was opened by an older looking woman dressed in a black robe with exotic, golden designs on the fabric. Her face seemed ancient, not just her wrinkles but also an essence that seemed to be emanating from her presence. I knew that I had to say something quickly. "I'm sorry to bother you, but I walk by this apartment building often. I have friends living on the second floor. And quite a few times I've seen this bright glow behind your window. I know it's none of my business, but I wondered if a photographer or a film maker lived here. I'm a filmmaker myself." Well, Fallacious is, anyway.

As I looked into her eyes, I felt mesmerized. Her eyes turned from a warm amber tone to a lovely blue, and I felt immediately at ease and comforted. When she spoke I felt a fulfilling feeling of well-being come over me. She seemed so caring, like someone I could trust with my life. She said in a gentle voice, "We know why you are here, and we know you do not have the ring with you, but we need it back. Please, you must give it back to us. The woman reached out and touched my hand. Her touch sent a warm and stimulating surge up my arm. Then she continued to speak, "We need the ring back. We have seen you with the man who found the ring and we know you have used the ring. We have not been able to locate the other man, but if you know where the ring is, please bring it back. It is a matter of extreme importance. We will not try to forcefully take the ring back from you, but you must give it back. We will be waiting here for your return. Go now in peace." Then she closed the door.

After I was on the street, I looked back up to the window and then decided for sure that I would tell Esola that the ring must be given back.

June 23 ~~ BILLY BUZZ OVERDOSES

I heard this afternoon that Billy overdosed and was in the hospital. I went to see how he was doing and ran into Livid. She was sitting in the lobby, crying.

"How's Billy," I asked.

"I don't know. He's unconscious. He's been unconscious for two days now."

I didn't know what to say. Billy has barely been conscious since I've known him, but it sounds like he just went over the edge.

Livid said, "I had just told Billy that I'd be buying our tickets this next week."

I sat with Livid for a while at the hospital. A doctor came out and said that Billy was in a coma and his condition had not changed. I asked Livid is she wanted me to walk with her anywhere. She said no, she had to go back to work. She said she needed to work to save some money for the medical expenses.

Now I'm in a coffee shop at the hospital. I see so many worried faces around me. I knew something like this might happen to Billy but it's sad to finally see it happen. I have this worried feeling that Livid would be staying here continuing working on the streets to help pay for Billy's care. I wouldn't like to see that happen but I can't do anything about it.

At least Billy is receiving medical care. Now that he's overdosed he might be forced into a detox and rehab center, if he survives. Maybe he will fall under some government program. Maybe Livid won't have to pay for it so she will be free to go back to Amsterdam if she wants.

June 25 ~~ WHO WILL SEE JUSTINE'S CANDLELIGHT IN THE WINDOW?

I was helping Justine unpack some candleholders today and she acted like a child opening a gift at Christmas. She said to me, "I have such romantic feelings about candleholders and candlelight. One time in a play my character said to her lover, 'I light candles to keep romance in my life. The romance of a candle in the window. The romance of the soft mesmerizing glow, bringing faces and figures out of the shadows, hinting at the pleasures of love, the pleasures of sensuality.'"

She stopped and looked at me, smiling, and said, "That's the way I feel. I light candles at special moments—at dinner, when I'm being cozy with friends or a lover, when I'm taking a bath. When new candleholders come into the store I have bought many of them. Some candleholders inspire me to create a fantasy or story." She looked at the ceramic candleholders she had just unpacked. "For example, I was told these candleholders come from a small village in France.

Look at the hearts and designs painted on them. Don't these look like tears? I imagine that this candleholder was owned by an upper-class French woman in the Middle Ages who lived in a castle across the river from a small peasant village. She has fallen in love with a man, a peasant, who lives in the village. Every night she puts the candle in the window and lights it, hoping that one night he will come and see the light and come for her."

She stopped talking. I waited for a while and finally asked, "Does he come for her?"

She smiled and said, "In my fantasy he certainly does, or someone equally special does. A woman can't wait around too long for one special person to notice the candlelight in the window."

"I thought with romantic love there's only one true love."

"No, no, I don't believe that. I think there can be many special people who can become a true love." She stopped and raised her eyebrows. "Generally one at a time though. Seriously, what's important is that when you love somebody you can only be so assertive. While I like the image of a woman yearning for love, but who has to wait, she can't wait forever for the man to respond to the light in the window." She was silent for a moment, looking at me with those beautiful dark eyes. Then she handed me the ceramic candleholder, turned and started walking away, saying over her shoulder, "After you clean those candleholders, Gibson, please leave them out on the table. I might take one for myself."

Who's she waiting for? I don't really want to know the answer to that question. I wish I felt ready to try to find the answer to that question.

June 26 ~~ TRYING TO MAKE BETTER SENSE OF MY RANTING AND RAVING

This morning I was sitting across from the Holy Skyscraper, enjoying the reflections of the blue sky and sun on the glass walls. I found myself feeling benevolent toward the building, and at first I felt angry that I would find something good with a structure that represents greed, misplaced resources, the worship of money that benefit the rich and powerful at the expense of the less fortunate. Then I challenged myself to get beyond my anger, and to try to be more reflective.

When I rant and rave about slave society, who or what am I blaming? Surely, I can't blame capitalism and Christianity for all the injustices in America. Up until this point I haven't even cared to make sense out of all this. That's why I haven't talked about this to that many people. I haven't wanted to ask questions.

But I do blame capitalism as it is now for most of the injustices of the world.

It's a system that builds on a master-slave relationship, productivity over human concerns, unrestricted accumulation of wealth and resources at the expense of others.

Could a different system be better? I believe that there has to be a better system. One that keeps some of the freedom and creativity of capitalism. But somehow there has to be a

recognition that we need a body of government that looks out for the welfare of the community, and we have to find ways to keep this kind of government from being bought by special interest groups. I think it's possible. I don't think it'd be easy to do these things but I think it's possible.

I don't want to get into why I'm down on Christianity—just to say that any religious or belief system that claims a monopoly on the spiritual experience is just another form of imperialism——where a group of people think they are better than others and therefore deserves to live better than others. And while I do think we have negative sides of ourselves I don't think a person's tendency to do bad things is stronger than his or her tendency to be caring and do positive things. The "evil" that people do has more to do with how few opportunities they have, how abused and how hungry they are, than it has to do with some innate tendency to be evil.

In a nutshell these are my thoughts on capitalism and Christianity—the two pillars that hold up our U.S. slave society. Can things get better? I have to answer this question in order to know where my new soul will live, how it will live, does it really have a future. Will I be out on the streets forever?

June 27 ~~ PROTECTING THE TREASURE MARKET IN MY DREAMS

Last night dragons appeared to me in the shape of beautiful women floating through the night sky, like ancient goddesses. I could almost believe they were real. And they were beckoning to me. I felt the loneliest I've ever felt and wanted to just accept their extended hands, but at the last moment I saw a faint light in a window of a building. I walked toward it. Eventually I realized the building was the Treasure Market, and I saw Justine in the window. She had just lit a candle. I looked back at the goddesses, and saw that they were not goddesses at all. They had changed back into their horrible night dragon shapes. I ran away. I did not want them to scorch the Treasure Market. With all my heart I did not want them to do that. I woke up and was surprised that I had not reached the end of my nightmare. It was the first time that Fallacious didn't carry me to my usual end.

~~ BILLY BUZZ AND LIVID

I went by the hospital today to see how Billy and Livid were doing. Livid said that the doctors told her that Billy probably wouldn't come out of the coma, that he was brain dead. She said that his father had come to the hospital and was handling the medical decisions.

"I'm going back to Amsterdam next week," she said. "I can't help Billy anymore here, and I decided that I am hurting myself if I stay any longer. If Billy comes out of his coma, I will try to come back for him."

"What are you going to do?"

"I'm going to live with my aunt in Amsterdam and go to school. But I'm going to stay as far away from the red-light district as I can. That's what I plan right now."

I wished her luck and felt good that she would be off the streets. Then I thought of Billy. Another street casualty. I see it happening all the time. I keep wondering if the slaves see it too because if they did see it, wouldn't they demand that these people get help? Right now, most Americans don't seem to give a goddamn about the poor and the sick. Survival of the fittest. The big scam. Keep everybody thinking that there's not enough to go around and then people will say it's ok to not help people in need. It'll leave more for everyone else. Not very humane or evolved thinking.

~~ I'M BEING TARGETED

I had just settled into the dirt and grime of an alley close to the freeway fields, making it my own dirty and grimy bedroom for the evening, when I heard what had to be members of some gang talking further down the alley. I looked into the darkness and thought I saw movement, but I couldn't be sure. Then I heard someone say, "Where is that Gibson asshole? I thought you said he'd be around here somewhere, man."

"Slow down your ass, man. We'll find him and do what we've been paid to do soon enough. I mean, he's homeless, asshole. He could be anywhere. He's just supposed to hang out around here. That's all I know."

I don't think I'll ever forget those words as long as I live. I knew that I wasn't popular with a few people, but I didn't think I was so unpopular that someone would pay a gang to attack me. Would they kill me or just make me an invalid? I sat there thinking to myself, "Is it my time to die?"

I was about ready to try to get away, even though I knew that they were close, when I heard them start yelling at someone, and heard grunts and sounds of fighting. I was still lying very still along the side of a building in the darkness of the alley. Suddenly I heard three or four people run by me yelling. I looked up to see them run out of the alley and turn the corner onto the street.

What had happened? Someone had attacked them. Two gangs fighting one another, or what? Maybe someone like Batman or the Flash came to save me. I lay in the darkness, and after a while when I hadn't heard anything, I got up and now I am sitting in the bright lights of a 7-11 store parking lot, trying to figure out who would hate me enough to send a gang of hoodlums after me. Surely the bag lady doesn't care that much. The Thai people would probably do it themselves. Same with Jerome. He sure as hell doesn't need a gang. What about Chris, Justine's ex. Maybe he thinks I destroyed their relationship. I guess that's a little far-fetched. The Butcher? That's probably who. The goddamn Butcher.

I'm just a peaceful, lonely outcast. I certainly don't mean harm to anyone. Why can't I just be left alone?

June 29 ~~ DREAM OF THE HOMELESS KILLER

Last night I had another dream of the Butcher killing a homeless man as he slept. Only this time I dreamed that someone was standing behind him. I could not see who this other person was, but it was the first time I had imagined someone else with the Butcher as he killed a sleeping homeless person.

Then this morning the local newspaper reported that another homeless man had been found murdered. With my dreams and visions and with what Carissa told me she saw in the Butcher's office, I believe it's the Butcher who is the killer. I know it could be some other insane person. It could even be the crazy old bag lady, or some crazed Iraqi vet, like Jerome. But I believe my visions come from more than my own fears and memories of what the Butcher did to me. I just can't prove it yet.

I am wondering who was standing behind the Butcher in my dream. Perhaps one of the other men who comes to his store in the middle of the night.

~~ CARISSA'S FEARS

When I saw Carissa today, she was really upset. She said that her mother can't come up with the rent. "We may be homeless," she said, and started crying. "We are about $300 short."

I asked her what her mother was doing. She said that her mother is trying to borrow some money from her friends. Carissa said that her mother sent her to see if she could get an advance at her job. She said she wouldn't have time to interview me today. I told her I would walk part way with her to Casey's. As we walked I tried to be as encouraging as I could. I said that I just couldn't imagine that a landlord would kick them out. Carissa said that they have been late in their rent so often that the landlord is tired of it all.

When we said goodbye, it seemed Carissa was feeling better. She said that she may be seeing me soon out on the streets. She was trying to smile through her tears, trying to seem brave. I waited around until she came back out of the store. She had a big smile on her face and ran up to me and told me that the owner's wife was there and talked the owner into giving her the money. She agreed to work extra hours this month to make it up. She asked if I could meet her tomorrow. I said ok and then she ran off to take the rent money to her mother.

July 2 ~~ ESOLA AND THE MYSTERIOUS RING

It's been over a week since I gave Esola the ring, and I can't believe the change that's come over her. She seems to have this glow about her. She has a bounce to her walk. I asked her about this, and she said something about it being even better than she could imagine, but she said that she couldn't talk about it right now. And then she said that she must see Walter. I told her that I hadn't been able to find him, and with the wave of her hand she told me to keep looking. I called after her that we must take the ring back, and she said she knows that, and we will. Soon. After we find Walter.

I was just beginning to feel upset that Esola was being so evasive, but then she turned around and looked at me. "Gibson, please be patient with me. I have made contact and I am working with them on something. Please trust me."

"What! You made contact with these beings? That's all you are going to say? I trust you Esola but I want to know more about what you are doing. After all I brought the ring to you. I experienced some things with the ring that I need to understand."

Esola thought for a moment and then asked me to follow her. When we reached one of the isolated back rooms, she said to me, "I have used the ring, and I had similar experiences that you did. Only I kept trying to communicate with them. Each time I awoke I looked into the ring again. Finally, they were able to speak to me, and I was able to speak to them with my thoughts. I am trying to convince the aliens that there are enough people here on earth who really do care. Who are ready to act for change that is out of the ordinary. Who are ready to take responsibility for taking action so that our societies do not continue to be harmful and disrespectful to earth and its inhabitants. But that these people may need their help to change things, or at least their guidance."

"Do you really believe there are enough people on earth who really care?" I asked. "Who care enough to act, to put their own self-interests aside and to change their excessive life styles?"

"Yes I do," she said firmly. "Gibson I can understand your focusing on people who have let themselves become slaves, how they have sold themselves and perhaps the earth and future generations. But you have to believe that people can be different if they are given the opportunity and some guidance, some true leadership. Not authoritarian leadership, but leadership that tries to help them understand. You have to be able to see the positive potentials of people. It's like this ring. If you look at the ring without looking into the darkness of the stone, all you will see is a piece of superficial jewelry. But if you look into the stone you will see so much more. The stone of the ring is like the souls of people. People have the potentials to care, and to act in ways that are for the good of everyone. People have the potential to rise above their cultural, racial or nationalistic biases. You have to look into the souls of people and see their positive potentials if you are going to help things get better. If you are going to help us, help them, and yourself."

I sat silent for a few moments thinking about what she had said. I knew it was true, and that people had the potential to be different, to care, but what was going to make them different? All I could see was our society becoming more and more materialistic. More and more war-like, more and more violent and class-oriented.

"Why do you think these space beings—why do you think they are evolved and have anything to teach us?"

"I believe they do. It is something that I know, and it is difficult to explain. I'm not talking about a blind faith in a god-figure. They have showed me their society. I have talked with many of their people. I believe they are living a highly spiritual life and can share some of what they've learned in ways that can help our species become more compassionate and caring not just for other humans but for all life forms on earth—and other places beyond earth."

"I'll have to think about what you're saying, Esola. You're right I am focusing on how horrible people can be, how uncaring and complacent they are. That's all I see."

"You need to try to focus your attention on the good that some people are doing, and the positive potentials that people are capable of developing in themselves and in society. You have to try looking into people's souls, not just their conditioned actions.

"By the way, Gibson. I've learned something about you I didn't know. And that you don't know. I wasn't going to share this with you until later, but since we are talking about these things, I think I need to tell you more about yourself."

I felt curious and a bit apprehensive. Esola continued. "Just as I thought, you are highly psychic. All these trances and fading out that you do apparently are caused by your psyche exploring new dimensions, new realities. You don't remember these experiences because other parts of your psyche aren't developed enough yet to handle these journeys into the unknown and into other realities. These special beings have told me you have visited them often, and they have shared even more of their way of life with you than they have with me. Only they acknowledge you are not ready to remember any of this yet."

As I listened to Esola, I felt peaceful. I knew what she was saying was true, but I didn't have anything to base this truth on except for my feelings. "I believe I understand what you are saying, Esola. But how do I become more ready? How do I start remembering these journeys my mind takes?"

"Gibson, just have patience. While I know some of these things, I don't have all the answers. I think you will need first to resolve your inner struggles and truly free yourself from your past conditioning. Then you need to study with someone who can teach you to use your special psychic abilities. You will need to work at it."

Despite the seriousness of this conversation, I smiled at Esola and said, "What kind of special preparation have you done to develop your psychic abilities?"

She laughed with me, and said, "Well, Gibson, that's one of the benefits of age perhaps. But I have worked for many years at developing my psychic abilities. I have spent years developing my spiritual life."

"You mean you don't just drink wine and dance," I teased.

"Dancing—and a little wine from time to time—has helped me develop my psychic abilities. Dancing will help you, too Gibson."

"I'll try doing that—with your help." I became serious again, and asked Esola what would happen next with her contact with these special beings.

"I'm trying to make a proposal to them. The proposal is that there are enough of us who care and who have the potential to make changes in society that will be for the good of all living species, not just for the good of a select few in our species. I am telling them that I know that our species must rise above our negative tendencies on our own, but that we could use their guidance. I am asking them to open channels of communication with a select few of us. Not just me, but others who have demonstrated their altruistic beliefs."

"What is their response," I asked.

"They have not responded. They keep asking me to tell them about people who have reached levels of altruistic consciousness and behavior. I tell them about people who I think have been trying to help others. But I'm trying to show them examples of behaviors in everyday people, behaviors which proves that all of us have the capacity to rise above our negative biases and selfishness."

"I wish I had your positive view of people," I said, but when I saw her expression I quickly added, "But I will be trying to see this potential in people now."

She laughed and hugged me. "You better. Now I have a lot to do. Don't tell anyone else about the ring. And find Walter. I want to meet Walter."

"I wonder why, Esola. I'm sure only for altruistic reasons. For the good of society. Right?"

"Only partly right, Gibson," Esola answered with a sly expression. "You know me better than that."

I started to walk away, and she asked me to wait. "Gibson, I've been told by these beings that you have identified someone you think might be killing homeless people in this city."

I was stunned. "Did I hear you correctly? They told you that I believe I know who is killing homeless people?"

"All I know is that you need to follow you intuitions about this matter to its conclusion. I was told that you are right, but not completely. It is important that you find the truth about this issue both to stop the homeless killings, but also to help you develop your true powers and potentials"

I started to ask her more, but she held up her hand to stop me from talking. "I'm sorry Gibson, that's all I can really tell you. But just be careful, and I will tell you more when I can."

I reluctantly went back to work overwhelmed with this last information Esola told me. The knowledge of these beings from another world was overwhelming in itself, but it's even more amazing to find out that they know what's in my mind. I now know that it is not some crazy part of me that is imagining fanciful and delusional things. I now know that I am a part of and connected to realities and beings beyond myself, beyond my family, my nation and beyond our time-space reality.

As I continued to work at the Treasure Market that afternoon, I tried to get more in touch with what could be gained by making contact with these beings. I was struck by how difficult it seemed to find a way to take advantage of breaking through to a new reality, and I realized how truly insecure the people of our world seem to be. Many peoples' insecurities and fears of losing their homes and financial well-being sometimes cause them to see people from other lands and cultures as threats. I know that most people have benefitted from living in today's mass media world and because of this exposure are able to have some understanding of people from other cultures—but if an alien from another planet landed in the middle of one of our American cities, there would probably be mass panic. Police and military forces would be called in to deal with what would be perceived as a threat.

I don't know. It's strange to think that I've made contact with beings from another planet or dimension, and then have to go back to dealing with everyday problems of survival. I just can't get over thinking that having made contact with otherworldly beings would enable me to rise above my circumstances, or at least provide me with more resources so that I could live in a house or an apartment without having my new creative self destroyed by society. But I think all this is just wishful thinking. I may know about these special beings, but I am not completely prepared to take advantage of this knowledge. I just have to get on with trying to prove that the Butcher is the killer of homeless people. Of course, my main purpose in life continues to be protecting my new self until it becomes strong enough to live in this society without being destroyed. Maybe by then I'll be able to develop the psychic powers that I'm told I have.

July 5 ~~ A COMMUNITY GATHERING ON HOMELESSNESS

I was dusting furniture on the display floor today at the Treasure Market, and I came up to the Grand Dragon Boat. I was standing there looking at it, almost fading into a trance, when Justine came into the room. She called my name, and I refocused and turned to see what she wanted.

"Gibson, I've been contacted by a coalition of non-profit community groups who want to use the Treasure Theater for an all-day conference focused on ways to help the homeless have access to housing and the other basics of life. I've agreed, and the conference will be held two weekends from now. I may need your help to get the theater ready a day or two before. Does that work for you?"

I realized that she did not ask me if I thought the conference was a good thing to do or not. Or if I would even come to the conference.

"Sure, I'll help to set it up."

"Great. You know, I wanted to let you know about this conference because even though you have your own schedule when you come to the Treasure Market, I will need you to show up here a few days before the conference. I'll try to remind you."

"That will be helpful, but I'm sure I will be able to remember."

"Gibson, you know, you are the reason I agreed to this conference. Oh, I may have agreed anyway. And even though I read about the increase in homelessness, knowing you and talking with you has made the loss of homes and basic resources for a growing number of people more real to me. I feel like I have to do something. I know that homelessness is a part of larger issues in our society, and I've decided to use the Treasure Theater more to host conferences like this, and to offer the theater to progressive organizations for planning and outreach purposes. I'm excited about this."

I was waiting for her to ask me what I thought about her doing this. But she didn't.

"OK, I've got to get back to work, Gibson. Thanks for agreeing to help me."

I nodded.

She turned to walk away, but then turned back, and said, "I hope to see you there at the conference if you feel you can be there."

She didn't wait for my answer, but left the room. She obviously didn't want to get into a conversation with me about her decision to become more active in community causes, starting with homelessness. Thinking back on this interaction, I am amazed that I only had a mild feeling that she was wasting her time. And now that I've thought more about it, I'm now admitting to myself that it could be a good thing. When I think of people like Charles and Louise, Billy Buzz and Livid, Carlos and his family and so many other homeless families with children who I've seen and met on the streets lately, I do support people like Justine and other like-minded people getting together to find ways to help. I like that Justine emphasized that homelessness is a part of larger issues confronting our society.

I don't know if I am going to actually feel like going to the conference. But I did do two things that surprised me. After work, I rummaged through my backpack, and found the old crumpled card of the advertising man who wanted to video me staring angrily at people passing by. I called him, and surprisingly got through to him. He said he remembered me, and I told him about this conference. He thanked me, and said he would be there. I didn't ask him about his project, but I was curious if he had done anything. Anyway, I also called Ken, the attorney who had given me some of his old clothes, and left a message on his phone about the conference.

OK, so I have done my part. Only because of Justine. And I don't want to dwell on whether or not this kind of community activism will do any good. I'm trying to embrace a new sense of optimism. I am trying to hope that something good will come of this gathering. Maybe I am able to feel this way because of my awareness that perhaps more evolved beings exist, and somehow this has made me believe that as a species we may be able to one day reach our own higher potentials.

July 10 ~~ JEREMIAH AND THE NEW CHRIST CHILD

I saw Jeremiah walking down the street this afternoon with his arm around Raul. I had this uneasy feeling that something was amiss. "No, no, Jeremiah," I thought. "Don't do it. Don't fall for it." When they came up to me I saw Raul tense as if he were going to run, but Jeremiah told him to relax.

"I gotta go man." Raul said staring uneasily at me.

"All right, Raul. You'll meet me later at the church?"

"Yeah, sure man."

When Raul had left Jeremiah turned to me with a glazed look in his eyes. "I think I found Him. I think I found Him. Raul was just outside the church I went to last Sunday and as I came out, he took my hand and knelt and said to me, 'You have been looking for me Jeremiah.' I felt elated but I'm also trying to remain skeptical. But it's just feels so good to think I have succeeded in my quest."

Something inside of me told me not to tell Jeremiah he was wrong, at least not now. I asked him, "What are you planning to do with Raul if he is the Christ child?"

"I know he is the Christ child. I just know it. What am I going to do? I'm going to take care of him. I'm going to find a place to rent. I'm going to get a job somehow and care for this child. I will learn from him, and perhaps I can provide him any help that he needs to achieve his purpose."

I then told Jeremiah that I had heard Raul was a wild kid and hustled basketball for money. Jeremiah said that Raul had told him that other people had made up stories about him and those things are not true.

"Haven't you ever heard of Raul? He's been around the Burnside shelter forever it seems."

"Yes, I'd seen Raul around but I never gave him much thought. He was always just playing and he seemed to be minding his own business. Now I know that he was just biding his time, a self-contained spiritual being, waiting for the right time."

"All I can say is that you'd better look into it a little more deeply." I knew it wouldn't matter what else I would say.

Now that I'm thinking about it more, I feel maybe something good could happen from this. Raul will be having some strange opportunity to be taken care of. He probably thinks of it is as a hustle, but perhaps he might benefit from Jeremiah's caring. The hustler and the Christ-child seeker. Seems a little sacrilegious, but I have to remain open to different spiritual paths. And after what I've seen recently, I'm not surprised by anything anymore.

July 16 ~~ JUSTINE'S CONCERNS

Yesterday, I helped Justine set up the theater for the conference on homelessness. After we finished, she told me that I seemed very tired and kind of distant. She asked me if I felt all right. I told her I actually did feel tired and that I haven't been getting very much sleep the last week, but I didn't tell her that dreams of the Butcher killing homeless people kept waking me up at night. I figured that I didn't want to discuss my suspicions with her until I really had some proof, and even if I had proof I don't know if I wanted to bring Justine into it. Now that I think of it, if I somehow was able to find that the Butcher is the killer, I don't know what I would do with it.

"You also seem so preoccupied," Justine said to me. "Are you dealing with something that maybe I could help you with?" She looked at me with so much concern and sincerity.

"One thing that has been bothering me is these murders of homeless people. I have to be more careful where I sleep, and I guess I've become more worried about who might be killed."

"I worried about that, too, Gibson. Every time I've read about some other homeless person murdered, I think about you. I hope this conference this weekend will focus on this issue. Why don't you take our offer to sleep in the room here at the store at night? Especially now with this killing going on."

I thought about it for a moment. I actually thought about it, but I knew I couldn't do it. "I can't do that right now, Justine. I just can't do it, but I appreciate you offering it to me again."

"It's a standing offer. Anytime you want to take us up on it, you can. But why can't you do it?"

"I'm sorry, I just can't talk about it right now either." I said, beginning to feel uneasy. I like Justine. I more than like Justine. I know that we have become closer, but I don't feel I can share my private battles, my private fears, with her now.

She seemed to be reading my mind. "If you can't talk about it, do you write about it in your journal? Do you write about why you can't sleep in beds? Why you can't be around people who care for you longer than a few hours at a time?"

"Justine, I still need to keep what I write in my journal private," I said. Suddenly I felt stubbornly protective, emotionally clamped up. When she started asking her questions it was like a switch was clicked in my emotions and a wall came up, and my mind had no control over my voice and actions. I had gone into emergency protective emotional defense.

But Justine shifted her approach. She must have been able tell she could not get anywhere with direct challenges. "I know, Gibson. but I care about you." She reached out and took my hands in her hands. "I don't mean to upset you. I'll leave you alone, but I just want you to be comfortable with life, with yourself. And to be safe."

Her new approach made a big difference to me. My clamped emotions began to loosen as I felt her touch and listened to her expression of caring. But I said to her, "Maybe it's still not time for me to be comfortable or to be safe. I just have to be out on the street right now. I can't explain it to you."

"I wish you could," she said. "But that's ok, do what you have to do. If you do ever feel like talking about it, I'd be willing to, anytime. Not as a judge, as a friend." She kissed me on my cheek and started to walk away. "I hope to see you at the conference tomorrow."

"What am I doing?" I screamed silently to myself as I was left alone. "Why can't I respond to her?"

Then I saw the image again of the Butcher standing over some helpless man sleeping in an alley, and I watched as the Butcher began to brutally attack the defenseless man in his sleep. Maybe Fallacious flashed this horrible scene to tear myself away from the spell that Justine just cast over me. I don't want him helping me in this way.

I know that Justine is letting me know that she wants to become more involved. She has changed her approach to me, especially since the play has been ended. I think she began to change before the play, but she still kept her distance. Now she is spending more time with me, sharing her thoughts, her feelings, herself. I have enjoyed it. She has demanded nothing of me until recently, and now I have to figure out what I'm going to do about it. Justine is presenting me with an amazing dilemma. I have always thought of Justine as being beyond me. Since I have had to be around her so much, I haven't allowed myself to create an emotional yearning to be with her, I think I have tried to just leave her alone and not consciously bring her into my imagination and my heart. But for the first time, I'm feeling bothered—extremely bothered—by my emotional blocks. I want to be able to share myself more with Justine.

When Justine walked away, I went back to work and finished what I wanted to do that day. Justine paid me, and before I left, I told her I appreciated her concern for me, and that I would think about what she said. I felt that I could not just leave without saying something to her.

~~ CONFRONTING AND CONTROLLING FALLACIOUS

I decided before going to sleep tonight that I needed to try to take control of Fallacious. I have to stop him from taking me into one of his movie trances any time he wants. I am realizing I don't want to miss important aspects of my day-to-day reality anymore. I don't want to just drift off without any say in the matter. In the process of wrestling with Fallacious, I've realized that I want to take control of him, but not destroy him. I have allowed him to just project things onto my mind any time he wanted whether I wanted it or not. I want to gain control of him, and for the first time, I believe I have the power to take control. I must be like a permissive parent who finally has to set limits to keep his child from harming himself and the parent.

I demanded to talk with him, but he would not show himself. I talked to him anyway, and told him that I wanted him remain in my mind, but that I want him to only show things to me when I ask for it. I told him if he did this for me, I would consult with him if I ever try to work on any creative projects. I do believe Fallacious could be an important resource to any future imaginative endeavors of mine.

I hope he takes me up on this offer. I'll see if I drift off into any of his movie trances in the coming days. Actually, I feel kind of excited about thinking I have control over Fallacious. It might prove to be a very creative collaboration between my new soul and him.

July 18 ~~ THE CONFERENCE ON HOMELESSNESS

The conference was scheduled to begin at 9:00 am, and to end at 4:00 pm. I didn't sleep well—I kept having visions of the Butcher killing homeless men and women as they slept. I have to do something about these dreams and visions. I finally fell deep asleep right before dawn and slept until noon. I walked to the Treasure Theater, not sure if I was actually going to go to the conference. A part of me watched one side of myself struggle with another side of myself about going or not going. Which one would win? I didn't really know which one would win until I found myself that afternoon standing in front of the theater.

I finally took a deep breath and walked inside. I found a chair in the back of the room. I looked at the program sheet given to me when I walked into the lobby of the theater.

When I arrived at the conference a speaker was talking about the need to address climate change. She described the terrible affects climate change is having on the homeless as well as on lower income individuals in general. She presented a PowerPoint slide show that was riveting in visually demonstrating the climate change damages to the environment, health, and livelihood around the nation and world. She also showed and discussed examples of constructive efforts many individuals and groups are making and discussed specific solutions that could make a difference in improving environmental conditions. I appreciated that she ended her talk on a positive and optimistic note.

Another speaker talked specifically about the systemic racial injustices affecting non-white races, including the large number of black and brown-skinned individuals and families who are homeless. His words affected me deeply as he described the daily fears blacks have related to police profiling and, so often, police brutality by some bad police officers. He described his organization's efforts to create alternative community responders who are able to provide medical and crisis interventions that can resolve many difficult situations without having to call the police. He said that the Portland Police Department, as well as the city council and mayor are supportive of working with their organization and are highly supportive. He then introduced the local police chief who discussed reforms within the department and with the police union to prevent unjust violent and racially discriminating behaviors by police officers, and when these actions occur to hold those police officers accountable. He said that he felt most of the police officers are supportive of these efforts, and he feels that the police union is realizing that their organization can't continue to be a barrier to weeding out bad and undisciplined officers. This was another informative and hopeful presentation.

The next speaker was probably the highlight of the conference for me. She was a woman in her 90s who had just written a book about the need for a new emphasis on non-violent social activism to transform the American militaristic, corporate society. She said this type of transformative activism has to be based upon values deeper than politics and economics. She feels to be effective today in helping to make our human endeavors more sustainable, we have to do more than be politically active—which she thinks is still important. She said that we have to focus on the development of our souls, our inner world and we need to get in touch with not just the importance, but the necessity of living together in an inter-connective, multicultural world.

She believes that we will have difficulty improving our social programs that can transform the inherent systemic racial injustices, and that can improve conditions for the homeless and those working in low-income jobs as well as the middle class…she maintained we will have difficulty improving our social programs and political policies until more people are willing to embrace each other and value each human being no matter their ethnic background or belief system.

She went on to say that the American Dream is dead and the American empire based upon dominating others to support a weapons industry and to control access to oil is unsustainable and is dying. She said we have to recognize that we need a new American Dream based upon a holistic balance between individual creativity and community creativity, and that this balance can only come from learning again how to connect and cooperate with each other. We have to rethink the concept of work so that its main goal is not just to make money, but to contribute to the well-being of others. She said we have to move beyond jobs that just turn us into consumers and rob us of our creativity and caring and our relationships to the community and nature around us.

She talked further, but my mind stayed with her use of the word, 'soul'. I felt inspired listening to her. I felt a sense of validation of what I was trying to do—to develop my new creative soul. I understood the importance of what she is saying—we have to develop more spiritually and get in touch with our inner world as a first step. Then, if we want to live in a better world we each have to take responsibility to join with others and to do each our own part—to contribute to the whole of society—to work toward making the changes in our politics and in our society that we feel need to be made. While I believe that to be true, I know I am not there yet. I am aware that I keep using the word 'yet', but I don't know what I would do to contribute to others. I just don't feel like joining a community or political group. I am painfully aware of how difficult it has been for me to be open to connecting with others.

But I do feel it was important I heard this amazing woman's speech. I felt like I was in the presence of a wise teacher, an elder of our world collective community. I was both surprised and impressed by her thoughts. I guess I had figured the conference would only be about issues like housing, nutrition, health care, better police protection—which were discussed at times during the day. I liked her viewpoint that we had to deal with what kind of society we valued and wanted before we could change it. She emphasized the importance of developing a society where caring for others, artistic creativity and taking care of Mother Earth, all more important than competing with others over how much money could be made and how much territory could be controlled for its non-renewable resources.

Throughout the rest of the conference I realized that it was so important for me that I came to this conference.

Later in the afternoon at a break, Esola came to sit by me. "Gibson, I'm so glad you came. And so is Justine," she said. "Justine said to say hello. She's backstage looking after the various speakers. All these speakers are saying the same thing. More people have to get involved in social and political activism." Then she turned to me and said, "Gibson, I believe that you have definitely become more involved in your own way. More involved in helping other people, and even in helping our society."

"How can you say that?" I protested. "I'm just as non-involved as I've always been." But I knew that wasn't true. I knew I've been changing—slowly.

"You told me you tried to help that kid who was on drugs. I think you said you gave some money to that couple from New Orleans. You're trying to do something about those homeless killings. You are here at this conference, aren't you? You wouldn't have come here a few months ago."

"I guess I have become more involved in those ways. But I don't think I'm able to do much more."

I braced for Esola to say, "Bullshit" or something like that. But she just smiled and said, "We'll see." That was an uncharacteristically tame and unsettling response. "By the way, Gibson, do you remember that you are scheduled for an astrology reading on Monday?"

I told her I remembered and that I would be there. I'm kind of looking forward to this reading now. I don't know what to expect, but I'm intrigued.

As I left the conference, I noticed that the advertising man I had called was interviewing somebody. I'm glad he showed up. I'm glad I showed up.

July 20 ~~ ASTROLOGY READING

Today was my astrology reading. It wasn't what I expected and as I think more about what I was told, I am feeling a whirlwind of emotions and thoughts.

I managed to arrive at the Treasure Market when I was supposed to. Both Justine and Esola were there waiting for me. Justine gave me a hug, and said it meant a lot to her that I came to the conference. Even though her hug was brief, the closeness I felt to her, not just to her body, has lingered with me through the day.

We talked briefly about the conference, and I let Justine know that I felt it was a valuable experience and I could see where some good could come from it.

Esola said that the astrologer was in the next room, and I told Justine and Esola that they could sit in on the reading. If I'd known what was going to be said I probably wouldn't have agreed to them being there. I thought the astrologer was just going to say something, like "This is a good time for romance. Be careful about arguments. Expect a letter from an old friend. Etc. Etc."

Justine and Esola took me into one of the backrooms where we could close the door. I saw a well-dressed woman in her fifties sitting at a dark wood table. In front of her on the table were a few books and some sheets of paper with diagrams and handwriting on them. She smiled at me as I walked into the room. Then she stood, walked over to me and held out her hand for me to shake. As I shook it, she said, "You must be Gibson Calhoun. My name is Sonja Parks. Please, you can have a seat here." She motioned to a chair on one side of the table near her. Then she asked that Justine and Esola sit on the other side of the table. Sonja continued, "I use astrology simply as a tool to help people understand themselves better, to understand their unique potentials. I help people to understand meaningful turning points in their lives and to get a better sense of timing in their lives."

I thought to myself that I've certainly been in a state of deprivation regarding how to understand my life. Maybe a little understanding would help me. I didn't know about my sense of timing. I didn't think I had a good sense of timing. I said to her, "I'm not sure if I know what you mean by special turning points and sense of timing."

"Astrology is the study of cycles. A person continually passes through meaningful phases and turning points of their life cycles. Think of the cycle of the seasons. The cycle of the seasons begins in the spring and most people feel a burst of new energy. Each phase of the cycle has a different quality to it as the new energy takes form as life activities, urges to act in certain ways and significant turning points. There are a number of other cycles besides the cycle of the seasons that are just as important in understanding what you are going though in your life. Astrology is the discipline of applying the understanding of these common and meaningful phases of these cycles in our solar system specifically to each individual's own personal rhythms and potentials for meaningful development."

"I think I know what you mean. In the spring time everything is growing and everyone feels excited by the warm weather coming. In the fall there is a sense of getting ready for the winter and there seems to be a lot of indoor social gatherings. Of course, for the homeless these seasons have a little different meaning. For the homeless it's either cold or not cold, rainy or not. But anyway, that's another issue."

Sonja said I was describing external weather patterns that are based on cycles of the seasons. She said that astrology allows us to become aware of internal cycles that allow us to forecast and understand changes in our internal weather patterns. On some days we feel sunny, other days we might experience more stormy feelings. She said that she was using a very simple analogy to describe something that is more complex. What she was saying was intriguing to me, and

I asked if she minded if I took notes in my journal. She said that was fine with her, and after I took out my journal, she said, "I want to start by interpreting your natal chart and discussing your innate potentials. Your chart shows you have a strong need to find your unique form of individual creativity and artistic expression. But you don't feel comfortable with art for art's sake. You feel a need to use whatever you create to help others. You have a progressive mind, looking for possibilities, concerned about the well-being of the masses, not just your own well-being.

"You also have a contradictory need for material security and success. This need may have overshadowed your creative needs. There is an indication that you had a major turning point about a year ago where you experienced many unsettling events. Old outdated patterns in your life were shattered. It may have been a difficult time for you but it began a transformative experience that I think you are still involved in."

"Is that why I'm homeless?" I asked. She had definitely sparked my curiosity, but I was still skeptical. "Am I homeless because of some planetary influence?"

"No, you're homeless because of the choices you made during this important turning point in your life. This doesn't mean you were in control of your choices but it doesn't mean some planet made the choice for you. You are homeless because you had lost touch with your inner needs—who you are inside. Your home did not reflect your inner soul and your true purpose in this lifetime. Your home, as well as your primary relationship and your career, were not built on a solid inner foundation. So when this powerful cyclical turning point arrived in your life, it had the effect of a psychic hurricane which just blew away your false home. A home needs to reflect what's emotionally inside of you, your motivations, what makes you feel internally secure and satisfied in your life. If you don't know what's inside how can you create a strong home? Another way of looking at this is that the side of you that you've repressed and ignored took advantage of this major turning point and said enough is enough. I want some attention and perhaps in a revengeful way rebelled against the parts of yourself that were striving for success at the expense of your creative side."

I instantly thought of the side of myself I have named Fallacious. I knew what she was saying was absolutely correct. Instead of acknowledging this I said, "Well, I think I'm homeless because I live in a society that doesn't provide for its people."

"That may be one part of it. But why are you one of the homeless? Did you have a good job?" I nodded. "Were you successful?"

"Sort of. But not successful enough. I was a sales manager. And then I was fired."

"I don't think lack of success was the important thing. Even if you had reached your high goals in terms of success and money you would have not been happy. You are homeless because you weren't attending to your artistic and creative needs. Your chart shows that one of your purposes in life is to develop your artistic creativity. Another important purpose for you is to contribute to improving social justice"

Even though what she was saying resonated with me, I began to feel frustrated. I felt then, and still feel overwhelmed, by the pressure. I didn't know if I was truly able to be creative with the purpose she described. I did not want to look at Justine or Esola. I said to Sonja, "I'm just trying to cope with surviving on the street. I am just trying to keep from starving, or getting sick. I can't create anything."

"You will have to one day. You have entered a very powerful but dangerous phase of your development. You have entered a state of consciousness that can allow you to travel beyond the here and now. But unless you anchor yourself to this reality in well-grounded, concrete ways you will find it more and more difficult to stay focused in the here and now. It is difficult to know how your psyche would react to being lost in the alternate realities without being anchored in this world in some practical or creative way."

I started to say, "You can see all that in my chart?" But I didn't want her to know how right what she was saying seemed to me. Instead I just shrugged.

She went on, "I see a tremendous source of pain in your chart."

"I thought you were already describing a pretty heavy source of pain," I said.

"You're right. I should have said another source of pain. But this may be more troubling for you. You have a strong need for emotional love and sharing. If you were able to respond to this need for love and deep emotional sharing, it seems you would be more able to resolve your other life challenges. You need to find a way to blend your solitary search with your need to share love, or whatever you do will seem hollow to you."

I managed to say, "You keep describing a lot of heavy consequences if I don't do the right thing."

"I don't often see a chart that reflects such powerful tensions and in which the present timings are adding to the tension in a way that could cause tremendous eruptions and/or transformative resolutions."

"You make me sound like a volcano."

"No, you are not a volcano, but you have emotions that may erupt like one if you don't find some release for your creative drives. And sexual drives, I might add. Or your consciousness may just dissolve under the pressure. Your chart shows you have an immense, almost untapped, source of creative power. You have a strong desire to use this creative power to help society change for the better. Use it. You must use your creative power. That's the first thing you must realize. The second thing is that you can't use it alone. You have to reach out to others and you have to open yourself to love."

She stopped for a moment and continued to study my chart. I remained silent. She described my struggles so accurately. I felt like saying that old cliché, "Well, that's easy for you to say…" But then I realized she wasn't trying to say my challenges are easy to resolve. She said that I have a lot to gain, and a lot to lose if I don't meet the challenges and develop what she has described are my life purposes.

Sonja finally continued. "One final thing. I see some patterns in the chart and in your timings that reflect unforeseen dangers and clashes of conflicting forces. Be careful. During the next few weeks don't put yourself in any unnecessary risk."

"Living on the street is always a risk, but thanks, I'll be careful. And you've given me a lot to think about." I was desperately trying to maintain my composure as we wrapped this up. I turned to Justine and Esola and told them I was going for a walk to think about what Sonja had told me and I left.

I've just been trying to continue to write down as much as I could remember about what she told me. I know damn well she was accurate about what's been going on with me. And I can agree with her about what I should be doing. But how do I get from here to there? I must not be ready, my creative soul must not be ready or I'd be able to act. I feel like I'm still waiting behind a huge black metal door in the darkness—waiting for the door to open. Maybe it will never open. Maybe I'll drift off into some catatonic state or erupt like a volcano, but it seems like I have no control over what's going to happen. But I have to admit, I haven't tried to open the door. It just seems like I wouldn't be able to budge it. Then I remembered I was able to eventually open the door to the pagoda cabin on the Grand Dragon boat and this gave me hope.

What's going to be really uncomfortable now is talking with Justine and Esola when I see them again. The astrology reading has supported what they have been telling me for these past months as they have tried to get me to come in from the streets, and "to get back into life," as Esola keeps saying to me.

~~ IS THIS THE TIME FOR ME TO ACT?

I've been sitting on a bench in a park by the river for an hour or so, and I can't stop thinking about the astrology reading. I've been sitting here brooding, upset that I still don't know the purpose of the new side of me—this new side that for the past eight or nine months I've been trying to protect so it can develop. What's the purpose of my new creative soul, and when will it be developed enough for me to take risks? What risks would I take? I realize it has been so comfortable for me to stay immersed in this protective, solitary mode—hiding so much of myself as I interact on my own terms with others on the street and with Justine and Esola. But the messages of the ninety year old woman at the conference and of the astrology reading seem to be that it is time for me to act—to somehow come back into society. I just don't think I can do it. I don't know how to do it. It makes me feel upset even thinking about it.

But then I just thought about Justine's curiosity about my writing. Has my new soul reached a stage where it has to do something to survive? Well, hell wouldn't I have known if it had reached that stage? Maybe that's what's happening to me now. My new soul is fighting me now, trying to break out. I'm not sure if I'm ready to let it break out.

July 21 ~~ A CHANGED MAN

Last night I was sleeping in one of the downtown alleys when I was awakened by someone shuffling toward me. I jumped up and tried to hide behind a dumpster as the man got closer and closer in the darkness. Whoever it was stopped a few feet on the other side of the dumpster. I couldn't see who it was from where I was hiding but I could see a grotesque shadow on the side of the brick wall of the building. I couldn't believe how frightened I felt. I wondered if I started running would I make it out of the alley before whoever it was could get me. I knew that if whoever it was walked a little farther he would see me. But I couldn't run. I decided to take a chance that the person would be going the other way.

He finally started walking again, and as he came by the dumpster in view of me, I tried to huddle back into the shadows, and I braced myself. But it turned out to be Walter.

Before I could say anything, he came up to where I was hiding, and said, "You don't have be afraid of me. I'm not the one you have to be afraid of."

"Did you know I was hiding here?" I asked.

"I knew that you were in the alley," he said, and then he smiled, "And I knew where I would have hid, except I might even have jumped into the dumpster."

It was then I noticed how good Walter looked. He was wearing his same type of clothes, but they seemed new and cleaner. His hair and beard seemed trimmed, and even in the darkness he looked healthier. I said something to him about how good he looked.

"I feel much better than I have in years, and I think I do look better. But, listen, Gibson, I need that ring. I know that you don't have it anymore, but you must take me to the person who has it, and who has been using it."

"I can take you to her, but how do you know I gave it to someone else? Where have you been, Walter? I have been looking all over for you."

"I was hiding, frightened of what I thought were evil beings from outer space. But I've been wrong. I know that now. I finally allowed them to communicate with me and I know what type of beings they are. I know by how they make me feel, and what they have shown me. All my beliefs have been expanded to take into account…the good of the universe, is the best way I can say it.. I now see that our life here on earth can truly be better, and my life can be better. It's just a wonderful feeling. But I need to find the ring and to give it back."

"In the morning I'll take you to the person I gave the ring to. Her name is Esola. She's been wanting to meet you anyway. I'm sure you two will have a lot to talk about."

Walter said he would come back to this alley in the morning, and he left. The next day after dawn, Walter came back. As we walked to get coffee, Walter asked me about Esola. He asked if she was a spiritual woman. I said yes, but that she was difficult to describe and that he would just have to meet her. On the way to the Treasure Market, I asked Walter if he had looked into the ring. He looked at me, shook his head, and asked if I had.

"I did and it caused me to travel to their planet or realm, I think. It was extremely exhilarating experience. Actually, it was probably the most spiritual experience I've ever had in my life."

"I know what you mean. I've been there too, but in a different way and I have felt that same wonderful, spiritual feeling. They have helped me see a lot of things. I think they have rehabilitated and healed me. Now I need to give them back the ring."

"Let me tell you, Walter, that Esola has some ideas about remaining in contact with the aliens. You should listen to her. She has some good reasons for keeping the ring long enough to convince the aliens that they should remain in contact with some humans."

"I will listen to her. These beings told me to find her and talk with her. They said that after I talked with her I should make my own decision. I have to admit that they are strange beings. They express what they want, but I didn't get the sense they would ever force me to do what they want or take what they want. After what they have done for me, I'd sure like to help them get the ring back because they said they need it."

"I'm sure Esola wants to help them, too, but I also think that she sees some good in these beings remaining in contact with humans."

When we arrived at the Treasure Market, Esola met us as soon as we walked in, and she led us to a room where we would have some privacy. I introduced Esola and Walter to each other and they instantly seemed to forget I was there.

"You've come for the ring," Esola said.

"Yes, I must take it back."

"I know, but we need to talk first. I think you might be interested in some proposals that I have been discussing with our friends."

"Yes, I would be very interested."

They stopped talking and looked at each other for a few moments. I was about ready to say something, when Esola turned to me and said that they needed to be alone now.

I protested, "I'd like to know about these beings—whoever they are, wherever they are from. I would want to know about them, too,"

"You'll learn more about these special beings, Gibson, but at this point they have to be convinced to continue their communications with us. I think Walter and I might be able to convince them. Of course, we are not the only ones on our earth that are communicating with them. It seems they have identified a vast number of people who are open—perhaps spiritually evolved—but who are able to listen and communicate in truly respectful and interactive manner. Anyway, when the time is right, you will be needed to help us communicate their guidance to the rest of the world. But please I have been waiting to meet Walter for a long time."

I reluctantly left, but felt all right about leaving it to Esola. I did trust her, and I knew that I had other things to deal with. Maybe these special beings were afraid to come to earth because there were too many people like the Butcher around. Perhaps if I could prove that the Butcher was involved in the killings, and if he were stopped then these beings might feel more comfortable at least visiting this city. I laughed to myself, knowing how ridiculous it was to think that by just stopping the Butcher it would make any real difference. Maybe it wouldn't make any difference to these beings, but it would make a lot of difference to me and to some of the other homeless people of the city.

I told Esola I'd be back tomorrow to put in some work.

Later during the early evening, I was washing my clothes in a laundromat in the Northwest. A lot of young people were around. At first I felt detached from everyone else. Not just physically detached but also emotionally detached. Everyone else in the laundryomat also seemed detached, sitting alone with their computers or smart phones. My life has been exposed to such broad and amazing spectrums recently, some out of this world, others very much a part of this world, and yet I felt frustrated that I was still a homeless man—alone, hungry, dirty most of the time. I know there are opportunities for me to live my life differently yet when I look around me I still see apathy and insensitivity and a lack of connection. But then I challenged myself to look at all of these people differently. I took time to look more closely at each person's face, and I could see shifts of emotions that I had not allowed myself to see before. I began to realize that these people were connecting with other people beyond their present space, just like I had used the ring to connect with other beings beyond where I was physically located at the time. I challenged myself to think differently, to be more open to positive potentials of those around me, just as I am trying to be more positive about my own potentials.

A young man, perhaps in his twenties looked up from his computer and noticed me looking at him. He smiled and I smiled back. I then did something I've avoided doing for so long. I walked over to him and engaged in conversation. He showed me what he was doing on the computer. He was planning a trip with his girlfriend to Egypt, and they wanted to find ways to become more involved in supporting movements for freedom in the middle east. He said that he was so inspired by what had been happening in that country he wanted to see it firsthand. He showed me photographs of the places he was going to visit. I visited with him until my laundry was done, and I became caught up in his enthusiasm and desire to connect with others who were fighting for freedom and a better life in this world.

When I left the laundromat I felt a surge of joy that I had been able to get beyond my fixation about the negative things in society. I had been able to connect emotionally with someone else and it felt so good.

July 24 ~~ JUSTINE SHARES HER SECRET ROOM WITH ME

Justine came up to me yesterday shortly after I got to work and stood very close to me while I was unpacking some glassware. I thought at first she was inspecting it, but then I felt her breast through her blouse as she leaned forward and whispered in my ear that she wanted to show me some very precious secrets. She asked if I would come with her. I whispered to her that I would come, and then we both laughed since there was really no reason to whisper. I put down the glass and followed her to the stairway and up to the top floor. She didn't offer any further explanation of where we were going and what her secret was, but I felt intrigued and excited. As we walked down a hallway on the top floor, I realized that I had not been to this part of the store before. I noticed that at a certain point, the hallway changed from just another storage area to a passage way had been creatively decorated. We walked on an Oriental rug rich with dark red-and-black patterns. On the walls were wonderful paintings and photographs in matching frames.

We stopped in front of a door, and Justine took out her keys to unlock it. I followed her into a broad, open room with large warehouse windows taking up half of one wall. They ran from the ceiling to mid-wall, and there were skylights in the ceiling. The room had a dark wood floor, and I could see that Justine had created various living areas within the large room by how she placed different types of rugs, furniture and lamps. She showed me to the living room area, which contained a sofa and chairs and pillows on the floor. Adjoining this area she had her desk and bookcases. She showed me the kitchen area and a door that led to the only separate room, the bathroom, where there was an old claw-foot tub and a shower. She showed me to the area where there was a brass bed with large pillows and featherbed covers. The room was full of wonderful furniture and art objects, yet it was so large that it didn't seem crowded. It seemed to me that no matter what direction I looked there were intricate layers of beautiful and exotic shapes and colors. It was obvious that in this room an artist had created a masterpiece of beauty and livability, a space that appealed to all the senses and even to the higher sensitivities.

Justine's expression showed how proud and happy she felt as she showed me around. "This room is my main secret, my special, private room," She said. "Even Esola doesn't come in here. When I was growing up this room was a playroom for my sister and me, and then as we became teenagers, we started playing house, only with real furniture. Then when I took over the store, I began to create this room."

"This is quite a secret," I said, completely enraptured by the exotic and comfortable atmosphere.

"This room is only one of my secrets, though. I have many other secrets to show you. Another one is over here." She took my hand and led me to a cabinet with a glass door. I have to admit that my focus at that point was entirely on how wonderful her touch felt. Inside the cabinet was an old hardcover book on a stand. "This book is one of the reasons I wanted to bring you up here."

I looked closer and read the title: Justine by Lawrence Durrell. I had heard of this author's name but I didn't know anything about him. Justine told me that the book was from the first printing of the novel, and explained to me that it is a part of the author's Alexandria Quartet, four books he wrote about characters who lived in Alexandria, Egypt. She said that her particular copy of the novel is worth a great deal of money now. Her mother and father named her after Justine, of Durrell's book. She told me a little about the romantic and political intrigues that Durrell wrote about and said that the author seemed to be saying that one could never be quite sure about the motives of people, that events had different meanings depending on the perspective of each individual.

"We are all very mysterious," Justine said, giving me a sensual, penetrating look, which made me feel that she can see all of me. She again was standing close to me with her shoulder touching mine, which made my body feel more alive than it had been for a long time. "I think you're mysterious, Gibson. What I learned about you over these past months has made me feel connected to you despite how protective you try to be. I want to know you in a deeper and fuller way."

"I would like that. I feel comfortable sharing with you. I like the sides of you that I know, but being in this room, it seems you may have more secrets than I have." I knew I was attempting to throw the spotlight of mystery back onto her.

"Maybe, but the difference might be that I'm willing to tell you all about me. And I'm willing to let you discover who I am." Her eyes seemed to be changing in their intensity to a silky and inviting softness trying to pull me into her. "I am willing to let you know my secrets. Are you willing to tell me all about yourself, to let me discover who you are? Are you willing to tell me your secrets?"

I didn't answer her, but I wanted to say yes. I think I was saying yes just by how I held her gaze and did not turn away. We stared at each other with an intensity of emotional connection that seemed to blend our souls.

She finally broke the spell by looking back to the book in the cabinet. She said that she loved the period of time in which this book was written. She said that she particularly liked writers like Anais Nin and Henry Miller. She said that she hadn't given Henry Miller a chance until she read Anais Nin's description of him. But she said that all these people lived such romantic, adventurous lives. She said they were willing to be outsiders, but still remain connected to other like-minded and creative people. She said that she thinks these writers, as well as others, have helped many others live more inspired and creative lives.

Justine then looked at me and said that I might not be as outrageous as Henry Miller, but that she thinks there might be similarities. "Haven't you ever thought of what you could do with your writing?" she asked.

This time I did look away and even walked over to the window and looked outside. The skyline of the city stretched out before me, and I thought for a moment that if these buildings were blades of grass, and this city were just a lawn on some wealthy person's estate, I would be just another bug crawling around in the dirt. Then I came out of my stupid, irrelevant reverie and said, "I don't know Justine. It seems like I don't have a lot of control over what I write and what I do and what my mind does."

"But what do you want to do, Gibson?"

"I want to keep a part of myself from dying. A part of myself I recognized during my breakdown. A part of myself that I had turned away through my twenties and early thirties in order to maintain my job and family obligations."

"But what do you want to do with this new creative part of yourself?" She came over and stood by me again.

"I don't know! I just don't know. I surprised myself at how much frustration I expressed. "I'm sorry, I...It's like asking a baby what it wants to do with its life."

"Gibson, maybe your new side is like a baby, but you have an essence within you that is mature and can make decisions about what you want to do. Let this center, this essence of you take its rightful control over your creative side and guide it, use it in ways you want. Don't you have to integrate this new side of yourself in a way that others can relate to, and that allows you to feel satisfied and purposeful?

"Those are nice ideas, but how? I just don't know how to bring the new creative side together with the rest of me. I don't even know if I can trust the rest of me. I suspect that the 'rest of me' is still too warped and conditioned by slave life, and would too easily forsake my new self if I reentered society.

"I don't think so, but I do believe you will have to take that risk one day. You can't just stay isolated from others, those who are your friends, those who love you." She took my hand and asked me to sit down beside her on one of the sofas in the room.

"Tell me about your street life. Describe it to me. Describe what you do to survive. Describe your feelings."

I attempted to describe these things to her. And I told her how I felt, the anger and bitterness at what I saw as sold-out, greedy, inhuman society.

She listened to me and after I was through she then asked, "Now can you tell me why you don't come back into regular life? Why you don't take up our offer for you to sleep in the bedroom in the store? Why you don't work more here, or do something else to get back into regular life?"

I hesitated at first. I told her that I didn't know if I could answer those questions.

She squeezed my hand. "Share with me, Gibson. You can trust me."

"I know I can. It's not you, it's anybody. I have this feeling that if I tell anybody about what's keeping me in the street, a part of me will be destroyed."

She asked me if I could write about it. I said that I have been. She asked if I could write a play about it. She said that she could help me write a play about it, and she would try to get it produced. "It could help you. And maybe it could reach some of the people who want to become more sensitive to others, who want to do their part of help society become better and more inclusive. You could help them understand the homeless, and what causes this condition, and what could be done about it."

I was almost convinced that I could do what she was saying, but then I felt so apprehensive. I stared straight ahead, thinking about what she was proposing. I told her that her idea did excite me, but that I was also afraid.

"What are you afraid of?" she asked.

"The death of my new self."

"How would it die?"

"Through opening myself and entering into relationships that would require me to reenter slave life."

"Isn't a slave someone who has no freedom?"

"It's all relative. Plantation slaves were free to walk around a small area, free to eat and sleep, free to fuck and be fucked. People today enjoy a little more freedom, but they still allow themselves to be fucked by the people who have all the power and wealth. Their chains allow them to walk around in larger areas, but the slaves are all still controlled by the masters. Most of the slaves are not truly able to share in the wealth in a way that would allow everyone to have a decent life. Today's slaves still have their opportunities limited by arbitrary economic injustices."

"Is this all there is—economic equality or isolation? What about love?"

"It's true that love can exist in the most horrible of circumstances. But when you love someone and you wish to live a life with that person, you have to think about what it's going to actually mean. How will you live your life on a daily basis when you have an on-going relationship with another slave? You have to become chained again to slave-like conditions. Love tends to shackle people and keep them from developing their true potential."

"So, you think I am a slave?" she asked, not at all defensively.

"I don't know," I said, smiling for the first time. "I can't figure you out."

"I may be a slave in some ways, but I think I am like a lot of other people. I know that I don't like a lot of things. I just don't know what I can do about it. I didn't know, but I think I do now, and you helped me figure it out. I think I can create and produce plays and media that help to wake people up and give them guidance to take creative community action. I think I can do other things, too. I can look at my life style and become more conscious about my life. But don't you see? Knowing you has helped me become more aware of my responsibilities, and you haven't even talked to me about these things." She took my hand and led me to the couch. "And another thing. Love doesn't have to be the way you describe. Two people can love each other in a way that is not possessive, in a way that encourages both people to follow the paths they need to. Gibson, let's start from this kind of love. I am willing to love you without putting any demands on you other than you being responsive to me when we are together. Let's just go step by step and see if we give each other what we need. Even if it works out for just a little while, it will have been worth it if we are able to share who we really are."

Then she leaned over and kissed me lightly on the lips. What she had been saying had brought a lot of questions to mind about how it could work, and what she was suggesting, but her kiss short-circuited my thoughts and dissolved all my tension and defensiveness. I put my arm around her and held her tightly and we kissed passionately. We both just let ourselves melt into the other. I felt a mixture of sensations, holding her body close to me, feeling the strength of her emotions, her kiss.

She drew me back on the sofa, on top of her, and from then on it seemed like our actions were following some larger purpose, some larger design. We helped each other out of our clothes, and our bodies flowed together. We lay touching, caressing, and kissing each other until we came together, and I lost the awareness of the separateness of myself as our passion and excitement grew and grew.

Afterwards we lay together, and at first I didn't question or doubt anything. It just happened, and I was clear Justine had wanted it to happen. I admitted to myself how much I had recently fantasized about this happening. I felt happy and deeply satisfied, so complete. Eventually I drifted off to sleep, which was a mistake because I allowed Fallacious to take control of my mind. He put a dream on his projector which cut through all my romantic feelings.

In my dream Queen Avarice had been sitting in a luxurious high back soft chair in front of a cozy, crackling fireplace, light dim and romantic. She looked as beautiful as she usually does. She wore a lavender blouse with white lace and delicate amaranth earrings.

I was sitting in a comfortable chair across from her. She leaned forward in her chair and said, "Gibson, I know you realize my name is not Queen Avarice."

I felt disturbed that she knew I called her that. How did she know I called her Queen Avarice?

She continued, "You know, Gibson, I can understand how disappointed you must have been losing your job, your wife, your home. I believe you turned this disappointment into anger and then projected this anger onto me. I don't take this personally, and I am willing to tell you my real name."

In my dream, I realized that I had become curious, "What is your real name?"

She smiled, "Now don't get angry, Gibson, but I won't tell you my real name until you agree to accept the position in our firm that we want to offer to you. After you accept our offer, and on your first day, I will tell you my name."

For some reason I realized that Queen Avarice never uses the word, "work." She never says, "when you come to work."

I asked her why she never uses the word, "work" when she says I should accept her offer.

She said, "Because we never think of what we do as work, Gibson. We feel we are accumulating what God has chosen to give us. Just as you have always thought, we are the privileged elite chosen by God to rule over the less deserving masses of people. You are one of us. You are also one of the chosen elite who lost your way. Your destiny is with us, not with the working or middle class, and definitely not on the street. We want you to come take the position that you are meant to have. "

"I can't accept your offer," I said.

"But don't you want to know my real name," she asked.

"Yes, I do…can't you just tell me?" I realized that I really wanted to know her name.

"Then all you have to do is come to me and let me know you are accepting our offer."

I was feeling it was very important to me to know her real name. It suddenly seemed a matter of life and death. I realized that maybe I did need to accept her offer. I started to tell her I would accept her as long as she would tell me her real name.

She smiled, and I woke up with feeling shocked and confused. I had been dreaming of Queen Avarice, but looked over at Justine lying asleep next to me in bed. The memory of making love with her filled me with such joy. Why would I be dreaming of Queen Avarice, especially on this night?

I was stunned to realize how much I had wanted to know her real name. In my dream I was willing to accept her offer just to know her real name. I felt so weak.

Looking at Justine, I knew I was in love with her. Yet I realized that somewhere in my psyche exists remnants of my past conditioning, hanging around, waiting to sabotage my efforts to live and love on my own terms. And I think these parts of my psyche have recruited Queen Avarice to represent them, to confuse my conscious mind. I have to find a way of eradicating Queen Avarice from my psyche. I have to dethrone her. But how?

I am in love with Justine. And maybe that should be enough. If I do what I want to do, and am open to developing a relationship with her, then maybe that will automatically dissolve Queen Avarice from dreams and thoughts. But maybe I have to do something more direct. More bold. Maybe I have to finally act in a bold way on my own behalf. Maybe I have to meet Queen Avarice—or whatever her name really is—face to face, in-person, and then maybe her spell over me will be broken. Why did I write "maybe?" What else could happen?

I'm going to do it. I'm going to go into the Holy Skyscraper, find her, meet her and bring closure to this illusion once and for all—no matter what may happen.

I gently got out of bed and quietly dressed. I went into the next room and tore a page from my journal. I wrote a note to Justine, telling her that I loved her and wanted to be in a relationship with her. But I told her that I had to resolve some things that needed to be dealt with before I could start a new life with her. I hoped she would understand. I laid the note on the table and left before she woke. I realized that I needed to leave before she woke up or I might not have been able to leave.

Now that I'm sitting alone away from Justine, a mixture of feelings are flowing through me. I feel a pleasant glow of love for Justine, and yet I feel that I have to break down some barriers within myself before I can fully share with her. I have to free myself from whatever attachments I have to the American Dream of becoming rich and powerful. I also have to follow-through with doing whatever I can to stop the homeless killings. To prove that the Butcher is the killer. He has to be the killer. I hope I will be able to prove it. I have to get these "simple" things done so I can get back to Justine. If she will have me back after leaving her like I did.

July 25 ~~ ANOTHER HOMELESS MAN MURDERED

I was walking around in my state of love reverie when I noticed the headlines of the evening daily newspaper. The huge headlines blared out, ANOTHER HOMELESS MAN MURDERED. I had the money so I bought a paper and read the story. As I read the details, I felt a dread, a sinking feeling. Another nameless person killed in his sleep. Hacked up. Goddamnit. It would be a horrible way to die. I could imagine being jarred awake with the force of a knife or hatchet, then feeling pain, disoriented, and then feeling terror.

I have to step back here. My imagination still just takes over. I've got to get control of myself. It wasn't me who was hacked up, yet for a moment, for a moment I felt, I felt the…knife. I felt the knife slicing into my skin.

I'll go to the Campfire tonight, and lay it all out in the open for everyone.

I can't stop writing in my journal right now. I can't put my pen away and close this journal. I know there is some part of me which wants to go back to Justine. To apologize for running out and to work through my feelings with her. But now isn't the time. I have to finish this thing with the killings of homeless people, and to prove one way or another if the Butcher is the killer. It just has to be him. Ransack will have to help me. He'll have to help me stop the Butcher. I know there is something else I have to deal with. I have to resolve this obsession I have with Queen Avarice. I have to free myself from what she represents. But right now I have to force myself to stop writing.

~~ THE FINAL STRAW

I feel so frustrated. I was just at the Campfire and still nobody believed me about the Butcher, even after I told them that Carissa had seen all of the newspaper articles about the killings on the wall of his office. Ransack was worse than all of them, which just pisses me off. He knows more than most about what a fanatic like the Butcher is capable of. He sat there by the fire, making jokes about how out of all of the millions of people in the Portland and surrounding area, I just happen to know who the killer of these homeless people is. "How likely that would be?" he asked derisively. "Not very likely."

Ransack turned back to me and said, "Besides Gibson, the killer has already been caught." Ransack could see that I did not know what he was talking about, so he began to explain. "Charlie was the homeless man killed last night, and the last person who was seen with Charlie was Ronald. They went off together because Ronald said he knew of a warm place where Charlie could sleep. Charlie had not been feeling well. When the cops came around earlier today, they found out that Ronald was the last person to see Charlie alive and they arrested him."

It was shocking that Charlie had been killed. I looked around for Louise, but I didn't see her. This must be devastating for her. Charlie had been her partner on the street for so many years. I really didn't know Charlie that well, but I did feel a connection to him. His death made me want even more to do something to stop the killings. I knew this was the last straw for me—it has increased my resolve to do something.

I thought of Ronald. I couldn't imagine that he was the one who had been killing the homeless. I turned to Ransack, and said, "It can't be Ronald. He's not the type who would be a serial killer."

"How do you know? Are you an expert on serial killers?" Ransack teased.

"No, but it just doesn't seem right. If there's a chance it isn't Ronald, shouldn't we try to prove it?" I desperately wanted his help to resolve this thing once and for all, and then perhaps my fears in the night would be resolved. Even if it were really Ronald, which I knew it wasn't, my mind still knew that the Butcher was somehow involved in these killings.

"What do you think we should do?" Ransack challenged.

"I don't know what you should do, but I'm going to break into the Butcher's store one night and see what I can find."

"Come on, Gibson, you're not that type of person. You'll just get caught or hurt, maybe killed for trespassing."

"We'll see," is all I answered. I stared at the fire for a little while, and watched the burning embers float up into the dark night sky and disappear. An individual's spark of life can be distinguished so quickly. Not just from a murder, but from so many other causes of death. I looked over at Jerome sitting with his back against his tree. I couldn't see his face clearly in the darkness, but I could see the rest of his body. He was sharpening his knife. I stared at his hands moving back and forth in a rhythmic, continual motion.

As I looked at Jerome I didn't feel he was the killer. I knew that he killed many enemy soldiers in Iraq, and it is clear he is carrying pent up rage and anger. Even though I have been scared of him—not knowing why he follows me—my intuition told me that he was not the killer, either. Anybody could be the killer. Ransack was right, and yet deep down I knew that the Butcher was the one. I just knew it. And I knew that I had to do something.

Now that I'm away from the Campfire sitting in a doorway of a desolate warehouse, I have to think of what I can do. I don't want to do anything courageous or anything life-threatening. I'm determined to figure out some plan of action tomorrow.

July 26 ~~ REACHING OUT FOR HELP

I woke up this morning realizing what I had to do. I will go see the lawyer who became more conscious to the needs of others after his wife left him. The one who gave me some of his old clothes. He wanted to know how he could help the world. How better could he help than to stop a brutal serial killer of the homeless? I couldn't remember his name though. I didn't even know if I could remember where he lives. Somewhere in the southwest near downtown. I don't hang out there that often. I just remembered that I had a few of his shirts. I looked on the collar, and his dry cleaners had his name, Ken Burnett, written on the inside collar in indelible ink. Even the dirt on the streets hadn't had an effect on it. I called him and asked to see him. Surprisingly, he remembered me right away. I told him that I had information about the homeless killings that I didn't think anyone would believe, and he said that he would see me as soon as I wanted. We agreed to meet by a fountain near his office in about an hour.

~~ MEETING WITH KEN

I could see Ken Burnett standing in his grey suit, fidgeting by the escalators as I came into the entrance from Park Street. I stood for a moment looking, wondering if I was wasting my time, but I thought that maybe he really could help me. He did express some sincere concerns to me when I last saw him, and he seemed to be glad to hear from me when I telephoned him just a little while ago.

I went up to him and before I could say anything he threw his arms around me and hugged me. "I'm happy you got in touch with me, Gibson. I wanted so much to thank you for helping to change my life. I wanted to let you know what I have done since I talked with you and you gave me that lecture. After you left that morning, I sat and thought about what you had said and realized you were right. I was living a phony, upscale life, and that I needed to change. I went through the house and chose things to give my ex-wife or to sell. I bought a low energy refrigerator, and don't keep the heat on at night. I have started shopping at the natural food stores to not to add to the use of chemicals negatively affecting our bodies and our earth's soil and waters. I've also volunteered at the local legal aid center to provide free or low cost legal advice to the needy. I know that this all may seem superficial, but I am sincere, really sincere. I realize I've just begun, and it hasn't been easy. I keep falling back into my old patterns, but I'm working on it. And I have been looking for you on the streets so I could tell you what you've meant to me. And to thank you. I got your message about the conference, but unfortunately I was out of town for work."

I told him I appreciated him telling me about what he was doing to change his life. I then told him that I thought I knew who was killing the homeless people. He was silent for a moment and then said, "Did you know that the police think they have arrested the person doing the killing?"

"Yes, I know that, but I think the police have the wrong person."

"Tell me what you have."

I didn't really know how to explain to him at first. I stumbled around saying I saw some men going into a store, which I could tell must have sounded a little silly. I finally was able to describe to him more coherently that I saw these men go into the Butcher's store in February. I explained how I had finally figured out that it was the same night as one of the killings by comparing my journal entry with the newspaper article at the library. I described to him how the Butcher had harassed homeless people who had walked in front of his store. I didn't tell him about Ransack. Why confuse the main issue? I told him what Carissa had seen on his office wall.

That information seemed to spark his interest, but he then asked me if I were taking drugs or drinking. I told him no, goddamnit, no. He apologized for asking me that question but said he had to assess all the facts. He said that he didn't think anything could be done unless there was more proof. He said that he would try to think of a way to force a search of the Butcher's premises, but he didn't think there would be legal grounds for such a search without more substantial proof.

After he left I walked around downtown thinking about how to get proof. I was disappointed that Ken couldn't help me, but I understood. I realized that I had to get into the Butcher's store to see if I could find some evidence about his involvement in the killings. I thought about how often Carissa says that she goes into the Butcher's store, and I decided to ask her if she could steal me a key or find a way of leaving a door or window open in the basement for me to go into the store late at night.

Ken had expressed concern about me doing something dangerous or illegal, and cautioned me against putting myself in those kinds of situations. I lied and told him that he had nothing to worry about, that I was not that foolish to try to do something on my own. At least part of it was a lie. I guess I am a bit of a fool at times, but I hope it's for the right reasons. I don't see any other way to get proof that the Butcher is the serial killer, and even if it may not be the right time to take a risk as the astrologer said, and even if it would be dangerous or illegal, I know I have to do something to try to stop these killings.

Now that I've decided to do something, I feel extremely restless. I couldn't sit still. I walked and I walked. And then I slowly began to feel scared. What am I doing? I mean, who do I think I am? Captain Courageous? Jason Bourne?

I do know that I'm going to try to find the evidence to prove my psychic perceptions are correct. I am going to ask Carissa if she could help me get into the Butcher's store. If I didn't act soon, I might talk myself out of attempting to prove that the Butcher is the killer.

~~ CARISSA'S UNREASONABLE DEMAND

I met Carissa after she got off work tonight and told her what I wanted to do and asked for her help. She instantly said she would help me. "You know I don't like that gross asshole," she said. "And after what I saw in his office, and just how mean and spiteful he is around others, I think he is capable of hurting and killing. I'll do anything to see if he's the killer, and if he is, to stop him."

She was silent for a moment and then looked at me. "I think I know how to help you, but I'll only do it on one condition."

I felt apprehensive. "What's your condition, Carissa?"

"I will help you if you let me come with you."

I looked at her and sighed. "Carissa, if I get caught, it will be bad enough for me, but if the police catch me, I'll get into more trouble if you are along. You're a minor. Besides, I don't want you to get in trouble, or hurt. If the Butcher catches us in his store, I have no doubt he would try to kill us."

"I know I'm only a teenager, but I know how to take care of myself. You will have a harder time getting into the store if you don't let me help you. You can't do this alone. I tell you what. I won't go into the store with you. I'll stand by the door to warn you if anyone comes. That way I won't be the one who is trespassing." She looked at me to see if I was agreeing with her. "Gibson, I think you need a lookout. Besides, I feel strongly about this. I won't help you unless you let me come with you."

"You can't be serious, Carissa. I can't let you come with me. Being a lookout would be just as dangerous as coming into the store with me. It just would not be safe."

"If I agree to help you by leaving a window open, I will know the night you are going to break into the Butcher's store. You won't be able to stop me from being there."

"You mean you would risk ruining this chance to see if he is the killer and to stop him."

"I don't think I would be ruining anything—again, I would stay outside, and just be a lookout.

"If you are willing to help me, fine. But I won't agree to you being there. If you insist on being there, all I ask is that you stay across the street. It's just too dangerous, Carissa. The Butcher or the police or some other of his friends could show up at the store."

She reluctantly agreed, and said she would try to open a basement window when she goes to the store tomorrow.

Later I went over to the Campfire and told Ransack what I was going to do. I asked him one more time if he would help me. He said no again, and said that if I went through with this break-in I'd probably get myself killed. However, I've already shrugged off Ransack's pessimism. What does he know? He may be a professional killer, but he's over the hill or he wouldn't be hanging out on street, telling stories to drugged and down-and-out street people around the Campfire.

I hope Fallacious leaves me alone tonight while I'm sleeping. I'm very vulnerable, even though I feel insanely determined. I don't want to dream about the night dragons, about Jerome stalking me, about the Butcher, about Queen Avarice—or especially about Justine. I miss her so. I just want a dreamless, blank night, or if I have to endure a dream, I want it to be something innocuous, like flying or running in place or something like that. Something I can deal with.

July 27 ~~ SURVIVING THE MYSTERY OF THE MURDERS

I have resolved one of the major self-imposed challenges of my present life. I have survived, barely survived, the most insane thing that I have ever gotten involved in. Insane because it is not me. I am not a hero. I am not a crime fighter. I am not an adventurer. I used to enjoy a good cop or adventure movie or book just like a lot of mainstream people do. Somehow these myths and fairy tales satisfied my repressed urges to battle the forces of evil—satisfied my fantasies about being a hero.

What I just went through wasn't a myth or a fairy tale. Some people got killed. Some people got hurt. And I have to live with this. I accomplished what I set out to do. But at what costs?

Once Carissa told me she could get me in the Butcher's store, we agreed to go the next night, after she got off work. It would be about 12:00 midnight. I went to sleep worrying about what dream Fallacious would project onto my mind, but I awoke the next morning pleasantly surprised. I had dreamed of lying in Justine's big, comfortable brass bed with her beside me. We were cuddling in the soft candlelight, and then suddenly we saw the night dragons come into the night sky in the distance. I sat up frightened, but Justine reached up and pulled me back down. "Don't be afraid," she said.

"But don't you see the night dragons coming?" I said lifting myself while pointing to towards the sky.

She looked out the window and said that she didn't see anything. I looked out the window again, and the night dragons were gone. I looked back at Justine, and she smiled at me. That's the way the dream ended. I woke to a sunny morning, feeling relieved.

Later I was sitting in front of the Holy Skyscraper when I saw Ransack and Jerome walking down the street toward me. As a twosome they look mean and powerful. I was happy I was friends with at least one of them. They walked up and stood in front of me on the steps.

"We want to talk with you," Ransack said. "I remembered that you usually hang out here on weekday mornings. Why, for god's sake, I don't know. Listen, Gibson, I changed my mind. I got to thinking about what you were saying, and even though I don't think it is this Butcher and his men who are doing the killings, I decided that those assholes should be investigated and if they're guilty, stopped. I talked with Jerome here and convinced him that we should be the ones to break into the store to see if we can find some proof about what they might be doing. Not you. With our skills, it would be so easy for Jerome and me to get in and out of his store, whereas you would probably wake up the whole city and get yourself arrested or killed. No offense."

"No offense, but I'm still going to go ahead with my plan. I'm going tonight, if you two want to come along."

Ransack frowned but said he'd do it with me even though he'd prefer not to. He looked at Jerome, who nodded. It was too good to be true. For just a second I felt a big weight had been lifted until I remembered that I was still going to be putting myself in danger. I told them about my plan, and at first they were bothered about Carissa's involvement. They said that they didn't need her to break into the store. I finally convinced them that we should let her get us in, and that it would be safe with her outside looking out in case someone came. Ransack reluctantly agreed, and Jerome didn't seem to care one way or the other. It was as though both were just wanting to get the whole thing over with.

We agreed to meet by the café that night around 12:00. I was ecstatic. I stayed at the Holy skyscraper for another hour or so but I didn't see Queen Avarice. I didn't mind. Queen Avarice would be here tomorrow or the next day. I just hoped I would be here also watching her, given what I was about to do. I definitely felt more optimistic now that Ransack and Jerome would be helping me.

I thought just for a moment about going to see Justine, but I knew I couldn't until I finished facing certain fears and conditionings with my psyche. I decided to just go somewhere and try to relax, and maybe get some sleep. I stopped by Powell's and drank coffee, looked at magazines, but I couldn't get interested in anything. The articles were so detached from reality, so superficial.

I was able to doze lightly for an hour or two that afternoon, but basically I was too excited. Maybe a little anxious. Scared shitless. What was I doing, I kept asking myself? Then a part of me said that with Ransack and Jerome along I should be safe. Unless Jerome is the killer, which I quickly refuted.

Finally, the time arrived for us to meet. I stood in the shadows across the street away from Casey's Cafe and the parking lot.

Ransack and Jerome finally arrived a little after 12:00. Carissa was late anyway, and didn't get off work until 12:15. She came up close to me, looked around quickly, and then took a small handgun out of her purse and handed it to me.

Astounded I stared at the gun for a few moments as though I didn't know what it was. Actually, I had only held real handguns a few times in my life. It felt light but solid. I finally looked at Carissa and asked where she had gotten this. She said that she had taken it out of her boss's desk drawer. She said that he wouldn't miss it and that she would put it back tomorrow, but she thought that we might need it.

Ransack asked to see the gun, and while he inspected it I explained to Carissa who Jerome and Ransack were. Ransack gave me back the gun and told me that it was loaded, and carefully showed me how to use the safety. He said that I should keep the safety on and keep the gun hidden and not pull it out unless I absolutely needed to. He said that he also had a gun so that I probably wouldn't need to use mine.

We didn't walk directly across the parking lot. Instead we walked down the street adjacent to the parking lot until we got to the building. The three of us stayed in the shadows hidden from view, while Carissa crawled along the side of the buildings until she got to the window behind the Butcher's store that she had left open. We could see her push the basement window open and crawl through.

One by one we started crawling along the building toward the Butcher's store. We knew that she would be opening the door soon. I got there first and saw that the door was opened a crack. I rolled onto the porch and scrambled inside, followed quickly by Ransack. But Jerome didn't come in behind him. We waited in silence at the top of the stair leading to the basement below for Jerome, staring at the outside door.

All of a sudden I felt someone behind me. I turned and saw a figure with a knife. I jumped back toward the outside door and would have yelled except that Ransack had put his hand over my mouth.

"Take it easy, take it easy," Jerome whispered, as he came out of the shadows of the basement stairway. "I climbed through the basement window to make sure everything was safe."

As I tried to catch my breath we took our bearings and realized that we were in the back room used as a meat cutting area. On one side of the room was a huge freezer door. Ransack motioned toward the basement and whispered that we should start our search. Jerome had already started back down the stairs.

Before I followed Jerome, I looked at Carissa and asked her to leave the building. She said that it would be safer for her to remain hidden just inside the back door. I reluctantly agreed because I just wanted to get in and get out. I should have made her leave.

I followed Jerome downstairs into the basement. Ransack came behind me. I could feel the gun in my jacket pocket and felt uncomfortable about it. Jerome turned on his flashlight when we got downstairs. A huge round table sat in a cleared space near the bottom of the stairs. On top of the table was a box. I opened the box and found a tray of poker chips and cards. Ransack and Jerome came over to look.

"That's what they're doing down here," Ransack said. "Playing poker. That's all. Just playing poker."

I felt embarrassed. But I also felt like this didn't prove that they weren't the killers involved in a fanatical conspiracy. The basement was a huge storeroom, with barrels and cabinets, machinery and boxes stored in a random order, it seemed. Ransack and I also had our flashlights, and the three of us went in different directions.

I don't really know what I was looking for. Perhaps some knives or guns or something that would link the Butcher and his gang to the killings of the homeless people. I opened boxes and looked in cabinets. But I found nothing. There was so much to look through. I didn't know how much time we would have, I was looking as quickly yet as thoroughly as I could. I realized at one point that I was feeling frantic and tried to step back and relax.

I was gradually making my way back to the center of the room when I heard something upstairs. I thought that it sounded like a yelp, a muffled yell. As I approached the center of the room I could see Jerome standing by the round table looking up the stairway. I was behind some barrels but I could still see the top of the stairs, and I saw the door open. I couldn't see Ransack, but I assumed he was somewhere on the other side of the storage room.

Then I saw the most frightening sight I have ever seen. The Butcher came through the door holding a gun to Carissa's head. He looked at Jerome and over at me.

"Don't any of you move," he said, "Or I will kill this girl."

He started down the stairway with Carissa. I could see how frightened she looked. I don't know if I can describe what happened next. Everything was so fast and frightening. First, I caught a flash of movement in Jerome's direction at the same time I heard a gunshot. I saw Jerome fall backward onto the table with blood spurting out of the side of his head. I started in his direction, but then I heard Carissa scream and looked back just in time to see the Butcher and her fall from the stairway to the concrete floor below. I scrambled back around the barrels over to them. The Butcher lay on his back with the large handle of Jerome's knife sticking out of his throat. Carissa lay beside him. I reached for her and turned her over. I could see a gash on the side of her head and could see that as she fell she had hit her head on the piece of metal equipment that was below the stairs. I quickly felt for her pulse and felt relieved that I could find one. I then looked around frantically for a piece of cloth or something to wrap around her head. I couldn't see anything. I saw that she was wearing a leather belt. I saw a storage area underneath the stairs where there were paper towels and toilet paper. I reached over and ripped open a pack and tore off one of the towels and folded it. I took off Carissa's belt and used it to keep the paper bandage on her gash. I had to tie the belt in an awkward knot but it seemed to work.

This took only seconds and while I worked my mind began to grasp what had happened. When Jerome started to throw his knife Ransack shot him but not in time to stop his throw. Ransack murdered Jerome and I realized that he may try to murder me. Why, I didn't know, but without thinking further, I started moving back toward the barrels. I heard another gunshot and heard metal clang close to where I had just been. I had just missed being shot. I instinctively reached into my jacket and pulled the handgun out, but I remember thinking, "What chance do I have against someone like Ransack? Why Ransack? Why did he kill Jerome and why was he trying to kill me?" I decided that I should just ask him. Hell, I had nothing to lose. Maybe I could find a way out of this.

"What's going on, Ransack?" I yelled. "Why are you trying to kill me? Why... Why did you kill Jerome?" I was surprised that my voice sounded in control and didn't squeak.

I heard Ransack laugh. Then when he spoke again his voice had changed. It was chilling and angry. "Gibson, you are the biggest asshole I know. I had a good thing going here until you came along with your fucking suspicions and ruined everything. I didn't want to have to kill Jerome. But of course Al couldn't let me handle this my own way, either, and had to come barging in here. He deserves what he got. Now you, Gibson. I've been standing here trying to decide whether or not to let you live or to kill you."

I huddled behind the barrels, tightly holding the handgun and tried to make sense out of what was happening. It seemed that Ransack and the Butcher had been working together. But why?

Ransack started talking again. "Gibson, I want you to just stay where you are until I decide what I am going to do. Your gun doesn't have any bullets in it anyway, if you're thinking of trying to use it. I took the bullets out earlier when you gave me the gun to inspect. So just sit there and wait."

I could hear him moving around somewhere in the darkness on the other side of the room.

I looked down at the handgun I was holding and shook my head. Then I remembered the Butcher's gun. I leaned out from the barrel I was hiding behind and looked over where the Butcher lay. I first looked at Carissa, who was still unconscious. I really didn't want to see the sight of the Butcher again with the knife in his throat but I had to locate his gun. My eyes skimmed across the Butchers contorted face and I felt no satisfaction whatsoever that he had been killed. I finally saw the gun which had fallen between the Butcher's body and the stairs. I would have to crawl about ten feet to get to it, and I wondered if Ransack would see me if I kept low. I didn't even know where the hell Ransack was but I knew that I had to do something. I knew I had to act quickly or I wouldn't do anything, so as quietly as I could I started crawling toward the Butcher's handgun.

After I had started crawling a few feet Ransack started talking again and at first I froze in my spot. "I've been standing over here smoking a cigarette, thinking about you, Gibson. And I've decided that I'm not going to kill you. Let me tell you why. Listen carefully. I want you to appreciate how important this decision I am making is for you. It's a life or death issue for you." He chuckled.

Despite what Ransack was saying, I knew I still had to get that gun. Apparently, he hadn't seen me so far, or he would have already shot me. I continued toward the gun, and was able to get it and crawl back to my hiding place behind the barrels while Ransack talked. Despite how scared I was and how focused I had been on getting the gun, a part of my mind was still listening to Ransack, and I was amazed at what he was saying.

"Gibson, ever since you came to me with your suspicions that the Butcher was involved in killings of homeless bums I've gone back and forth in my mind about killing you. I ultimately decided not to kill you because I have chosen you to be the chronicler of my life. I have invested a great deal of time telling you my story and I want you to live to write it. I haven't changed my mind despite what's gone on here. I will soon be making a telephone call and by tomorrow morning this incident in Al's store will just be listed as a burglary and murder. Some crazy Iraqi vet will be listed as having blown his cork and burglarized this store. He was caught in the act by the owner and they killed each other. Just another inner-city crime story.

"Before I go, I'd like to let you know what was really happening here. I wish you had your journal with you. You better have a good memory because I want you to write all of what I am going to tell you down. The first thing you should know is that you were partly correct about the Butcher, as you call him, and his group of fanatical men. They wanted to do something about the street people, who they considered a threat to their businesses, and perhaps to America in some pathetic way, as if a group of poor people could interfere with the powerful money and military machines that run this society. Anyway, when you asked me to stop the Butcher from harassing homeless people, you did me a favor. I went to him and told him that I could solve his problems about homelessness for a sizeable fee. That was when he called together his group of men and they each came up with part of my fee, which, by the way, I will be using to leave this country and live in a more luxurious style than I've been living in recently. Nothing personal, but I've had it with hiding out among the poor in America.

"I never planned on killing more than a few of the homeless anyway, even though I convinced Al's gang that I would keep it up indefinitely. I told Al that after a series of murders, the homeless would probably avoid the streets of the inner city and the city council would pass laws to keep them off the streets. Not solve the problem, mind you, but it would reduce the number of homeless on the streets. I was actually only planning to kill a few more homeless people over the next few weeks, and then by that time I would have all the money I needed. I have enough now, I guess, but it would have been better if I'd been able to kill a few more. But then you came along and wanted to break into the store. Shit, even had the police thinking that they had caught the killer. I knew Ronald would have to be released soon because there is really no evidence against him, and I was going to wait until after he was released before I killed again. I really didn't need to have the police pin the murders on the wrong person, but at the same time I welcomed it. It's in my training to be thorough in erasing any chance of the authorities finding out about my involvement in something like this.

"All I really wanted to do was to come along tonight and make sure you didn't find anything, and then leave. I felt that you would then decide that you were wrong and would stop pestering us. I'd be able to finish my job and leave the country in three or four weeks. But the stupid fuck, Al, apparently couldn't stay away from the store. Well, so he paid the price. He lost more than I lost."

I closed my eyes and felt a deep despair. It was Ransack who had been killing all along, and I was the one who had introduced him to the Butcher.

"Now I realize that you may think I'm quite heartless to kill a homeless man while he's sleeping. You surely know by now that I have no qualms about killing anybody, anytime, if it's going to advance my purposes. I'm a product of the people who trained me and, I suppose, of my early years when my father and uncles would beat the shit out of me if I showed any sign of weakness or sympathy for the niggers and others they despised. The truth of the matter is, I don't really value human life that much. You can't if you're in the business that I've been in for all these years. It's like war. What does it matter if it's five thousand or twenty thousand or a hundred thousand who get killed? That's the cost of survival! I entered into an arrangement with the Butcher because I needed to get out of the country. I needed to survive. I could have gotten out some other way. I could have stolen something but there was an opportunity so I took it. The truth of the matter is that I actually like killing in this way. I like conspiracies. I like manipulating people's fears and prejudices.

"I want you to write the truth about what I did and include it with all the other things I've told you. Most people don't realize how many people are walking around in this country who simply don't have to follow the rules and regulations that the average American does. The world is a different place than what most people think. We moved beyond national interests and there is a ruling elite of wealthy, powerful people who operate in a very manipulative and bloodthirsty manner. But I want you to understand, I'm not asking you to write about these things to help Americans understand the real power in their so-called land of freedom. I really don't think most Americans want to face what these kinds of things mean to them. I just want you to write about me. I haven't been telling you my life story to expose something about secret organizations and groups that are running the show. I think Americans have had many opportunities to acknowledge this reality. Almost every Hollywood movie or national best seller over the past 40 years has been dealing with this idea. Americans have had their chance to wake up. Let the secret organizations control everyone. All I'm interested in is being immortalized. And getting out of the country so I can enjoy the rest of my life in comfort and ease on a secluded beach somewhere."

I studied the Butcher's handgun in my hand and wondered if I would be able to use it. Ransack was saying he was going to let me live. It made sense but I couldn't trust him. Besides something else was beginning to form in my mind. An uncharacteristic thought. I was beginning think I should try to stop him. I was being drawn to this notion even as a part of me was trying to resist it.

Ransack continued to talk, "You may wonder why I can allow you to live since you know what happened here and you know all about me and that I did all this as well as kill all the homeless. The answer is simple. Even though certain government agencies want to find me, they don't want me exposed. They won't allow this potentially messy situation to become public and be pinned on me. Besides I am in the process of negotiating with some corporations to be contracted for mercenary work, and once I get on their payrolls, the agencies trying to find me will leave me alone. I just don't want to go to work again too soon. I'd like to enjoy the money I've been stashing away. Ellen will be meeting me where I'm going so I should have an enjoyable extended vacation living in luxury and sin." He chuckled again. He was enjoying his monologue.

He also would be enjoying his luxuries at the expense of homeless people he's murdered.

"Another reason I'm not worried about you knowing is that you still don't really know who I am. I have gone through so many identities in my time of being undercover that I've almost forgotten who I really am. I've had more plastic surgeries, hair dyes and implants than most of the residents of Beverly Hills have had. I don't even have my fingerprints on file anymore. I wasn't real when I worked for those secret government agencies and I'm not real now. The police would be frustrated as hell trying to locate me in their databases.

"I do want to leave a picture of the real me here with you. I was going to give you a picture of me anyway. I know that nobody will really know who I am except a few of my colleagues but I just think that it would be a kick to be a subject of a book and have my picture in it. I'd like people to see how I looked when I worked for the Special Forces. Short hair. In combat gear, even though I spent a lot of time wearing suits. I'll leave this picture on the stairs when I go.

"Now Gibson I'm going to promise you something. I promise you that if you don't write about me and get the book published, I'll come back and I won't just kill you. You'll spend the rest of your life in the most horrible pain you can imagine after I'm through with you. I hope this promise will provide you with the proper motivation to complete a book about me." He laughed again. I almost couldn't believe what I had just heard.

I could hear him moving. I wondered for just a moment whether or not I would try to stop him as he walked up the stairs, and I started to shake my head angrily asking myself who I thought I was. Ransack just said that he is willing to let me live. Let him go. Let him go. But then some side of me, a side that I know doesn't always look out for my best interests, was telling me that I couldn't let him go. I made a commitment to stop the killing of the homeless, and I had to stop Ransack who was the actual serial killer. I was sitting there listening in disbelief to my inner dialogue when Ransack started talking again.

"In just a minute I'm going to walk up those stairs and out the door. I want you to count to 500, and then get up and leave. I hope you take my advice not to try anything. I'd hate to have to kill you after all this time I have taken to tell you about myself. I'd be really pissed and I'd make it hurt.

"Oh, by the way, you were partly right and partly wrong about Jerome. It was true that he was following you but he was trying to protect you, the dumb shit. He told me once that you reminded him of a friend of his who had been killed in Iraq. His friend wrote journals, and apparently more than a couple of times his friend had saved Jerome's life but Jerome couldn't save his. So when Jerome saw you he kind of adopted you and began following you around. He said that a couple of times he had to fight off gangs to keep them from attacking you. It seems that your journal, my friend, has been lucky for you. Remember, you'd better write my story and get it published or I'm going to come back."

Ransack's voice had taken on threatening overtones with that last statement, but then his voice took on this eerie, friendly overtone, as if he were saying goodbye to a drinking buddy at a bar.

"Well, I'm going to take off now. Remember, count to five hundred."

I could hear Ransack start to walk, and again I felt a strong drive to do something to stop him. He had killed all of these homeless people, for god's sake. How could I just let him go? But did I want to get myself killed? What match would I be for him? I kept telling myself that I wasn't a hero but then some voice inside myself said, "It has nothing to do with being a hero. Sooner or later you're going to have do something to try to make a difference about how terrible you think things are or you might as well lie down in some gutter and let yourself be swept down the drain with the rest of the sludge and industrial wastes."

I have to admit that I was getting myself psyched up to try to stop Ransack with all my self-talk. Then I realized that I wasn't able to hear any movement. I couldn't hear Ransack walking. I couldn't tell if he was on the stairs yet. I began to think I was letting him get away. I looked down at the gun in my hand, I looked over at Jerome lying dead on the table, and then at Carissa who still had not regained consciousness, and something in me screamed, "DO SOMETHING!"

I made sure that the safety was off on the handgun, and I leaned out from the barrel and at the same time pointed the gun toward the stairs. Nobody was there.

I didn't have time to wonder where Ransack was because I felt the barrel of a gun at the back of my head. "Hold it Gibson. Don't move a goddamn inch. Not one fraction of an inch." I tried not to move. I think I even stopped breathing. "You're just goddamn lucky you can do no wrong, Gibson. In a way I'm proud of you. I have to admire your courage even if it's stupid courage. Even though you must have known you'd be no match for me, you tried. That took balls. Of course, I remembered that the Butcher had a gun. I thought I heard you crawling around when I was talking to you. And I just never take chances."

He said he wasn't going to kill me. I believed him but then I felt pissed off. "You mean you killed those homeless people just for the money?" I asked.

"Yep. That's all I did it for."

"You couldn't have needed the money that badly."

"Someone in my position can't get enough money, Gibson. It was such easy money. Besides, in all the wars we fight, we lose thousands of good soldiers. What's few goddamn homeless bums matter?

"Why did you have to kill Jerome?"

"Once Al came into the store holding Carissa, Jerome became a liability. He would know what was going on here. Besides, Jerome never let anything bad happen to you if he could help it. It wouldn't have been helpful to have him continue to be your protector. You have me as a protector, but for my purposes. Anyway I have a lot to do so I can't visit with you anymore. By the way I'm not going to kill the girl because she doesn't really know what has happened here. It's up to you to keep it that way. You'd better warn her not to say anything if you want her to stay alive. Part of me says to kill her but I do have some limits—I've never liked killing children or women even when I've had to." He stopped talking. All this time he still had the gun pointed to my head but then I felt him move it back and that's the last thing I remember about being in the Butcher's store. I don't remember pain, I don't remember a sound or anything.

July 28 ~~ WAKING UP FROM A NIGHTMARE

When I woke up, I could feel grass underneath my body, and Carissa was kneeling over me. It was not until a few moments later that my mind had cleared enough to see that Carissa was barely conscious herself. When I sat up I felt a sharp pain that extended from the base of my skull deep into my shoulder. But I quickly forgot about it as I attended to Carissa. I helped her to lay back down and asked how she felt. She said her right arm was terribly painful and she felt nauseated. Her arm was probably broken and she could have a concussion. I told her I'd be calling for help right away.

I looked around and realized Ransack had somehow gotten us to a park. I recognized it was the park four or five blocks from Casey's Cafe and the Butcher's Store where Carissa and I met often. Ransack had set us down near the swings. He had told me what Carissa's story should be. That she got off work, and decided to walk to the park. She got this quirky urge to play around. She played on the swing and on the merry go around, but when she decided to use the slide, she fell off. Okay so maybe it's not the best story but who's going to really question her.

Why would she be in the park alone? She wouldn't. Let her say she was with some friends or some families who were still in the park so she thought it was safe. But it didn't matter. Let them lecture her. Carissa seemed coherent enough. I explained to her that we could not say we were in the Butcher's store. I told her what to say and she said she understood. I told her I'd explain what happened later to her. I asked her to stay where she was while I called 911. Before I left I asked her to tell me the address of her house so I could go tell her mother. I had to ask her a few times so I knew she must have still been in shock. Then I went to the edge of the park, telephoned 911 police and said that I was a homeless man who noticed that a girl was lying unconscious in a park and I told them the cross streets. After I hung up I walked a few blocks away and waited.

When I heard the sirens and saw the flashing lights I started walking toward Carissa's house. It was on this side of the city, not too far away. I wanted to tell her mother right away. I walked to one of the main streets and found a store where I could see a clock. It was almost 4:00 a.m. I had been unconscious for about two or three hours.

I decided to walk around for a while before talking to Carissa's mother. I needed to just get off by myself and get myself together. I think that I was both in shock and a state of denial. Two people had been killed and one special person hurt, and another person had been operating above the law. Ransack had been killing the homeless men and had threatened to kill me if I didn't write about him.

Then I thought about myself. If what Ransack had said was true then I'm the one who started the whole thing by telling him to go meet the Butcher. As I thought about that I was surprised that I didn't have any real feeling of remorse or guilt. I was aware that I didn't feel discouraged, depressed, angry or happy from all that that happened in the last few hours. That's when I knew I was in some kind of shock or denial. But I knew I did feel something. Even one person's death for these reasons is horrible and I feel affected by it.

Suddenly I remembered that the killings of the homeless had started before Ransack had met the Butcher and his gang. Maybe I didn't recognize this until now because everything has happened so fast and has been so traumatic. Had the Butcher actually been killing the homeless before he met Ransack? Or was there another serial killer still out there? If I had made the connection last night I would have asked Ransack about this. Then I realized that in some ways it didn't matter. The homeless in this city and around the world have been neglected and allowed to die or be killed before the Butcher and Ransack came along, and more homeless will continue to die of poverty or be killed by fanatics until our society becomes more humane and inclusive. What's important for me is

I know I am now willing and feel able to become more involved in helping to find solutions to these terrible problems related to homelessness. I won't allow myself to fear one serial killer. I want to do my part to help all of us rise above the dark sides of ourselves. I know I have to start with myself.

~~ CARISSA'S MOTHER

Around 6:00 a.m., I went back to Carissa's house and walked up to the door. I had to knock a couple of times before the living room light came on, and the door was opened by a boy who looked about ten or eleven. He was rubbing his eyes. He was very thin and had features that reminded me of Carissa. He looked up at me sleepily, questioningly. I told him I was friend of Carissa's and asked him if he would go get his mother, and without saying anything he turned and ran back toward the hallway on the other side of the living room. I could see him run down the hallway and into a room. I walked inside the house, closed the door, and looked around the living room. It was clean, and on the mantle I could see some pictures. I walked closer and could see pictures of Carissa. Then I noticed that in one of the pictures the man who was holding Carissa was the same man in the picture she had been showing around, her friend's father. I heard someone open the door in the hallway, and I hurried back to stand by the front door.

A woman appeared in her night robe, looking quite haggard and disheveled. As she came closer to me I could smell alcohol. She looked at me, squinting. "You say you are a friend of Carissa's? Isn't she in her room? What's this all about?" As she talked, she lit a cigarette she had taken out of a pack she had in her robe. The small boy waited in the entrance way.

"I came to tell you that after work last night she was playing around in the park and fell off the slide. She hit her head and hurt her arm. I had been standing across the street from the park and when I saw it happen, I telephoned the police. I wanted to tell you but I couldn't get over here any sooner."

She looked like she was thinking, and after a few moments she looked back at me and asked,

"Now who are you? And how did you know where I live?"

I told her that I was a homeless man who hangs out around Casey's Cafe. I told her that Carissa had given me food from time to time and that she had been interviewing me for a school project. I told her that before the ambulance came Carissa told me her address, and I wanted to let her know what had happened. While I was explaining who I was, Carissa's mother walked over by the fireplace and flipped some ashes into the opening. Suddenly she started crying. "What happened to my little girl?" she said, looking at me imploringly. Her son started crying as he stood in the hallway entrance.

"She hit her head in a fall," I repeated. "I don't think she is hurt too badly."

"Carissa takes such good care of me, you know," she said, as if she had regressed to a ten-year-old. "She does everything around here, and she goes to school and she works. I'm not a very good mother."

"That's not what she says."

Her mother looked at me, surprised. "What does she say?"

"She says that you do your best to look after her and her brother, and that she really loves and appreciates you. She told me she knows you are going through a rough time now that your husband died, and that it's just a matter of time before you find work."

"Wait, wait a second," she interrupted. "What did you say about her father?"

"She said that he died. Carissa really misses him. She talks about him a lot."

"He didn't die, the bum. I kicked him out. He was a drunk. I didn't really start drinking until… well, until I was alone with the kids. I feel so helpless—I can barely make the rent. I have to rely on Carissa working. What kind of mother lets her kid work to help pay rent? The last time I saw her father, a couple years ago, he was lying drunk on the sidewalk on Burnside."

She noticed that I was looking at the picture on the mantle.

"Yeah, that's her father. You wonder why I keep these pictures of him on the mantle. Carissa won't let me take them down. I did take them down and threw them away, but I didn't know that Carissa had gotten them out of the trash at the time, and had kept them hidden for over a year. Then one day they were put back up there and Carissa stood her ground, saying that she was not going to let me take them down." I smiled to myself as I thought about Carissa's firmness that I knew so well. "I was too drunk to care. And, you know, I do miss the bum. Sometimes I wish I hadn't kicked him out. He was a good man. It was just that he got involved in a small business that failed, and it shattered him. He was never the same after. He couldn't pick himself up and go back to a regular job. But he was good to the kids. Now I've become like him, probably worse than him. I may be out on the street with him soon. Maybe Carissa will kick me out."

"Even if Carissa could, she would never do that," I said trying to reassure her. "Is her father still in Portland?"

"How the hell should I know? I don't get out that much anymore and I certainly don't go looking around the places where the street bums hang out. Oh, he used to call me but after I hung up on him a number of times he finally stopped calling. Carissa thinks he is still in Portland, which is why she's doing this school project on the homeless. She's been interviewing a number of homeless people, like yourself, and showing pictures of her father to them all, but she hasn't found anyone who has seen him yet. She wants to find him. Let her find him. I don't care. Maybe I even want her to find him. Sometimes I think I want her to find him and go live with him even if it's on the street. At other times I want her to find him so he can move back in with us if he would."

"I don't think Carissa wants to live on the street," I said. "She's very frightened of you not being able to make ends meet."

Carissa's mother seemed to lapse back into her little-girl behavior. "I try to find a job. I just can't handle a job right now. I try to find a job…" She was shaking her head, staring down at the floor.

"Listen…what's your name?" I interrupted her.

She looked up at me. "Linda."

"Listen, Linda. The right thing now for you to do is to find out where they've taken Carissa and to go to her. Do you have transportation?"

"Yes, I have a car. You're right. I'll get dressed and I'll go to her but…which hospital did you say they took her to?"

"I said I didn't know which hospital. Why don't you call the police and find out?"

"We don't have a telephone. The phone company disconnected it a few months ago, the bastards. How do they expect me to find work with no telephone…

"Linda…" I interrupted sternly. "Where is the closest telephone?"

"I can go wake up the neighbors," she said in her little girl voice. "They've said I could use their telephone in an emergency."

Linda got dressed and went next door. When she came back she said that they had taken Carissa to Good Samaritan Hospital. She thanked me for coming to talk with her, and I left.

I walked slowly back to the river. I felt drained and sad about Carissa's home situation. Her mother is in a mess, and her father, not dead but a street person, like myself. I probably should have known, but Carissa was pretty clever about how she kept the search for her father seemingly secondary to our interviews. As I thought about Carissa, I realized how attached I felt to her. She lied about her father, but that's understandable. In a way he had died, as far as not being available to her, but she was trying to find a way of resurrecting him, of bringing him back to life. I admired her sense of purpose. I admired her determination.

I realized how special I think Carissa is. Somehow I knew that she would be a part of my life even though this school project about the homeless won't any longer be the main reason for our getting together. Maybe I thought of her as a daughter, but regardless, she has certainly become a good friend. I figured that I would try to get some sleep and then later in the afternoon I'd go see how she was doing.

~~ NOT A FUTILE EFFORT

While I stood on the corner of Stark and Grand, waiting for the light to turn, I began to feel more positive about things. It was a sunny day. My feelings were similar to the feelings I'd had when I was a twelve-year-old child after our family survived the hurricane. The hurricane would create a tremendous mess of broken trees and houses, but afterwards when it stopped, the sky and the silence that followed made me feel safe. And later, I played among the broken fences and tree limbs, happy to be alive.

Like I feel now, but I my feelings are fuller now, based on an awareness of positive choices I've been able to make. I realize that I have actually done something to stop the homeless killings. Even though the man who did the killings is still free, the killings will stop, at least the killings by this group of fanatics. I thought about how I had somehow acted, however unplanned and out of control, to try to stop someone who had skills and power way beyond me in the area of physical force. Ransack is as big and powerful as the night dragons in my nightmares. But I was beginning to feel different about what I felt I was capable of, what I felt I could do, what I wanted to do.

I know I feel good because I feel involved. Involved in the struggle. Involved with other good people who care for the well-being of everyone and who try to fight the advocates of prejudice, privilege and greed. Even if I didn't win against Ransack and the violent forces he represents, I want to be able to join with others to help grow the caring human spirit.

I made a decision to reach out again for help. I walked to a pay telephone and called Ken. Woke him up. Told him I needed for him to come pick me up right away. I told him enough of what happened to make sure he got his butt moving. He picked me up about a half hour later and we drove back to his house.

As we drove, I told him what had happened. When we arrived at his place we sat in the car until I finished my story. Ken listened and asked questions. After I finished, he sat silently for a few minutes thinking. I had asked Ken if we should notify the police about what had happened. Finally he turned to me and said he'd have to think about what I had told him and whether or not we should notify the authorities.

He asked me if I wanted to get some sleep while he figured out what to do. When he said the word, "sleep", it was like he cast a spell on me. I suddenly felt so unbelievably tired. He showed me to his guest room, and without question, without hesitation, without debate within my mind, I undressed, pulled back the covers, got into the bed and fell immediately to sleep.

When I woke it was dark out again. I later found out I had slept about 8 hours. And I hadn't had one dream. In a way I was disappointed but I got up, took a shower and found Ken sitting in his living room. He fixed me some soup and as I ate he told me that during the day he had made a number of telephone calls to friends who worked for the police and in other areas of government. He was told that a murder had occurred at Al's Meat Store last night. The police had been called when workers opened the store this morning. Initial police reports are calling it a burglary and that both the burglar and Al were killed when Al caught the thief in the act.

After Ken told me this he said, "I'm not going to say anything about what really happened right now. This man who you call Ransack probably did work for some secret forces in the government. But since you don't have proof he was there you'd probably be the one blamed for the murders if we came forward with the truth."

"I know but I've decided that I am going to write the book that Ransack wants me to write, and I will tell the truth in the book."

Ken shook his head. "I don't know if that's wisest thing to do."

"I have to do it. I have to do it anyway to keep Ransack from coming to torture and kill me. But I'm going to do it for another reason. Jerome saved my life many times. I can't let him be blamed for this murder."

I told Ken that I would not be writing positively about Ransack but I didn't think that mattered to him. Actions that I think make him horrible, Ransack thinks make him a hero. I'm sure a lot of people will see him as a hero but if I'm successful with the way I want to write the book I hope to force people to see how disgusting this man and what he represents is. Ken smiled at one point and asked, "Does this mean you are returning to the world?"

"You mean the slave life? Hell no."

"Aren't you going to come in out of the streets?"

"I don't know. Just because I am becoming more involved doesn't mean I have to live in a house or sleep in a bed."

Ken challenged me, "It doesn't mean you have to sell your soul to live in a little bit of comfort and convenience."

"I'm not sure. It's not the living in a house or an apartment. It's what you have to do to afford the house or apartment. I don't know if I can even be a part of this society again. Unless it really changes. It's an inhuman, uncaring society."

"But you know there are a lot of people who are caring."

"Well they have to start showing themselves. They have to do more than throw token crumbs to the poor and disadvantaged while they continue their lavish life styles. They have to join more in the outcry against the raping of the earth."

Ken said he understood my thoughts and feelings. He still considered himself a part of the mainstream. He has his career, his salary, his possession, his stocks and bonds. He is successful. Yet he said that he thinks he is finding a way to make a difference and to do his part to help society become more caring and human without having to sacrifice everything that he has attained. "It just takes time," he said. "I'm going to continue to work within the system, and if you feel more comfortable, work outside it."

"Or at least on the edge," I thought.

I was able to tell Ken that I did feel he was doing his part and that he did seem to be trying in good faith to find a way to help people in need and to change society. "I just don't think it can be done only working through the system. The system has been rigged. It has become so inaccessible it's impossible to make major changes. It takes millions of dollars to even get noticed today in politics. Only the corporations have millions of dollars. And they certainly don't want change to occur that will require them to share their wealth."

After I left Ken's place I thought more about Ransack. I decided it didn't really matter whether or not he was ever caught. I just wanted people to know. Perhaps many Americans don't care how crooked and rotten their government is, but I think some do care.

~~ QUEEN AVARICE'S POWER

I found an isolated place not too far away from Ken's house and fixed my bed. I still felt exhausted even though I had slept so long. As I lay in my bed I first thought about Carissa and decided that I would go see her when I woke up the next day. Then before dropping off to sleep I remember thinking that if I could survive the encounter with someone so powerful as Ransack, I should be able to scale the heights of the Holy Skyscraper and make some kind of contact with Queen Avarice. But during my sleep I had another wonderful dream of Justine. I woke up with another affirmation of my love for Justine, yet I also knew that I needed to at least go into the Holy Skyscraper and introduce myself to Queen Avarice.

Queen Avarice must still have power over part of my psyche. Compared to Justine she now seemed wispy to me in my mind. Unreal. During these past months my fantasies of her still has helped to sustain me, even if it has been in an unhealthy manner. I decided that I wanted to make her real. A part of me argued that I should just let Queen Avarice remain the unreal image that's she's been, but I knew I didn't want to leave it that way. And the Holy Skyscraper. I knew that I couldn't just walk away from it. I have to go into it and face whatever I might encounter inside the building, inside myself. And I knew that I had to do this soon, to take advantage of the illusion of how invincible I was feeling after surviving the ordeal at the Butcher's shop. I also did not want to risk losing Justine. I wanted so much to share what I was going through with her.

I worried that I would be invading Queen Avarice's privacy, but, hell, I already have been invading her privacy. She just hasn't known it. I had tried to do it respectfully. I've tried to be a respectful eavesdropper, and if I do try to meet her I hope I will be able to find a way to not make her defensive. All I want is to come face-to-face with the real person behind the Queen Avarice mask that I've constructed for her.

July 29 ~~ VISITING CARISSA IN THE HOSPITAL

On my way to the Holy Skyscraper, I stopped by the hospital to see Carissa. When I got to Carissa's room I stood by the open door for a moment looking at her. Her head was bandaged, and her arm was in a cast, but she had the earphones of her Walkman around her head, and she looked like some kind of strange, young, beautiful space being. Now that I'm an expert on space beings.

It was good to see her, and to see that she was all right. I walked into the room, and stood in front of the bed. Her eyes had been closed, but then she opened them, and when she saw me, she smiled broadly. I walked over to her and gave her a hug. She took her earphones off and said how glad she was that I was there.

"How are you Carissa? You looked pretty bandaged up."

"I'm ok. My head hurts and my arm hurts, but I'm supposed to be released later today, so I'm so happy you came by before I left. I have so much to ask you. Was anyone arrested? I know I'm not supposed to tell anyone that I was at the store that night, so I have not been able to find out what happened."

"Carissa, you have to listen very carefully to what I am about to say and to trust me. For your own safety you cannot know what else happened at the store. You cannot talk about my suspicions or what you saw in the Butcher's office. You cannot ever say you were at the store that night. Just know that the homeless killings will stop. I'm sorry but if you let anyone else know even the little that you do, your life and mine might be in danger. I wish I had not agreed to let you come with me."

"But if I hadn't have been there, you might have been killed. Maybe I saved your life. All of us needed to be there."

"Well, I won't argue with you. I'm just happy that you're all right. Will you promise me not to ask any more questions about what went on that night, and especially not to talk to anyone else about your involvement."

"I promise I won't say anything about that night. It scares me to think I could have been killed or hurt worse. I kind of want to know what happened, but I trust you that I can't know. I won't say anything else about it. I can keep secrets."

I smiled at her. "Yes, I know you can. I am a little upset with you." She looked at me questioningly. "You didn't tell me about your father."

She looked down before she started talking. "I know. I'm sorry. Before I met you I had developed this story about my father because I felt embarrassed that he was a drunk and a bum and he left us. Then when I met you and got to know you better, I was embarrassed to tell you that I had been lying."

"The important thing is that I know the truth and I will be keeping an eye out for your father. You know that I know how tough it is to survive the pressures of this crazy society, and that some of the most sensitive and best people fall to the streets. Look at me."

I smiled. She smiled back at me even though she had tears in her eyes. I asked her how her mother was doing. She shook her head and frowned. "The same. She has visited me but not for long. I think she's home drinking. I'm not sure what I'm going to do."

"I know she cares for you and your brother. Maybe you can get her to go to a rehab program.

I visited with Carissa for a little while longer, and then told her that I would be coming by and visiting her at her house soon. I told her I wanted us to stay in contact with each other. She beamed and said she did too. I left the hospital relieved that Carissa had not been hurt too badly. I knew Carissa was strong enough to survive, and maybe one day she will be able to encourage her mother to help herself.

After going by the hospital to see Carissa, I rested for the rest of the day. I almost called Justine, but decided that I would call her as soon as I finished my visit to the Holy Skyscraper to meet Queen Avarice.

~~ ENTERING THE HOLY SKYSCRAPER

I stood across the street looking at the Holy Skyscraper, waiting for Queen Avarice to come to work. I had my "good jacket" on, one of the windbreakers Ken had given me. I reserved it for special occasions when I felt that I had to look nicer than usual in order to be served at a café a notch up from the dives where I usually went. I had taken a shower at Ken's this morning, so I figured I looked probably like a common worker/slave, maybe a delivery man, or a janitor, or a repairman of some type.

Yesterday when I was preparing for this monumental meeting, I decided that I would give Queen Avarice back her scarf. I took it to a one-hour dry cleaners and now it was cleaned and pressed in a plastic bag inside in my jacket pocket.

Finally, I saw the limousine arrive, and Queen Avarice emerged from the back with her usual grace. I thought for a moment that perhaps I should just walk away, let this fantasy dissolve in a different manner. But I was afraid that it wouldn't dissolve. I needed to just go in there, ride the elevator to whatever floor Queen Avarice worked on, walk up to her, and say hello to her and to any of the other kings, princes, princesses, who were around. And if I weren't sent to the tower to await beheading, or struck by a lightning bolt, then maybe I could continue our conversation, or at least walk away. I could prove to myself that I could just walk away and not be caught up in the slave life again.

I ran across the street and followed her as she walked across the front patio. I was about fifteen feet behind her. As we got closer to the building I could feel the pace of my heart beat increase and I began to feel like I did when right before the performance of Justine's play. It felt kind of nice to remember the play, and when I noticed that I was smiling to myself I relaxed a little bit. I also imagined myself with a protective shield around me. I thought about the fact that I had traveled to a distant planet, helped a wonderful Thai woman escape her dictatorial parent, and uncovered and stopped a secret organization that was killing homeless men. Certainly I deserved to walk into this building of financial royalty and material priests and priestesses. Certainly I belonged in the same company of these people, even though I didn't really think I wanted to stay around them too long. I wanted to be a part of a different land, a different society. But I needed to travel to this land of the Holy Skyscraper so that I could free my old soul. Simply free my old soul. To let it go.

Queen Avarice pushed the glass entry door to the Holy Skyscraper open, and a few steps later I did the same. I was inside the huge lobby with its marble floors, tall plants in huge pots, and expensive-looking sculptures. Directly across from me was an escalator going to the mezzanine. Queen Avarice was just stepping on the escalator. I followed her to the escalator and stepped on, too. When she reached the top I saw her turn right, walk about twenty feet, and turn a corner. When I got to the top I quickly stepped off and hurried in the same direction. I had to see where she was going, into an elevator or office. If I lost her now I knew that I'd have to wait until another day to locate her.

When I turned the corner I saw Queen Avarice had just walked into an elevator about three doors down. A few people were behind her still walking. I started running and just as the doors were about to close I put my hand in between the rubber door stoppers and they opened again. It was full of people who stared at me with big frowns, but I didn't care. Fuck it. I was doing this. I had made it into the Holy Skyscraper and I had survived so far, even though I felt like I might be attacked in this elevator. But I knew I would be able to survive. I was feeling the excitement of the moment. Queen Avarice was standing on the other side of the elevator behind a few other people. We were so close.

At the top floor, Queen Avarice stepped out, and I followed her as she walked down the hall to her office. I thought about trying to talk with her before she got there, but then I decided, no—it would probably feel safer to her if she were in her office. I wanted to do everything I could to keep her from feeling she needed to protect herself from some maniac. I might still be crazy, and as a matter of fact I'm sure I am somewhat, but I am not a psychotic maniac. I might even be a higher being—well, that's what Esola would lead me to believe…

I walked into her office and went up to the receptionist who was reading a book titled What You Can Do to Help the Economically Disadvantaged. I decided that I liked her already. She didn't seem to be dressed as expensively as Queen Avarice. She wore a very plain skirt and blouse that seemed to set off her fresh complexion nicely. She looked up at me and smiled and asked gently if she could help me. I told her that I was looking for a woman who had just come into this office.

I told her I had found a scarf of hers that she dropped and I would like to give it back to her and talk with her a few moments. I noticed a nameplate on the counter which read Sue Catlin. Sue was saying to me, "You must mean Catherine Harper. Just one moment please. I'll ring her." She spoke into the intercom and told Catherine that someone was here to see her. Someone who said that he found something she lost.

I sat down on the plush sofa and tried to reassign the face of the woman who had been like a fantasy Siren for me all these months to the name Catherine. Her real name still had a regal sound to it.

Finally, she came around the corner and walked up to me. I hoped that I was going to be able to speak clearly and coherently. She was smiling and exhibiting the warmth that she usually displays. "Sue said that you found something that I lost."

"Yes," I said and pulled out the blue scarf. She looked perplexed, and the smile lost a little of its shine. "Why I lost that scarf months ago," she said.

"I know. I found it months ago right after you lost it, but I was afraid to give it back to you."

She looked even more perplexed and cocked her head questioningly. Her face took on a suspicious expression, which rather darkened her smile. Her disposition began to cloud. "What's going on here? What do you want?"

"Please let me explain. I am a homeless man, and most mornings I sit on the steps across the street watching people come to work. When I saw you drop your scarf I picked it up, but I couldn't give it back to you for reasons that are difficult for me to explain. But I decided that I did want to give this scarf back to you. I also wanted to meet you because you've stood out to me during these last few months. You seem so professional and you are a very attractive woman."

I realized immediately I shouldn't have said that I thought she was attractive. I could tell she was becoming more and more suspicious of me. When I finished she stood looking at the scarf for a few minutes, and then she said, "I don't know what you are trying to pull, but I want you to take that scarf and get out of here. I don't want to even touch it. I don't want to even see it anymore. There's no telling where it has been. I want you out of my sight immediately, or I'm going to call security. And if I ever see you spying on me again, I will call the police and have you arrested. Is that clear?"

As she talked I watched her expression and noticed that she seemed to grow fangs from her mouth. I saw that her eyes became slits and her face turned into a hideous, grotesque mask. Then all that disappeared, and I saw that she was just very uptight, and frightened and concerned that someone had invaded her privacy.

"I'm sorry," I said. "I'm sorry you feel the way you do. I don't want anything. I just wanted to give this scarf back to you, and to meet you."

Queen Avarice had turned her attention away from me, and started talking with Sue. "Call security right away. I want to make sure this man leaves the building, and I want to also complain about them just letting anyone come up here to these offices."

I turned and walked toward the door, but then I heard Sue say, "Ms. Harper, I'm sure security won't be necessary. He's just a homeless man, for god's sake. Why are you so upset? Just let him go."

"I won't tolerate anyone spying on me."

"I don't think he's spying on you." Sue said. "He said that he noticed how professional you look as you come to work. That's a compliment."

"What is your name?" Catherine asked the receptionist, despite the name plate and despite the fact that she had called her Sue just a few minutes earlier.

Sue picked up her name plate and pointed to it.

"Sue, you can be sure that you won't be in this position very long after I talk with Mr. Baker."

"Don't bother, Catherine. Tell Mr. Baker that I quit. I've been having a difficult time working for such an arrogant prima donna like you, and I've been meaning to quit for the last week or two. I think this is a good time." She picked up her bag, and turned to me. "Wait a second. I'll go down with you."

On the elevator down to the lobby, Sue asked me if I wanted a cup of coffee. She took me to a restaurant on the main floor. It was rather fancy and the hostess looked at me a little funny, wondering how in the hell I found my way in there.

After we were seated, Sue told me more about why she had been thinking of quitting that job anyway. "Catherine is not the owner of the business but because the two males who do own the business are either sleeping with her or hoping that she will let them sleep with her one day, she has been given tremendous power to do anything she damn well pleases. She is a horrible person to work for. She is so arrogant and insensitive. You sure have been fantasizing about the wrong type of woman, a real bitch."

"Perhaps that's the advantage of a fantasy. It doesn't necessarily depend on reality. It is its own reality."

"Then why did you bother to come in and try to meet her? Why didn't you just leave well enough alone?"

"It's complicated, but I think it's because I don't need or want this fantasy anymore, and…well, this building, what it represents to me is beyond the fantasy world. What it represents in the real world has had a hold on me for a long time. Everything in this building, including Queen Avarice—that's what I call her—seemed larger than life, larger than me, and I just wanted to learn that I was the same size as some of the people in the building. I haven't been able to come in here before, and I'm at a point where I think that I am ready to move on in my life. I had to say goodbye to this building and the only way I could let it go was to walk through it and to meet Queen Avarice."

Sue laughed, "Queen Avarice. That's such an appropriate name! But what if she had been more friendly to you, and even had invited you into her office to talk? What if she had been everything you fantasized about her?"

"I'm sure that couldn't have happened. Anyway, it wouldn't have mattered. There is another woman in my life, in my here-and-now reality. And I love this woman very much."

"For a homeless man you're not doing too bad, it seems." She looked at me, smiling.

"It's not what it seems. I've been a lonely and down-and-out homeless man for quite a few months, but things might be looking up. You know, you are really friendly. I have to say that meeting you has been just as important—no, more important to me—than meeting Queen Avarice or rather Catherine."

"I like Queen Avarice as a name for her better. But thank you."

"I feel bad about causing you to lose your job."

"Don't. Like I said, I needed to leave that job. And listen, I have no problem getting work. I have excellent qualifications and experience."

I told Sue that I've felt recently the kind of work that people have to do in society these days is slave work, and that society treats people like slaves. She said that she agrees, sort of, but that she feels the slaves are freeing themselves little by little. Maybe they can only run from one slave job to another at this point, but that she's hoping that one day there will be changes. She said that it seems people have been looking for leaders who will make things better, but she thinks that it is going to take regular people connecting with each other and making sure that government represents the common person rather than the rich. She said that is what she is doing—trying to connect with others in support of causes she thinks are important.

As we said goodbye to each other, I expressed to Sue how inspiring it was for me to have met her, and I appreciated so much that she took the time to talk with me. I left the Holy Skyscraper and walked back across the street. I stood looking at it. I figured that I would still call this thing the Holy Skyscraper. Why not? I really didn't feel that it controlled me anymore, but it still meant something to me. It still represented the kind of wealth and power than has been concentrated in the hands of just a few. I wanted to do something about this, work toward changing it, and I felt that the name Holy Skyscraper was still an appropriate name for it.

~~ LIBERATION FROM THE AMERICAN MONEY DREAM

I'm by the park near the river close to the Burnside Bridge, sitting on a bench, feeling amazed with my life. Feeling excited with some opportunities that I see. Feeling free from certain demons I've been battling, trying to hide from. I can remember my past. I can see potential for the future. I still am angry with the society we live in and people who are complacent. But I don't have to deal in black and whites, exaggerations, and generalizations anymore to protect myself.

Justine was right about what I could be doing. She was right about so many things. I couldn't accept them at the time, but somehow the events of these past months and especially these past few days have helped me to be able to accept that she is right. She saw in me my new self, and she recognized that my new self could make a difference. She was willing to help me. She told me of her willingness to help me produce some plays about the homeless condition and about what people can do to change things.

Maybe my new creative soul has developed enough to take some action on its own. Maybe I have to get out of its way. I should let it take over my mind and let my old soul dissolve or be transformed. I feel the urge to do something, to become more involved. I don't feel the Holy Skyscraper and what it represents as having any real power or irrational lure for me anymore. I don't feel like I will ever return totally to what I once was, a man concerned with material success and status at the expense of everything else, especially compassion for others, love for special people in my life and my own creativity. Perhaps my new soul has already taken over my old soul.

I've stood up to what I saw was an immediate injustice and threat to the homeless. It didn't turn out the way I had hoped, but at least the main killers were stopped. Then I stood up to my fantasy Queen and the pseudo-spiritual shrine that had held me under its control for so long. I freed myself from these false images, from these symbols of everything that I will be fighting to change.

Seeing how Carissa has survived and remained strong, seeing how people like Ken, Justine, Sue, the receptionist at the Holy Skyscraper, are all striving to retain their independence from slavery—these people give me hope, even make me humble. I could be doing more. I can't remain in my cocoon forever. As the astrologer said, I have been undergoing a major transformation, a major death-and-rebirth process. So I've died and have been reborn, and have needed to nurture my new self until it has gotten stronger and clearer in my consciousness. That phase has finished and now I need to move on.

Before I do anything else, I want to go to Justine. I finally feel capable of sharing my feelings, my thoughts—all of whom I am—with Justine. I hope it's not too late.

~~ REACHING OUT TO JUSTINE

I sent red roses and a note to Justine. I wrote in the note that if she could forgive me for running away like I did, would she please meet me in the kitchen at the back of the store tonight? I said I would be there at 8:00 pm. I told her that if she decided that she didn't want to see me, I would put the key on the kitchen table and leave.

I arrived a little before 8:00 pm, opened the door and looked into the kitchen. I walked to the adjacent bedroom and it was empty. My heart sank. I walked back to the table to put the key on it, and then I noticed a note. It had been written by Justine, and said, "Dear Gibson, I would like to meet you but in my secret room where we will have more privacy. I will be waiting for you. Love, Justine."

I felt someone else had come into the room and looked up. Esola was standing in the doorway. Smiling she came to me and hugged me. "I'm happy that you and Justine are in love. I'm happy it is you that she loves. I'm happy you came back."

"Thank you Esola. I'm glad you know about us, but I'm not sure where this is leading to."

She patted me on the cheek. "It will lead to nice things. Wonderful things. I know it will."

"What about you, Esola? What has happened?"

"I'm leaving on my journey in the next few days. Walter is coming with me. Maybe when we get back Walter and I might spend more time together. He is a good man." She laughed. "He is attractive for an old man, and for what's he's been through. If our journey is successful, we will be helping to begin a new glorious and compassionate age."

"I hope you are successful Esola. You are looking so good. So vibrant."

"I feel that way. By the way, you will have an important role to play in the coming changes our society will be going through. I'm happy you are not only recognizing what you have to contribute, but you are willing to lend your talents and skills. Now you go on to Justine. You have been keeping her waiting too long."

"I know. I know, I agreed, hugging Esola goodbye.

I walked up to the top floor, down the hallway, and opened the door to her private room. A lamp by the couch cast a warm light on Justine, who was sitting on the couch reading. She was wearing blue jeans and a white blouse. When she saw me she stood up and ran to me. We stood hugging for a long time. I was overwhelmed by how much I had been waiting for this moment. I had missed her so much during the wild events over these last few days.

We sat down on the couch and Justine asked me to tell her what had happened to me. I told her about the Butcher, Ransack and Jerome. I told her what had happened to Carissa. I even told her about the Holy Skyscraper and Queen Avarice/Catherine. She smiled as I told her about Queen Avarice/Catherine, and said that she often wondered if she were competing with anyone in the role of a muse. I told her that Queen Avarice was the dark muse and I had freed myself from her powers. I told Justine that she was my love and life muse, who has been inspiring me to get in touch with the full and wonderful possibilities of living in this reality, especially with her as a friend and a lover.

She asked me what I wanted to do now, and I told her that I had thought a lot about what she had said to me about my writing and about becoming involved in plays and that I wanted to do that with her if she still wanted to do it. I said that in my writings I wanted to combine my concerns about our society with stories and plays about the positive things people are doing to change things. I told her I also want to write about the alternate realities that I am becoming more aware of during this time I have been on the streets and psychologically lost. I told Justine that I didn't know if I had psychologically found my way back to a balance, but that at least I felt more in control of myself and my life purpose.

I told her that I would like to move into the room downstairs, and continue to work for her on a more regular basis if she needs me. Then I told her that most importantly I wanted to be a part of her life. I wanted to take the next steps of my life knowing that I was holding her hand and walking with her.

After I finished, I waited for her response. She leaned over and kissed me, and said that she had been waiting for me to open myself to her. We held each other and I felt a wonderful emotional blending between us. Then she pulled back from me and looked into my eyes. She said, "Gibson, If we are going to share time together, it has to be different than it has been. It can't be a one-way communication anymore. You will have to share your feelings and thoughts with me."

I reached out and touched her cheek. "Yes, I want this too. I feel I'm ready to share my feelings, my hopes and desires…and my insecurities and doubts with you. I love you."

She looked intensely at me for a few moments, then stood up, and started taking off her clothes. She said, 'Some famous author once wrote, 'There's a time for talking and there's a time for making love.' I want to get as close as I can to you before we start talking." We spent the evening getting exquisitely close together and enjoying our new sharing. And we talked. We talked through the night and it felt so wonderful to share words, physical touch, emotions, passion with a woman who I'm in love with and who loves me.

August 6 ~~ FEELING AT HOME

I'm sitting at Justine's desk in our private room, looking out over the city. She's sitting on the couch a short distance away from me also writing notes on a new project we want to work on together. We have decided to start a community project where we organize and sponsor theater productions, primarily focusing on issues and life struggles related to homelessness. We want to focus not only on the problems of income inequality, systematic racial injustices and climate change, but also explore and highlight positive solutions to these challenges. We want to involve homeless people in these productions as writers, actors, music composers, visual artists, set designers and stage hands—and we want to involve people from all genders, races, and from different spiritual, religious and even political orientations. It's been amazing working together with Justine planning these projects. It's been fulfilling being with her, sharing our dreams as well as the everyday tasks that have to be done to reach our dreams.

In terms of my own writing, I have a few ideas for my first play. I have been attempting to describe my visions and inner journeys in poetry and I'm enjoying sharing these writings with Justine.

I have continued to meditate on the Grand Dragon boat, and have visited often with the inner guide in the pagoda cabin. He has been giving me exercises to develop my psychic abilities. He has also said that if I am able to continue to develop my abilities, I will be able to contribute the tumultuous, but eventually positive transformative changes that will be coming to the societies of this world. He has encouraged me to continue to develop my rational mental abilities to serve as receptors and transformers to communicate my visions and psychic insights to the peoples of my world.

Justine gets up from the couch, comes over and stands behind me. She reaches around me as I write and hugs me. She says she is going downstairs to start dinner. I tell her that I will finish these thoughts, and will be right down to cook with her.

When she leaves, I look around this room for a few moments and I am struck by how at home I feel. I feel at home with Justine. I feel at home with my new and old self. I feel at home with my new purpose. I feel all the emotional security and well-being that a home can give. I know I will be carrying these feelings within my heart and soul.

CPSIA information can be obtained
at www.ICGtesting.com
Printed in the USA
BVHW081325301120
594475BV00003B/149